Drama & Lyric

Old Western Culture Reader

Volume 2

DRAMA & LYRIC

A Selection of Greek Drama and Poetry

OLD WESTERN CULTURE READER
VOLUME 2

Companion to *Old Western Culture,*
a great books curriculum by Roman Roads Press

ROMAN ROADS PRESS

MOSCOW, IDAHO

Drama and Lyric: Old Western Culture Reader, Volume 2

Fourth Edition

Copyright ©2020 by Roman Roads Media, LLC
Copyright ©2017 by Roman Roads Media, LLC
Copyright ©2016 by Roman Roads Media, LLC
Copyright ©2013 by Roman Roads Media, LLC

Published by Roman Roads Press
Moscow, Idaho
info@romanroadsmedia.com | romanroadspress.com

General Editors: Daniel Foucachon and Wesley Callihan
Editors: George Callihan and E. Gunn Wilson
Cover Design: Daniel Foucachon and Rachel Rosales
Interior Layout: E. Gunn Wilson and Carissa Hale

Printed in the United States of America

Drama and Lyric: Old Western Culture Reader, Volume 2
Roman Roads Media, LLC
ISBN: 978-1-944482-26-8 (paperback)

Version 4.0.0   December 2020

This is a companion reader for the *Old Western Culture* curriculum
by Roman Roads Press. To find out more about this course,
visit www.romanroadspress.com.

OLD WESTERN CULTURE
Great Books Reader Series

THE GREEKS

VOLUME 1	*The Epics*
VOLUME 2	*Drama & Lyric*
VOLUME 3	*The Histories*
VOLUME 4	*The Philosophers*

THE ROMANS

VOLUME 5	*The Aeneid*
VOLUME 6	*The Historians*
VOLUME 7	*Early Christianity*
VOLUME 8	*Nicene Christianity*

CHRISTENDOM

VOLUME 9	*Early Medievals*
VOLUME 10	*Defense of the Faith*
VOLUME 11	*The Medieval Mind*
VOLUME 12	*The Reformation*

EARLY MODERNS

VOLUME 13	*Rise of England*
VOLUME 14	*Poetry and Politics*
VOLUME 15	*The Enlightenment*
VOLUME 16	*The Novels*

NOTE ABOUT LINE NUMBERS.

The line numbers in this text match the English translation, which in most cases lines up closely with the original Greek line numbers. We also include the original Greek line numbers, indicated by a darker font, placed further from the text in the margins, and spaced more widely apart. Below is an example.

This allows readers to find their way in original texts or to compare with other editions which also indicate Greek line numbers.

Of her curtains backward rolled,
And to sea, to sea, she threw her
In the West Wind's giant hold;

710   And with spear and sword behind her
Came the hunters in a flood,
Down the oarblade's viewless trail
Tracking, till in Simoïs' vale
Through the leaves they crept to find her,
A Wrath, a seed of blood.
(The Trojans welcomed her with triumph and praised Alexander till at last their song changed and they saw another meaning in Alexander's name also.)

700   So the Name to Ilion came
On God's thought-fulfilling flame,

720   She a vengeance and a token
Of the unfaith to bread broken,
Of the hearth of God betrayed,
Against them whose voices swelled
Glorying in the prize they held

CONTENTS

AESCHYLUS

Aeschylus

•

The Oresteia

Agamemnon

Translated By Gilbert Murray

Dramatis Personae

AGAMEMNON
son of Atreus and King of Argos and Mycenae;
Commander-in-Chief of the Greek armies
in the War against Troy.

CLYTEMNESTRA
daughter of Tyndareus, sister of Helen;
wife to Agamemnon.

AEGISTHUS
son of Thyestes, cousin and blood-enemy to
Agamemnon, lover to Clytemnestra.

CASSANDRA
daughter of Priam, King of Troy, a prophetess;
now slave to Agamemnon.

A WATCHMAN

A HERALD

CHORUS
Argive Elders, faithful to Agamemnon.

[The Scene represents a space in front of the Palace of Agamemnon in Argos, with an Altar of Zeus in the centre and many other altars at the sides. On a high terrace of the roof stands a watchman. It is night.]

Watchman

This waste of year-long vigil I have prayed
God for some respite, watching elbow-stayed,
As sleuthhounds watch, above the Atreidae's hall,
Till well I know yon midnight festival
Of swarming stars, and them that lonely go,
Bearers to man of summer and of snow,
Great lords and shining, throned in heavenly fire.
And still I await the sign, the beacon pyre
That bears Troy's capture on a voice of flame
Shouting o'erseas. So surely to her aim   10
Cleaveth a woman's heart, man-passioned!
And when I turn me to my bed—my bed
Dew-drenched and dark and stumbling, to which near
Cometh no dream nor sleep, but alway Fear
Breathes round it, warning, lest an eye once fain
To close may close too well to wake again;
Think I perchance to sing or troll a tune
For medicine against sleep, the music soon
Changes to sighing for the tale untold
Of this house, not well mastered as of old.   20
Howbeit, may God yet send us rest, and light
The flame of good news flashed across the night.

[He is silent, watching. Suddenly at a distance in the night there is a glimmer of fire, increasing presently to a blaze.]

Ha!
O kindler of the dark, O daylight birth
Of dawn and dancing upon Argive earth
For this great end! All hail!—What ho, within!
What ho! Bear word to Agamemnon's queen

To rise, like dawn, and lift in answer strong
To this glad lamp her women's triumph-song,
If verily, verily, Ilion's citadel
Is fallen, as yon beacons flaming tell.
And I myself will tread the dance before
All others; for my master's dice I score
Good, and mine own to-night three sixes plain.

[Lights begin to show in the Palace.]

Oh, good or ill, my hand shall clasp again
My dear lord's hand, returning! Beyond that
I speak not. A great ox hath laid his weight
Across my tongue. But these stone walls know well,
If stones had speech, what tale were theirs to tell.
For me, to him that knoweth I can yet
Speak; if another questions I forget.

[Exit into the Palace. The women's "Ololûgê" or tri-umph-cry, is heard within and then repeated again and again further off in the City. Handmaids and Attendants come from the Palace, bearing torches, with which they kin-dle incense on the altars. Among them comes Clytemnestra, who throws herself on her knees at the central Altar in an agony of prayer.

Presently from the further side of the open space appear the Chorus of Elders and move gradually into position in front of the Palace. The day begins to dawn.]

Chorus

Ten years since Ilion's righteous foes,
  The Atreidae strong,
Menelaüs and eke Agamemnon arose,
Two thrones, two sceptres, yoked of God;
And a thousand galleys of Argos trod
  The seas for the righting of wrong;
And wrath of battle about them cried,
  As vultures cry,

Whose nest is plundered, and up they fly   50
In anguish lonely, eddying wide,
Great wings like oars in the waste of sky,
Their task gone from them, no more to keep
Watch o'er the vulture babes asleep.
But One there is who heareth on high
Some Pan or Zeus, some lost Apollo—
That keen bird-throated suffering cry
Of the stranger wronged in God's own sky;
And sendeth down, for the law transgressed,
  The Wrath of the Feet that follow.   60

So Zeus the Watcher of Friend and Friend,
Zeus who Prevaileth, in after quest
For One Belovèd by Many Men
On Paris sent the Atreidae twain;
Yea, sent him dances before the end
  For his bridal cheer,
Wrestlings heavy and limbs forespent
For Greek and Trojan, the knee earth-bent,
The bloody dust and the broken spear.
He knoweth, that which is here is here,   70
And that which Shall Be followeth near;
He seeketh God with a great desire,
He heaps his gifts, he essays his pyre
With torch below and with oil above,
With tears, but never the wrath shall move
Of the Altar cold that rejects his fire.

We saw the Avengers go that day,
And they left us here; for our flesh is old
And serveth not; and these staves uphold
A strength like the strength of a child at play.   80
For the sap that springs in the young man's hand
And the valour of age, they have left the land.
And the passing old, while the dead leaf blows
And the old staff gropeth his three-foot way,
Weak as a babe and alone he goes,
A dream left wandering in the day.

[Coming near the Central Altar they see Clytemnestra,

7

who is still rapt in prayer.]

But thou, O daughter of Tyndareus,
Queen Clytemnestra, what need? What news?
What tale or tiding hath stirred thy mood
90 To send forth word upon all our ways
For incensed worship? Of every god
That guards the city, the deep, the high,
Gods of the mart, gods of the sky,
   The altars blaze.
   One here, one there,
To the skyey night the firebrands flare,
Drunk with the soft and guileless spell
Of balm of kings from the inmost cell.
Tell, O Queen, and reject us not,
100 All that can or that may be told,
And healer be to this aching thought,
Which one time hovereth, evil-cold,
And then from the fires thou kindlest
Will Hope be kindled, and hungry Care
Fall back for a little while, nor tear
The heart that beateth below my breast.

*[Clytemnestra rises silently, as though unconscious of their
presence, and goes into the House. The Chorus take posi-
tion and begin their first Stasimon, or Standing-song.]*

Chorus

   (The sign seen on the way; Eagles tearing a hare with young.)

It is ours to tell of the Sign of the War-way given,
   To men more strong,
(For a life that is kin unto ours yet breathes from heaven
110   A spell, a Strength of Song:)
How the twin-throned Might of Achaia, one Crown divided
   Above all Greeks that are,
With avenging hand and spear upon Troy was guided
   By the Bird of War.
'Twas a King among birds to each of the Kings of the Sea,
   One Eagle black, one black but of fire-white tail,

By the House, on the Spear-hand, in station that all might see;
And they tore a hare, and the life in her womb that grew,
Yea, the life unlived and the races unrun they slew.
    Sorrow, sing sorrow: but good prevail, prevail!   120

(How Calchas read the sign; his Vision of the Future.)

And the War-seer wise, as he looked on the Atreid Yoke
   Twain-tempered, knew
Those fierce hare-renders the lords of his host; and spoke,
   Reading the omen true.
"At the last, the last, this Hunt hunteth Ilion down,
     Yea, and before the wall
Violent division the fulness of land and town
     Shall waste withal;
If only God's eye gloom not against our gates,
  And the great War-curb of Troy, fore-smitten, fail.   130
For Pity lives, and those wingèd Hounds she hates,
  Which tore in the Trembler's body the unborn beast.
And Artemis abhorreth the eagles' feast."
    Sorrow, sing sorrow: but good prevail, prevail!

(He prays to Artemis to grant the fulfilment of the Sign, but, as his vision increases, he is afraid and calls on Paian, the Healer, to hold her back.)

"Thou beautiful One, thou tender lover
   Of the dewy breath of the Lion's child;
  Thou the delight, through den and cover,
   Of the young life at the breast of the wild,
Yet, oh, fulfill, fulfill The sign of the Eagles' Kill!
Be the vision accepted, albeit horrible....   140
But I-ê, I-ê! Stay her, O Paian, stay!
For lo, upon other evil her heart she setteth,
  Long wastes of wind, held ship and unventured sea,
On, on, till another Shedding of Blood be wrought:
They kill but feast not; they pray not; the law is broken;
Strife in the flesh, and the bride she obeyeth not,
And beyond, beyond, there abideth in wrath reawoken—
It plotteth, it haunteth the house, yea, it never forgetteth—
    Wrath for a child to be."

150   So Calchas, reading the wayside eagles' sign,
      Spake to the Kings, blessings and words of bale;
        And like his song be thine,
    Sorrow, sing sorrow: but good prevail, prevail!

*(Such religion belongs to old and barbarous gods, and brings no peace. I
turn to Zeus, who has shown man how to Learn by Suffering.)*

Zeus! Zeus, whate'er He be,
If this name He love to hear
This He shall be called of me.
Searching earth and sea and air

Refuge nowhere can I find
Save Him only, if my mind
160   Will cast off before it die
The burden of this vanity.

One there was who reigned of old,
Big with wrath to brave and blast,
Lo, his name is no more told!
And who followed met at last
His Third-thrower, and is gone.
Only they whose hearts have known
Zeus, the Conqueror and the Friend,
They shall win their vision's end;

170   Zeus the Guide, who made man turn
Thought-ward, Zeus, who did ordain
Man by Suffering shall Learn.
So the heart of him, again
Aching with remembered pain,
Bleeds and sleepeth not, until
Wisdom comes against his will.
'Tis the gift of One by strife
Lifted to the throne of life.

*(Agamemnon accepted the sign. Then came long delay, and storm while the
fleet lay at Aulis.)*

So that day the Elder Lord,

Marshal of the Achaian ships, 180
Strove not with the prophet's word,
Bowed him to his fate's eclipse,
When with empty jars and lips
Parched and seas impassable
Fate on that Greek army fell,
Fronting Chalcis as it lay,
By Aulis in the swirling bay.

(Till at last Calchas answered that Artemis was wroth and demanded the death of Agamemnon's daughter. The King's doubt and grief.)

And winds, winds blew from Strymon River,
Unharboured, starving, winds of waste endeavour,
Man-blinding, pitiless to cord and bulwark, 190
 And the waste of days was made long, more long,
Till the flower of Argos was aghast and withered;
 Then through the storm rose the War-seer's song,
And told of medicine that should tame the tempest, 200
 But bow the Princes to a direr wrong.
Then "Artemis" he whispered, he named the name;
And the brother Kings they shook in the hearts of them,
And smote on the earth their staves, and the tears came.

But the King, the elder, hath found voice and spoken:
"A heavy doom, sure, if God's will were broken; 200
But to slay mine own child, who my house delighteth,
 Is that not heavy? That her blood should flow
On her father's hand, hard beside an altar?
 My path is sorrow wheresoe'er I go.
Shall Agamemnon fail his ships and people,
 And the hosts of Hellas melt as melts the snow?
They cry, they thirst, for a death that shall break the spell,
For a Virgin's blood: 'tis a rite of old, men tell.
And they burn with longing.—O God may the end be well!"

(But ambition drove him, till he consented to the sin of slaying his daughter, Iphigenia, as a sacrifice.)

To the yoke of Must-Be he bowed him slowly, 210
 And a strange wind within his bosom tossed,

11

A wind of dark thought, unclean, unholy;
  And he rose up, daring to the uttermost.
For men are boldened by a Blindness, straying
  Toward base desire, which brings grief hereafter,
    Yea, and itself is grief;
So this man hardened to his own child's slaying,
  As help to avenge him for a woman's laughter
  And bring his ships relief!

220   Her "Father, Father," her sad cry that lingered,
  Her virgin heart's breath they held all as naught,
Those bronze-clad witnesses and battle-hungered;
  And there they prayed, and when the prayer was wrought
He charged the young men to uplift and bind her,
  As ye lift a wild kid, high above the altar,
    Fierce-huddling forward, fallen, clinging sore
To the robe that wrapt her; yea, he bids them hinder
  The sweet mouth's utterance, the cries that falter,
    —His curse for evermore!—

230   With violence and a curb's voiceless wrath.
  Her stole of saffron then to the ground she threw,
And her eye with an arrow of pity found its path
  To each man's heart that slew:
A face in a picture, striving amazedly;
  The little maid who danced at her father's board,
The innocent voice man's love came never nigh,
Who joined to his her little paean-cry
  When the third cup was poured....

What came thereafter I saw not neither tell.
240   But the craft of Calchas failed not.—'Tis written, He
Who Suffereth Shall Learn; the law holdeth well.
  And that which is to be,
Ye will know at last; why weep before the hour?
For come it shall, as out of darkness dawn.
Only may good from all this evil flower;
So prays this Heart of Argos, this frail tower
  guarding the land alone.

[As they cease, Clytemnestra comes from the Palace with

*Attendants. She has finished her prayer and sacrifice, and
is now wrought up to face the meeting with her husband.
The Leader approaches her.]*

Leader

> Before thy state, O Queen, I bow mine eyes.
> 'Tis written, when the man's throne empty lies,
> The woman shall be honoured.—Hast thou heard   250
> Some tiding sure? Or is it Hope, hath stirred
> To fire these altars? Dearly though we seek
> To learn, 'tis thine to speak or not to speak.

Clytemnestra

> Glad-voiced, the old saw telleth, comes this morn,
> The Star-child of a dancing midnight born,
> And beareth to thine ear a word of joy
> Beyond all hope: the Greek hath taken Troy.

Leader

> How?
> Thy word flies past me, being incredible.

Clytemnestra

> Ilion is ours. No riddling tale I tell.

Leader

> Such joy comes knocking at the gate of tears.   260

Clytemnestra

> Aye, 'tis a faithful heart that eye declares.

Leader

> What warrant hast thou? Is there proof of this?

Clytemnestra

> There is; unless a God hath lied there is.

Leader

Some dream-shape came to thee in speaking guise?

Clytemnestra

Who deemeth me a dupe of drowsing eyes?

Leader

Some word within that hovereth without wings?

Clytemnestra

Am I a child to hearken to such things?

Leader

Troy fallen?—But how long? When fell she, say?

Clytemnestra

The very night that mothered this new day.

Leader

270   And who of heralds with such fury came?

Clytemnestra

A Fire-god, from Mount Ida scattering flame.
Whence starting, beacon after beacon burst
In flaming message hitherward. Ida first
Told Hermes' Lemnian Rock, whose answering sign
Was caught by towering Athos, the divine,
With pines immense—yea, fishes of the night
Swam skyward, drunken with that leaping light,
Which swelled like some strange sun, till dim and far
Makistos' watchmen marked a glimmering star;
280   They, nowise loath nor idly slumber-won,
Spring up to hurl the fiery message on,
And a far light beyond the Eurîpus tells
That word hath reached Messapion's sentinels.
They beaconed back, then onward with a high
Heap of dead heather flaming to the sky.
And onward still, not failing nor aswoon,

14

Across the Asôpus like a beaming moon
The great word leapt, and on Kithairon's height
Uproused a new relay of racing light.
His watchers knew the wandering flame, nor hid   290   *300*
Their welcome, burning higher than was bid.
Out over Lake Gorgôpis then it floats,
To Aigiplanctos, waking the wild goats,
Crying for "Fire, more Fire!" And fire was reared,
Stintless and high, a stormy streaming beard,
That waved in flame beyond the promontory
Rock-ridged, that watches the Saronian sea,
Kindling the night: then one short swoop to catch
The Spider's Crag, our city's tower of watch;
Whence hither to the Atreidae's roof it came,   300
A light true-fathered of Idaean flame.
Torch-bearer after torch-bearer, behold
The tale thereof in stations manifold,
Each one by each made perfect ere it passed,
And Victory in the first as in the last.
These be my proofs and tokens that my lord
From Troy hath spoke to me a burning word.

Leader

Woman, speak on. Hereafter shall my prayer
Be raised to God; now let me only hear,
Again and full, the marvel and the joy.   310

Clytemnestra

Now, even now, the Achaian holdeth Troy!
Methinks there is a crying in her streets
That makes no concord. When sweet unguent meets
With vinegar in one phial, I warrant none
Shall lay those wranglers lovingly at one.
So conquerors and conquered shalt thou hear,
Two sundered tones, two lives of joy or fear.
  Here women in the dust about their slain,
Husbands or brethren, and by dead old men
Pale children who shall never more be free,   320
For all they loved on earth cry desolately.
And hard beside them war-stained Greeks, whom stark

Battle and then long searching through the dark
Hath gathered, ravenous, in the dawn, to feast
At last on all the plenty Troy possessed,
No portion in that feast nor ordinance,
But each man clutching at the prize of chance.
Aye, there at last under good roofs they lie
Of men spear-quelled, no frosts beneath the sky,
330   No watches more, no bitter moony dew....
How blessèd they will sleep the whole night through!
Oh, if these days they keep them free from sin
Toward Ilion's conquered shrines and Them within
Who watch unconquered, maybe not again
The smiter shall be smit, the taker ta'en.
May God but grant there fall not on that host
The greed of gold that maddeneth and the lust
To spoil inviolate things! But half the race
Is run which windeth back to home and peace.
340   Yea, though of God they pass unchallengèd,
Methinks the wound of all those desolate dead
Might waken, groping for its will....Ye hear
A woman's word, belike a woman's fear.
May good but conquer in the last incline
Of the balance! Of all prayers that prayer is mine.

Leader

O Woman, like a man faithful and wise
Thou speakest. I accept thy testimonies
And turn to God with praising, for a gain
Is won this day that pays for all our pain.

*[Clytemnestra returns to the Palace. The Chorus take up
their position for the Second Stasimon.]*

An Elder

350   O Zeus, All-ruler, and Night the Aid,
Gainer of glories, and hast thou thrown
Over the towers of Ilion
Thy net close-laid,
That none so nimble and none so tall
Shall escape withal

The snare of the slaver that claspeth all?

Another

And Zeus the Watcher of Friend and Friend
I also praise, who hath wrought this end.
Long since on Paris his shaft he drew,
And hath aimèd true,   360
Not too soon falling nor yet too far,
The fire of the avenging star.

Chorus

*(This is God's judgement upon Troy. May it not be too fierce! Gold cannot
save one who spurneth Justice.)*

The stroke of Zeus hath found them! Clear this day
  The tale, and plain to trace.
He judged, and Troy hath fallen.—And have men said
That God not deigns to mark man's hardihead,
  Trampling to earth the grace
Of holy and delicate things?—Sin lies that way.
For visibly Pride doth breed its own return
  On prideful men, who, when their houses swell   370
    With happy wealth, breathe ever wrath and blood.
Yet not too fierce let the due vengeance burn;
  Only as deemeth well
  One wise of mood.

Never shall state nor gold
  Shelter his heart from aching
Whoso the Altar of Justice old
  Spurneth to Night unwaking.

*(The Sinner suffers in his longing till at last Temptation overcomes him;
as longing for Helen overcame Paris.)*

The tempting of misery forceth him, the dread
  Child of fore-scheming Woe!   380
And help is vain; the fell desire within
Is veilèd not, but shineth bright like Sin:
  And as false gold will show

17

Black where the touchstone trieth, so doth fade
His honour in God's ordeal. Like a child,
    Forgetting all, he hath chased his wingèd bird,
    And planted amid his people a sharp thorn.
And no God hears his prayer, or, have they heard,
    The man so base-beguiled
        They cast to scorn.
        Paris to Argos came;
        Love of a woman led him;
    So God's altar he brought to shame,
        Robbing the hand that fed him.

390

400

(Helen's flight; the visions seen by the King's seers; the phantom of Helen and the King's grief.)

She hath left among her people a noise of shield and sword,
A tramp of men armed where the long ships are moored;
She hath ta'en in her goings Desolation as a dower;
She hath stept, stept quickly, through the great gated Tower,
    And the thing that could not be, it hath been!
And the Seers they saw visions, and they spoke of strange ill:
    "A Palace, a Palace; and a great King thereof:
    A bed, a bed empty, that was once pressed in love:
And thou, thou, what art thou? Let us be, thou so still,
    Beyond wrath, beyond beseeching, to the lips reft of thee!"
For she whom he desireth is beyond the deep sea,
    And a ghost in his castle shall be queen.

400

Images in sweet guise
    Carven shall move him never,
Where is Love amid empty eyes?
    Gone, gone for ever!

410

(His dreams and his suffering; but the War that he made caused greater and wider suffering.)

But a shape that is a dream, 'mid the phantoms of the night,
Cometh near, full of tears, bringing vain vain delight:
For in vain when, desiring, he can feel the joy's breath
—Nevermore! Nevermore!—from his arms it vanisheth,
    On wings down the pathways of sleep.

In the mid castle hall, on the hearthstone of the Kings,
These griefs there be, and griefs passing these,
But in each man's dwelling of the host that sailed the seas,
A sad woman waits; she has thoughts of many things,
   And patience in her heart lieth deep.   420
Knoweth she them she sent,
  Knoweth she? Lo, returning,
Comes in stead of the man that went
  Armour and dust of burning.

(The return of the funeral urns; the murmurs of the People.)

And the gold-changer, Ares, who changeth quick for dead,
Who poiseth his scale in the striving of the spears,
Back from Troy sendeth dust, heavy dust, wet with tears,
Sendeth ashes with men's names in his urns neatly spread.
And they weep over the men, and they praise them one by
one,   430
How this was a wise fighter, and this nobly-slain—
  "Fighting to win back another's wife!"
Till a murmur is begun,
  And there steals an angry pain
    Against Kings too forward in the strife.

There by Ilion's gate
   Many a soldier sleepeth,
Young men beautiful; fast in hate
   Troy her conqueror keepeth.

*(For the Shedder of Blood is in great peril, and not unmarked by God.
May I never be a Sacker of Cities!)*

But the rumour of the People, it is heavy, it is chill;   440
And tho' no curse be spoken, like a curse doth it brood;
And my heart waits some tiding which the dark holdeth still,
For of God not unmarked is the shedder of much blood.
And who conquers beyond right ... Lo, the life of man decays;
  There be Watchers dim his light in the wasting of the years;
    He falls, he is forgotten, and hope dies.
There is peril in the praise
  Over-praised that he hears;

For the thunder it is hurled from God's eyes.
450   Glory that breedeth strife,
    Pride of the Sacker of Cities;
Yea, and the conquered captive's life,
    Spare me, O God of Pities!

Diverse Elders

—The fire of good tidings it hath sped the city through,
But who knows if a god mocketh? Or who knows if all be
true?
    'Twere the fashion of a child,
    Or a brain dream-beguiled,
    To be kindled by the first
460   Torch's message as it burst,
And thereafter, as it dies, to die too.

—'Tis like a woman's sceptre, to ordain
Welcome to joy before the end is plain!

—Too lightly opened are a woman's ears;
Her fence downtrod by many trespassers,
    And quickly crossed; but quickly lost
The burden of a woman's hopes or fears.

*[Here a break occurs in the action, like the descent of the
curtain in a modern theatre. A space of some days is as-
sumed to have passed and we find the Elders again assem-
bled.]*

Leader

Soon surely shall we read the message right;
Were fire and beacon-call and lamps of light
470 True speakers, or but happy lights, that seem
And are not, like sweet voices in a dream.
I see a Herald yonder by the shore,
Shadowed with olive sprays. And from his sore
Rent raiment cries a witness from afar,
Dry Dust, born brother to the Mire of war,
That mute he comes not, neither through the smoke

Of mountain forests shall his tale be spoke;
But either shouting for a joyful day,
Or else…. But other thoughts I cast away.
As good hath dawned, may good shine on, we pray!   480   *500*
—And whoso for this City prayeth aught
 Else, let him reap the harvest of his thought!

[Enter the Herald, running. His garments are torn and war-stained. He falls upon his knees and kisses the Earth, and salutes each Altar in turn.]

Herald

Land of my fathers! Argos! Am I here …
Home, home at this tenth shining of the year,
And all Hope's anchors broken save this one!
For scarcely dared I dream, here in mine own
Argos at last to fold me to my rest….
But now—All Hail, O Earth! O Sunlight blest!
And Zeus Most High!

[Checking himself as he sees the altar of Apollo]

   And thou, O Pythian Lord;   490
No more on us be thy swift arrows poured!
Beside Scamander well we learned how true
Thy hate is. Oh, as thou art Healer too,
Heal us! As thou art Saviour of the Lost,
Save also us, Apollo, being so tossed
With tempest! … All ye Daemons of the Pale!
And Hermes! Hermes, mine own guardian, hail!
Herald beloved, to whom all heralds bow….
Ye Blessèd Dead that sent us, receive now
In love your children whom the spear hath spared.   500
 O House of Kings, O roof-tree thrice-endeared,
O solemn thrones! O gods that face the sun!
Now, now, if ever in the days foregone,
After these many years, with eyes that burn,
Give hail and glory to your King's return!
For Agamemnon cometh! A great light

21

Cometh to men and gods out of the night.
　Grand greeting give him—aye, it need be grand—
Who, God's avenging mattock in his hand,
510　　Hath wrecked Troy's towers and digged her soil beneath,
Till her gods' houses, they are things of death;
Her altars waste, and blasted every seed
Whence life might rise! So perfect is his deed,
So dire the yoke on Ilion he hath cast,
The first Atreides, King of Kings at last,
And happy among men! To whom we give
Honour most high above all things that live.
　For Paris nor his guilty land can score
The deed they wrought above the pain they bore.
520　　"Spoiler and thief," he heard God's judgement pass;
Whereby he lost his plunder, and like grass
Mowed down his father's house and all his land;
And Troy pays twofold for the sin she planned.

Leader

Be glad, thou Herald of the Greek from Troy!

Herald

So glad, I am ready, if God will, to die!

Leader

Did love of this land work thee such distress?

Herald

The tears stand in mine eyes for happiness.

Leader

Sweet sorrow was it, then, that on you fell.

Herald

How sweet? I cannot read thy parable.

Leader

530　　To pine again for them that loved you true.

22

Herald

> Did ye then pine for us, as we for you?

Leader

> The whole land's heart was dark, and groaned for thee.

Herald

> Dark? For what cause? Why should such darkness be?

Leader

> Silence in wrong is our best medicine here.

Herald

> Your kings were gone. What others need you fear?

Leader

> 'Tis past! Like thee now, I could gladly die.

Herald

> Even so! 'Tis past, and all is victory.
> And, for our life in those long years, there were
> Doubtless some grievous days, and some were fair.
> Who but a god goes woundless all his way?....   540
> Oh, could I tell the sick toil of the day,
> The evil nights, scant decks ill-blanketed;
> The rage and cursing when our daily bread
> Came not! And then on land 'twas worse than all.
> Our quarters close beneath the enemy's wall;
> And rain—and from the ground the river dew—
> Wet, always wet! Into our clothes it grew,
> Plague-like, and bred foul beasts in every hair.
> Would I could tell how ghastly midwinter
> Stole down from Ida till the birds dropped dead!   550
> Or the still heat, when on his noonday bed
> The breathless blue sea sank without a wave!....
> Why think of it? They are past and in the grave,
> All those long troubles. For I think the slain
> Care little if they sleep or rise again;

And we, the living, wherefore should we ache
With counting all our lost ones, till we wake
The old malignant fortunes? If Good-bye
Comes from their side, Why, let them go, say I.
560   Surely for us, who live, good doth prevail
Unchallenged, with no wavering of the scale;
Wherefore we vaunt unto these shining skies,
As wide o'er sea and land our glory flies:
"By men of Argolis who conquered Troy,
These spoils, a memory and an ancient joy,
Are nailed in the gods' houses throughout Greece."
Which whoso readeth shall with praise increase
Our land, our kings, and God's grace manifold
Which made these marvels be.—My tale is told.

Leader

570   Indeed thou conquerest me. Men say, the light
In old men's eyes yet serves to learn aright.
But Clytemnestra and the House should hear
These tidings first, though I their health may share.

[During the last words Clytemnestra has entered from the Palace.]

Clytemnestra

Long since I lifted up my voice in joy,
When the first messenger from flaming Troy
Spake through the dark of sack and overthrow.
And mockers chid me: "Because beacons show
On the hills, must Troy be fallen? Quickly born
Are women's hopes!" Aye, many did me scorn;
580   Yet gave I sacrifice; and by my word
Through all the city our woman's cry was heard,
Lifted in blessing round the seats of God,
And slumbrous incense o'er the altars glowed
In fragrance. And for thee, what need to tell
Thy further tale? My lord himself shall well
600   Instruct me. Yet, to give my lord and king
All reverent greeting at his homecoming—
What dearer dawn on woman's eyes can flame

24

Than this, which casteth wide her gate to acclaim
The husband whom God leadeth safe from war?—   590
Go, bear my lord this prayer: That fast and far
He haste him to this town which loves his name;
And in his castle may he find the same
Wife that he left, a watchdog of the hall,
True to one voice and fierce to others all;
A body and soul unchanged, no seal of his
Broke in the waiting years.—No thought of ease
Nor joy from other men hath touched my soul,
Nor shall touch, until bronze be dyed like wool.
A boast so faithful and so plain, I wot,   600
Spoke by a royal Queen doth shame her not.

[Exit Clytemnestra.]

Leader

Let thine ear mark her message. 'Tis of fair
Seeming, and craves a clear interpreter....
But, Herald, I would ask thee; tell me true
Of Menelaus. Shall he come with you,
Our land's belovèd crown, untouched of ill?

Herald

I know not how to speak false words of weal
For friends to reap thereof a harvest true.

Leader

Canst speak of truth with comfort joined? Those two
Once parted, 'tis a gulf not lightly crossed.   610

Herald

Your king is vanished from the Achaian host,
He and his ship! Such comfort have I brought.

Leader

Sailed he alone from Troy? Or was he caught
By storms in the midst of you, and swept away?

Herald

> Thou hast hit the truth; good marksman, as men say!
> And long to suffer is but brief to tell.

Leader

> How ran the sailors' talk? Did there prevail
> One rumour, showing him alive or dead?

Herald

> None knoweth, none hath tiding, save the head
> Of Helios, ward and watcher of the world.

620

Leader

> Then tell us of the storm. How, when God hurled
> His anger, did it rise? How did it die?

Herald

> It likes me not, a day of presage high
> With dolorous tongue to stain. Those twain, I vow,
> Stand best apart. When one with shuddering brow,
> From armies lost, back beareth to his home
> Word that the terror of her prayers is come;
> One wound in her great heart, and many a fate
> For many a home of men cast out to sate
> The two-fold scourge that worketh Ares' lust,
> Spear crossed with spear, dust wed with bloody dust;
> Who walketh laden with such weight of wrong,
> Why, let him, if he will, uplift the song
> That is Hell's triumph. But to come as I
> Am now come, laden with deliverance high,
> Home to a land of peace and laughing eyes,
> And mar all with that fury of the skies
> Which made our Greeks curse God—how should this be?
> Two enemies most ancient, Fire and Sea,
> A sudden friendship swore, and proved their plight
> By war on us poor sailors through that night
> Of misery, when the horror of the wave
> Towered over us, and winds from Strymon drave
> Hull against hull, till good ships, by the horn

630

640

26

Of the mad whirlwind gored and overborne,
One here, one there, 'mid rain and blinding spray,
Like sheep by a devil herded, passed away.
And when the blessèd Sun upraised his head,
We saw the Aegean waste a-foam with dead,
Dead men, dead ships, and spars disasterful.   650
Howbeit for us, our one unwounded hull
Out of that wrath was stolen or begged free
By some good spirit—sure no man was he!—
Who guided clear our helm; and on till now
Hath Saviour Fortune throned her on the prow.
No surge to mar our mooring, and no floor
Of rock to tear us when we made for shore.
Till, fled from that sea-hell, with the clear sun
Above us and all trust in fortune gone,
We drove like sheep about our brain the thoughts   660
Of that lost army, broken and scourged with knouts
Of evil. And, methinks, if there is breath
In them, they talk of us as gone to death—
How else?—and so say we of them! For thee,
Since Menelaüs thy first care must be,
If by some word of Zeus, who wills not yet
To leave the old house for ever desolate,
Some ray of sunlight on a far-off sea
Lights him, yet green and living ... we may see
His ship some day in the harbour!—'Twas the word   670
Of truth ye asked me for, and truth ye have heard!

*[Exit Herald. The Chorus take position for the Third
Stasimon.]*

Chorus

    *(Surely there was mystic meaning in the name Helena, meaning which was
    fulfilled when she fled to Troy.)*

    Who was He who found for thee
      That name, truthful utterly—
    Was it One beyond our vision
    Moving sure in pre-decision
      Of man's doom his mystic lips?—

Calling thee, the Battle-wed,
Thee, the Strife-encompassèd,
Helen? Yea, in fate's derision,
680   Hell in cities, Hell in ships,
Hell in hearts of men they knew her,
    When the dim and delicate fold
    Of her curtains backward rolled,
And to sea, to sea, she threw her
    In the West Wind's giant hold;
And with spear and sword behind her
    Came the hunters in a flood,
Down the oarblade's viewless trail
Tracking, till in Simoïs' vale
690 Through the leaves they crept to find her,
    A Wrath, a seed of blood.

(The Trojans welcomed her with triumph and praised Alexander till at last their song changed and they saw another meaning in Alexander's name also.)

700

So the Name to Ilion came
    On God's thought-fulfilling flame,
She a vengeance and a token
Of the unfaith to bread broken,
    Of the hearth of God betrayed,
        Against them whose voices swelled
        Glorying in the prize they held
And the Spoiler's vaunt outspoken
700   And the song his brethren made
    'Mid the bridal torches burning;
    Till, behold, the ancient City
Of King Priam turned, and turning
Took a new song for her learning,
    A song changed and full of pity,
    With the cry of a lost nation;
        And she changed the bridegroom's name:
Called him Paris Ghastly-wed;
    For her sons were with the dead,
710   And her life one lamentation,
        'Mid blood and burning flame.

(Like a lion's whelp reared as a pet and turning afterwards to a great beast of prey)

Lo, once there was a herdsman reared
 In his own house, so stories tell,
 A lion's whelp, a milk-fed thing
 And soft in life's first opening
 Among the sucklings of the herd;
  The happy children loved him well,
 And old men smiled, and oft, they say,
 In men's arms, like a babe, he lay,
Bright-eyed, and toward the hand that teased him   720
 Eagerly fawning for food or play.

Then on a day outflashed the sudden
 Rage of the lion brood of yore;
 He paid his debt to them that fed
 With wrack of herds and carnage red,
 Yea, wrought him a great feast unbidden,
  Till all the house-ways ran with gore;
 A sight the thralls fled weeping from,
 A great red slayer, beard a-foam,
High-priest of some blood-cursèd altar   730
 God had uplifted against that home.

(So was it with Helen in Troy.)

 And how shall I call the thing that came
  At the first hour to Ilion city?
 Call it a dream of peace untold,
 A secret joy in a mist of gold,
 A woman's eye that was soft, like flame,
  A flower which ate a man's heart with pity.

But she swerved aside and wrought to her kiss a bitter ending,
And a wrath was on her harbouring, a wrath upon her
fristaten friending,   740
When to Priam and his sons she fled quickly o'er the deep,
With the god to whom she sinned for her watcher on the wind,
A death-bride, whom brides long shall weep.

(Men say that Good Fortune wakes the envy of God; not so; Good Fortune may be innocent, and then there is no vengeance.)

A grey word liveth, from the morn
  Of old time among mortals spoken,
That man's Wealth waxen full shall fall
  Not childless, but get sons withal;
And ever of great bliss is born
  A tear unstanched and a heart broken.

750   But I hold my thought alone and by others unbeguiled;
'Tis the deed that is unholy shall have issue, child on child,
Sin on sin, like his begetters; and they shall be as they were.
  But the man who walketh straight,
    and the house thereof, tho' Fate
Exalt him, the children shall be fair.

(It is Sin, it is Pride and Ruthlessness, that beget children like themselves till Justice is fulfilled upon them.)

But Old Sin loves, when comes the hour again,
  To bring forth New,
Which laugheth lusty amid the tears of men;
Yea, and Unruth, his comrade, wherewith none

760   May plead nor strive, which dareth on and on,
  Knowing not fear nor any holy thing;
Two fires of darkness in a house, born true,
  Like to their ancient spring.

But Justice shineth in a house low-wrought
  With smoke-stained wall,
And honoureth him who filleth his own lot;
But the unclean hand upon the golden stair
With eyes averse she flieth, seeking where
  Things innocent are; and, recking not the power

770   Of wealth by man misgloried, guideth all
  To her own destined hour.

[*Here, amid a great procession, enters Agamemnon on a Chariot. Behind him on another Chariot is Cassandra. The Chorus approach and make obeisance. Some of*

30

*Agamemnon's men have on their shields a White Horse,
some a Lion. Their arms are rich and partly barbaric.]*

Leader

> All hail, O King! Hail, Atreus' Son!
> Sacker of Cities! Ilion's bane!
> With what high word shall I greet thee again,
> How give thee worship, and neither outrun
> The point of pleasure, nor stint too soon?
> For many will cling to fair seeming
> The faster because they have sinned erewhile;
> And a man may sigh with never a sting
> Of grief in his heart, and a man may smile   780
> With eyes unlit and a lip that strains.
> But the wise Shepherd knoweth his sheep,
>   And his eyes pierce deep
> The faith like water that fawns and feigns.
>
> But I hide nothing, O King. That day
> When in quest of Helen our battle array   800
> Hurled forth, thy name upon my heart's scroll
> Was deep in letters of discord writ;
>   And the ship of thy soul,
> Ill-helmed and blindly steered was it,   790
> Pursuing ever, through men that die,
> One wild heart that was fain to fly.
>   But on this new day,
> From the deep of my thought and in love, I say
>   "Sweet is a grief well ended;"
> And in time's flow Thou wilt learn and know
>   The true from the false,
> Of them that were left to guard the walls
>   Of thine empty Hall unfriended.

[During the above Clytemnestra has appeared on the Palace steps, with a train of Attendants, to receive her Husband.]

Agamemnon

800

To Argos and the gods of Argolis
All hail, who share with me the glory of this
Home-coming and the vengeance I did wreak
On Priam's City! Yea, though none should speak,
The great gods heard our cause, and in one mood
Uprising, in the urn of bitter blood,
That men should shriek and die and towers should burn,
Cast their great vote; while over Mercy's urn
Hope waved her empty hands and nothing fell.
Even now in smoke that City tells her tale;

810

The wrack-wind liveth, and where Ilion died
The reek of the old fatness of her pride
From hot and writhing ashes rolls afar.
For which let thanks, wide as our glories are,
Be uplifted; seeing the Beast of Argos hath
Round Ilion's towers piled high his fence of wrath
And, for one woman ravished, wrecked by force
A City. Lo, the leap of the wild Horse
in darkness when the Pleiades were dead;
A mailed multitude, a Lion unfed,

820

Which leapt the tower and lapt the blood of Kings!

Lo, to the Gods I make these thanksgivings.
But for thy words: I marked them, and I mind
Their meaning, and my voice shall be behind
Thine. For not many men, the proverb saith,
Can love a friend whom fortune prospereth
Unenvying; and about the envious brain
Cold poison clings, and doubles all the pain
Life brings him. His own woundings he must nurse,
And feels another's gladness like a curse.

830

Well can I speak. I know the mirrored glass
Called friendship, and the shadow shapes that pass
And feign them a King's friends. I have known but one—
Odysseus, him we trapped against his own
Will!—who once harnessed bore his yoke right well ...
Be he alive or dead of whom I tell
The tale. And for the rest, touching our state
And gods, we will assemble in debate

A concourse of all Argos, taking sure
Counsel, that what is well now may endure
Well, and if aught needs healing medicine, still   840
By cutting and by fire, with all good will,
I will essay to avert the after-wrack
Such sickness breeds. Aye, Heaven hath led me back;
And on this hearth where still my fire doth burn
I will go pay to heaven my due return,
Which guides me here, which saved me far away.
    O Victory, now mine own, be mine alway!

[Clytemnestra, at the head of her retinue, steps forward.
She controls her suspense with difficulty but gradually gains
courage as she proceeds.]

Clytemnestra

Ye Elders, Council of the Argive name
Here present, I will no more hold it shame
To lay my passion bare before men's eyes.   850
There comes a time to a woman when fear dies
For ever. None hath taught me. None could tell,
Save me, the weight of years intolerable
I lived while this man lay at Ilion.
That any woman thus should sit alone
In a half-empty house, with no man near,
Makes her half-blind with dread! And in her ear
Alway some voice of wrath; now messengers
Of evil; now not so; then others worse,
Crying calamity against mine and me.   860
    Oh, had he half the wounds that variously
Came rumoured home, his flesh must be a net,
All holes from heel to crown! And if he met
As many deaths as I met tales thereon,
Is he some monstrous thing, some Gêryon
Three-souled, that will not die, till o'er his head,
Three robes of earth be piled, to hold him dead?
    Aye, many a time my heart broke, and the noose
Of death had got me; but they cut me loose.
It was those voices alway in mine ear.   870

33

For that, too, young Orestes is not here
Beside me, as were meet, seeing he above
All else doth hold the surety of our love;
Let not thy heart be troubled. It fell thus:
Our loving spear-friend took him, Strophius
The Phocian, who forewarned me of annoy
Two-fronted, thine own peril under Troy,
And ours here, if the rebel multitude
Should cast the Council down. It is men's mood
880   Alway, to spurn the fallen. So spake he,
And sure no guile was in him. But for me,
The old stormy rivers of my grief are dead
Now at the spring; not one tear left unshed.
Mine eyes are sick with vigil, endlessly
Weeping the beacon-piles that watched for thee
For ever answerless. And did I dream,
A gnat's thin whirr would start me, like a scream
Of battle, and show me thee by terrors swept,
Crowding, too many for the time I slept.

890   From all which stress delivered and free-souled,
I greet my lord: O watchdog of the fold,
O forestay sure that fails not in the squall,
O strong-based pillar of a towering hall;
O single son to a father age-ridden;
900   O land unhoped for seen by shipwrecked men;
Sunshine more beautiful when storms are fled;
Spring of quick water in a desert dead ....
How sweet to be set free from any chain!

These be my words to greet him home again.
900   No god shall grudge them. Surely I and thou
Have suffered in time past enough! And now
Dismount, O head with love and glory crowned,
From this high car; yet plant not on bare ground
Thy foot, great King, the foot that trampled Troy.
  Ho, bondmaids, up! Forget not your employ,
A floor of crimson broideries to spread
For the King's path. Let all the ground be red
Where those feet pass; and Justice, dark of yore,
Home light him to the hearth he looks not for!

What followeth next, our sleepless care shall see   910
Ordered as God's good pleasure may decree.

*[The attendants spread tapestries of crimson and gold from
the Chariot to the Door of the Palace. Agamemnon does
not move.]*

Agamemnon

Daughter of Leda, watcher of my fold,
In sooth thy welcome, grave and amply told,
Fitteth mine absent years. Though it had been
Seemlier, methinks, some other, not my Queen,
Had spoke these honours. For the rest, I say,
Seek not to make me soft in woman's way;
Cry not thy praise to me wide-mouthed, nor fling
Thy body down, as to some barbarous king.
Nor yet with broidered hangings strew my path,   920
To awake the unseen ire. 'Tis God that hath
Such worship; and for mortal man to press
Rude feet upon this broidered loveliness ...
I vow there is danger in it. Let my road
Be honoured, surely; but as man, not god.
Rugs for the feet and yonder broidered pall ...
The names ring diverse!... Aye, and not to fall
Suddenly blind is of all gifts the best
God giveth, for I reckon no man blest
Ere to the utmost goal his race be run.   930
  So be it; and if, as this day I have done,
I shall do always, then I fear no ill.

Clytemnestra

Tell me but this, nowise against thy will ...

Agamemnon

My will, be sure, shall falter not nor fade.

Clytemnestra

Was this a vow in some great peril made?

Agamemnon

> Enough! I have spoke my purpose, fixed and plain.

Clytemnestra

> Were Priam the conqueror ... Think, would he refrain?

Agamemnon

> Oh, stores of broideries would be trampled then!

Clytemnestra

> Lord, care not for the cavillings of men!

Agamemnon

940

> The murmur of a people hath strange weight.

Clytemnestra

> Who feareth envy, feareth to be great.

Agamemnon

> 'Tis graceless when a woman strives to lead.

Clytemnestra

> When a great conqueror yields, 'tis grace indeed,

Agamemnon

> So in this war thou must my conqueror be?

Clytemnestra

> Yield! With good will to yield is victory!

Agamemnon

> Well, if I needs must ... Be it as thou hast said!
>   Quick! Loose me these bound slaves on which I tread,
> And while I walk yon wonders of the sea
> God grant no eye of wrath be cast on me

950

> From far!

[The Attendants untie his shoes]

For even now it likes me not
To waste mine house, thus marring underfoot
The pride thereof, and wondrous broideries
Bought in far seas with silver. But of these
Enough.—And mark, I charge thee, this princess
Of Ilion; tend her with all gentleness.
God's eye doth see, and loveth from afar,
The merciful conqueror. For no slave of war
Is slave by his own will. She is the prize
And chosen flower of Ilion's treasuries,   960
Set by the soldiers' gift to follow me.
Now therefore, seeing I am constrained by thee
And do thy will, I walk in conqueror's guise
Beneath my Gate, trampling sea-crimson dyes.

*[As he dismounts and sets foot on the Tapestries Clytem-
nestra's women utter again their Cry of Triumph. The
people bow or kneel as he passes.]*

Clytemnestra

There is the sea—its caverns who shall drain?—
Breeding of many a purple-fish the stain
Surpassing silver, ever fresh renewed,
For robes of kings. And we, by right indued,
Possess our fill thereof. Thy house, O King,
Knoweth no stint, nor lack of anything.   970
  What trampling of rich raiment, had the cry
So sounded in the domes of prophesy,
Would I have vowed these years, as price to pay
For this dear life in peril far away!
Where the root is, the leafage cometh soon
To clothe an house, and spread its leafy boon
Against the burning star; and, thou being come,
Thou, on the midmost hearthstone of thy home,
Oh, warmth in winter leapeth to thy sign.
And when God's summer melteth into wine   980
The green grape, on that house shall coolness fall
Where the true man, the master, walks his hall.

Zeus, Zeus! True Master, let my prayers be true!
And, oh, forget not that thou art willed to do!

*[She follows Agamemnon into the Palace. The retinues
of both King and Queen go in after them. Cassandra re-
mains.]*

Chorus

[Strophe 1.]

What is this that evermore,
　A cold terror at the door
Of this bosom presage-haunted,
　Pale as death hovereth?
While a song unhired, unwanted,
By some inward prophet chanted,
　Speaks the secret at its core;
　And to cast it from my blood
　Like a dream not understood
　No sweet-spoken Courage now
　Sitteth at my heart's dear prow.

Yet I know that manifold
　Days, like sand, have waxen old

Since the day those shoreward-thrown
　Cables flapped and line on line
Standing forth for Ilion
　The long galleys took the brine

[Antistrophe 1.]

And in harbour—mine own eye
Hath beheld—again they lie;
Yet that lyreless music hidden
　Whispers still words of ill,
'Tis the Soul of me unbidden,
Like some Fury sorrow-ridden,
　Weeping over things that die.
　Neither waketh in my sense

38

Ever Hope's dear confidence;   1010
For this flesh that groans within,
And these bones that know of Sin,
This tossed heart upon the spate
Of a whirpool that is Fate,
Surely these lie not. Yet deep
   Beneath hope my prayer doth run,
All will die like dreams, and creep
   To the unthought of and undone.   *1000*

[Strophe 2.]

  —Surely of great Weal at the end of all
    Comes not Content; so near doth Fever crawl,   1020
    Close neighbour, pressing hard the narrow wall.

  —Woe to him who fears not fate!
    'Tis the ship that forward straight
    Sweepeth, strikes the reef below;
    He who fears and lightens weight,
    Casting forth, in measured throw,
    From the wealth his hand hath got …
    His whole ship shall founder not,
    With abundance overfraught,
    Nor deep seas above him flow.   1030
  —Lo, when famine stalketh near,
    One good gift of Zeus again
  From the furrows of one year
    Endeth quick the starving pain;

[Antistrophe 2.]

  —But once the blood of death is fallen, black
    And oozing at a slain man's feet, alack!
    By spell or singing who shall charm it back?

  —One there was of old who showed
    Man the path from death to day;
  But Zeus, lifting up his rod,   1040
    Spared not, when he charged him stay.

—Save that every doom of God
Hath by other dooms its way
Crossed, that none may rule alone,
In one speech-outstripping groan
Forth had all this passion flown,
Which now murmuring hides away,
Full of pain, and hoping not
Ever one clear thread to unknot

1050 From the tangle of my soul,
From a heart of burning coal.

[Suddenly Clytemnestra appears standing in the Doorway.]

Clytemnestra

Thou likewise, come within! I speak thy name,
Cassandra;

*[Cassandra trembles, but continues to stare in front of her,
as though not hearing Clytemnestra.]*

seeing the Gods—why chafe at them?—
Have placed thee here, to share within these walls
Our lustral waters, 'mid a crowd of thralls
Who stand obedient round the altar-stone
Of our Possession. Therefore come thou down,
And be not over-proud. The tale is told

1060 How once Alcmena's son himself, being sold,
Was patient, though he liked not the slaves' mess.
   And more, if Fate must bring thee to this stress,
Praise God thou art come to a House of high report
And wealth from long ago. The baser sort,
Who have reaped some sudden harvest unforeseen,
Are ever cruel to their slaves, and mean
In the measure. We shall give whate'er is due.

[Cassandra is silent.]

Leader

To thee she speaks, and waits ... clear words and true!
Oh, doom is all around thee like a net;

1070 Yield, if thou canst.... Belike thou canst not yet.

Clytemnestra

> Methinks, unless this wandering maid is one
> Voiced like a swallow-bird, with tongue unknown
> And barbarous, she can read my plain intent.
> I use but words, and ask for her consent.

Leader

> Ah, come! Tis best, as the world lies to-day.
> Leave this high-throned chariot, and obey!

Clytemnestra

> How long must I stand dallying at the Gate?
> Even now the beasts to Hestia consecrate
> Wait by the midmost fire, since there is wrought
> This high fulfilment for which no man thought.   1080
> Wherefore, if 'tis thy pleasure to obey
> Aught of my will, prithee, no more delay!
> If, dead to sense, thou wilt not understand...

[To the Leader of the Chorus]

> Thou show her, not with speech but with brute hand!

Leader

> The strange maid needs a rare interpreter.
> She is trembling like a wild beast in a snare.

Clytemnestra

> 'Fore God, she is mad, and heareth but her own
> Folly! A slave, her city all o'erthrown,
> She needs must chafe her bridle, till this fret
> Be foamed away in blood and bitter sweat.   1090
> I waste no more speech, thus to be defied.

[She goes back inside the Palace.]

Leader

> I pity thee so sore, no wrath nor pride
> Is in me.—Come, dismount! Bend to the stroke

Fate lays on thee, and learn to feel thy yoke.

[*He lays his hand softly on Cassandra's shoulder*]

Cassandra [*moaning to herself*]

Otototoi … Dreams. Dreams.
Apollo. O Apollo!

Second Elder

Why sob'st thou for Apollo? It is writ,
He loves not grief nor lendeth ear to it.

Cassandra

1100
        Otototoi … Dreams. Dreams.
Apollo. O Apollo!

Leader

Still to that god she makes her sobbing cry
Who hath no place where men are sad, or die.

Cassandra

Apollo, Apollo! Light of the Ways of Men!
  Mine enemy!
Hast lighted me to darkness yet again?

Second Elder

How? Will she prophesy about her own
Sorrows? That power abides when all is gone!

Cassandra

Apollo, Apollo! Light of all that is! Mine enemy!
Where hast thou led me? … Ha! What house is this?

Leader

1110
        The Atreidae's castle. If thou knowest not, I
Am here to help thee, and help faithfully.

Cassandra [whispering]

> Nay, nay. This is the house that God hateth.
> There be many things that know its secret; sore
> And evil things; murders and strangling death.
> 'Tis here they slaughter men...A splashing floor.

Second Elder

> Keen-sensed the strange maid seemeth, like a hound
> For blood.—And what she seeks can sure be found!

Cassandra

> The witnesses ... I follow where they lead.
> The crying ... of little children ... near the gate:
> Crying for wounds that bleed: 1120
> And the smell of the baked meats their father ate.

Second Elder [recognizing her vision, and repelled]

> Word of thy mystic power had reached our ear
> Long since. Howbeit we need no prophets here.

Cassandra

> Ah, ah! What would they? A new dreadful thing.   *1100*
> A great great sin plots in the house this day;
> Too strong for the faithful, beyond medicining ...
> And help stands far away.

Leader

> This warning I can read not, though I knew
> That other tale. It rings the city through.

Cassandra

> O Woman, thou! The lord who lay with thee!   1130
> Wilt lave with water, and then ... How speak the end?
> It comes so quick. A hand ... another hand ...
> That reach, reach gropingly....

Leader

> I see not yet. These riddles, pierced with blind

43

Gleams of foreboding, but bemuse my mind.

Cassandra

Ah, ah! What is it? There; it is coming clear.
A net ... some net of Hell.
Nay, she that lies with him ... is she the snare?
And half of his blood upon it. It holds well....
1140   O Crowd of ravening Voices, be glad, yea, shout
And cry for the stoning, cry for the casting out!

Second Elder

What Fury Voices call'st thou to be hot
Against this castle? Such words like me not.

And deep within my breast I felt that sick
  And saffron drop, which creepeth to the heart
  To die as the last rays of life depart.
    Misfortune comes so quick.

Cassandra

Ah, look! Look! Keep his mate from the Wild Bull!
  A tangle of raiment, see;
1150   A black horn, and a blow, and he falleth, full
  In the marble amid the water. I counsel ye.
  I speak plain ... Blood in the bath and treachery!

Leader

No great interpreter of oracles
Am I; but this, I think, some mischief spells.

What spring of good hath seercraft ever made
  Up from the dark to flow?
'Tis but a weaving of words, a craft of woe,
  To make mankind afraid.

Cassandra

Poor woman! Poor dead woman! ... Yea, it is I,
1160   Poured out like water among them. Weep for me....

Ah! What is this place? Why must I come with thee....
⠀⠀To die, only to die?

Leader

⠀⠀Thou art borne on the breath of God, thou spirit wild,
⠀⠀⠀⠀For thine own weird to wail,
⠀⠀Like to that wingèd voice, that heart so sore
⠀⠀Which, crying alway, hungereth to cry more,
⠀⠀"Itylus, Itylus," till it sing her child
⠀⠀⠀⠀Back to the nightingale.

Cassandra

⠀⠀Oh, happy Singing Bird, so sweet, so clear!
⠀⠀⠀⠀Soft wings for her God made,⠀⠀⠀⠀⠀⠀⠀⠀⠀⠀⠀⠀1170
⠀⠀And an easy passing, without pain or tear ...
⠀⠀For me 'twill be torn flesh and rending blade.

Second Elder

⠀⠀Whence is it sprung, whence wafted on God's breath,
⠀⠀⠀⠀This anguish reasonless?
⠀⠀This throbbing of terror shaped to melody,
⠀⠀Moaning of evil blent with music high?
⠀⠀Who hath marked out for thee that mystic path
⠀⠀⠀⠀Through thy woe's wilderness?

Cassandra

⠀⠀Alas for the kiss, the kiss of Paris, his people's bane!
⠀⠀Alas for Scamander Water, the water my fathers drank!⠀⠀⠀1180
⠀⠀Long, long ago, I played about thy bank,
⠀⠀⠀⠀And was cherished and grew strong;
⠀⠀Now by a River of Wailing, by shores of Pain,
⠀⠀⠀⠀Soon shall I make my song.

Leader

⠀⠀⠀⠀How sayst thou? All too clear,
⠀⠀This ill word thou hast laid upon thy mouth!
⠀⠀⠀⠀A babe could read thee plain.
⠀⠀It stabs within me like a serpent's tooth,
⠀⠀The bitter thrilling music of her pain:

45

1190   I marvel as I hear.

Cassandra

Alas for the toil, the toil of a City, worn unto death!
Alas for my father's worship before the citadel,
The flocks that bled and the tumult of their breath!
  But no help from them came
To save Troy Towers from falling as they fell!...
And I on the earth shall writhe, my heart aflame.

Second Elder

Dark upon dark, new ominous words of ill!
  Sure there hath swept on thee some Evil Thing,
    Crushing, which makes thee bleed
1200   And in the torment of thy vision sing
These plaining death-fraught oracles ... Yet still, still,
    Their end I cannot read!

*Cassandra [By an effort she regains mastery of herself, and speaks directly to the
Leader.]*

'Fore God, mine oracle shall no more hide
With veils his visage, like a new-wed bride!
A shining wind out of this dark shall blow,
Piercing the dawn, growing as great waves grow,
To burst in the heart of sunrise ... stronger far
Than this poor pain of mine. I will not mar
With mists my wisdom. Be near me as I go,
1210 Tracking the evil things of long ago,
And bear me witness. For this roof, there clings
Music about it, like a choir which sings
One-voiced, but not well-sounding, for not good
The words are. Drunken, drunken, and with blood,
To make them dare the more, a revelling rout
Is in the rooms, which no man shall cast out,
Of sister Furies. And they weave to song,
Haunting the House, its first blind deed of wrong,
Spurning in turn that King's bed desecrate,
1220 Defiled, which paid a brother's sin with hate....

46

Hath it missed or struck, mine arrow? Am I a poor
Dreamer, that begs and babbles at the door?
Give first thine oath in witness, that I know
Of this great dome the sins wrought long ago.

Elder

And how should oath of mine, though bravely sworn,
Appease thee? Yet I marvel that one born
Far over seas, of alien speech, should fall   *1200*
So apt, as though she had lived here and seen all.

Cassandra

The Seer Apollo made me too to see.

Elder [in a low voice]

Was the God's heart pierced with desire for thee?   1230

Cassandra

Time was, I held it shame hereof to speak.

Elder

Ah, shame is for the mighty, not the weak.

Cassandra

We wrestled, and his breath to me was sweet.

Elder

Ye came to the getting of children, as is meet?

Cassandra

I swore to Loxias, and I swore a lie.

Elder

Already thine the gift of prophecy?

Cassandra

Already I showed my people all their path.

Elder

And Loxias did not smite thee in his wrath?

Cassandra

After that sin ... no man believed me more.

Elder

1240   Nay, then, to us thy wisdom seemeth sure.

Cassandra

Oh, oh! Agony, agony!
Again the awful pains of prophecy
Are on me, maddening as they fall....
Ye see them there ... beating against the wall?
So young ... like shapes that gather in a dream ...
Slain by a hand they loved. Children they seem,
Murdered ... and in their hands they bear baked meat:
I think it is themselves. Yea, flesh; I see it;
And inward parts.... Oh, what a horrible load
1250   To carry! And their father drank their blood.

From these, I warn ye, vengeance broodeth still,
A lion's rage, which goes not forth to kill
But lurketh in his lair, watching the high
Hall of my war-gone master ... Master? Aye;
Mine, mine! The yoke is nailed about my neck....
Oh, lord of ships and trampler on the wreck
Of Ilion, knows he not this she-wolf's tongue,
Which licks and fawns, and laughs with ear up-sprung,
To bite in the end like secret death?—And can
1260   The woman? Slay a strong and armèd man? ...
    What fangèd reptile like to her doth creep?
Some serpent amphisbene, some Skylla, deep
Housed in the rock, where sailors shriek and die,
Mother of Hell blood-raging, which doth cry
On her own flesh war, war without alloy ...
God! And she shouted in his face her joy,
Like men in battle when the foe doth break.
And feigns thanksgiving for his safety's sake!

48

What if no man believe me? 'Tis all one.
The thing which must be shall be; aye, and soon   1270
Thou too shalt sorrow for these things, and here
Standing confess me all too true a seer.

Leader

The Thyestean feast of children slain
I understood, and tremble. Aye, my brain
Reels at these visions, beyond guesswork true.
But after, though I heard, I had lost the clue.

Cassandra

Man, thou shalt look on Agamemnon dead.

Leader

Peace, Mouth of Evil! Be those words unsaid!

Cassandra

No god of peace hath watch upon that hour.

Leader

If it must come. Forefend it, Heavenly Power!   1280

Cassandra

They do not think of prayer; they think of death.

Leader

They? Say, what man this foul deed compasseth?

Cassandra

Alas, thou art indeed fallen far astray!

Leader

How could such deed be done? I see no way.

Cassandra

Yet know I not the Greek tongue all too well?

Leader

> Greek are the Delphic dooms, but hard to spell.

Cassandra

> Ah! Ah! There!
> What a strange fire! It moves ... It comes at me.
> O Wolf Apollo, mercy! O agony! ...
> 1290 Why lies she with a wolf, this lioness lone,
> Two-handed, when the royal lion is gone?
> God, she will kill me! Like to them that brew
> Poison, I see her mingle for me too
> A separate vial in her wrath, and swear,
> Whetting her blade for him, that I must share
> His death ... because, because he hath dragged me here!
>   Oh, why these mockers at my throat? This gear
> Of wreathèd bands, this staff of prophecy?
> I mean to kill you first, before I die.
> 1300 Begone!

[She tears off her prophetic habiliments; and presently throws them on the ground, and stamps on them.]

> Down to perdition! ... Lie ye so?
> So I requite you! Now make rich in woe
> Some other Bird of Evil, me no more!

[Coming to herself]

> Ah, see! It is Apollo's self, hath tore
> His crown from me! Who watched me long ago
> In this same prophet's robe, by friend, by foe,
> All with one voice, all blinded, mocked to scorn:
> "A thing of dreams," "a beggar-maid outworn,"
> Poor, starving and reviled, I endured all;
> 1310 And now the Seer, who called me till my call
> Was perfect, leads me to this last dismay....
> 'Tis not the altar-stone where men did slay
> My father; 'tis a block, a block with gore
> Yet hot, that waits me, of one slain before.
>   Yet not of God unheeded shall we lie.
> There cometh after, one who lifteth high

The downfallen; a branch where blossometh
A sire's avenging and a mother's death.
Exiled and wandering, from this land outcast,
One day He shall return, and set the last   1320
Crown on these sins that have his house downtrod.
For, lo, there is a great oath sworn of God,
His father's upturned face shall guide him home.
　Why should I grieve? Why pity these men's doom?
I who have seen the City of Ilion
Pass as she passed; and they who cast her down
Have thus their end, as God gives judgement sure....
　I go to drink my cup. I will endure
To die. O Gates, Death-Gates, all hail to you!
Only, pray God the blow be stricken true!   1330
Pray God, unagonized, with blood that flows
Quick unto friendly death, these eyes may close!

Leader

O full of sorrows, full of wisdom great,
Woman, thy speech is a long anguish; yet,
Knowing thy doom, why walkst thou with clear eyes,
Like some god-blinded beast, to sacrifice?

Cassandra

There is no escape, friends; only vain delay.

Leader

Is not the later still the sweeter day?   1300

Cassandra

The day is come. Small profit now to fly.

Leader

Through all thy griefs, Woman, thy heart is high.   1340

Cassandra

Alas! None that is happy hears that praise.

Leader

> Are not the brave dead blest in after days?

Cassandra

> O Father! O my brethren brave, I come!

[She moves towards the House, but recoils shuddering.]

Leader

> What frights thee? What is that thou startest from?

Cassandra

> Ah, faugh! Faugh!

Leader

> What turns thee in that blind
> Horror? Unless some loathing of the mind ...

Cassandra

> Death drifting from the doors, and blood like rain!

Leader

> 'Tis but the dumb beasts at the altar slain.

Cassandra

1350
> And vapours from a charnel-house ... See there!

Leader

> 'Tis Tyrian incense clouding in the air.

Cassandra [recovering herself again]

> So be it!—I will go, in yonder room
> To weep mine own and Agamemnon's doom.
> May death be all! Strangers, I am no bird
> That pipeth trembling at a thicket stirred
> By the empty wind. Bear witness on that day
> When woman for this woman's life shall pay,

And man for man ill-mated low shall lie:
I ask this boon, as being about to die.

Leader

Alas, I pity thee thy mystic fate!   1360

Cassandra

One word, one dirge-song would I utter yet
O'er mine own corpse. To this last shining Sun
I pray that, when the Avenger's work is done,
His enemies may remember this thing too,
This little thing, the woman slave they slew!

O world of men, farewell! A painted show
Is all thy glory; and when life is low
The touch of a wet sponge out-blotteth all.
Oh, sadder this than any proud man's fall!

[She goes into the House.]

Chorus

Great Fortune is an hungry thing,   1370
  And filleth no heart anywhere,
Though men with fingers menacing
  Point at the great house, none will dare,
When Fortune knocks, to bar the door
Proclaiming: "Come thou here no more!"
Lo, to this man the Gods have given
  Great Ilion in the dust to tread
And home return, emblazed of heaven;
If it is writ, he too shall go
Through blood for blood spilt long ago;   1380
If he too, dying for the dead,
  Should crown the deaths of alien years,
  What mortal afar off, who hears,
Shall boast him Fortune's Child, and led
Above the eternal tide of tears?

[A sudden Cry from within.]

Voice

> Ho! Treason in the house! I am wounded: slain.

Leader

> Hush! In the castle! 'Twas a cry
> Of some man wounded mortally.

Voice

> Ah God, another! I am stricken again.

Leader

1390

> I think the deed is done. It was the King
> Who groaned.... Stand close, and think if anything....

[The Old Men gather together under the shock, and debate confusedly.]

Elder B

> I give you straight my judgement. Summon all
> The citizens to rescue. Sound a call!

Elder C

> No, no! Burst in at once without a word!
> In, and convict them by their dripping sword!

Elder D

> Yes; that or something like it. Quick, I say,
> Be doing! 'Tis a time for no delay.

Elder E

> We have time to think. This opening ... They have planned
> Some scheme to make enslavement of the land.

Elder F

1400

> Yes, while we linger here! They take no thought
> Of lingering, and their sword-arm sleepeth not!

Elder G

> I have no counsel. I can speak not. Oh,
> Let him give counsel who can strike a blow!

Elder H

> I say as this man says. I have no trust
> In words to raise a dead man from the dust.

Elder I

> How mean you? Drag out our poor lives, and stand
> Cowering to these defilers of the land?

Elder J

> Nay, 'tis too much! Better to strive and die!
> Death is an easier doom than slavery.

Elder K

> We heard a sound of groaning, nothing plain,   1410
> How know we—are we seers?—that one is slain?

Elder L

> Oh, let us find the truth out, ere we grow
> Thus passionate! To surmise is not to know.

Leader

> Break in, then! 'Tis the counsel ye all bring,
> And learn for sure, how is it with the King.

[They cluster up towards the Palace Door, as though to force an entrance, when the great Door swings open, revealing Clytemnestra, who stands, axe in hand, over the dead bodies of Agamemnon and Cassandra. The body of Agamemnon is wrapped in a rich crimson web. There is blood on Clytemnestra's brow, and she speaks in wild triumph.]

Clytemnestra

> Oh, lies enough and more have I this day

55

Spoken, which now I shame not to unsay.
How should a woman work, to the utter end,
Hate on a damnèd hater, feigned a friend;

1420   How pile perdition round him, hunter-wise,
Too high for overleaping, save by lies?
To me this hour was dreamed of long ago;
A thing of ancient hate. 'Twas very slow
In coming, but it came. And here I stand
Even where I struck, with all the deed I planned
Done! 'Twas so wrought—what boots it to deny?—
The man could neither guard himself nor fly.
An endless web, as by some fisher strung,
A deadly plenteousness of robe, I flung

1430   All round him, and struck twice; and with two cries
His limbs turned water and broke; and as he lies
I cast my third stroke in, a prayer well-sped
To Zeus of Hell, who guardeth safe his dead!
So there he gasped his life out as he lay;
And, gasping, the blood spouted ... Like dark spray
That splashed, it came, a salt and deathly dew;
Sweet, sweet as God's dear rain-drops ever blew
O'er a parched field, the day the buds are born! ...
Which things being so, ye Councillors high-born,

1440   Depart in joy, if joy ye will. For me,
I glory. Oh, if such a thing might be
As o'er the dead thank-offering to outpour,
On this dead it were just, aye, just and more,
Who filled the cup of the House with treacheries
Curse-fraught, and here hath drunk it to the lees!

Leader

We are astonished at thy speech. To fling,
1400   Wild mouth! such vaunt over thy murdered King!

Clytemnestra

Wouldst fright me, like a witless woman? Lo,
This bosom shakes not. And, though well ye know,
1450   I tell you ... Curse me as ye will, or bless,
'Tis all one ... This is Agamemnon; this,
My husband, dead by my right hand, a blow

Struck by a righteous craftsman. Aye, 'tis so.

Chorus

Woman, what evil tree,
  What poison grown of the ground
Or draught of the drifting sea
  Way to thy lips hath found,
Making thee clothe thy heart
  In rage, yea, in curses burning
When thine own people pray?   1460
Thou hast hewn, thou hast cast away;
And a thing cast away thou art,
  A thing of hate and a spurning!

Clytemnestra

Aye, now, for me, thou hast thy words of fate;
Exile from Argos and the people's hate
For ever! Against him no word was cried,
When, recking not, as 'twere a beast that died,
With flocks abounding o'er his wide domain,
He slew his child, my love, my flower of pain, ...
Great God, as magic for the winds of Thrace!   1470
Why was not he man-hunted from his place,
To purge the blood that stained him? ... When the deed
Is mine, oh, then thou art a judge indeed!
But threat thy fill. I am ready, and I stand
Content; if thy hand beateth down my hand,
Thou rulest. If aught else be God's decree,
Thy lesson shall be learned, though late it be.

Chorus

Thy thought, it is very proud;
  Thy breath is the scorner's breath;
Is not the madness loud   1480
  In thy heart, being drunk with death?
Yea, and above thy brow
  A star of the wet blood burneth!
Oh, doom shall have yet her day,
The last friend cast away,
When lie doth answer lie

57

And a stab for a stab returneth!

Clytemnestra

And hoark what Oath-gods gather to my side!
By my dead child's Revenge, now satisfied,
1490 By Mortal Blindness, by all Powers of Hell
Which Hate, to whom in sacrifice he fell,
My Hope shall walk not in the house of Fear,
While on my hearth one fire yet burneth clear,
One lover, one Aigisthos, as of old!
What should I fear, when fallen here I hold
This foe, this scorner of his wife, this toy
And fool of each Chryseis under Troy;
And there withal his soothsayer and slave,
His chanting bed-fellow, his leman brave,
1500 Who rubbed the galleys' benches at his side.
But, oh, they had their guerdon as they died!
For he lies thus, and she, the wild swan's way,
Hath trod her last long weeping roundelay,
And lies, his lover, ravisht o'er the main
For his bed's comfort and my deep disdain.

Chorus [Some Elders]

Would God that suddenly
With no great agony,
  No long sick-watch to keep,
My hour would come to me,
1510 My hour, and presently
Bring the eternal, the
  Unwaking Sleep,
Now that my Shepherd, he
Whose love watched over me,
  Lies in the deep!

Another

For woman's sake he endured and battled well,
  And by a woman's hand he fell.

Others

What hast thou done, O Helen blind of brain,

O face that slew the souls on Ilion's plain,
One face, one face, and many a thousand slain?   1520
  The hate of old that on this castle lay,
Builded in lust, a husband's evil day,
Hath bloomed for thee a perfect flower again
And unforgotten, an old and burning stain
  Never to pass away.

Clytemnestra

Nay, pray not for the hour of death, being tried
  Too sore beneath these blows
Neither on Helen turn thy wrath aside,
The Slayer of Men, the face which hath destroyed
Its thousand Danaan souls, and wrought a wide   1530
  Wound that no leech can close.

Chorus

—Daemon, whose heel is set
  On the House and the twofold kin
    Of the high Tantalidae,
A power, heavy as fate,
  Thou wieldest through woman's sin,
    Piercing the heart of me!

—Like a raven swoln with hate
  He hath set on the dead his claw,
He croaketh a song to sate   1540
  His fury, and calls it Law!

Clytemnestra

Ah, call upon Him! Yea, call—
  And thy thought hath found its path—
The Daemon who haunts this hall,
  The thrice-engorged Wrath;

From him is the ache of the flesh
  For blood born and increased;
Ere the old sore hath ceased
  It oozeth afresh.

Chorus

1550
 —Indeed He is very great,
  And heavy his anger, He,
  The Daemon who guides the fate
  Of the old Tantalidae:
 Alas, alas, an evil tale ye tell
 Of desolate angers and insatiable!

 —Ah me,
  And yet 'tis all as Zeus hath willed,
  Doer of all and Cause of all;
  By His Word every chance doth fall,
1560
  No end without Him is fulfilled;
  What of these things
 But cometh by high Heaven's counsellings?

[A band of Mourners has gathered within the House.]

Mourners

 Ah, sorrow, sorrow! My King, my King!
  How shall I weep, what word shall I say?
 Caught in the web of this spider thing,
  In foul death gasping thy life away!
 Woe's me, woe's me, for this slavish lying,
 The doom of craft and the lonely dying,
  The iron two-edged and the hands that slay!

Clytemnestra

1570
  And criest thou still this deed hath been
  My work? Nay, gaze, and have no thought
  That this is Agamemnon's Queen.
  'Tis He, 'tis He, hath round him wrought
1500
  This phantom of the dead man's wife;
 He, the old Wrath, the Driver of Men astray,
  Pursuer of Atreus for the feast defiled;
  To assoil an ancient debt he hath paid this life;
 A warrior and a crowned King this day
  Atones for a slain child.

60

Chorus

—That thou art innocent herein,   1580
  What tongue dare boast? It cannot be,
Yet from the deeps of ancient sin
  The Avenger may have wrought with thee.

—On the red Slayer crasheth, groping wild
  For blood, more blood, to build his peace again,
And wash like water the old frozen stain
    Of the torn child.

Mourners

Ah, sorrow, sorrow! My King, my King!
  How shall I weep, what word shall I say?
Caught in the web of this spider thing,   1590
  In foul death gasping thy life away.
Woe's me, woe's me, for this slavish lying,
The doom of craft and the lonely dying,
  The iron two-edged and the hands that slay!

Clytemnestra

And what of the doom of craft that first
He planted, making the House accurst?
What of the blossom, from this root riven,
Iphigenîa, the unforgiven?
Even as the wrong was, so is the pain:
He shall not laugh in the House of the slain,   1600
  When the count is scored;
He hath but spoilèd and paid again
  The due of the sword.

Chorus

I am lost; my mind dull-eyed
  Knows not nor feels
Whither to fly nor hide
  While the House reels.
The noise of rain that falls
  On the roof affrighteth me,
Washing away the walls;   1610
  Rain that falls bloodily.

61

Doth ever the sound abate?
Lo, the next Hour of Fate
Whetting her vengeance due
On new whet-stones, for new
    Workings of hate.

Mourners

Would thou hadst covered me, Earth, O Earth,
    Or e'er I had looked on my lord thus low,
In the pallèd marble of silvern girth!
1620   What hands may shroud him, what tears may flow?
Not thine, O Woman who dared to slay him,
    Thou durst not weep to him now, nor pray him,
Nor pay to his soul the deep unworth
    Of gift or prayer to forget thy blow.

—Oh, who with heart sincere
    Shall bring praise or grief
To lay on the sepulchre
    Of the great chief?

Clytemnestra

His burial is not thine to array.
1630   By me he fell, by me he died,
    I watch him to the grave, not cried
By mourners of his housefolk; nay,
His own child for a day like this
    Waits, as is seemly, and shall run
    By the white waves of Acheron
To fold him in her arms and kiss!

Chorus

Lo, she who was erst reviled
    Revileth; and who shall say?
Spoil taken from them that spoiled,
1640   Life-blood from them that slay!
Surely while God ensueth
    His laws, while Time doth run
'Tis written: On him that doeth
    It shall be done.

This is God's law and grace,
Who then shall hunt the race
Of curses from out this hall?
The House is sealed withal
    To dreadfulness.

Clytemnestra

Aye, thou hast found the Law, and stept   1650
    In Truth's way.—Yet even now I call
    The Living Wrath which haunts this hall
To truce and compact. I accept
All the affliction he doth heap
    Upon me, and I charge him go
    Far off with his self-murdering woe
To strange men's houses. I will keep
Some little dower, and leave behind
    All else, contented utterly.
    I have swept the madness from the sky   1660
Wherein these brethren slew their kind.

*[As she ceases, exhausted and with the fire gone out of
her, Aegisthus, with Attendants, bursts triumphantly in.]*

Aegisthus

O shining day, O dawn of righteousness
Fulfilled! Now, now indeed will I confess
That divine watchers o'er man's death and birth
Look down on all the anguish of the earth,
Now that I see him lying, as I love
To see him, in this net the Furies wove,
To atone the old craft of his father's hand.
    For Atreus, this man's father, in this land
Reigning, and by Thyestes in his throne   1670
Challenged—he was his brother and mine own
Father From home and city cast him out;
And he, after long exile, turned about
And threw him suppliant on the hearth, and won
Promise of so much mercy, that his own
Life-blood should reek not in his father's hall.
Then did that godless brother, Atreus, call,

To greet my sire—More eagerness, O God,
Was there than love!—a feast of brotherhood.
1680 And, feigning joyous banquet, laid as meat
Before him his dead children. The white feet
And finger-fringèd hands apart he set,
Veiled from all seeing, and made separate
The tables. And he straightway, knowing naught,
Took of those bodies, eating that which wrought
No health for all his race. And when he knew
The unnatural deed, back from the board he threw,
1600 Spewing that murderous gorge, and spurning brake
The table, to make strong the curse he spake:
1690 "Thus perish all of Pleisthenês begot!"
      For that lies this man here; and all the plot
Is mine, most righteously. For me, the third,
When butchering my two brethren, Atreus spared
And cast me with my broken sire that day,
A little thing in swaddling clothes, away
To exile; where I grew, and at the last
Justice hath brought me home! Yea though outcast
In a far land, mine arm hath reached this king;
My brain, my hate, wrought all the counselling;
1700 And all is well. I have seen mine enemy
Dead in the snare, and care not if I die!

Leader

Aegisthus, to insult over the dead
I like not. All the counsel, thou hast said,
Was thine alone; and thine the will that spilled
This piteous blood. As justice is fulfilled,
Thou shalt not 'scape—so my heart presageth—
The day of cursing and the hurlèd death.

Aegisthus

How, thou poor oarsman of the nether row,
When the main deck is master? Sayst thou so?...
1710 To such old heads the lesson may prove hard,
I fear me, when Obedience is the word.
But hunger, and bonds, and cold, help men to find
Their wits.—They are wondrous healers of the mind!

Hast eyes and seest not this?—Against a spike
Kick not, for fear it pain thee if thou strike.

Leader [*turning from him to Clytemnestra*]

Woman! A soldier fresh from war! To keep
Watch o'er his house and shame him in his sleep...
To plot this craft against a lord of spears...

[*Clytemnestra, as though in a dream, pays no heed. Ae-
gisthus interupts.*]

Aegisthus

These be the words, old man, that lead to tears!
Thou hast an opposite to Orpheus' tongue,   1720
Who chained all things with his enchanting song,
For thy mad noise will put the chains on thee.
Enough! Once mastered thou shalt tamer be.

Leader

Thou master? Is old Argos so accurst?
Thou plotter afar off, who never durst
Raise thine own hand to affront and strike him down...

Aegisthus

To entice him was the wife's work. I was known
By all men here, his old confessed blood-foe.
Howbeit, with his possessions I will know
How to be King. And who obeys not me   1730
Shall be yoked hard, no easy trace-horse he,
Corn-flushed. Hunger, and hunger's prison mate,
The clammy murk, shall see his rage abate.

Leader

Thou craven soul! Why not in open strife
Slay him? Why lay the blood-sin on his wife,
Staining the Gods of Argos, making ill
The soil thereof?...But young Orestes still
Liveth. Oh, Fate will guide him home again,
Avenging, conquering, home to kill these twain!

Aegisthus

1740
      'Fore God, if 'tis your pleasure
      Thus to speak and do, ye soon shall hear!
      Ho there, my trusty pikes, advance!
      There cometh business for the spear.

[A body of Spearmen, from concealment outside, rush in and dominate the stage.]

Leader

      Ho there, ye Men of Argos! Up!
      Stand and be ready, sword from sheath!

Aegisthus

      By Heaven, I also, sword in hand,
      Am ready, and refuse not death!

Leader

      Come, find it! We accept thy word.
      Thou offerest what we hunger for.

[Some of the Elders draw swords with the Leader; others have collapsed with weakness. Men from Agamemnon's retinue have gathered and prepare for battle, when, before they can come to blows, Clytemnestra breaks from her exhausted silence.]

Clytemnestra

1750
      Nay, peace, O best-belovèd! Peace!
      And let us work no evil more.
      Surely the reaping of the past
      Is a full harvest, and not good,
      And wounds enough are everywhere.—
      Let us not stain ourselves with blood.
      Ye reverend Elders, go your ways,
      To his own dwelling every one,
      Ere things be wrought for which men suffer.—

What we did must needs be done.
And if of all these strifes we now   1760
May have no more, oh, I will kneel
And praise God, bruisèd though we be
Beneath the Daemon's heavy heel.
This is the word a woman speaks,
To hear if any man will deign.

Aegisthus

And who are these to burst in flower
Of folly thus of tongue and brain,
And utter words of empty sound
And perilous, tempting Fortune's frown,
And leave wise counsel all forgot,   1770
And gird at him who wears the crown?

Leader

To cringe before a caitiff's crown,
It squareth not with Argive ways.

Aegisthus [sheathing his sword and turning from them]

Bah, I will be a hand of wrath
To fall on thee in after days.

Leader

Not so, if God in after days
Shall guide Orestes home again!

Aegisthus

I know how men in exile feed on dreams...
And know such food is vain.

Leader

Go forward and wax fat!   1780
Defile the right for this thy little hour!

Aegisthus

I spare thee now.

Know well for all this folly thou shalt feel my power.

Leader

Aye, vaunt thy greatness,
As a bird beside his mate doth vaunt and swell.

Clytemnestra

Vain hounds are baying round thee;
Oh, forget them! Thou and I shall dwell
As Kings in this great House. We two
At last will order all things well.

*[The Elders and the remains of Agamemnon's retinue
retire sullenly, leaving the Spearmen in possession. Clytem-
nestra and Aegisthus turn and enter the Palace.]*

The Libation Bearers

Translated By E.D.A. Morshead

Dramatis Personae

ORESTES
son of Agamemnon and Clytemnestra

CHORUS OF CAPTIVE WOMEN

ELECTRA
sister of Orestes

A NURSE

CLYTEMNESTRA

AEGISTHUS

AN ATTENDANT

PYLADES
friend of Orestes

[The Scene is the Tomb of Agamemnon at Mycenae; after-
wards, the Palace of Atreus, hard by the Tomb.]

Orestes

    Lord of the shades and patron of the realm
    That erst my father swayed, list now my prayer,
    Hermes, and save me with thine aiding arm,
    Me who from banishment returning stand
    On this my country; lo, my foot is set
    On this grave-mound, and herald-like, as thou,
    Once and again, I bid my father hear.
    And these twin locks, from mine head shorn, I
    bring,
    And one to Inachus the river-god,   10
    My young life's nurturer, I dedicate,
    And one in sign of mourning unfulfilled
    I lay, though late, on this my father's grave.
    For O my father, not beside thy corpse
    Stood I to wail thy death, nor was my hand
    Stretched out to bear thee forth to burial.

    What sight is yonder? what this woman-throng
    Hitherward coming, by their sable garb
    Made manifest as mourners? What hath chanced?
    Doth some new sorrow hap within the home?   20
    Or rightly may I deem that they draw near
    Bearing libations, such as soothe the ire
    Of dead men angered, to my father's grave?
    Nay, such they are indeed; for I descry
    Electra mine own sister pacing hither,
    In moody grief conspicuous. Grant, O Zeus,
    Grant me my father's murder to avenge—
    Be thou my willing champion!
                Pylades,
    Pass we aside, till rightly I discern   30
    Wherefore these women throng in suppliance.

*[Exeunt Pylades and Orestes; enter the Chorus bearing
vessels for libation; Electra follows them; they pace slowly
towards the tomb of Agamemnon.]*

Chorus

Forth from the royal halls by high command
I bear libations for the dead.
Rings on my smitten breast my smiting hand,
    And all my cheek is rent and red,
Fresh-furrowed by my nails, and all my soul
This many a day doth feed on cries of dole.
    And trailing tatters of my vest,
In looped and windowed raggedness forlorn,
    Hang rent around my breast,
Even as I, by blows of Fate most stern
Saddened and torn.

Oracular thro' visions, ghastly clear,
Bearing a blast of wrath from realms below,
And stiffening each rising hair with dread,
    Came out of dream-land Fear,
    And, loud and awful, bade
The shriek ring out at midnight's witching hour,
    And brooded, stern with woe,
Above the inner house, the woman's bower.
And seers inspired did read the dream on oaths,
    Chanting aloud *In realms below*
     The dead are wroth;
Against their slayers yet their ire doth glow.

Therefore to bear this gift of graceless worth—
    O Earth, my nursing mother!—
The woman god-accurs'd doth send me forth.
    Lest one crime bring another.
Ill is the very word to speak, for none
     Can ransom or atone
For blood once shed and darkening the plain.
    O hearth of woe and bane,
    O state that low doth lie!
Sunless, accursed of men, the shadows brood

40

50

60

Above the home of murdered majesty.

Rumour of might, unquestioned, unsubdued,
Pervading ears and soul of lesser men,
   Is silent now and dead.
   Yet rules a viler dread;
  For bliss and power, however won,   70
As gods, and more than gods, dazzle our mortal
ken.

Justice doth mark, with scales that swiftly sway,
  Some that are yet in light;
  Others in interspace of day and night,
   Till Fate arouse them, stay;
And some are lapped in night, where all things are
undone.

On the life-giving lap of Earth
  Blood hath flowed forth;   80
And now, the seed of vengeance, clots the plain—
  Unmelting, uneffaced the stain.
And Atè tarries long, but at the last
    The sinner's heart is cast
Into pervading, waxing pangs of pain.

Lo, when man's force doth ope
The virgin doors, there is nor cure nor hope
  For what is lost,—even so, I deem,
Though in one channel ran Earth's every stream,
  Laving the hand defiled from murder's stain,   90
    It were vain.

And upon me—ah me!—the gods have laid
  The woe that wrapped round Troy,
What time they led down from home and kin
    Unto a slave's employ—
   The doom to bow the head
   And watch our master's will
    Work deeds of good and ill—
To see the headlong sway of force and sin,
  And hold restrained the spirit's bitter hate,   100

Wailing the monarch's fruitless fate,
Hiding my face within my robe, and fain
Of tears, and chilled with frost of hidden pain.

Electra

Handmaidens, orderers of the palace-halls,
Since at my side ye come, a suppliant train,
Companions of this offering, counsel me
As best befits the time: for I, who pour
Upon the grave these streams funereal,
With what fair word can I invoke my sire?
110   Shall I aver, *Behold, I bear these gifts*
From well-beloved wife unto her well-beloved lord,
When 'tis from her, my mother, that they come?
I dare not say it: of all words I fail
Wherewith to consecrate unto my sire
These sacrificial honours on his grave.
Or shall I speak this word, as mortals use—
Give back, to those who send these coronals
Full recompense—of ills for acts malign?
Or shall I pour this draught for Earth to drink,
120   Sans word or reverence, as my sire was slain,
And homeward pass with unreverted eyes,
Casting the bowl away, as one who flings
The household cleansings to the common road?
100   Be art and part, O friends, in this my doubt,
Even as ye are in that one common hate
Whereby we live attended: fear ye not
The wrath of any man, nor hide your word
Within your breast: the day of death and doom
Awaits alike the freeman and the slave.
130   Speak, then, if aught thou know'st to aid us more.

Chorus

Thou biddest; I will speak my soul's thought out,
Revering as a shrine thy father's grave.

Electra

Say then thy say, as thou his tomb reverest.

Chorus

    Speak solemn words to them that love, and pour.

Electra

    And of his kin whom dare I name as kind?

Chorus

    Thyself; and next, whoe'er Aegisthus scorns.

Electra

    Then 'tis myself and thou, my prayer must name.

Chorus

    Whoe'er they be, 'tis thine to know and name them.

Electra

    Is there no other we may claim as ours?

Chorus

    Think of Orestes, though far-off he be.   140

Electra

    Right well in this too hast thou schooled my thought.

Chorus

    Mindfully, next, on those who shed the blood—

Electra

    Pray on them what? expound, instruct my doubt.

Chorus

    This, *Upon them some god or mortal come*——

Electra

    As judge or as avenger? speak thy thought.

77

Chorus

Pray in set terms, *Who shall the slayer slay.*

Electra

Beseemeth it to ask such boon of heaven?

Chorus

How not, to wreak a wrong upon a foe?

Electra

O mighty Hermes, warder of the shades,
150   Herald of upper and of under world,
Proclaim and usher down my prayer's appeal
Unto the gods below, that they with eyes
Watchful behold these halls, my sire's of old—
And unto Earth, the mother of all things,
And foster-nurse, and womb that takes their seed.

Lo, I that pour these draughts for men now dead,
Call on my father, who yet holds in ruth
Me and mine own Orestes, Father, speak—
How shall thy children rule thine halls again?
160   Homeless we are and sold; and she who sold
Is she who bore us; and the price she took
Is he who joined with her to work thy death,
Aegisthus, her new lord. Behold me here
Brought down to slave's estate, and far away
Wanders Orestes, banished from the wealth
That once was thine, the profit of thy care,
Whereon these revel in a shameful joy.
Father, my prayer is said; 'tis thine to hear—
Grant that some fair fate bring Orestes home,
170   And unto me grant these—a purer soul
Than is my mother's, a more stainless hand.

These be my prayers for us; for thee, O sire,
I cry that one may come to smite thy foes,
And that the slayers may in turn be slain.
Cursed is their prayer, and thus I bar its path,

Praying mine own, a counter-curse on them.
And thou, send up to us the righteous boon
For which we pray: thine aids be heaven and earth,
And justice guide the right to victory,

[To the Chorus.]

Thus have I prayed, and thus I shed these streams,　　　　180
And follow ye the wont, and as with flowers
Crown ye with many a tear and cry the dirge,
Your lips ring out above the dead man's grave.

[She pours the libations.]

Chorus

　　　Woe, woe, woe!
Let the teardrop fall, splashing on the ground
　　　Where our lord lies low:
Fall and cleanse away the cursed libation's stain,
　　　Shed on this grave-mound,
Fenced wherein together, gifts of good or bane
　　　From the dead are found.　　　　190
　　　Lord of Argos, hearken!
Though around thee darken
　Mist of death and hell, arise and hear!
Hearken and awaken to our cry of woe!
　　　Who with might of spear
　　　Shall our home deliver?
　　　Who like Ares bend until it quiver,
　　　Bend the northern bow?
Who with hand upon the hilt himself will thrust
with glaive,　　　　200
　　　Thrust and slay and save?

Electra

　　　Lo! the earth drinks them, to my sire they pass—
　　　Learn ye with me of this thing new and strange.

Chorus

　　　Speak thou; my breast doth palpitate with fear.

Electra

I see upon the tomb a curl new shorn.

Chorus

Shorn from what man or what deep-girded maid?

Electra

That may he guess who will; the sign is plain.

Chorus

Let me learn this of thee; let youth prompt age.

Electra

None is there here but I, to clip such gift.

Chorus

210   For they who thus should mourn him hate him sore.

Electra

And lo! in truth the hair exceeding like—

Chorus

Like to what locks and whose? instruct me that.

Electra

Like unto those my father's children wear.

Chorus

Then is this lock Orestes' secret gift?

Electra

Most like it is unto the curls he wore,

Chorus

Yet how dared he to come unto his home?

Electra

> He hath but sent it, clipt to mourn his sire.

Chorus

> It is a sorrow grievous as his death,
> That he should live yet never dare return.

Electra

> Yea, and my heart o'erflows with gall of grief,   220
> And I am pierced as with a cleaving dart;
> Like to the first drops after drought, my tears
> Fall down at will, a bitter bursting tide,
> As on this lock I gaze; I cannot deem
> That any Argive save Orestes' self
> Was ever lord thereof; nor, well I wot,
> Hath she, the murd'ress, shorn and laid this lock
> To mourn him whom she slew—my mother she,
> Bearing no mother's heart, but to her race
> A loathing spirit, loathed itself of heaven!   230
> Yet to affirm, as utterly made sure,
> That this adornment cometh of the hand
> Of mine Orestes, brother of my soul,
> I may not venture, yet hope flatters fair!
> Ah well-a-day, that this dumb hair had voice
> To glad mine ears, as might a messenger,
> Bidding me sway no more 'twixt fear and hope,
> Clearly commanding, Cast me hence away,
> Clipped was I from some head thou lovest not;
> Or, I am kin to thee, and here, as thou,   240
> I come to weep and deck our father's grave.   *200*
> Aid me, ye gods! for well indeed ye know
> How in the gale and counter-gale of doubt,
> Like to the seaman's bark, we whirl and stray.
> But, if God will our life, how strong shall spring,
> From seed how small, the new tree of our
> home!—
> Lo ye, a second sign—these footsteps, look,—
> Like to my own, a corresponsive print;
> And look, another footmark,—this his own,   250
> And that the foot of one who walked with him.

Mark, how the heel and tendons' print combine,
Measured exact, with mine coincident!
Alas! for doubt and anguish rack my mind.

Orestes [approaching suddenly]

Pray thou, in gratitude for prayers fulfilled,
Fair fall the rest of what I ask of heaven.

Electra

Wherefore? what win I from the gods by prayer?

Orestes

This, that thine eyes behold thy heart's desire.

Electra

On whom of mortals know'st thou that I call?

Orestes

260 I know thy yearning for Orestes deep.

Electra

Say then, wherein event hath crowned my prayer?

Orestes

I, I am he; seek not one more akin.

Electra

Some fraud, O stranger, weavest thou for me?

Orestes

Against myself I weave it, if I weave.

Electra

Ah thou hast mind to mock me in my woe!

Orestes

'Tis at mine own I mock then, mocking thine.

Electra

    Speak I with thee then as Orestes' self?

Orestes

    My very face thou see'st and know'st me not,
    And yet but now, when thou didst see the lock
    Shorn for my father's grave, and when thy quest   270
    Was eager on the footprints I had made,
    Even I, thy brother, shaped and sized as thou,
    Fluttered thy spirit, as at sight of me!
    Lay now this ringlet whence 'twas shorn, and
    judge,
    And look upon this robe, thine own hands' work,
    The shuttle-prints, the creature wrought there-
    on—
    Refrain thyself, nor prudence lose in joy,
    For well I wot, our kin are less than kind.   280

Electra

    O thou that art unto our father's home
    Love, grief and hope, for thee the tears ran down,
    For thee, the son, the saviour that should be;
    Trust thou thine arm and win thy father's halls!
    O aspect sweet of fourfold love to me,
    Whom upon thee the heart's constraint bids call
    As on my father, and the claim of love
    From me unto my mother turns to thee,
    For she is very hate; to thee too turns
    What of my heart went out to her who died   290
    A ruthless death upon the altar-stone;
    And for myself I love thee—thee that wast
    A brother leal, sole stay of love to me.
    Now by thy side be strength and right, and Zeus
    Saviour almighty, stand to aid the twain!

Orestes

    Zeus, Zeus! look down on our estate and us,
    The orphaned brood of him, our eagle-sire,
    Whom to his death a fearful serpent brought
    Enwinding him in coils; and we, bereft

300

And foodless, sink with famine, all too weak
To bear unto the eyrie, as he bore,
Such quarry as he slew. Lo! I and she,
Electra, stand before thee, fatherless,
And each alike cast out and homeless made.

Electra

And if thou leave to death the brood of him
Whose altar blazed for thee, whose reverence
Was thine, all thine,—whence, in the after years,
Shall any hand like his adorn thy shrine
With sacrifice of flesh? the eaglets slain,

310

Thou wouldst not have a messenger to bear
Thine omens, once so clear, to mortal men;
So, if this kingly stock be withered all,
None on high festivals will fend thy shrine
Stoop thou to raise us! strong the race shall show,
Though puny now it seem, and fallen low.

Chorus

O children, saviours of your father's home,
Beware ye of your words, lest one should hear
And bear them, for the tongue hath lust to tell,
Unto our masters—whom God grant to me

320

In pitchy reek of fun'ral flame to see!

Orestes

Nay, mighty is Apollo's oracle
And shall not fail me, whom it bade to pass
Thro' all this peril; clear the voice rang out
With many warnings, sternly threatening
To my hot heart the wintry chill of pain,
Unless upon the slayers of my sire
I pressed for vengeance: this the god's com-
mand—
That I, in ire for home and wealth despoiled,

330

Should with a craft like theirs the slayers slay:
Else with my very life I should atone
This deed undone, in many a ghastly wise

For he proclaimed unto the ears of men
That offerings, poured to angry power of death,
Exude again, unless their will be done,
As grim disease on those that poured them
forth—
As leprous ulcers mounting on the flesh
And with fell fangs corroding what of old
Wore natural form; and on the brow arise   340
White poisoned hairs, the crown of this disease.
He spake moreover of assailing fiends
Empowered to quit on me my father's blood,
Wreaking their wrath on me, what time in night
Beneath shut lids the spirit's eye sees clear.
The dart that flies in darkness, sped from hell
By spirits of the murdered dead who call
Unto their kin for vengeance, formless fear,
The night-tide's visitant, and madness' curse
Should drive and rack me; and my tortured frame 350
Should be chased forth from man's community
As with the brazen scorpions of the scourge.
For me and such as me no lustral bowl
Should stand, no spilth of wine be poured to God
For me, and wrath unseen of my dead sire
Should drive me from the shrine; no man should
dare
To take me to his hearth, nor dwell with me:
Slow, friendless, cursed of all should be mine end,
And pitiless horror wind me for the grave,   360
This spake the god—this dare I disobey?
Yea, though I dared, the deed must yet be done;
For to that end diverse desires combine,—
The god's behest, deep grief for him who died, *300*
And last, the grievous blank of wealth
despoiled—
All these weigh on me, urge that Argive men,
Minions of valour, who with soul of fire
Did make of fencéd Troy a ruinous heap,
Be not left slaves to two and each a woman! 370
For he, the man, wears woman's heart; if not
Soon shall he know, confronted by a man.

85

*[Orestes, Electra, and the Chorus gather round the tomb of
Agamemnon for the invocation which follows.]*

Chorus

Mighty Fates, on you we call!
Bid the will of Zeus ordain
Power to those, to whom again
Justice turns with hand and aid!
Grievous was the prayer one made—
Grievous let the answer fall!
Where the mighty doom is set,
380   Justice claims aloud her debt
Who in blood hath dipped the steel,
Deep in blood her meed shall feel!
List an immemorial word—
  Whosoe'er shall take the sword
  Shall perish by the sword.

Orestes

Father, unblest in death, O father mine!
  What breath of word or deed
Can I waft on thee from this far confine
  Unto thy lowly bed,—
390   Waft upon thee, in midst of darkness lying,
  Hope's counter-gleam of fire?
Yet the loud dirge of praise brings grace undying
  Unto each parted sire.

Chorus

O child, the spirit of the dead,
Altho' upon his flesh have fed
  The grim teeth of the flame,
Is quelled not; after many days
The sting of wrath his soul shall raise,
  A vengeance to reclaim!
400   To the dead rings loud our cry—
Plain the living's treachery—
Swelling, shrilling, urged on high,

The vengeful dirge, for parents slain
Shall strive and shall attain.

Electra

Hear me too, even me, O father, hear!
Not by one child alone these groans, these tears
are shed
 Upon thy sepulchre.
Each, each, where thou art lowly laid,
Stands, a suppliant, homeless made: 410
 Ah, and all is full of ill,
Comfort is there none to say!
Strive and wrestle as we may,
 Still stands doom invincible.

Chorus

Nay, if so he will, the god
 Still our tears to joy can turn
He can bid a triumph-ode
 Drown the dirge beside this urn;
He to kingly halls can greet
The child restored, the homeward-guided feet. 420

Orestes

Ah my father! hadst thou lain
 Under Ilion's wall,
By some Lycian spearman slain,
 Thou hadst left in this thine hall
Honour; thou hadst wrought for us
Fame and life most glorious.
 Over-seas if thou had'st died,
Heavily had stood thy tomb,
 Heaped on high; but, quenched in pride,
Grief were light unto thy home.   430

Chorus

Loved and honoured hadst thou lain
 By the dead that nobly fell,
In the under-world again,

87

Where are throned the kings of hell,
  Full of sway adorable
Thou hadst stood at their right hand—
Thou that wert, in mortal land,
  By Fate's ordinance and law,
King of kings who bear the crown
  And the staff, to which in awe
Mortal men bow down.

Electra

Nay O father, I were fain
Other fate had fallen on thee.
  Ill it were if thou hadst lain
One among the common slain,
  Fallen by Scamander's side—
Those who slew thee there should be!
Then, untouched by slavery,
  We had heard as from afar
Deaths of those who should have died
  'Mid the chance of war.

Chorus

O child, forbear! things all too high thou sayest.
  Easy, but vain, thy cry!
A boon above all gold is that thou prayest,
  An unreached destiny,
As of the blessèd land that far aloof
  Beyond the north wind lies;
Yet doth your double prayer ring loud reproof;
  A double scourge of sighs
Awakes the dead; th' avengers rise, though late;
  Blood stains the guilty pride
Of the accursed who rule on earth, and Fate
  Stands on the children's side.

Electra

That hath sped thro' mine ear,
Like a shaft from a bow!

440

450

460

Zeus, Zeus! it is thou who dost send from below
A doom on the desperate doer—ere long
On a mother a father shall visit his wrong.

Chorus

Be it mine to upraise thro' the reek of the pyre
The chant of delight, while the funeral fire   470
   Devoureth the corpse of a man that is slain
    And a woman laid low!
For who bids me conceal it! out-rending control,
Blows ever stern blast of hate thro' my soul,
   And before me a vision of wrath and of bane
    Flits and waves to and fro.

Orestes

Zeus, thou alone to us art parent now.
   Smite with a rending blow
  Upon their heads, and bid the land be well:
Set right where wrong hath stood; and thou give   480
ear,
   O Earth, unto my prayer—
Yea, hear O mother Earth, and monarchy of hell!

Chorus

Nay, the law is sternly set—   400
  Blood-drops shed upon the ground
Plead for other bloodshed yet;
  Loud the call of death doth sound,
Calling guilt of olden time,
A Fury, crowning crime with crime.

Electra

Where, where are ye, avenging powers,   490
  Puissant Furies of the slain?
  Behold the relics of the race
  Of Atreus, thrust from pride of place!
O Zeus, what home henceforth is ours,
  What refuge to attain?

Chorus

Lo, at your wail my heart throbs, wildly stirred;
 Now am I lorn with sadness,
Darkened in all my soul, to hear your sorrow's
    word
 Anon to hope, the seat of strength, I rise,—
 She, thrusting grief away, lifts up mine eyes
  To the new dawn of gladness.

Orestes

Skills it to tell of aught save wrong on wrong,
 Wrought by our mother's deed?
Though now she fawn for pardon, sternly strong
 Standeth our wrath, and will nor hear nor heed;
Her children's soul is wolfish, born from hers,
 And softens not by prayers.

Chorus

 I dealt upon my breast the blow
 That Asian mourning women know;
 Wails from my breast the fun'ral cry,
 The Cissian weeping melody;
Stretched rendingly forth, to tatter and tear,
My clenched hands wander, here and there,
From head to breast; distraught with blows
 Throb dizzily my brows.

Electra

 Aweless in hate, O mother, sternly brave!
 As in a foeman's grave
Thou laid'st in earth a king, but to the bier
 No citizen drew near,—
Thy husband, thine, yet for his obsequies,
 Thou bad'st no wail arise!

Orestes

Alas the shameful burial thou dost speak!
Yet I the vengeance of his shame will wreak—

That do the gods command!
That shall achieve mine hand!
Grant me to thrust her life away, and I
    Will dare to die!

Chorus

List thou the deed! Hewn down and foully torn,
    He to the tomb was borne; 530
Yea, by her hand, the deed who wrought,
With like dishonour to the grave was brought,
And by her hand she strove, with strong desire,
Thy life to crush, O child, by murder of thy sire:
  Bethink thee, hearing, of the shame, the pain
    Wherewith that sire was slain!

Electra

Yea, such was the doom of my sire; well-a-day,
    I was thrust from his side,—
As a dog from the chamber they thrust me away,
And in place of my laughter rose sobbing and 540
tears
    As in darkness I lay.
O father, if this word can pass to thine ears,
    To thy soul let it reach and abide!

Chorus

Let it pass, let it pierce, through the sense of thine
ear,
  To thy soul, where in silence it waiteth the hour!
The past is accomplished; but rouse thee to hear
What the future prepareth; awake and appear, 550
    Our champion, in wrath and in power!

Orestes

O father, to thy loved ones come in aid.

Electra

With tears I call on thee.

Chorus

> Listen and rise to light!
> Be thou with us, be thou against the foe!
> Swiftly this cry arises—even so
>   Pray we, the loyal band, as we have prayed!

Orestes

> Let their might meet with mine, and their right with my right.

Electra

> O ye Gods, it is yours to decree.

Chorus

> Ye call unto the dead; I quake to hear.
> Fate is ordained of old, and shall fulfil your prayer.

560

Electra

> Alas, the inborn curse that haunts our home,
>   Of Atè's bloodstained scourge the tuneless
> sound!
> Alas, the deep insufferable doom,
>   The stanchless wound!

Orestes

> It shall be stanched, the task is ours,—
>   Not by a stranger's, but by kindred hand,
> Shall be chased forth the blood-fiend of our land.
>   Be this our spoken spell, to call Earth's nether powers!

Chorus

570

> Lords of a dark eternity,
> To you has come the children's cry,
> Send up from hell, fulfil your aid
>   To them who prayed.

Orestes

> O father, murdered in unkingly wise,
> Fulfil my prayer, grant me thine halls to sway.

Electra

> To me too, grant this boon—dark death to deal
> Unto Aegisthus, and to 'scape my doom.

Orestes

> So shall the rightful feasts that mortals pay
> Be set for thee; else, not for thee shall rise
> The scented reek of altars fed with flesh,
> But thou shall lie dishonoured: hear thou me!

580

Electra

> I too, from my full heritage restored,
> Will pour the lustral streams, what time I pass
> Forth as a bride from these paternal halls,
> And honour first, beyond all graves, thy tomb.

Orestes

> Earth, send my sire to fend me in the fight!

Electra

> Give fair-faced fortune, O Persephone!

Orestes

> Bethink thee, father, in the laver slain—

Electra

> Bethink thee of the net they handselled for thee!

Orestes

> Bonds not of brass ensnared thee, father mine.

590

Electra

> Yea, the ill craft of an enfolding robe.

Orestes

> By this our bitter speech arise, O sire!

Electra

Raise thou thine head at love's last, dearest call!

Orestes

Yea, speed forth Right to aid thy kinsmen's cause;
Grip for grip, let them grasp the foe, if thou
Willest in triumph to forget thy fall.

Electra

500

600

Hear me, O father, once again hear me.
Lo! at thy tomb, two fledglings of thy brood—
A man-child and a maid; hold them in ruth,
Nor wipe them out, the last of Pelops' line.
For while they live, thou livest from the dead;
Children are memory's voices, and preserve
The dead from wholly dying: as a net
Is ever by the buoyant corks upheld,
Which save the flaxen mesh, in the depth sub-
merged.
Listen, this wail of ours doth rise for thee,
And as thou heedest it thyself art saved.

Chorus

610

In sooth, a blameless prayer ye spake at length—
The tomb's requital for its dirge denied:
Now, for the rest, as thou art fixed to do,
Take fortune by the hand and work thy will.

Orestes

620

The doom is set; and yet I fain would ask—
Not swerving from the course of my resolve,—
Wherefore she sent these offerings, and why
She softens all too late her cureless deed?
An idle boon it was, to send them here
Unto the dead who recks not of such gifts.
I cannot guess her thought, but well I ween
Such gifts are skill-less to atone such crime.
Be blood once spilled, an idle strife he strives
Who seeks with other wealth or wine outpoured

94

To atone the deed. So stands the word, nor fails.
Yet would I know her thought; speak, if thou
knowest.

Chorus

I know it, son; for at her side I stood.
'Twas the night-wandering terror of a dream
That flung her shivering from her couch, and bade
her—
Her, the accursed of God—these offerings send.   630

Orestes

Heard ye the dream, to tell it forth aright?

Chorus

Yea, from herself; her womb a serpent bare.

Orestes

What then the sum and issue of the tale?

Chorus

Even as a swaddled child, she lull'd the thing.

Orestes

What suckling craved the creature, born full-fanged?

Chorus

Yet in her dreams she proffered it the breast.

Orestes

How? did the hateful thing not bite her teat?

Chorus

Yea, and sucked forth a blood-gout in the milk.

Orestes

Not vain this dream—it bodes a man's revenge.

Chorus

640   Then out of sleep she started with a cry,
                And thro' the palace for their mistress' aid
                Full many lamps, that erst lay blind with night
                Flared into light; then, even as mourners use,
                She sends these offerings, in hope to win
                A cure to cleave and sunder sin from doom.

Orestes

                Earth and my father's grave, to you I call—
                Give this her dream fulfilment, and thro' me.
                I read it in each part coincident,
                With what shall be; for mark, that serpent sprang
650   From the same womb as I, in swaddling bands
                By the same hands was swathed, lipped the same
                breast.
                And sucking forth the same sweet mother's-milk
                Infused a clot of blood; and in alarm
                She cried upon her wound the cry of pain.
                The rede is clear: the thing of dread she nursed,
                The death of blood she dies; and I, 'tis I,
                In semblance of a serpent, that must slay her.
                Thou art my seer, and thus I read the dream.

Chorus

660   So do; yet ere thou doest, speak to us,
                Siding some act, some, by not acting, aid.

Orestes

                Brief my command: I bid my sister pass
                In silence to the house, and all I bid
                This my design with wariness conceal,
                That they who did by craft a chieftain slay
                May by like craft and in like noose be ta'en
                Dying the death which Loxias foretold—
                Apollo, king and prophet undisproved.
                I with this warrior Pylades will come
670   In likeness of a stranger, full equipt
                As travellers come, and at the palace gates

Will stand, as stranger yet in friendship's bond
Unto this house allied; and each of us
Will speak the tongue that round Parnassus sounds,
Feigning such speech as Phocian voices use.
And what if none of those that tend the gates
Shall welcome us with gladness, since the house
With ills divine is haunted? if this hap,
We at the gate will bide, till, passing by,   680
Some townsman make conjecture and proclaim,
How? is Aegisthus here, and knowingly
Keeps suppliants aloof, by bolt and bar?
Then shall I win my way; and if I cross
The threshold of the gate, the palace' guard,
And find him throned where once my father sat—
Or if he come anon, and face to face
Confronting, drop his eyes from mine—I swear
He shall not utter, *Who art thou and whence?*
Ere my steel leap, and compassed round with   690
death
Low he shall lie: and thus, full-fed with doom,
The Fury of the house shall drain once more
A deep third draught of rich unmingled blood.
But thou, O sister, look that all within
Be well prepared to give these things event.
And ye—I say 'twere well to bear a tongue
Full of fair silence and of fitting speech
As each beseems the time; and last, do thou,
Hermes the warder-god, keep watch and ward,   700
And guide to victory my striving sword.

[Exit with Pylades.]

Chorus

Many and marvellous the things of fear
  Earth's breast doth bear;
And the sea's lap with many monsters teems,
And windy levin-bolts and meteor gleams
  Breed many deadly things—
Unknown and flying forms, with fear upon their

wings,
And in their tread is death;
710 And rushing whirlwinds, of whose
blasting breath
Man's tongue can tell.
But who can tell aright the fiercer thing,
The aweless soul, within man's breast
inhabiting?
Who tell, how, passion-fraught and
love-distraught
The woman's eager, craving thought
600 Doth wed mankind to woe and ruin fell?
720 Yea, how the loveless love that doth possess
The woman, even as the lioness,
Doth rend and wrest apart, with eager strife,
The link of wedded life?

Let him be the witness, whose thought is not
borne on light wings thro' the air,
But abideth with knowledge, what thing was
wrought by Althea's despair;
For she marr'd the life-grace of her son, with ill
counsel rekindled the flame
730 That was quenched as it glowed on the brand,
what time from his mother he came,
With the cry of a new-born child; and the brand
from the burning she won,
For the Fates had foretold it coeval, in life and in
death, with her son.
Yea, and man's hate tells of another, even Scylla of
murderous guile,
Who slew for an enemy's sake her father, won o'er
by the wile
740 And the gifts of Cretan Minos, the gauds of the
high-wrought gold;
For she clipped from her father's head the lock
that should never wax old,
As he breathed in the silence of sleep, and knew
not her craft and her crime—
But Hermes, the guard of the dead, doth grasp
her, in fulness of time.

And since of the crimes of the cruel I tell, let my
singing record
The bitter wedlock and loveless, the curse on these   750
halls outpoured,
The crafty device of a woman, whereby did a
chieftain fall,
A warrior stern in his wrath; the fear of his ene-
mies all,—
A song of dishonour, untimely! and cold is the
hearth that was warm
And ruled by the cowardly spear, the woman's
unwomanly arm.

But the summit and crown of all crimes is that   760
which in Lemnos befell;
A woe and a mourning it is, a shame and a spitting
to tell;
And he that in after time doth speak of his deadli-
est thought,
Doth say, *It is like to the deed that of old time
in Lemnos was wrought*;
And loathed of men were the doers, and perished,
they and their seed,
For the gods brought hate upon them;   770
none loveth the impious deed.

It is well of these tales to tell; for the sword in the
grasp of Right
With a cleaving, a piercing blow to the innermost
heart doth smite,
And the deed unlawfully done is not trodden
down nor forgot,
When the sinner out-steppeth the law and heedeth
the high God not;
But Justice hath planted the anvil, and Destiny   780
forgeth the sword
That shall smite in her chosen time; by her is the
child restored;
And, darkly devising, the Fiend of the house,
world-cursed, will repay
The price of the blood of the slain that was shed

in the bygone day.

[Enter Orestes and Pylades, in guise of travellers.]

Orestes [knocking at the palace gate]

What ho! slave, ho! I smite the palace gate
In vain, it seems; what ho, attend within,—
Once more, attend; come forth and ope the halls
If yet Aegisthus holds them hospitable.

Slave [from within]

Anon, anon!

[Opens the door]

Speak, from what land art thou, and sent from
whom?

Orestes

Go, tell to them who rule the palace-halls,
Since 'tis to them I come with tidings new—
(Delay not—Night's dark car is speeding on,
And time is now for wayfarers to cast
Anchor in haven, wheresoe'er a house
Doth welcome strangers)—that there now come
forth
Some one who holds authority within—
The queen, or, if some man, more seemly were it;
For when man standeth face to face with man,
No stammering modesty confounds their speech,
But each to each doth tell his meaning clear.

[Enter Clytemnestra.]

Clytemnestra

Speak on, O strangers; have ye need of aught?
Here is whate'er beseems a house like this—
Warm bath and bed, tired Nature's soft restorer,

And courteous eyes to greet you; and if aught 810
Of graver import needeth act as well,
That, as man's charge, I to a man will tell.

Orestes

A Daulian man am I, from Phocis bound,
And as with mine own travel-scrip self-laden
I went toward Argos, parting hitherward
With travelling foot, there did encounter me
One whom I knew not and who knew not me,
But asked my purposed way nor hid his own,
And, as we talked together, told his name—
Strophius of Phocis; then he said, "Good sir, 820
Since in all case thou art to Argos bound,
Forget not this my message, heed it well,
Tell to his own, *Orestes is no more.*
And—whatsoe'er his kinsfolk shall resolve,
Whether to bear his dust unto his home,
Or lay him here, in death as erst in life
Exiled for aye, a child of banishment—
Bring me their hest, upon thy backward road;
For now in brazen compass of an urn
His ashes lie, their dues of weeping paid." 830
So much I heard, and so much tell to thee,
Not knowing if I speak unto his kin
Who rule his home; but well, I deem, it were,
Such news should earliest reach a parent's ear.

Clytemnestra

Ah woe is me! thy word our ruin tells; 700
From roof-tree unto base are we despoiled.—
O thou whom nevermore we wrestle down,
Thou Fury of this home, how oft and oft
Thou dost descry what far aloof is laid,
Yea, from afar dost bend th' unerring bow 840
And rendest from my wretchedness its friends;
As now Orestes—who, a brief while since,
Safe from the mire of death stood warily,—
Was the home's hope to cure th' exulting wrong;
Now thou ordainest, *Let the ill abide.*

Orestes

> To host and hostess thus with fortune blest,
> Lief had I come with better news to bear
> Unto your greeting and acquaintanceship;
> For what goodwill lies deeper than the bond
850 > Of guest and host? and wrong abhorred it were,
> As well I deem, if I, who pledged my faith
> To one, and greetings from the other had,
> Bore not aright the tidings 'twixt the twain.

Clytemnestra

> Whate'er thy news, thou shalt not welcome lack,
> Meet and deserved, nor scant our grace shall be.
> Hadst them thyself not come, such tale to tell
> Another, sure, had borne it to our ears.
> But lo! the hour is here when travelling guests
> Fresh from the daylong labour of the road,
860 > Should win their rightful due. Take him within

[To the slave]

> To the man-chamber's hospitable rest—
> Him and these fellow-farers at his side;
> Give them such guest-right as beseems our halls;
> I bid thee do as thou shalt answer for it.
> And I unto the prince who rules our home
> Will tell the tale, and, since we lack not friends,
> With them will counsel how this hap to bear.

[Exit Clytemnestra.]

Chorus

> So be it done—
> Sister-servants, when draws nigh
870 > Time for us aloud to cry
> Orestes and his victory?

> O holy earth and holy tomb
> Over the grave-pit heaped on high,
> Where low doth Agamemnon lie,

The king of ships, the army's lord!
Now is the hour—give ear and come,
  For now doth Craft her aid afford,
And Hermes, guard of shades in hell,
Stands o'er their strife, to sentinel
  The dooming of the sword.   880
I wot the stranger worketh woe within—
For lo! I see come forth, suffused with tears,
Orestes' nurse. What ho, Kilissa—thou
Beyond the doors? Where goest thou? Methinks
Some grief unbidden walketh at thy side.

[*Enter Kilissa, a nurse.*]

Kilissa

My mistress bids me, with what speed I may,
Call in Aegisthus to the stranger guests,
That he may come, and standing face to face,
A man with men, may thus more clearly learn
This rumour new. Thus speaking, to her slaves   890
She hid beneath the glance of fictive grief
Laughter for what is wrought—to her desire
Too well; but ill, ill, ill besets the house,
Brought by the tale these guests have told so clear.
And he, God wot, will gladden all his heart
Hearing this rumour. Woe and well-a-day!
The bitter mingled cup of ancient woes,
Hard to be borne, that here in Atreus' house
Befell, was grievous to mine inmost heart,
But never yet did I endure such pain.   900
All else I bore with set soul patiently;
But now—alack, alack!—Orestes dear,
The day and night-long travail of my soul!
Whom from his mother's womb, a new-born
child,
I clasped and cherished! Many a time and oft
Toilsome and profitless my service was,
When his shrill outcry called me from my couch!
For the young child, before the sense is born,
Hath but a dumb thing's life, must needs be   910

nursed
As its own nature bids. The swaddled thing
Hath nought of speech, whate'er discomfort
come—
Hunger or thirst or lower weakling need,—
For the babe's stomach works its own relief.
Which knowing well before, yet oft surprised,
'Twas mine to cleanse the swaddling clothes—
poor I
920   Was nurse to tend and fuller to make white;
Two works in one, two handicrafts I took,
When in mine arms the father laid the boy.
And now he's dead—alack and well-a-day!
Yet must I go to him whose wrongful power
Pollutes this house—fair tidings these to him!

Chorus

Say then, with what array she bids him come?

Kilissa

What say'st thou! Speak more clearly for mine ear.

Chorus

Bids she bring henchmen, or to come alone?

Kilissa

She bids him bring a spear-armed body-guard.

Chorus

930   Nay, tell not that unto our loathèd lord,
But speed to him, put on the mien of joy,
Say, *Come along, fear nought, the news is good.*
A bearer can tell straight a twisted tale.

Kilissa

Does then thy mind in this new tale find joy?

Chorus

What if Zeus bid our ill wind veer to fair?

Kilissa

> And how? the home's hope with Orestes dies.

Chorus

> Not yet—a seer, though feeble, this might see.

Kilissa

> What say'st thou? Know'st thou aught, this tale belying?

Chorus

> Go, tell the news to him, perform thine hest,—
> What the gods will, themselves can well provide.   940

Kilissa

> Well, I will go, herein obeying thee;
> And luck fall fair, with favour sent from heaven.

[Exit.]

Chorus

> Zeus, sire of them who on Olympus dwell,
>   Hear thou, O hear my prayer!
> Grant to my rightful lords to prosper well
>   Even as their zeal is fair!
> For right, for right goes up aloud my cry—
>   Zeus, aid him, stand anigh!
>
> Into his father's hall he goes
>   To smite his father's foes.   950
> Bid him prevail! by thee on throne of triumph set,
> Twice, yea and thrice with joy shall he acquit the
> debt.
> Bethink thee, the young steed, the orphan foal
>   Of sire beloved by thee, unto the car
>   Of doom is harnessed fast.
> Guide him aright, plant firm a lasting goal,
> Speed thou his pace,—O that no chance may mar
>   The homeward course, the last!

105

And ye who dwell within the inner chamber
  Where shines the storèd joy of gold—
Gods of one heart, O hear ye, and remember;
Up and avenge the blood shed forth of old,
    With sudden rightful blow;
  Then let the old curse die, nor be renewed
    With progeny of blood,—
  Once more, and not again, be latter guilt laid low!

O thou who dwell'st in Delphi's mighty cave,
  Grant us to see this home once more restored
970   Unto its rightful lord!
  Let it look forth, from veils of death, with joyous
eye
    Unto the dawning light of liberty;
  And Hermes, Maia's child, lend hand to save,
    Willing the right, and guide
Our state with Fortune's breeze adown the
favouring tide.
    Whate'er in darkness hidden lies,
    He utters at his will;
980 He at his will throws darkness on our eye
  By night and eke by day inscrutable.

Then, then shall wealth atone
  The ills that here were done.
    Then, then will we unbind,
    Fling free on wafting wind
Of joy, the woman's voice that waileth now
In piercing accents for a chief laid low;
    And this our song shall be—
  Hail to the commonwealth restored!
990   Hail to the freedom won to me!
All hail! for doom hath passed from him, my well-
loved lord!

And thou, O child, when Time and Chance agree,
Up to the deed that for thy sire is done!
And if she wail unto thee, *Spare, O son*—
Cry, *Aid, O father*—and achieve the deed,
The horror of man's tongue, the gods' great need!

Hold in thy breast such heart as Perseus had,
The bitter woe work forth,
Appease the summons of the dead,   1000
The wrath of friends on earth;
Yea, set within a sign of blood and doom,
And do to utter death him that pollutes thy home.

[Enter Aegisthus.]

Aegisthus

Hither and not unsummoned have I come;
For a new rumour, borne by stranger men
Arriving hither, hath attained mine ears,
Of hap unwished-for, even Orestes' death.
This were new sorrow, a blood-bolter'd load
Laid on the house that doth already bow
Beneath a former wound that festers deep.   1010
Dare I opine these words have truth and life?
Or are they tales, of woman's terror born,
That fly in the void air, and die disproved?
Canst thou tell aught, and prove it to my soul?

Chorus

What we have heard, we heard; go thou within
Thyself to ask the strangers of their tale.
Strengthless are tidings, thro' another heard;
Question is his, to whom the tale is brought.

Aegisthus

I too will meet and test the messenger,
Whether himself stood witness of the death,   1020
Or tells it merely from dim rumour learnt:
None shall cheat me, whose soul hath watchful
eyes.

[Exit.]

Chorus

Zeus, Zeus! what word to me is given?

107

What cry or prayer, invoking heaven,
Shall first by me be uttered?
What speech of craft? nor all revealing,
Nor all too warily concealing?
Ending my speech, shall aid the deed?
1030   For lo! in readiness is laid
The dark enterprise, the rending blade;
Blood-dropping daggers shall achieve
The dateless doom of Atreus' name,
Or—kindling torch and joyful flame
In sign of new-won liberty—
Once more Orestes shall retrieve
His father's wealth, and, throned on high,
Shall hold the city's fealty.
So mighty is the grasp whereby,
1040   Heaven-holpen, he shall trip and throw,
Unseconded, a double foe
Ho for the victory!

[A loud cry within.]

Voice of Aegisthus

Help, help, alas!

Chorus

Ho there, ho! how is't within?
Is't done? is't over? Stand we here aloof
While it is wrought, that guiltless we may seem
Of this dark deed; with death is strife fulfilled.

[Enter a slave.]

Slave

O woe, O woe, my lord is done to death!
Woe, woe, and woe again, Aegisthus gone!
1050   Hasten, fling wide the doors, unloose the bolts
Of the queen's chamber.
O for some young strength
To match the need! but aid availeth nought

To him laid low for ever. Help, help, help!
Sure to deaf ears I shout, and call in vain
To slumber ineffectual. What ho!
The queen! how fareth Clytemnestra's self?
Her neck too, hers, is close upon the steel,
And soon shall sink, hewn thro' as justice wills.

[Enter Clytemnestra.]

Clytemnestra

What ails thee, raising this ado for us?   1060

Slave

I say the dead are come to slay the living.

Clytemnestra

Alack, I read thy riddles all too clear—
We slew by craft and by like craft shall die.
Swift, bring the axe that slew my lord of old;
I'll know anon or death or victory—
So stands the curse, so I confront it here.

[Enter Orestes, his sword dropping with blood.]

Orestes

Thee too I seek: for him what's done will serve.

Clytemnestra

Woe, woe! Aegisthus, spouse and champion, slain!

Orestes

What lov'st the man? then in his grave lie down,
Be his in death, desert him nevermore!   1070

Clytemnestra

Stay, child, and fear to strike. O son, this breast
Pillowed thine head full oft, while, drowsed with

109

sleep,
Thy toothless mouth drew mother's milk from me.

Orestes

900

Can I my mother spare? speak, Pylades,

Pylades

Where then would fall the hest Apollo gave
At Delphi, where the solemn compact sworn?
Choose thou the hate of all men, not of gods.

Orestes

Thou dost prevail; I hold thy counsel good.

[To Clytemnestra]

1080

Follow; I will slay thee at his side.
With him whom in his life thou lovedst more
Than Agamemnon, sleep in death, the meed
For hate where love, and love where hate was due!

Clytemnestra

I nursed thee young; must I forego mine eld?

Orestes

Thou slew'st my father; shalt thou dwell with me?

Clytemnestra

Fate bore a share in these things, O my child!

Orestes

Fate also doth provide this doom for thee.

Clytemnestra

Beware, O my child, a parent's dying curse.

Orestes

A parent who did cast me out to ill!

Clytemnestra

    Not cast thee out, but to a friendly home.   1090

Orestes

    Born free, I was by twofold bargain sold.

Clytemnestra

    Where then the price that I received for thee?

Orestes

    The price of shame; I taunt thee not more plainly.

Clytemnestra

    Nay, but recount thy father's lewdness too.

Orestes

    Home-keeping, chide not him who toils without.

Clytemnestra

    'Tis hard for wives to live as widows, child.

Orestes

    The absent husband toils for them at home.

Clytemnestra

    Thou growest fain to slay thy mother, child.

Orestes

    Nay, 'tis thyself wilt slay thyself, not I.

Clytemnestra

    Beware thy mother's vengeful hounds from hell.   1100

Orestes

    How shall I 'scape my father's, sparing thee?

Clytemnestra

Living, I cry as to a tomb, unheard.

Orestes

My father's fate ordains this doom for thee.

Clytemnestra

Ah, me! this snake it was I bore and nursed.

Orestes

Ay, right prophetic was thy visioned fear.
Shameful thy deed was—die the death of shame!

[Exit, driving Clytemnestra before him.]

Chorus

Lo, even for these I mourn, a double death:
Yet since Orestes, driven on by doom,
Thus crowns the height of murders manifold,
I say, 'tis well—that not in night and death
Should sink the eye and light of this our home.

There came on Priam's race and name
A vengeance; though it tarried long,
With heavy doom it came.
Came, too, on Agamemnon's hall
A lion-pair, twin swordsmen strong.
And last, the heritage doth fall
To him, to whom from Pythian cave
The god his deepest counsel gave.
Cry out, rejoice! our kingly hall
Hath 'scaped from ruin—ne'er again
Its ancient wealth be wasted all
By two usurpers, sin-defiled—
An evil path of woe and bane!
On him who dealt the dastard blow
Comes Craft, Revenge's scheming child.
And hand in hand with him doth go,
Eager for fight,

112

The child of Zeus, whom men below
  Call Justice, naming her aright.   1130
    And on her foes her breath
    Is as the blast of death;
For her the god who dwells in deep recess
    Beneath Parnassus' brow,
    Summons with loud acclaim
    To rise, though late and lame,
And come with craft that worketh righteousness.

For even o'er Powers divine this law is strong—
  Thou shalt not serve the wrong.
To that which ruleth heaven beseems it that we   1140
bow.
    Lo, freedom's light hath come!
    Lo, now is rent away
The grim and curbing bit that held us dumb.
  Up to the light, ye halls! this many a day
    Too low on earth ye lay.
  And Time, the great Accomplisher,
  Shall cross the threshold, whensoe'er
  He choose with purging hand to cleanse
  The palace, driving all pollution thence.   1150
  And fair the cast of Fortune's die
  Before our state's new lords shall lie,
  Not as of old, but bringing fairer doom
    Lo, freedom's light hath come!

*[The scene opens, disclosing Orestes standing over the
corpses of Aegisthus and Clytemnestra; in one hand he
holds his sword, in the other the robe in which Agamemnon
was entangled and slain.]*

Orestes

  There lies our country's twofold tyranny,
  My father's slayers, spoilers of my home.
  Erst were they royal, sitting on the throne,
  And loving are they yet,—their common fate
  Tells the tale truly, shows their trothplight firm.
  They swore to work mine ill-starred father's death,   1160

They swore to die together; 'tis fulfilled.
O ye who stand, this great doom's witnesses,
Behold this too, the dark device which bound
My sire unhappy to his death,—behold
The mesh which trapped his hands, enwound his
feet!
Stand round, unfold it—'tis the trammel-net
That wrapped a chieftain; holds it that he see,
The father—not my sire, but he whose eye

1170

Is judge of all things, the all-seeing Sun!
Let him behold my mother's damnèd deed,
Then let him stand, when need shall be to me,
Witness that justly I have sought and slain
My mother; blameless was Aegisthus' doom—
He died the death law bids adulterers die.
But she who plotted this accursèd thing
To slay her lord, by whom she bare beneath
Her girdle once the burden of her babes,
Beloved erewhile, now turned to hateful foes—

1180

What deem ye of her? or what venomed thing,
Sea-snake or adder, had more power than she
To poison with a touch the flesh unscarred?
So great her daring, such her impious will.
How name her, if I may not speak a curse?
A lion-springe! a laver's swathing cloth,

1000

Wrapping a dead man, twining round his feet—
A net, a trammel, an entangling robe?
Such were the weapon of some strangling thief,
The terror of the road, a cut-purse hound—

1190

With such device full many might he kill,
Full oft exult in heat of villainy.
Ne'er have my house so cursed an indweller—
Heaven send me, rather, childless to be slain!

Chorus

Woe for each desperate deed!
Woe for the queen, with shame of life bereft!
And ah, for him who still is left,
Madness, dark blossom of a bloody seed!

Orestes

>Did she the deed or not? this robe gives proof,
>Imbrued with blood that bathed Aegisthus' sword;
>Look, how the spurted stain combines with time   1200
>To blur the many dyes that once adorned
>Its pattern manifold! I now stand here,
>Made glad, made sad with blood, exulting, wailing—
>Hear, O thou woven web that slew my sire!
>I grieve for deed and death and all my home—
>Victor, pollution's damnèd stain for prize.

Chorus

>Alas, that none of mortal men
>Can pass his life untouched by pain!
>Behold, one woe is here—
>Another loometh near.   1210

Orestes

>Hark ye and learn—for what the end shall be
>For me I know not: breaking from the curb
>My spirit whirls me off, a conquered prey,
>Borne as a charioteer by steeds distraught
>Far from the course, and madness in my breast
>Burneth to chant its song, and leap, and rave—
>Hark ye and learn, friends, ere my reason goes!
>I say that rightfully I slew my mother,
>A thing God-scorned, that foully slew my sire
>And chiefest wizard of the spell that bound me   1220
>Unto this deed I name the Pythian seer
>Apollo, who foretold that if I slew,
>The guilt of murder done should pass from me;
>But if I spared, the fate that should be mine
>I dare not blazon forth—the bow of speech
>Can reach not to the mark, that doom to tell.
>And now behold me, how with branch and crown
>I pass, a suppliant made meet to go
>Unto Earth's midmost shrine, the holy ground
>Of Loxias, and that renownèd light   1230
>Of ever-burning fire, to 'scape the doom
>Of kindred murder: to no other shrine

(So Loxias bade) may I for refuge turn.
Bear witness, Argives, in the after time,
How came on me this dread fatality.
Living, I pass a banished wanderer hence,
To leave in death the memory of this cry.

Chorus

Nay, but the deed is well; link not thy lips
To speech ill-starred, nor vent ill-boding words—
1240 Who hast to Argos her full freedom given,
Lopping two serpents' heads with timely blow.

Orestes

Look, look, alas!
Handmaidens, see—what Gorgon shapes throng up;
Dusky their robes and all their hair enwound—
Snakes coiled with snakes—off, off, I must away!

Chorus

Most loyal of all sons unto thy sire,
What visions thus distract thee? Hold, abide;
Great was thy victory, and shalt thou fear?

Orestes

These are no dreams, void shapes of haunting ill,
1250 But clear to sight my mother's hell-hounds come!

Chorus

Nay, the fresh bloodshed still imbrues thine hands,
And thence distraction sinks into thy soul.

Orestes

O king Apollo—see, they swarm and throng—
Black blood of hatred dripping from their eyes!

Chorus

One remedy thou hast; go, touch the shrine
Of Loxias, and rid thee of these woes.

Orestes

>Ye can behold them not, but I behold them.
>Up and away! I dare abide no more.

[Exit.]

Chorus

>Farewell then as thou mayst,—the god thy friend
>Guard thee and aid with chances favouring.   1260
>
>Behold, the storm of woe divine
>That the raves and beats on Atreus' line
> Its great third blast hath blown.
>First was Thyestes' loathly woe—
>The rueful feast of long ago,
> On children's flesh, unknown.
>And next the kingly chief's despite,
>When he who led the Greeks to fight
> Was in the bath hewn down.
>And now the offspring of the race   1270
>Stands in the third, the saviour's place,
> To save—or to consume?
>O whither, ere it be fulfilled,
>Ere its fierce blast be hushed and stilled,   *1075*
> Shall blow the wind of doom?

[Exeunt.]

The Eumenides

Translated By E.D.A Morshead

Dramatis Personae

THE PYTHIAN PRIESTESS

APOLLO

ORESTES

THE GHOST OF CLYTEMNESTRA

CHORUS OF FURIES

ATHENA

ATTENDANTS OF ATHENA

TWELVE ATHENIAN CITIZENS

*[The Scene of the Drama is the Temple of Apollo, at
Delphi: afterwards the Temple of Athena, on the Acropo-
lis of Athens, and the adjoining Areopagus.]*

[The Temple at Delphi]

The Pythian Priestess

> First, in this prayer, of all the gods I name
> The prophet mother Earth; and Themis next,
> Second who sat—for so with truth is said—
> On this her mother's shrine oracular.
> Then by her grace, who unconstrained allowed,
> There sat thereon another child of Earth—
> Titanian Phoebe. She, in after time,
> Gave o'er the throne, as birthgift to a god,
> Phoebus, who in his own bears Phoebe's name.
> He from the lake and ridge of Delos' isle   10
> Steered to the port of Pallas' Attic shores,
> The home of ships; and thence he passed and came
> Unto this land and to Parnassus' shrine.
> And at his side, with awe revering him,
> There went the children of Hephaestus' seed,
> The hewers of the sacred way, who tame
> The stubborn tract that erst was wilderness.
> And all this folk, and Delphos, chieftain-king
> Of this their land, with honour gave him home;
> And in his breast Zeus set a prophet's soul,   20
> And gave to him this throne, whereon he sits,
> Fourth prophet of the shrine, and, Loxias hight,
> Gives voice to that which Zeus his sire decrees.
>
> Such gods I name in my preluding prayer,
> And after them, I call with honour due
> On Pallas, wardress of the fane, and Nymphs
> Who dwell around the rock Corycian,
> Where in the hollow cave, the wild birds' haunt,
> Wander the feet of lesser gods; and there,

121

30 Right well I know it, Bromian Bacchus dwells,
Since he in godship led his Maenad host,
Devising death for Pentheus, whom they rent
Piecemeal, as hare among the hounds. And last,
I call on Pleistus' springs, Poseidon's might,
And Zeus most high, the great Accomplisher.
Then as a seeress to the sacred chair
I pass and sit; and may the powers divine
Make this mine entrance fruitful in response
Beyond each former advent, triply blest.
40 And if there stand without, from Hellas bound,
Men seeking oracles, let each pass in
In order of the lot, as use allows;
For the god guides whate'er my tongue proclaims.

[She goes into the interior of the temple; after a short inter-
val, she returns in great fear.]

Things fell to speak of, fell for eyes to see,
Have sped me forth again from Loxias' shrine,
With strength unstrung, moving erect no more,
But aiding with my hands my failing feet,
Unnerved by fear. A beldame's force is naught—
Is as a child's, when age and fear combine.
50 For as I pace towards the inmost fane
Bay-filleted by many a suppliant's hand,
Lo, at the central altar I descry
One crouching as for refuge—yea, a man
Abhorred of heaven; and from his hands, wherein
A sword new-drawn he holds, blood reeked and fell:
A wand he bears, the olive's topmost bough,
Twined as of purpose with a deep close tuft
Of whitest wool. This, that I plainly saw,
Plainly I tell. But lo, in front of him,
60 Crouched on the altar-steps, a grisly band
Of women slumbers—not like women they,
But Gorgons rather; nay, that word is weak,
Nor may I match the Gorgons' shape with theirs!
Such have I seen in painted semblance erst—
Winged Harpies, snatching food from Phineus' board,—
But these are wingless, black, and all their shape

The eye's abomination to behold.
Fell is the breath—let none draw nigh to it—
Wherewith they snort in slumber; from their eyes
Exude the damned drops of poisonous ire: 70
And such their garb as none should dare to bring
To statues of the gods or homes of men.
I wot not of the tribe wherefrom can come
So fell a legion, nor in what land Earth
Could rear, unharmed, such creatures, nor avow
That she had travailed and brought forth death.
But, for the rest, be all these things a care
Unto the mighty Loxias, the lord
Of this our shrine: healer and prophet he,
Discerner he of portents, and the cleanser   80
Of other homes—behold, his own to cleanse!

[Exit.]

[The scene opens, disclosing the interior of the temple: Orestes clings to the central altar; the Furies lie slumbering at a little distance; Apollo and Hermes appear from the innermost shrine.]

Apollo

Lo, I desert thee never: to the end,
Hard at thy side as now, or sundered far,
I am thy guard, and to thine enemies
Implacably oppose me: look on them,
These greedy fiends, beneath my craft subdued!
See, they are fallen on sleep, these beldames old,
Unto whose grim and wizened maidenhood
Nor god nor man nor beast can e'er draw near.
Yea, evil were they born, for evil's doom,   90
Evil the dark abyss of Tartarus
Wherein they dwell, and they themselves the hate
Of men on earth, and of Olympian gods.
But thou, flee far and with unfaltering speed;
For they shall hunt thee through the mainland wide
Where'er throughout the tract of travelled earth

Thy foot may roam, and o'er and o'er the seas
And island homes of men. Faint not nor fail,
Too soon and timidly within thy breast
100   Shepherding thoughts forlorn of this thy toil;
But unto Pallas' city go, and there
Crouch at her shrine, and in thine arms enfold
Her ancient image: there we well shall find
Meet judges for this cause and suasive pleas,
Skilled to contrive for thee deliverance
From all this woe. Be such my pledge to thee,
For by my hest thou didst thy mother slay.

Orestes

O king Apollo, since right well thou know'st
What justice bids, have heed, fulfill the same,—
110   Thy strength is all-sufficient to achieve.

Apollo

Have thou too heed, nor let thy fear prevail
Above thy will. And do thou guard him, Hermes,
Whose blood is brother unto mine, whose sire
The same high God. Men call thee guide and guard,
Guide therefore thou and guard my suppliant;
For Zeus himself reveres the outlaw's right,
Boon of fair escort, upon man conferred.

*[Exeunt Apollo, Hermes, and Orestes. The Ghost of
Clytemnestra near.]*

Ghost of Clytemnestra

Sleep on! awake! what skills your sleep to me—
Me, among all the dead by you dishonoured—
120   Me from whom never, in the world of death,
Dieth this curse, 'Tis she who smote and slew,
And shamed and scorned I roam? Awake, and hear
My plaint of dead men's hate intolerable.
Me, sternly slain by them that should have loved,
Me doth no god arouse him to avenge,
Hewn down in blood by matricidal hands.

100

Mark ye these wounds from which the heart's blood ran,
And by whose hand, bethink ye! for the sense
When shut in sleep hath then the spirit-sight,
But in the day the inward eye is blind. 130
List, ye who drank so oft with lapping tongue
The wineless draught by me outpoured to soothe
Your vengeful ire! how oft on kindled shrine
I laid the feast of darkness, at the hour
Abhorred of every god but you alone!
Lo, all my service trampled down and scorned!
And he hath baulked your chase, as stag the hounds;
Yea, lightly bounding from the circling toils,
Hath wried his face in scorn, and flieth far.
Awake and hear—for mine own soul I cry— 140
Awake, ye powers of hell! the wandering ghost
That once was Clytemnestra calls—Arise!

[The Furies mutter grimly, as in a dream.]

Mutter and murmur! He hath flown afar— My kin
have gods to guard them, I have none!

[The Furies mutter as before.]

O drowsed in sleep too deep to heed my pain!
Orestes flies, who me, his mother, slew.

[The Furies give a confused cry.]

Yelping, and drowsed again? Up and be doing
That which alone is yours, the deed of hell!

[The Furies give another cry.]

Lo, sleep and toil, the sworn confederates,
Have quelled your dragon-anger, once so fell! 150

The Furies *[muttering more fiercely and loudly]*

Seize, seize, seize, seize—mark, yonder!

Ghost

In dreams ye chase a prey, and like some hound,

That even in sleep doth ply his woodland toil,
Ye bell and bay. What do ye, sleeping here?
Be not o'ercome with toil, nor sleep-subdued,
Be heedless of my wrong. Up! thrill your heart
With the just chidings of my tongue,—such words
Are as a spur to purpose firmly held.
Blow forth on him the breath of wrath and blood,
160   Scorch him with reek of fire that burns in you,
Waste him with new pursuit—swift, hound him down!

[Ghost sinks.]

First Fury [awaking]

Up! rouse another as I rouse thee; up!
Sleep'st thou? Rise up, and spurning sleep away,
See we if false to us this prelude rang.

Chorus of Furies

Alack, alack, O sisters, we have toiled,
   O much and vainly have we toiled and borne!
Vainly! and all we wrought the gods have foiled,
   And turnèd us to scorn!
He hath slipped from the net, whom we chased:
170   He hath 'scaped us who should be our prey—
O'ermastered by slumber we sank,
   And our quarry hath stolen away!
Thou, child of the high God Zeus, Apollo,
   Hast robbed us and wronged;
Thou, a youth, hast down-trodden the right
   That to godship more ancient belonged;
Thou hast cherished thy suppliant man;
   The slayer the God-forsaken,
The bane of a parent, by craft
180   From out of our grasp thou hast taken:
A god, thou hast stolen from us the avengers a matricide son—
And who shall consider thy deed and say, It is rightfully done?
   The sound of chiding scorn
     Came from the land of dream;
Deep to mine inmost heart I felt it thrill and burn,
    Thrust as a strong-grasped goad, to urge

    Onward the chariot's team.
     Thrilled, chilled with bitter inward pain
  I stand as one beneath the doomsman's scourge.
  Shame on the younger gods who tread down right,   190
     Sitting on thrones of might!
  Woe on the altar of earth's central fane!
     Clotted on step and shrine,
  Behold, the guilt of blood, the ghastly stain!
    Woe upon thee, Apollo! uncontrolled,
     Unbidden, hast thou, prophet-god, imbrued
     The pure prophetic shrine with wrongful blood!
    For thou too heinous a respect didst hold
  Of man, too little heed of powers divine!
    And us the Fates, the ancients of the earth,   200
     Didst deem as nothing worth.
  Scornful to me thou art, yet shalt not fend
   My wrath from him; though unto hell he flee,
     There too are we!
  And he the blood defiled, should feel and rue,
  Though I were not, fiend-wrath that shall not end,
  Descending on his head who foully slew.

[Re-enter Apollo from the inner shrine.]

Apollo

    Out! I command you. Out from this my home—
    Haste, tarry not! Out from the mystic shrine,
    Lest thy lot be to take into thy breast   210
    The winged bright dart that from my golden string
    Speeds hissing as a snake,—lest, pierced and thrilled
    With agony, thou shouldst spew forth again
    Black frothy heart's-blood, drawn from mortal men,
    Belching the gory clots sucked forth from wounds.
    These be no halls where such as you can prowl—
    Go where men lay on men the doom of blood,
    Heads lopped from necks, eyes from their spheres plucked out,
    Hacked flesh, the flower of youthful seed crushed out
    Feet hewn away, and hands, and death beneath   220
    The smiting stone, low moans and piteous
    Of men impaled—Hark, hear ye for what feast

Ye hanker ever, and the loathing gods
Do spit upon your craving? Lo, your shape
Is all too fitted to your greed; the cave
Where lurks some lion, lapping gore, were home
More meet for you. Avaunt from sacred shrines,
Nor bring pollution by your touch on all
That nears you. Hence! and roam unshepherded—
No god there is to tend such herd as you.

230

Chorus

O king Apollo, in our turn hear us.
Thou hast not only part in these ill things,
But art chief cause and doer of the same.

200

Apollo

How? stretch thy speech to tell this, and have done.

Chorus

Thine oracle bade this man slay his mother.

Apollo

I bade him quit his sire's death,—wherefore not?

Chorus

Then didst thou aid and guard red-handed crime.

Apollo

Yea, and I bade him to this temple flee.

Chorus

And yet forsooth dost chide us following him!

Apollo

240

Ay—not for you it is, to near this fane.

Chorus

Yet is such office ours, imposed by fate.

128

Apollo

> What office? vaunt the thing ye deem so fair.

Chorus

> From home to home we chase the matricide.

Apollo

> What? to avenge a wife who slays her lord?

Chorus

> That is not blood outpoured by kindred hands.

Apollo

> How darkly ye dishonour and annul
> The troth to which the high accomplishers,
> Hera and Zeus, do honour. Yea, and thus
> Is Aphrodite to dishonour cast,
> The queen of rapture unto mortal men.   250
> Know, that above the marriage-bed ordained
> For man and woman standeth Right as guard,
> Enhancing sanctity of troth-plight sworn;
> Therefore, if thou art placable to those
> Who have their consort slain, nor will'st to turn
> On them the eye of wrath, unjust art thou
> In hounding to his doom the man who slew
> His mother. Lo, I know thee full of wrath
> Against one deed, but all too placable
> Unto the other, minishing the crime.   260
> But in this cause shall Pallas guard the right.

Chorus

> Deem not my quest shall ever quit that man.

Apollo

> Follow then, make thee double toil in vain!

Chorus

> Think not by speech mine office to curtail.

Apollo

None hast thou, that I would accept of thee!

Chorus

Yea, high thine honour by the throne of Zeus:
But I, drawn on by scent of mother's blood,
Seek vengeance on this man and hound him down.

Apollo

But I will stand beside him; 'tis for me
To guard my suppliant: gods and men alike
Do dread the curse of such an one betrayed,
And in me Fear and Will say *Leave him not.*

*[Exeunt omnes. The scene changes to Athens. In the fore-
ground, the Temple of Athena on the Acropolis; her statue
stands in the centre; Orestes is seen clinging to it.]*

Orestes

Look on me, queen Athena; lo, I come
By Loxias' behest; thou of thy grace
Receive me, driven of avenging powers—
Not now a red-hand slayer unannealed,
But with guilt fading, half-effaced, outworn
On many homes and paths of mortal men.
For to the limit of each land, each sea,
I roamed, obedient to Apollo's hest,
And come at last, O Goddess, to thy fane,
And clinging to thine image, bide my doom.

[Enter the Chorus of Furies, questing like hounds]

Chorus

Ho! clear is here the trace of him we seek:
Follow the track of blood, the silent sign!
Like to some hound that hunts a wounded fawn,
We snuff along the scent of dripping gore,
And inwardly we pant, for many a day

Toiling in chase that shall fordo the man;
For o'er and o'er the wide land have I ranged,
And o'er the wide sea, flying without wings,   290
Swift as a sail I pressed upon his track,
Who now hard by is crouching, well I wot,
For scent of mortal blood allures me here.
    Follow, seek him—round and round
Scent and snuff and scan the ground,
Lest unharmed he slip away,
    He who did his mother slay!
Hist—he is there! See him his arms entwine
Around the image of the maid divine—
    Thus aided, for the deed he wrought   300
Unto the judgment wills he to be brought.

It may not be! a mother's blood, poured forth
    Upon the stainèd earth,
None gathers up: it lies—bear witness, Hell!—
    For aye indelible!
And thou who sheddest it shalt give thine own
    That shedding to atone!
Yea, from thy living limbs I suck it out,
    Red, clotted, gout by gout,—
A draught abhorred of men and gods; but I   310
    Will drain it, suck thee dry;
Yea, I will waste thee living, nerve and vein;
    Yea, for thy mother slain,
Will drag thee downward, there where thou shalt dree
    The weird of agony!
And thou and whatsoe'er of men hath sinned—
    Hath wronged or God, or friend,
Or parent,—learn ye how to all and each
    The arm of doom can reach!
Sternly requiteth, in the world beneath,   320
    The judgment-seat of Death;
Yea, Death, beholding every man's endeavour
    Recordeth it for ever.

Orestes

I, schooled in many miseries, have learnt
How many refuges of cleansing shrines

There be; I know when law alloweth speech
And when imposeth silence. Lo, I stand
Fixed now to speak, for he whose word is wise
Commands the same. Look, how the stain of blood
330 Is dull upon mine hand and wastes away,
And laved and lost therewith is the deep curse
Of matricide; for while the guilt was new,
'Twas banished from me at Apollo's hearth,
Atoned and purified by death of swine.
Long were my word if I should sum the tale,
How oft since then among my fellow-men
I stood and brought no curse. Time cleanses all—
Time, the coeval of all things that are.
Now from pure lips, in words of omen fair,
340 I call Athena, lady of this land,
To come, my champion: so, in aftertime,
She shall not fail of love and service leal,
Not won by war, from me and from my land
And all the folk of Argos, vowed to her.
Now, be she far away in Libyan land
Where flows from Triton's lake her natal wave,—
Stand she with planted feet, or in some hour
Of rest conceal them, champion of her friends
Where'er she be,—or whether o'er the plain
350 Phlegraean she look forth, as warrior bold—
I cry to her to come, where'er she be,
(And she, as goddess, from afar can hear,)
And aid and free me, set among my foes.

Chorus

Thee not Apollo nor Athena's strength
300 Can save from perishing, a castaway
Amid the Lost, where no delight shall meet
Thy soul—a bloodless prey of nether powers,
A shadow among shadows. Answerest thou
Nothing? dost cast away my words with scorn,
360 Thou, prey prepared and dedicate to me?
Not as a victim slain upon the shrine,
But living shalt thou see thy flesh my food.
Hear now the binding chant that makes thee mine.

Weave the weird dance,—behold the hour
  To utter forth the chant of hell,
  Our sway among mankind to tell,
The guidance of our power.
Of Justice are we ministers,
  And whosoe'er of men may stand
  Lifting a pure unsullied hand,   370
That man no doom of ours incurs,
  And walks thro' all his mortal path
  Untouched by woe, unharmed by wrath.
But if, as yonder man, he hath
Blood on the hands he strives to hide,
  We stand avengers at his side,
Decreeing, *Thou hast wronged the dead:*
 We are doom's witnesses to thee.
The price of blood, his hands have shed,
We wring from him; in life, in death,   380
  Hard at his side are we!

Night, Mother Night, who brought me forth, a torment
    To living men and dead,
Hear me, O hear! by Leto's stripling son
    I am dishonourèd:
He hath ta'en from me him who cowers in refuge,
    To me made consecrate,—
A rightful victim, him who slew his mother.
    Given o'er to me and fate.

Hear the hymn of hell,   390
    O'er the victim sounding,—
Chant of frenzy, chant of ill,
    Sense and will confounding!
Round the soul entwining
    Without lute or lyre—
Soul in madness pining,
    Wasting as with fire!

Fate, all-pervading Fate, this service spun, commanding
    That I should bide therein:
Whosoe'er of mortals, made perverse and lawless,   400
    Is stained with blood of kin,

By his side are we, and hunt him ever onward,
    Till to the Silent Land,
The realm of death, he cometh; neither yonder
    In freedom shall he stand.
    Hear the hymn of hell,
      O'er the victim sounding,—
    Chant of frenzy, chant of ill,
      Sense and will confounding!
410   Round the soul entwining
      Without lute or lyre—
    Soul in madness pining,
      Wasting as with fire!

When from womb of Night we sprang, on us this labour
    Was laid and shall abide.
Gods immortal are ye, yet beware ye touch not
    That which is our pride!
None may come beside us gathered round the blood feast—
    For us no garments white
420   Gleam on a festal day; for us a darker fate is,
    Another darker rite.
That is mine hour when falls an ancient line—
    When in the household's heart
The god of blood doth slay by kindred hands,—
    Then do we bear our part:
On him who slays we sweep with chasing cry:
    Though he be triply strong,
We wear and waste him; blood atones for blood,
    New pain for ancient wrong.

430   I hold this task—'tis mine, and not another's.
    The very gods on high,
Though they can silence and annul the prayers
    Of those who on us cry,
They may not strive with us who stand apart,
    A race by Zeus abhorred,
Blood-boltered, held unworthy of the council
    And converse of Heaven's lord.
Therefore the more I leap upon my prey;
    Upon their head I bound;
440   My foot is hard; as one that trips a runner

134

I cast them to the ground;
Yea, to the depth of doom intolerable;
And they who erst were great,
And upon earth held high their pride and glory,
Are brought to low estate.
In underworld they waste and are diminished,
The while around them fleet
Dark wavings of my robes, and, subtly woven,
The paces of my feet.

Who falls infatuate, he sees not, neither knows he   450
That we are at his side;
So closely round about him, darkly flitting,
The cloud of guilt doth glide.
Heavily 'tis uttered, how around his hearthstone
The mirk of hell doth rise.
Stern and fixed the law is; we have hands t'achieve it,
Cunning to devise.
Queens are we and mindful of our solemn vengeance.
Not by tear or prayer
Shall a man avert it. In unhonoured darkness,   460
Far from gods, we fare,
Lit unto our task with torch of sunless regions,
And o'er a deadly way—
Deadly to the living as to those who see not
    Life and light of day—
Hunt we and press onward. Who of mortals hearing
    Doth not quake for awe,
Hearing all that Fate thro' hand of God hath given us
    For ordinance and law?
Yea, this right to us, in dark abysm and backward   470
    Of ages it befell:
None shall wrong mine office, tho' in nether regions
    And sunless dark I dwell.

[Enter Athena from above]

Athena

Far off I heard the clamour of your cry,
As by Scamander's side I set my foot

135

Asserting right upon the land given o'er
To me by those who o'er Achaia's host
Held sway and leadership: no scanty part
Of all they won by spear and sword, to me
They gave it, land and all that grew theron,
As chosen heirloom for my Theseus' clan.
Thence summoned, sped I with a tireless foot,—
Hummed on the wind, instead of wings, the fold
Of this mine aegis, by my feet propelled,
As, linked to mettled horses, speeds a car.
And now, beholding here Earth's nether brood,
I fear it nought, yet are mine eyes amazed
With wonder. Who are ye? of all I ask,
And of this stranger to my statue clinging.
But ye—your shape is like no human form,
Like to no goddess whom the gods behold,
Like to no shape which mortal women wear.
Yet to stand by and chide a monstrous form
Is all unjust—from such words Right revolts.

Chorus

O child of Zeus, one word shall tell thee all.
We are the children of eternal Night,
And Furies in the underworld are called.

Athena

I know your lineage now and eke your name.

Chorus

Yea, and soon after indeed my rights shalt know.

Athena

Fain would I learn them; speak them clearly forth.

Chorus

We chase from home the murderers of men.

Athena

And where at last can he that slew make pause?

Chorus

Where this is law—All joy abandon here.

Athena

Say, do ye bay this man to such a flight?

Chorus

Yea, for of choice he did his mother slay.

Athena

Urged by no fear of other wrath and doom?

Chorus

What spur can rightly goad to matricide?

Athena

Two stand to plead—one only have I heard.

Chorus

He will not swear nor challenge us to oath.

Athena

The form of justice, not its deed, thou willest.   510

Chorus

Prove thou that word; thou art not scant of skill.

Athena

I say that oaths shall not enforce the wrong.

Chorus

Then test the cause, judge and award the right.

Athena

Will ye to me then this decision trust?

Chorus

Yea, reverencing true child of worthy sire.

Athena [to Orestes]

> O man unknown, make thou thy plea in turn
> Speak forth thy land, thy lineage, and thy woes;
> Then, if thou canst, avert this bitter blame—
> If, as I deem, in confidence of right
> Thou sittest hard beside my holy place,
> Clasping this statue, as Ixion sat,
> A sacred suppliant for Zeus to cleanse,—
> To all this answer me in words made plain.

520

Orestes

> O queen Athena, first from thy last words
> Will I a great solicitude remove.
> Not one blood-guilty am I; no foul stain
> Clings to thine image from my clinging hand;
> Whereof one potent proof I have to tell.
> Lo, the law stands—The slayer shall not plead,
> Till by the hand of him who cleanses blood
> A suckling creature's blood besprinkle him.
> Long since have I this expiation done—
> In many a home, slain beasts and running streams
> Have cleansed me. Thus I speak away that fear.
> Next, of my lineage quickly thou shalt learn:
> An Argive am I, and right well thou know'st
> My sire, that Agamemnon who arrayed
> The fleet and them that went therein to war—
> That chief with whom thy hand combined to crush
> To an uncitied heap what once was Troy;
> That Agamemnon, when he homeward came,
> Was brought unto no honourable death,
> Slain by the dark-souled wife who brought me forth
> To him,—enwound and slain in wily nets,
> Blazoned with blood that in the laver ran.
> And I, returning from an exiled youth,
> Slew her, my mother—lo, it stands avowed!
> With blood for blood avenging my loved sire;
> And in this deed doth Loxias bear part,
> Decreeing agonies, to goad my will,
> Unless by me the guilty found their doom.
> Do thou decide if right or wrong were done—
> Thy dooming, whatsoe'er it be, contents me.

530

540

550

Athena

Too mighty is this matter, whatsoe'er
Of mortals claims to judge hereof aright.
Yea, me, even me, eternal Right forbids
To judge the issues of blood-guilt, and wrath
That follows swift behind. This too gives pause,
That thou as one with all due rites performed
Dost come, unsinning, pure, unto my shrine.   560
Whate'er thou art, in this my city's name,
As uncondemned, I take thee to my side,—
Yet have these foes of thine such dues by fate,
I may not banish them: and if they fail,
O'erthrown in judgment of the cause, forthwith
Their anger's poison shall infect the land—
A dropping plague-spot of eternal ill.
Thus stand we with a woe on either hand:
Stay they, or go at my commandment forth,
Perplexity or pain must needs befall.   570
Yet, as on me Fate hath imposed the cause,
I choose unto me judges that shall be
An ordinance for ever, set to rule
The dues of blood-guilt, upon oath declared.
But ye, call forth your witness and your proof,
Words strong for justice, fortified by oath;
And I, whoe'er are truest in my town,
Them will I chose and bring, and straitly charge,
Look on this cause, discriminating well,
And pledge your oath to utter nought of wrong.   580

[Exit Athena.]

Chorus

Now are they all undone, the ancient laws,
  If here the slayer's cause
Prevail; new wrong for ancient right shall be
  If matricide go free.
Henceforth a deed like his by all shall stand,
  Too ready to the hand:
Too oft shall parents in the aftertime
  Rue and lament this crime,—

Taught, not in false imagining, to feel
590   Their children's thrusting steel:
No more the wrath, that erst on murder fell
500   From us, the queens of Hell.
Shall fall, no more our watching gaze impend—
  Death shall smite unrestrained.

Henceforth shall one unto another cry
Lo, they are stricken, lo, they fall and die
  Around me! and that other answers him,
O thou that lookest that thy woes should cease,
  Behold, with dark increase
600 *They throng and press upon thee; yea, and dim*
  Is all the cure, and every comfort vain!
Let none henceforth cry out, when falls the blow
  Of sudden-smiting woe,
   Cry out in sad reiterated strain
O Justice, aid! aid, O ye thrones of Hell!
   So though a father or a mother wail
  New-smitten by a son, it shall no more avail,
Since, overthrown by wrong, the fane of Justice fell!

Know, that a throne there is that may not pass away,
610   And one that sitteth on it—even Fear,
Searching with steadfast eyes man's inner soul:
  Wisdom is child of pain, and born with many a tear;
   But who henceforth,
What man of mortal men, what nation upon earth,
  That holdeth nought in awe nor in the light
  Of inner reverence, shall worship Right
   As in the older day?

Praise not, O man, the life beyond control,
  Nor that which bows unto a tyrant's sway.
620   Know that the middle way
Is dearest unto God, and they thereon who wend,
  They shall achieve the end;
  But they who wander or to left or right
   Are sinners in his sight.
   Take to thy heart this one, this soothfast word—
   Of wantonness impiety is sire;

Only from calm control and sanity unstirred
Cometh true weal, the goal of every man's desire.

Yea, whatsoe'er befall, hold thou this word of mine:
  Bow down at Justice' shrine,   630
   Turn thou thine eyes away from earthly lure,
  Nor with a godless foot that altar spurn.
  For as thou dost shall Fate do in return,
   And the great doom is sure.
  Therefore let each adore a parent's trust,
   And each with loyalty revere the guest
    That in his halls doth rest.
 For whoso uncompelled doth follow what is just,
  He ne'er shall be unblest;
   Yea, never to the gulf of doom   640
    That man shall come.
But he whose will is set against the gods,
 Who treads beyond the law with foot impure,

Till o'er the wreck of Right confusion broods—
  Know that for him, though now he sail secure,
The day of storm shall be; then shall he strive and fail,
  Down from the shivered yard to furl the sail,
And call on Powers, that heed him nought, to save
  And vainly wrestle with the whirling wave,
   Hot was his heart with pride—   650
   I shall not fall, he cried.
  But him with watching scorn
  The god beholds, forlorn,
  Tangled in toils of Fate beyond escape,
  Hopeless of haven safe beyond the cape—
Till all his wealth and bliss of bygone day
  Upon the reef of Rightful Doom is hurled,
   And he is rapt away
Unwept, for ever, to the dead forgotten world.

[Re-enter Athena, with twelve Athenian citizens.]

Athena

  O herald, make proclaim, bid all men come.   660

Then let the shrill blast of the Tyrrhene trump,
Fulfilled with mortal breath, thro' the wide air
Peal a loud summons, bidding all men heed.
For, till my judges fill this judgment-seat,
Silence behoves,—that this whole city learn,
What for all time mine ordinance commands,
And these men, that the cause be judged aright.

[Apollo approaches.]

Chorus

O king Apollo, rule what is thine own,
But in this thing what share pertains to thee?

Apollo

670

First, as a witness come I, for this man
Is suppliant of mine by sacred right,
Guest of my holy hearth and cleansed by me
Of blood-guilt: then, to set me at his side
And in his cause bear part, as part I bore
Erst in his deed, whereby his mother fell.
Let whoso knoweth now announce the cause.

Athena [to the Chorus]

'Tis I announce the cause—first speech be yours;
For rightfully shall they whose plaint is tried
Tell the tale first and set the matter clear.

Chorus

680

Though we be many, brief shall be our tale.

[To Orestes]

Answer thou, setting word to match with
word;
And first avow—hast thou thy mother slain?

Orestes

I slew her. I deny no word hereof.

142

Chorus

Three falls decide the wrestle—this is one.

Orestes

Thou vauntest thee—but o'er no final fall.

Chorus

Yet must thou tell the manner of thy deed.

Orestes

Drawn sword in hand, I gashed her neck. Tis told.

Chorus

But by whose word, whose craft, wert thou impelled?

Orestes

By oracles of him who here attests me.   690

Chorus

The prophet-god bade thee thy mother slay?

Orestes

Yea, and thro' him less ill I fared, till now.

Chorus

If the vote grip thee, thou shalt change that word.

Orestes

Strong is my hope; my buried sire shall aid.

Chorus

Go to now, trust the dead, a matricide!

Orestes

Yea, for in her combined two stains of sin.   600

Chorus

How? speak this clearly to the judges' mind.

143

Orestes

Slaying her husband, she did slay my sire.

Chorus

Therefore thou livest; death assoils her deed.

Orestes

700   Then while she lived why didst thou hunt her not?

Chorus

She was not kin by blood to him she slew.

Orestes

And I, am I by blood my mother's kin?

Chorus

O cursed with murder's guilt, how else wert thou
The burden of her womb? Dost thou forswear
Thy mother's kinship, closest bond of love?

Orestes

It is thine hour, Apollo—speak the law,
Averring if this deed were justly done;
For done it is, and clear and undenied.
But if to thee this murder's cause seem right
710   Or wrongful, speak—that I to these may tell.

Apollo

To you, Athena's mighty council-court,
Justly for justice will I plead, even I,
The prophet-god, nor cheat you by one word.
For never spake I from my prophet-seat
One word, of man, of woman, or of state,
Save what the Father of Olympian gods
Commanded unto me. I rede you then,
Bethink you of my plea, how strong it stands,
And follow the decree of Zeus our sire,—
720   For oaths prevail not over Zeus' command.

Chorus

> Go to; thou sayest that from Zeus befell
> The oracle that this Orestes bade
> With vengeance quit the slaying of his sire,
> And hold as nought his mother's right of kin!

Apollo

> Yea, for it stands not with a common death,
> That he should die, a chieftain and a king
> Decked with the sceptre which high heaven confers—
> Die, and by female hands, not smitten down
> By a far-shooting bow, held stalwartly
> By some strong Amazon. Another doom   730
> Was his: O Pallas, hear, and ye who sit
> In judgment, to discern this thing aright!—
> She with a specious voice of welcome true
> Hailed him, returning from the mighty mart
> Where war for life gives fame, triumphant home;
> Then o'er the laver, as he bathed himself,
> She spread from head to foot a covering net,
> And in the endless mesh of cunning robes
> Enwound and trapped her lord, and smote him down.
> Lo, ye have heard what doom this chieftain met,   740
> The majesty of Greece, the fleet's high lord:
> Such as I tell it, let it gall your ears,
> Who stand as judges to decide this cause.

Chorus

> Zeus, as thou sayest, holds a father's death
> As first of crimes,—yet he of his own act
> Cast into chains his father, Cronos old:
> How suits that deed with that which now ye tell?
> O ye who judge, I bid ye mark my words!

Apollo

> O monsters loathed of all, O scorn of gods,
> He that hath bound may loose: a cure there is,   750
> Yea, many a plan that can unbind the chain.
> But when the thirsty dust sucks up man's blood

Once shed in death, he shall arise no more.
No chant nor charm for this my Sire hath wrought.
All else there is, he moulds and shifts at will,
Not scant of strength nor breath, whate'er he do.

Chorus

Think yet, for what acquittal thou dost plead:
He who hath shed a mother's kindred blood,
Shall he in Argos dwell, where dwelt his sire?
760　　How shall he stand before the city's shrines,
How share the clansmen's holy lustral bowl?

Apollo

This too I answer; mark a soothfast word,
Not the true parent is the woman's womb
That bears the child; she doth but nurse the seed
New-sown: the male is parent; she for him,
As stranger for a stranger, hoards the germ
Of life; unless the god its promise blight.
And proof hereof before you will I set.
Birth may from fathers, without mothers, be:
770　　See at your side a witness of the same,
Athena, daughter of Olympian Zeus,
Never within the darkness of the womb
Fostered nor fashioned, but a bud more bright
Than any goddess in her breast might bear.
And I, O Pallas, howsoe'er I may,
Henceforth will glorify thy town, thy clan,
And for this end have sent my suppliant here
Unto thy shrine; that he from this time forth
Be loyal unto thee for evermore,
780　　O goddess-queen, and thou unto thy side
Mayst win and hold him faithful, and his line,
And that for aye this pledge and troth remain
To children's children of Athenian seed.

Athena

Enough is said; I bid the judges now
With pure intent deliver just award.

Chorus

> We too have shot our every shaft of speech,
> And now abide to hear the doom of law.

Athena [to Apollo and Orestes]

> Say, how ordaining shall I 'scape your blame?

Apollo

> I spake, ye heard; enough. O stranger men,
> Heed well your oath as ye decide the cause.   790

Athena

> O men of Athens, ye who first do judge
> The law of bloodshed, hear me now ordain.
> Here to all time for Aegeus' Attic host
> Shall stand this council-court of judges sworn,
> Here the tribunal, set on Ares' Hill
> Where camped of old the tented Amazons,
> What time in hate of Theseus they assailed
> Athens, and set against her citadel
> A counterwork of new sky-pointing towers,
> And there to Ares held their sacrifice,   800
> Where now the rock hath name, even Ares' Hill.
> And hence shall Reverence and her kinsman Fear
> Pass to each free man's heart, by day and night
> Enjoining, Thou shalt do no unjust thing,
> So long as law stands as it stood of old
> Unmarred by civic change. Look you, the spring
> Is pure; but foul it once with influx vile
> And muddy clay, and none can drink thereof.
> Therefore, O citizens, I bid ye bow
> In awe to this command, Let no man live   810
> Uncurbed by law nor curbed by tyranny;
> Nor banish ye the monarchy of Awe
> Beyond the walls; untouched by fear divine,
> No man doth justice in the world of men.   700
> Therefore in purity and holy dread
> Stand and revere; so shall ye have and hold
> A saving bulwark of the state and land,

147

Such as no man hath ever elsewhere known,
Nor in far Scythia, nor in Pelops' realm.
820   Thus I ordain it now, a council-court
Pure and unsullied by the lust of gain,
Sacred and swift to vengeance, wakeful ever
To champion men who sleep, the country's guard.
Thus have I spoken, thus to mine own clan
Commended it for ever. Ye who judge,
Arise, take each his vote, mete out the right,
Your oath revering. Lo, my word is said.

*[The twelve judges come forward, one by one, to the urns
of decision; the first votes; as each of the others follows, the
Chorus and Apollo speak alternately.]*

Chorus

I rede ye well, beware! nor put to shame,
In aught, this grievous company of hell.

Apollo

830   I too would warn you, fear mine oracles—
From Zeus they are,—nor make them void of fruit.

Chorus

Presumptuous is thy claim, blood-guilt to judge,
And false henceforth thine oracles shall be.

Apollo

Failed then the counsels of my sire, when turned
Ixion, first of slayers, to his side?

Chorus

These are but words; but I, if justice fail me,
Will haunt this land in grim and deadly deed.

Apollo

Scorn of the younger and the elder gods
Art thou: 'tis I that shall prevail anon.

Chorus

> Thus didst thou too of old in Pheres' halls,
> O'errcaching Fate to make a mortal deathless.

840

Apollo

> Was it not well, my worshipper to aid,
> Then most of all when hardest was the need?

Chorus

> I say thou didst annul the lots of life,
> Cheating with wine the deities of eld.

Apollo

> I say thou shalt anon, thy pleadings foiled,
> Spit venom vainly on thine enemies.

Chorus

> Since this young god o'errides mine ancient right
> I tarry but to claim your law, not knowing
> If wrath of mine shall blast your state or spare.

850

Athena

> Mine is the right to add the final vote,
> And I award it to Orestes' cause.
> For me no mother bore within her womb,
> And, save for wedlock evermore eschewed,
> I vouch myself the champion of the man,
> Not of the woman, yea, with all my soul,—
> In heart, as birth, a father's child alone.
> Thus will I not too heinously regard
> A woman's death who did her husband slay,
> The guardian of her home; and if the votes
> Equal do fall, Orestes shall prevail.
> Ye of the judges who are named thereto,
> Swiftly shake forth the lots from either urn.

860

[Two judges come forward, one to each urn.]

Orestes

O bright Apollo, what shall be the end?

Chorus

O Night, dark mother mine, dost mark these things?

Orestes

Now shall my doom be life, or strangling cords.

Chorus

And mine, lost honour or a wider sway.

Apollo

O stranger judges, sum aright the count
Of votes cast forth, and, parting them, take heed
870   Ye err not in decision. The default
Of one vote only bringeth ruin deep,
One, cast aright, doth stablish house and home.

Athena

Behold, this man is free from guilt of blood,
For half the votes condemn him, half set free!

Orestes

O Pallas, light and safety of my home,
Thou, thou hast given me back to dwell once more
In that my fatherland, amerced of which
I wandered; now shall Grecian lips say this,
The man is Argive once again, and dwells
880   *Again within his father's wealthy hall,*
By Pallas saved, by Loxias, and by Him,
The great third saviour, Zeus omnipotent—
Who thus in pity for my father's fate
Doth pluck me from my doom, beholding these,
Confederates of my mother. Lo, I pass
To mine own home, but proffering this vow
Unto thy land and people: Nevermore,
Thro' all the manifold years of Time to be,

Shall any chieftain of mine Argive land
Bear hitherward his spears for fight arrayed.   890
For we, though lapped in earth we then shall lie,
By thwart adversities will work our will
On them who shall transgress this oath of mine,
Paths of despair and journeyings ill-starred
For them ordaining, till their task they rue.
But if this oath be rightly kept, to them
Will we the dead be full of grace, the while
With loyal league they honour Pallas' town.
And now farewell, thou and thy city's folk—
Firm be thine arm's grasp, closing with thy foes   900
And, strong to save, bring victory to thy spear.

[Exit Orestes, with Apollo.]

Chorus

Woe on you, younger gods! the ancient right
Ye have o'erridden, rent it from my hands.

I am dishonoured of you, thrust to scorn!
   But heavily my wrath
Shall on this land fling forth the drops that blast and burn
   Venom of vengeance, that shall work such scathe
   As I have suffered; where that dew shall fall,
      Shall leafless blight arise,
   Wasting Earth's offspring,—Justice, hear my call!—   910
And through all the land in deadly wise
Shall scatter venom, to exude again
      In pestilence on men.
What cry avails me now, what deed of blood,
Unto this land what dark despite?
      Alack, alack, forlorn
Are we, a bitter injury have borne!
Alack, O sisters, O dishonoured brood
      Of mother Night!

Athena

Nay, bow ye to my words, chafe not nor moan: 920
Ye are not worsted nor disgraced; behold,

With balanced vote the cause had issue fair,
Nor in the end did aught dishonour thee.
But thus the will of Zeus shone clearly forth,
And his own prophet-god avouched the same,
Orestes slew: his slaying is atoned.
Therefore I pray you, not upon this land
Shoot forth the dart of vengeance; be appeased,
Nor blast the land with blight, nor loose thereon
Drops of eternal venom, direful darts
Wasting and marring nature's seed of growth.

For I, the queen of Athens' sacred right,
Do pledge to you a holy sanctuary
Deep in the heart of this my land, made just
By your indwelling presence, while ye sit
Hard by your sacred shrines that gleam with oil
Of sacrifice, and by this folk adored.

Chorus

Woe on you, younger gods! the ancient right
Ye have o'erridden, rent it from my hands.

I am dishonoured of you, thrust to scorn!
  But heavily my wrath
Shall on this land fling forth the drops that blast and burn.
  Venom of vengeance, that shall work such scathe
  As I have suffered; where that dew shall fall,
    Shall leafless blight arise,
  Wasting Earth's offspring,—Justice, hear my call!—
And through all the land in deadly wise
Shall scatter venom, to exude again
  In pestilence of men.
What cry avails me now, what deed of blood,
Unto this land what dark despite?
  Alack, alack, forlorn
Are we, a bitter injury have borne!
Alack, O sisters, O dishonoured brood
  Of mother Night!

Athena

Dishonoured are ye not; turn not, I pray,

As goddesses your swelling wrath on men,
Nor make the friendly earth despiteful to them.
I too have Zeus for champion—'tis enough—
I only of all goddesses do know.   960
To ope the chamber where his thunderbolts
Lie stored and sealed; but here is no such need.
Nay, be appeased, nor cast upon the ground
The malice of thy tongue, to blast the world;
Calm thou thy bitter wrath's black inward surge,
For high shall be thine honour, set beside me
For ever in this land, whose fertile lap
Shall pour its teeming firstfruits unto you,
Gifts for fair childbirth and for wedlock's crown:
Thus honoured, praise my spoken pledge for aye.   970

Chorus

I, I dishonoured in this earth to dwell,—
Ancient of days and wisdom! I breathe forth
Poison and breath of frenzied ire. O Earth,
   Woe, woe, for thee, for me!
From side to side what pains be these that thrill?
Hearken, O mother Night, my wrath, mine agony!
Whom from mine ancient rights the gods have thrust
   And brought me to the dust—
Woe, woe is me!—with craft invincible.   *900*

Athena

Older art thou than I, and I will bear   980
With this thy fury. Know, although thou be
More wise in ancient wisdom, yet have I
From Zeus no scanted measure of the same,
Wherefore take heed unto this prophecy—
If to another land of alien men
Ye go, too late shall ye feel longing deep
For mine. The rolling tides of time bring round
A day of brighter glory for this town;
And thou, enshrined in honour by the halls
Where dwelt Erechtheus, shalt a worship win   990
From men and from the train of womankind,
Greater than any tribe elsewhere shall pay.
Cast thou not therefore on this soil of mine

153

Whetstones that sharpen souls to bloodshedding.
The burning goads of youthful hearts, made hot
With frenzy of the spirit, not of wine.
Nor pluck as 'twere the heart from cocks that strive,
To set it in the breasts of citizens
Of mine, a war-god's spirit, keen for fight,
1000 Made stern against their country and their kin.
The man who grievously doth lust for fame,
War, full, immitigable, let him wage
Against the stranger; but of kindred birds
I hold the challenge hateful. Such the boon
I proffer thee—within this land of lands,
Most loved of gods, with me to show and share
Fair mercy, gratitude and grace as fair.

Chorus

I, I dishonoured in this earth to dwell,—
Ancient of days and wisdom! I breathe forth
1010 Poison and breath of frenzied ire. O Earth,
    Woe, woe for thee, for me!
From side to side what pains be these that thrill?
Hearken, O mother Night, my wrath, mine agony!
Whom from mine ancient rights the gods have thrust,
    And brought me to the dust—
Woe, woe is me!—with craft invincible.

Athena

I will not weary of soft words to thee,
That never mayst thou say,
Behold me spurned, an elder by a younger deity,
1020 *And from this land rejected and forlorn,*
Unhonoured by the men who dwell therein.
But, if Persuasion's grace be sacred to thee,
Soft in the soothing accents of my tongue,
Tarry, I pray thee; yet, if go thou wilt,
Not rightfully wilt thou on this my town
Sway down the scale that beareth wrath and teen
Or wasting plague upon this folk. 'Tis thine,
If so thou wilt, inheritress to be
Of this my land, its utmost grace to win.

Chorus

> O queen, what refuge dost thou promise me?   1030

Athena

> Refuge untouched by bale: take thou my boon.

Chorus

> What, if I take it, shall mine honour be?

Athena

> No house shall prosper without grace of thine.

Chorus

> Canst thou achieve and grant such power to me?

Athena

> Yea, for my hand shall bless thy worshippers.

Chorus

> And wilt thou pledge me this for time eterne?

Athena

> Yea: none can bid me pledge beyond my power.

Chorus

> Lo, I desist from wrath, appeased by thee.

Athena

> Then in the land's heart shalt thou win thee friends.

Chorus

> What chant dost bid me raise, to greet the land?   1040

Athena

> Such as aspires towards a victory
> Unrued by any: chants from breast of earth,
> From wave, from sky; and let the wild winds' breath

Pass with soft sunlight o'er the lap of land,—
Strong wax the fruits of earth, fair teem the kine,
Unfailing, for my town's prosperity,
And constant be the growth of mortal seed.
But more and more root out the impious,
For as a gardener fosters what he sows,
So foster I this race, whom righteousness
Doth fend from sorrow. Such the proffered boon.
But I, if wars must be, and their loud clash
And carnage, for my town, will ne'er endure
That aught but victory shall crown her fame.

1050

Chorus

Lo, I accept it; at her very side
   Doth Pallas bid me dwell:
  I will not wrong the city of her pride,
Which even Almighty Zeus and Ares hold
   Heaven's earthly citadel,
Loved home of Grecian gods, the young, the old,
   The sanctuary divine,
   The shield of every shrine!
For Athens I say forth a gracious prophecy,—
  The glory of the sunlight and the skies
   Shall bid from earth arise
Warm wavelets of new life and glad prosperity.

1060

Athena

Behold, with gracious heart well pleased
   I for my citizens do grant
   Fulfilment of this covenant:
And here, their wrath at length appeased,
   These mighty deities shall stay,
   For theirs it is by right to sway
The lot that rules our mortal day,
   And he who hath not inly felt
   Their stern decree, ere long on him,
   Not knowing why and whence, the grim
   Life-crushing blow is dealt.
   The father's sin upon the child
   Descends, and sin is silent death,

1070

And leads him on the downward path,   1080
  By stealth beguiled,
   Unto the Furies: though his state
On earth were high, and loud his boast,
  Victim of silent ire and hate
    He dwells among the Lost.

Chorus

To my blessing now give ear.—
Scorching blight nor singèd air
Never blast thine olives fair!
Drought, that wasteth bud and plant,
Keep to thine own place. Avaunt,   1090
Famine fell, and come not hither
Stealthily to waste and wither!
Let the land, in season due,
Twice her waxing fruits renew;
Teem the kine in double measure;
Rich in new god-given treasure;
Here let men the powers adore
For sudden gifts unhoped before!

Athena

O hearken, warders of the wall
  That guards mine Athens, what a dower   1100
  Is unto her ordained and given!
For mighty is the Furies' power,
  And deep-revered in courts of heaven
And realms of hell; and clear to all
  They weave thy doom, mortality!
And some in joy and peace shall sing;
But unto other some they bring
  Sad life and tear-dimmed eye.

Chorus

And far away I ban thee and remove,
  Untimely death of youths too soon brought low!   1110
And to each maid, O gods, when time is come for love,
  Grant ye a warrior's heart, a wedded life to know.
Ye too, O Fates, children of mother Night,

157

Whose children too are we, O goddesses
Of just award, of all by sacred right
Queens who in time and in eternity
Do rule, a present power for righteousness,
Honoured beyond all Gods, hear ye and grant my cry!

Athena

And I too, I with joy am fain,
1120 Hearing your voice this gift ordain
Unto my land. High thanks be thine,
Persuasion, who with eyes divine
Into my tongue didst look thy strength,
To bend and to appease at length
Those who would not be comforted.
Zeus, king of parley, doth prevail,
And ye and I will strive nor fail,
That good may stand in evil's stead,
And lasting bliss for bale.

Chorus

1130 And nevermore these walls within
Shall echo fierce sedition's din
Unslaked with blood and crime;
The thirsty dust shall nevermore
Suck up the darkly streaming gore
Of civic broils, shed out in wrath
And vengeance, crying death for death!
But man with man and state with state
Shall vow, *The pledge of common hate*
And common friendship, that for man
1140 *Hath oft made blessing out of ban,*
Be ours unto all time.

Athena

Skill they, or not, the path to find
Of favouring speech and presage kind?
Yea, even from these, who, grim and stern,
Glared anger upon you of old,
O citizens, ye now shall earn
A recompense right manifold.

158

Deck them aright, extol them high,
Be loyal to their loyalty,
  And ye shall make your town and land   1150
  Sure, propped on Justice' saving hand,
And Fame's eternity.

Chorus

Hail ye, all hail! and yet again, all hail
  O Athens, happy in a weal secured!
O ye who sit by Zeus' right hand, nor fail
  Of wisdom set among you and assured,
Loved of the well-loved Goddess-Maid! the King   *1000*
Of gods doth reverence you, beneath her guarding wing.

Athena

All hail unto each honoured guest!
Whom to the chambers of your rest   1160
'Tis mine to lead, and to provide
The hallowed torch, the guard and guide.
Pass down, the while these altars glow
With sacred fire, to earth below
  And your appointed shrine.
There dwelling, from the land restrain
The force of fate, the breath of bane,
But waft on us the gift and gain
  Of Victory divine!
And ye, the men of Cranaos' seed,   1170
I bid you now with reverence lead
These alien Powers that thus are made
Athenian evermore. To you
Fair be their will henceforth, to do
  Whate'er may bless and aid!

Chorus

Hail to you all! hail yet again,
All who love Athens, Gods and men,
  Adoring her as Pallas' home!
And while ye reverence what ye grant—
My sacred shrine and hidden haunt—   1180
  Blameless and blissful be your doom!

Athena

> Once more I praise the promise of your vows,
> And now I bid the golden torches' glow
> Pass down before you to the hidden depth
> Of earth, by mine own sacred servants borne,
> My loyal guard of statue and of shrine.
> Come forth, O flower of Theseus' Attic land,
> O glorious band of children and of wives,
> And ye, O train of matrons crowned with eld!
> 1190 Deck you with festal robes of scarlet dye
> In honour of this day: O gleaming torch,
> Lead onward, that these gracious powers of earth
> Henceforth be seen to bless the life of men.

[Athena leads the procession downwards into the Cave of the Furies, under Areopagus: as they go, the escort of women and children chant aloud.]

Chant

> With loyalty we lead you; proudly go,
> Night's childless children, to your home below!
> (O citizens, awhile from words forbear!)
> To darkness' deep primeval lair,
> Far in Earth's bosom, downward fare,
> Adored with prayer and sacrifice.
> 1200 (O citizens, forbear your cries!)
> Pass hitherward, ye powers of Dread,
> With all your former wrath allayed,
> Into the heart of this loved land;
> With joy unto your temple wend,
> The while upon your steps attend
> The flames that fed upon the brand—
> (Now, now ring out your chant, your joy's acclaim!)
> Behind them, as they downward fare,
> Let holy hands libations bear,
> 1210 And torches' sacred flame.
> All-seeing Zeus and Fate come down
> To battle fair for Pallas' town!
> Ring out your chant, ring out your joy's acclaim!

[Exeunt omnes.]

SOPHOCLES

Sophocles

•

Three Theban Plays

Oedipus the King

Translated By F. Storr

Dramatis Personae

OEDIPUS
king of Thebes

THE PRIEST OF ZEUS

CREON
brother-in-law of Oedipus

CHORUS OF THEBAN ELDERS

TEIRESIAS
a blind seer

JOCASTA
queen of Thebes and
wife of Oedipus

MESSENGER

SHEPHERD OF LAIUS

*[Thebes. Before the Palace of Oedipus. Suppliants of all
ages are seated round the altar at the palace doors, at their
head a Priest of Zeus. To them enter Oedipus.]*

Oedipus

> My children, latest born to Cadmus old,
> Why sit ye here as suppliants, in your hands
> Branches of olive filleted with wool?
> What means this reek of incense everywhere,
> And everywhere laments and litanies?
> Children, it were not meet that I should learn
> From others, and am hither come, myself,
> I Oedipus, your world-renowned king.
> Ho! aged sire, whose venerable locks
> Proclaim thee spokesman of this company,   10
> Explain your mood and purport. Is it dread
> Of ill that moves you or a boon ye crave?
> My zeal in your behalf ye cannot doubt;
> Ruthless indeed were I and obdurate
> If such petitioners as you I spurned.

Priest

> Yea, Oedipus, my sovereign lord and king,
> Thou seest how both extremes of age besiege
> Thy palace altars—fledglings hardly winged,
> And greybeards bowed with years, priests, as am I
> Of Zeus, and these the flower of our youth.   20
> Meanwhile, the common folk, with wreathed boughs
> Crowd our two market-places, or before
> Both shrines of Pallas congregate, or where
> Ismenus gives his oracles by fire.
> For, as thou seest thyself, our ship of State,
> Sore buffeted, can no more lift her head,
> Foundered beneath a weltering surge of blood.
> A blight is on our harvest in the ear,
> A blight upon the grazing flocks and herds,
> A blight on wives in travail; and withal   30

Armed with his blazing torch the God of Plague
Hath swooped upon our city emptying
The house of Cadmus, and the murky realm
Of Pluto is full fed with groans and tears.

Therefore, O King, here at thy hearth we sit,
I and these children; not as deeming thee
A new divinity, but the first of men;
First in the common accidents of life,
And first in visitations of the Gods.
40   Art thou not he who coming to the town
Of Cadmus freed us from the tax we paid
To the fell songstress? Nor hadst thou received
Prompting from us or been by others schooled;
No, by a god inspired (so all men deem,
And testify) didst thou renew our life.
And now, O Oedipus, our peerless king,
All we thy votaries beseech thee, find
Some succor, whether by a voice from heaven
Whispered, or haply known by human wit.
50   Tried counselors, methinks, are aptest found
To furnish for the future pregnant rede.
Upraise, O chief of men, upraise our State!
Look to thy laurels! for thy zeal of yore
Our country's savior thou art justly hailed:
O never may we thus record thy reign:—
"He raised us up only to cast us down."
Uplift us, build our city on a rock.
Thy happy star ascendant brought us luck,
O let it not decline! If thou wouldst rule
60   This land, as now thou reignest, better sure
To rule a peopled than a desert realm.
Nor battlements nor galleys aught avail,
If men to man and guards to guard them tail.

Oedipus

Ah! my poor children, known, ah, known too well,
The quest that brings you hither and your need.
Ye sicken all, well wot I, yet my pain,
How great soever yours, outtops it all.
Your sorrow touches each man severally,

Him and none other, but I grieve at once
Both for the general and myself and you. 70
Therefore ye rouse no sluggard from day-dreams.
Many, my children, are the tears I've wept,
And threaded many a maze of weary thought.
Thus pondering one clue of hope I caught,
And tracked it up; I have sent Menoeceus' son,
Creon, my consort's brother, to inquire
Of Pythian Phoebus at his Delphic shrine,
How I might save the State by act or word.
And now I reckon up the tale of days
Since he set forth, and marvel how he fares. 80
'Tis strange, this endless tarrying, passing strange.
But when he comes, then I were base indeed,
If I perform not all the god declares.

Priest

Thy words are well timed; even as thou speakest
That shouting tells me Creon is at hand.

Oedipus

O King Apollo! may his joyous looks
Be presage of the joyous news he brings!

Priest

As I surmise, 'tis welcome; else his head
Had scarce been crowned with berry-laden bays.

Oedipus

We soon shall know; he's now in earshot range. 90

[Enter Creon.]

My royal cousin, say, Menoeceus' child,
What message hast thou brought us from the god?

Creon

Good news, for e'en intolerable ills,
Finding right issue, tend to naught but good.

Oedipus

> How runs the oracle? thus far thy words
> Give me no ground for confidence or fear.

Creon

> If thou wouldst hear my message publicly,
> I'll tell thee straight, or with thee pass within.

Oedipus

> Speak before all; the burden that I bear
> Is more for these my subjects than myself.

100

Creon

> Let me report then all the god declared.
> King Phoebus bids us straitly extirpate
> A fell pollution that infests the land,
> And no more harbor an inveterate sore.

Oedipus

> What expiation means he? What's amiss?

Creon

100

> Banishment, or the shedding blood for blood.
> This stain of blood makes shipwreck of our state.

Oedipus

> Whom can he mean, the miscreant thus denounced?

Creon

> Before thou didst assume the helm of State,
> The sovereign of this land was Laius.

110

Oedipus

> I heard as much, but never saw the man.

Creon

> He fell; and now the god's command is plain:
> Punish his takers-off, whoe'er they be.

Oedipus

> Where are they? Where in the wide world to find
> The far, faint traces of a bygone crime?

Creon

> In this land, said the god; "who seeks shall find;
> Who sits with folded hands or sleeps is blind."

Oedipus

> Was he within his palace, or afield,
> Or traveling, when Laius met his fate?

Creon

> Abroad; he started, so he told us, bound   120
> For Delphi, but he never thence returned.

Oedipus

> Came there no news, no fellow-traveler
> To give some clue that might be followed up?

Creon

> But one escaped, who flying for dear life,
> Could tell of all he saw but one thing sure.

Oedipus

> And what was that? One clue might lead us far,
> With but a spark of hope to guide our quest.

Creon

> Robbers, he told us, not one bandit but
> A troop of knaves, attacked and murdered him.

Oedipus

> Did any bandit dare so bold a stroke,   130
> Unless indeed he were suborned from Thebes?

Creon

> So 'twas surmised, but none was found to avenge

His murder mid the trouble that ensued.

Oedipus

What trouble can have hindered a full quest,
When royalty had fallen thus miserably?

Creon

The riddling Sphinx compelled us to let slide
The dim past and attend to instant needs.

Oedipus

Well, I will start afresh and once again
Make dark things clear. Right worthy the concern
140   Of Phoebus, worthy thine too, for the dead;
I also, as is meet, will lend my aid
To avenge this wrong to Thebes and to the god.
Not for some far-off kinsman, but myself,
Shall I expel this poison in the blood;
For whoso slew that king might have a mind
To strike me too with his assassin hand.
Therefore in righting him I serve myself.
Up, children, haste ye, quit these altar stairs,
Take hence your suppliant wands, go summon hither
150   The Theban commons. With the god's good help
Success is sure; 'tis ruin if we fail.

[Exeunt Oedipus and Creon.]

Priest

Come, children, let us hence; these gracious words
Forestall the very purpose of our suit.
And may the god who sent this oracle
Save us withal and rid us of this pest.

[Exeunt Priest and Suppliants.]

Chorus

[strophe 1]

Sweet-voiced daughter of Zeus
   From thy gold-paved Pythian shrine
      Wafted to Thebes divine,
What dost thou bring me?
   My soul is racked and shivers with fear.   160
      Healer of Delos, hear!
Hast thou some pain unknown before,
Or with the circling years renewest a penance of yore?
Offspring of golden Hope, thou voice immortal, O tell me.

[antistrophe 1]

First on Athene I call; O Zeus-born goddess, defend!
   Goddess and sister, befriend,
Artemis, Lady of Thebes, high-throned in the midst of our
mart!
   Lord of the death-winged dart!
Your threefold aid I crave   170
   From death and ruin our city to save.
If in the days of old when we nigh had perished,
Ye drave from our land the fiery plague,
      Be near us now
      And defend us!

[strophe 2]

Ah me, what countless woes are mine!
All our host is in decline;
Weaponless my spirit lies.
Earth her gracious fruits denies;
Women wail in barren throes;   180
Life on life downstriken goes,
Swifter than the wind bird's flight,
Swifter than the Fire-God's might,
To the westering shores of Night.

[antistrophe 2]

Wasted thus by death on death
All our city perisheth.
Corpses spread infection round;
None to tend or mourn is found.
Wailing on the altar stair

190 Wives and grandams rend the air—
Long-drawn moans and piercing cries
Blent with prayers and litanies.
Golden child of Zeus, O hear
Let thine angel face appear!

[strophe 3]

And grant that Ares whose hot breath I feel,
Though without target or steel
He stalks, whose voice is as the battle shout,
May turn in sudden rout,
To the unharbored Thracian waters sped,
200 Or Amphitrite's bed.
For what night leaves undone,
Smit by the morrow's sun
Perisheth. Father Zeus, whose hand
Doth wield the lightning brand,
Slay him beneath thy levin bold, we pray,
Slay him, O slay!

[antistrophe 3]

O that thine arrows too, Lycean King,
From that taut bow's gold string,
Might fly abroad, the champions of our rights;
210 Yea, and the flashing lights
Of Artemis, wherewith the huntress sweeps
Across the Lycian steeps.
Thee too I call with golden-snooded hair,
Whose name our land doth bear,
Bacchus to whom thy Maenads "Evoe" shout;
Come with thy bright torch, rout,
Blithe god whom we adore,
The god whom gods abhor.

[Enter Oedipus.]

Oedipus

Ye pray; 'tis well, but would ye hear my words
220 And heed them and apply the remedy,

174

Ye might perchance find comfort and relief.
Mind you, I speak as one who comes a stranger
To this report, no less than to the crime;
For how unaided could I track it far
Without a clue? Which lacking (for too late
Was I enrolled a citizen of Thebes)
This proclamation I address to all:—
Thebans, if any knows the man by whom
Laius, son of Labdacus, was slain,
I summon him to make clean shrift to me.   230
And if he shrinks, let him reflect that thus
Confessing he shall 'scape the capital charge;
For the worst penalty that shall befall him
Is banishment—unscathed he shall depart.
But if an alien from a foreign land
Be known to any as the murderer,
Let him who knows speak out, and he shall have
Due recompense from me and thanks to boot.
But if ye still keep silence, if through fear
For self or friends ye disregard my hest,   240
Hear what I then resolve; I lay my ban
On the assassin whosoe'er he be.
Let no man in this land, whereof I hold
The sovereign rule, harbor or speak to him;
Give him no part in prayer or sacrifice
Or lustral rites, but hound him from your homes.
For this is our defilement, so the god
Hath lately shown to me by oracles.
Thus as their champion I maintain the cause
Both of the god and of the murdered King.   250
And on the murderer this curse I lay
(On him and all the partners in his guilt):—
Wretch, may he pine in utter wretchedness!
And for myself, if with my privity
He gain admittance to my hearth, I pray
The curse I laid on others fall on me.
See that ye give effect to all my hest,
For my sake and the god's and for our land,
A desert blasted by the wrath of heaven.
For, let alone the god's express command,   260
It were a scandal ye should leave unpurged

The murder of a great man and your king,
Nor track it home. And now that I am lord,
Successor to his throne, his bed, his wife,
(And had he not been frustrated in the hope
Of issue, common children of one womb
Had forced a closer bond twixt him and me,
But Fate swooped down upon him), therefore I
His blood-avenger will maintain his cause
270 As though he were my sire, and leave no stone
Unturned to track the assassin or avenge
The son of Labdacus, of Polydore,
Of Cadmus, and Agenor first of the race.
And for the disobedient thus I pray:
May the gods send them neither timely fruits
Of earth, nor teeming increase of the womb,
But may they waste and pine, as now they waste,
Aye and worse stricken; but to all of you,
My loyal subjects who approve my acts,
280 May Justice, our ally, and all the gods
Be gracious and attend you evermore.

Chorus

The oath thou profferest, sire, I take and swear.
I slew him not myself, nor can I name
The slayer. For the quest, 'twere well, methinks
That Phoebus, who proposed the riddle, himself
Should give the answer—who the murderer was.

Oedipus

Well argued; but no living man can hope
To force the gods to speak against their will.

Chorus

May I then say what seems next best to me?

Oedipus

290 Aye, if there be a third best, tell it too.

Chorus

My liege, if any man sees eye to eye

176

With our lord Phoebus, 'tis our prophet, lord
Teiresias; he of all men best might guide
A searcher of this matter to the light.

Oedipus

Here too my zeal has nothing lagged, for twice
At Creon's instance have I sent to fetch him,
And long I marvel why he is not here.

Chorus

I mind me too of rumors long ago—
Mere gossip.

Oedipus

Tell them, I would fain know all.   300

Chorus

'Twas said he fell by travelers.

Oedipus

So I heard,
But none has seen the man who saw him fall.

Chorus

Well, if he knows what fear is, he will quail
And flee before the terror of thy curse.

Oedipus

Words scare not him who blenches not at deeds.

Chorus

But here is one to arraign him. Lo, at length
They bring the god-inspired seer in whom
Above all other men is truth inborn.

[Enter Teiresias, led by a boy.]

Oedipus

Teiresias, seer who comprehendest all,
Lore of the wise and hidden mysteries,
High things of heaven and low things of the earth,
Thou knowest, though thy blinded eyes see naught,
What plague infects our city; and we turn
To thee, O seer, our one defense and shield.
The purport of the answer that the God
Returned to us who sought his oracle,
The messengers have doubtless told thee—how
One course alone could rid us of the pest,
To find the murderers of Laius,
And slay them or expel them from the land.
Therefore begrudging neither augury
Nor other divination that is thine,
O save thyself, thy country, and thy king,
Save all from this defilement of blood shed.
On thee we rest. This is man's highest end,
To others' service all his powers to lend.

320

Teiresias

Alas, alas, what misery to be wise
When wisdom profits nothing! This old lore
I had forgotten; else I were not here.

330

Oedipus

What ails thee? Why this melancholy mood?

Teiresias

Let me go home; prevent me not; 'twere best
That thou shouldst bear thy burden and I mine.

Oedipus

For shame! no true-born Theban patriot
Would thus withhold the word of prophecy.

Teiresias

Thy words, O king, are wide of the mark, and I
For fear lest I too trip like thee...

Oedipus

> Oh speak,
> Withhold not, I adjure thee, if thou know'st,
> Thy knowledge. We are all thy suppliants.   340

Teiresias

> Aye, for ye all are witless, but my voice
> Will ne'er reveal my miseries—or thine.

Oedipus

> What then, thou knowest, and yet willst not speak!
> Wouldst thou betray us and destroy the State?

Teiresias

> I will not vex myself nor thee. Why ask
> Thus idly what from me thou shalt not learn?

Oedipus

> Monster! thy silence would incense a flint.
> Will nothing loose thy tongue? Can nothing melt thee,
> Or shake thy dogged taciturnity?

Teiresias

> Thou blam'st my mood and seest not thine own   350
> Wherewith thou art mated; no, thou taxest me.

Oedipus

> And who could stay his choler when he heard
> How insolently thou dost flout the State?

Teiresias

> Well, it will come what will, though I be mute.

Oedipus

> Since come it must, thy duty is to tell me.

Teiresias

> I have no more to say; storm as thou willst,

179

And give the rein to all thy pent-up rage.

Oedipus

Yea, I am wroth, and will not stint my words,
But speak my whole mind. Thou methinks thou art he,
360   Who planned the crime, aye, and performed it too,
All save the assassination; and if thou
Hadst not been blind, I had been sworn to boot
That thou alone didst do the bloody deed.

Teiresias

Is it so? Then I charge thee to abide
By thine own proclamation; from this day
Speak not to these or me. Thou art the man,
Thou the accursed polluter of this land.

Oedipus

Vile slanderer, thou blurtest forth these taunts,
And think'st forsooth as seer to go scot free.

Teiresias

370   Yea, I am free, strong in the strength of truth.

Oedipus

Who was thy teacher? not methinks thy art.

Teiresias

Thou, goading me against my will to speak.

Oedipus

What speech? repeat it and resolve my doubt.

Teiresias

Didst miss my sense wouldst thou goad me on?

Oedipus

I but half caught thy meaning; say it again.

Teiresias

> I say thou art the murderer of the man
> Whose murderer thou pursuest.

Oedipus

> Thou shalt rue it
> Twice to repeat so gross a calumny.

Teiresias

> Must I say more to aggravate thy rage? 380

Oedipus

> Say all thou wilt; it will be but waste of breath.

Teiresias

> I say thou livest with thy nearest kin
> In infamy, unwitting in thy shame.

Oedipus

> Think'st thou for aye unscathed to wag thy tongue?

Teiresias

> Yea, if the might of truth can aught prevail.

Oedipus

> With other men, but not with thee, for thou
> In ear, wit, eye, in everything art blind.

Teiresias

> Poor fool to utter gibes at me which all
> Here present will cast back on thee ere long.

Oedipus

> Offspring of endless Night, thou hast no power 390
> O'er me or any man who sees the sun.

Teiresias

> No, for thy weird is not to fall by me.
> I leave to Apollo what concerns the god.

Oedipus

> Is this a plot of Creon, or thine own?

Teiresias

> Not Creon, thou thyself art thine own bane.

Oedipus

> O wealth and empiry and skill by skill
> Outwitted in the battlefield of life,
> What spite and envy follow in your train!
> See, for this crown the State conferred on me.
> A gift, a thing I sought not, for this crown
> The trusty Creon, my familiar friend,
> Hath lain in wait to oust me and suborned
> This mountebank, this juggling charlatan,
> This tricksy beggar-priest, for gain alone
> Keen-eyed, but in his proper art stone-blind.
> Say, sirrah, hast thou ever proved thyself
> A prophet? When the riddling Sphinx was here
> Why hadst thou no deliverance for this folk?
> And yet the riddle was not to be solved
> By guess-work but required the prophet's art;
> Wherein thou wast found lacking; neither birds
> Nor sign from heaven helped thee, but I came,
> The simple Oedipus; I stopped her mouth
> By mother wit, untaught of auguries.
> This is the man whom thou wouldst undermine,
> In hope to reign with Creon in my stead.
> Methinks that thou and thine abettor soon
> Will rue your plot to drive the scapegoat out.
> Thank thy grey hairs that thou hast still to learn
> What chastisement such arrogance deserves.

400

410

400

420

Chorus

> To us it seems that both the seer and thou,

O Oedipus, have spoken angry words.
This is no time to wrangle but consult
How best we may fulfill the oracle.

Teiresias

King as thou art, free speech at least is mine
To make reply; in this I am thy peer.
I own no lord but Loxias; him I serve
And ne'er can stand enrolled as Creon's man.
Thus then I answer: since thou hast not spared
To twit me with my blindness—thou hast eyes,   430
Yet see'st not in what misery thou art fallen,
Nor where thou dwellest nor with whom for mate.
Dost know thy lineage? Nay, thou know'st it not,
And all unwitting art a double foe
To thine own kin, the living and the dead;
Aye and the dogging curse of mother and sire
One day shall drive thee, like a two-edged sword,
Beyond our borders, and the eyes that now
See clear shall henceforward endless night.
Ah whither shall thy bitter cry not reach,   440
What crag in all Cithaeron but shall then
Reverberate thy wail, when thou hast found
With what a hymeneal thou wast borne
Home, but to no fair haven, on the gale!
Aye, and a flood of ills thou guessest not
Shall set thyself and children in one line.
Flout then both Creon and my words, for none
Of mortals shall be stricken worse than thou.

Oedipus

Must I endure this fellow's insolence?
A murrain on thee! Get thee hence! Begone   450
Avaunt! and never cross my threshold more.

Teiresias

I ne'er had come hadst thou not bidden me.

Oedipus

I knew not thou wouldst utter folly, else

183

Long hadst thou waited to be summoned here.

Teiresias

Such am I—as it seems to thee a fool,
But to the parents who begat thee, wise.

Oedipus

What sayest thou—"parents"? Who begat me, speak?

Teiresias

This day shall be thy birth-day, and thy grave.

Oedipus

Thou lov'st to speak in riddles and dark words.

Teiresias

In reading riddles who is so skilled as thou?

Oedipus

Twit me with that wherein my greatness lies.

Teiresias

And yet this very greatness proved thy bane.

Oedipus

No matter if I saved the commonwealth.

Teiresias

'Tis time I left thee. Come, boy, take me home.

Oedipus

Aye, take him quickly, for his presence irks
And lets me; gone, thou canst not plague me more.

Teiresias

I go, but first will tell thee why I came.
Thy frown I dread not, for thou canst not harm me.

Hear then: this man whom thou hast sought to arrest
With threats and warrants this long while, the wretch   470
Who murdered Laius—that man is here.
He passes for an alien in the land
But soon shall prove a Theban, native born.
And yet his fortune brings him little joy;
For blind of seeing, clad in beggar's weeds,
For purple robes, and leaning on his staff,
To a strange land he soon shall grope his way.
And of the children, inmates of his home,
He shall be proved the brother and the sire,
Of her who bare him son and husband both,   480
Co-partner, and assassin of his sire.
Go in and ponder this, and if thou find
That I have missed the mark, henceforth declare
I have no wit nor skill in prophecy.

[Exeunt Teiresias and Oedipus.]

Chorus

[strophe 1]

Who is he by voice immortal
Named from Pythia's rocky cell,
Doer of foul deeds of bloodshed,
Hhorrors that no tongue can tell?
A foot for flight he needs
Fleeter than storm-swift steeds,   490
For on his heels doth follow,
Armed with the lightnings of his Sire, Apollo.
Like sleuth-hounds too
The Fates pursue.

[antistrophe 1]

Yea, but now flashed forth
    The summons from Parnassus' snowy peak,
"Near and far the undiscovered
    Doer of this murder seek!"

500

Now like a sullen bull he roves
Through forest brakes and upland groves,
And vainly seeks to fly
The doom that ever nigh
Flits o'er his head,
Still by the avenging Phoebus sped,
The voice divine,
From Earth's mid shrine.

[strophe 2]

510

Sore perplexed am I
 By the words of the master seer.
Are they true, are they false?
 I know not and bridle my tongue for fear,
Fluttered with vague surmise;
 Nor present nor future is clear.
Quarrel of ancient date or in days still near know I none
Twixt the Labdacidan house and our ruler, Polybus' son.
Proof is there none:
How then can I challenge our King's good name,
How in a blood-feud join for an untracked deed of shame?

[antistrophe 2]

520

500

All wise are Zeus and Apollo,
And nothing is hid from their ken;
They are gods; and in wits
A man may surpass his fellow men;
But that a mortal seer
Knows more than I know—where
 Hath this been proven?
Or how without sign assured, can I blame
Him who saved our State when the winged songstress came,
Tested and tried in the light of us all, like gold assayed?
How can I now assent when a crime is on Oedipus laid?

Creon

530

Friends, countrymen, I learn King Oedipus
Hath laid against me a most grievous charge,
And come to you protesting. If he deems
That I have harmed or injured him in aught

By word or deed in this our present trouble,
I care not to prolong the span of life,
Thus ill-reputed; for the calumny
Hits not a single blot, but blasts my name,
If by the general voice I am denounced
False to the State and false by you my friends.

Chorus

This taunt, it well may be, was blurted out
In petulance, not spoken advisedly.   540

Creon

Did any dare pretend that it was I
Prompted the seer to utter a forged charge?

Chorus

Such things were said; with what intent I know not.

Creon

Were not his wits and vision all astray
When upon me he fixed this monstrous charge?

Chorus

I know not; to my sovereign's acts I am blind.
But lo, he comes to answer for himself.

[Enter Oedipus.]

Oedipus

Sirrah, what mak'st thou here? Dost thou presume
To approach my doors, thou brazen-faced rogue,
My murderer and the filcher of my crown?   550
Come, answer this, didst thou detect in me
Some touch of cowardice or witlessness,
That made thee undertake this enterprise?
I seemed forsooth too simple to perceive
The serpent stealing on me in the dark,
Or else too weak to scotch it when I saw.

This thou art witless seeking to possess
Without a following or friends the crown,
A prize that followers and wealth must win.

Creon

560   Attend me. Thou hast spoken, 'tis my turn
To make reply. Then having heard me, judge.

Oedipus

Thou art glib of tongue, but I am slow to learn
Of thee; I know too well thy venomous hate.

Creon

First I would argue out this very point.

Oedipus

O argue not that thou art not a rogue.

Creon

If thou dost count a virtue stubbornness,
Unschooled by reason, thou art much astray.

Oedipus

If thou dost hold a kinsman may be wronged,
And no pains follow, thou art much to seek.

Creon

570   Therein thou judgest rightly, but this wrong
That thou allegest—tell me what it is.

Oedipus

Didst thou or didst thou not advise that I
Should call the priest?

Creon

Yes, and I stand to it.

Oedipus

Tell me how long is it since Laius...

Creon

> Since Laius...? I follow not thy drift.

Oedipus

> By violent hands was spirited away.

Creon

> In the dim past, a many years agone.

Oedipus

> Did the same prophet then pursue his craft?

Creon

> Yes, skilled as now and in no less repute.   580

Oedipus

> Did he at that time ever glance at me?

Creon

> Not to my knowledge, not when I was by.

Oedipus

> But was no search and inquisition made?

Creon

> Surely full quest was made, but nothing learnt.

Oedipus

> Why failed the seer to tell his story then?

Creon

> I know not, and not knowing hold my tongue.

Oedipus

> This much thou knowest and canst surely tell.

Creon

> What's mean'st thou? All I know I will declare.

Oedipus

But for thy prompting never had the seer
Ascribed to me the death of Laius.

Creon

If so he thou knowest best; but I
Would put thee to the question in my turn.

Oedipus

Question and prove me murderer if thou canst.

Creon

Then let me ask thee, didst thou wed my sister?

Oedipus

A fact so plain I cannot well deny.

Creon

And as thy consort queen she shares the throne?

Oedipus

I grant her freely all her heart desires.

Creon

And with you twain I share the triple rule?

Oedipus

Yea, and it is that proves thee a false friend.

Creon

Not so, if thou wouldst reason with thyself,
As I with myself. First, I bid thee think,
Would any mortal choose a troubled reign
Of terrors rather than secure repose,
If the same power were given him? As for me,
I have no natural craving for the name
Of king, preferring to do kingly deeds,

And so thinks every sober-minded man.
Now all my needs are satisfied through thee,
And I have naught to fear; but were I king,
My acts would oft run counter to my will.   610
How could a title then have charms for me
Above the sweets of boundless influence?
I am not so infatuated as to grasp
The shadow when I hold the substance fast.
Now all men cry me Godspeed! wish me well,
And every suitor seeks to gain my ear,
If he would hope to win a grace from thee.
Why should I leave the better, choose the worse?
That were sheer madness, and I am not mad.
No such ambition ever tempted me,   620   600
Nor would I have a share in such intrigue.
And if thou doubt me, first to Delphi go,
There ascertain if my report was true
Of the god's answer; next investigate
If with the seer I plotted or conspired,
And if it prove so, sentence me to death,
Not by thy voice alone, but mine and thine.
But O condemn me not, without appeal,
On bare suspicion. 'Tis not right to adjudge
Bad men at random good, or good men bad.   630
I would as lief a man should cast away
The thing he counts most precious, his own life,
As spurn a true friend. Thou wilt learn in time
The truth, for time alone reveals the just;
A villain is detected in a day.

Chorus

To one who walketh warily his words
Commend themselves; swift counsels are not sure.

Oedipus

When with swift strides the stealthy plotter stalks
I must be quick too with my counterplot.
To wait his onset passively, for him   640
Is sure success, for me assured defeat.

Creon

What then's thy will? To banish me from the land?

Oedipus

I would not have thee banished, no, but dead,
That men may mark the wages envy reaps.

Creon

I see thou wilt not yield, nor credit me.

Oedipus

None but a fool would credit such as thou.

Creon

Thou art not wise.

Oedipus

Wise for myself at least.

Creon

Why not for me too?

Oedipus

650 Why for such a knave?

Creon

Suppose thou lackest sense.

Oedipus

Yet kings must rule.

Creon

Not if they rule ill.

Oedipus

Oh my Thebans, hear him!

Creon

Thy Thebans? am not I a Theban too?

Chorus

Cease, princes;
Lo there comes, and none too soon,
Jocasta from the palace. Who so fit
As peacemaker to reconcile your feud?

[Enter Jocasta.]

Jocasta

Misguided princes, why have ye upraised   660
This wordy wrangle? Are ye not ashamed,
While the whole land lies stricken, thus to voice
Your private injuries? Go in, my lord;
Go home, my brother, and forebear to make
A public scandal of a petty grief.

Creon

My royal sister, Oedipus, thy lord,
Hath bid me choose (O dread alternative!)
An outlaw's exile or a felon's death.

Oedipus

Yes, lady; I have caught him practicing
Against my royal person his vile arts.   670

Creon

May I ne'er speed but die accursed, if I
In any way am guilty of this charge.

Jocasta

Believe him, I adjure thee, Oedipus,
First for his solemn oath's sake, then for mine,
And for thine elders' sake who wait on thee.

Chorus

[strophe 1]

Hearken, King, reflect, we pray thee,

Be not stubborn but relent.

Oedipus

Say to what should I consent?

Chorus

Respect a man whose probity and troth
680   Are known to all and now confirmed by oath.

Oedipus

Dost know what grace thou cravest?

Chorus

Yea, I know.

Oedipus

Declare it then and make thy meaning plain.

Chorus

Brand not a friend whom babbling tongues assail;
Let not suspicion 'gainst his oath prevail.

Oedipus

Bethink you that in seeking this ye seek
In very sooth my death or banishment?

Chorus

No, by the leader of the host divine!

[strophe 2]

Witness, thou Sun, such thought was never mine,
690   Unblest, unfriended may I perish,
If ever I such wish did cherish!
But O my heart is desolate
Musing on our stricken State,
Doubly fall'n should discord grow
Twixt you twain, to crown our woe.

Oedipus

> Well, let him go, no matter what it cost me,
> Or certain death or shameful banishment,
> For your sake I relent, not his; and him,
> Where'er he be, my heart shall still abhor.

Creon

> Thou art as sullen in thy yielding mood   700
> As in thine anger thou wast truculent.
> Such tempers justly plague themselves the most.

Oedipus

> Leave me in peace and get thee gone.

Creon

> I go,
> By thee misjudged, but justified by these.

[Exeunt Creon.]

Chorus

[antistrophe 1]

> Lady, lead indoors thy consort;
> Wherefore longer here delay?

Jocasta

> Tell me first how rose the fray.

Chorus

> Rumors bred unjust suspicioun and injustice rankles sore.

Jocasta

> Were both at fault?   710

Chorus

> Both.

Jocasta

What was the tale?

Chorus

Ask me no more. The land is sore distressed;
'Twere better sleeping ills to leave at rest.

Oedipus

Strange counsel, friend! I know thou mean'st me well,
And yet would'st mitigate and blunt my zeal.

Chorus

[antistrophe 2]

King, I say it once again,
Witless were I proved, insane,
If I lightly put away
720 Thee my country's prop and stay,
Pilot who, in danger sought,
To a quiet haven brought
Our distracted State; and now
Who can guide us right but thou?

Jocasta

Let me too, I adjure thee, know, O king,
What cause has stirred this unrelenting wrath.

Oedipus

700 I will, for thou art more to me than these.
Lady, the cause is Creon and his plots.

Jocasta

But what provoked the quarrel? make this clear.

Oedipus

730 He points me out as Laius' murderer.

Jocasta

Of his own knowledge or upon report?

196

Oedipus

> He is too cunning to commit himself,
> And makes a mouthpiece of a knavish seer.

Jocasta

> Then thou mayest ease thy conscience on that score.
> Listen and I'll convince thee that no man
> Hath scot or lot in the prophetic art.
> Here is the proof in brief. An oracle
> Once came to Laius (I will not say
> 'Twas from the Delphic god himself, but from
> His ministers) declaring he was doomed   740
> To perish by the hand of his own son,
> A child that should be born to him by me.
> Now Laius—so at least report affirmed—
> Was murdered on a day by highwaymen,
> No natives, at a spot where three roads meet.
> As for the child, it was but three days old,
> When Laius, its ankles pierced and pinned
> Together, gave it to be cast away
> By others on the trackless mountain side.
> So then Apollo brought it not to pass   750
> The child should be his father's murderer,
> Or the dread terror find accomplishment,
> And Laius be slain by his own son.
> Such was the prophet's horoscope. O king,
> Regard it not. Whate'er the god deems fit
> To search, himself unaided will reveal.

Oedipus

> What memories, what wild tumult of the soul
> Came o'er me, lady, as I heard thee speak!

Jocasta

> What mean'st thou? What has shocked and startled thee?

Oedipus

> Methought I heard thee say that Laius   760
> Was murdered at the meeting of three roads.

197

Jocasta

So ran the story that is current still.

Oedipus

Where did this happen? Dost thou know the place?

Jocasta

Phocis the land is called; the spot is where
Branch roads from Delphi and from Daulis meet.

Oedipus

And how long is it since these things befell?

Jocasta

'Twas but a brief while before thou wast proclaimed
Our country's ruler that the news was brought.

Oedipus

O Zeus, what hast thou willed to do with me!

Jocasta

770   What is it, Oedipus, that moves thee so?

Oedipus

Ask me not yet; tell me the build and height
Of Laius? Was he still in manhood's prime?

Jocasta

Tall was he, and his hair was lightly strewn
With silver; and not unlike thee in form.

Oedipus

O woe is me! Mehtinks unwittingly
I laid but now a dread curse on myself.

Jocasta

What say'st thou? When I look upon thee, my king,
I tremble.

Oedipus

> 'Tis a dread presentiment
> That in the end the seer will prove not blind.   780
> One further question to resolve my doubt.

Jocasta

> I quail; but ask, and I will answer all.

Oedipus

> Had he but few attendants or a train
> Of armed retainers with him, like a prince?

Jocasta

> They were but five in all, and one of them
> A herald; Laius in a mule-car rode.

Oedipus

> Alas! 'tis clear as noonday now. But say,
> Lady, who carried this report to Thebes?

Jocasta

> A serf, the sole survivor who returned.

Oedipus

> Haply he is at hand or in the house?   790

Jocasta

> No, for as soon as he returned and found
> Thee reigning in the stead of Laius slain,
> He clasped my hand and supplicated me
> To send him to the alps and pastures, where
> He might be farthest from the sight of Thebes.
> And so I sent him. 'Twas an honest slave
> And well deserved some better recompense.

Oedipus

> Fetch him at once. I fain would see the man.

Jocasta

He shall be brought; but wherefore summon him?

Oedipus

800   Lady, I fear my tongue has overrun
Discretion; therefore I would question him.

Jocasta

Well, he shall come, but may not I too claim
To share the burden of thy heart, my king?

Oedipus

And thou shalt not be frustrated of thy wish.
Now my imaginings have gone so far.
Who has a higher claim than thou to hear
My tale of dire adventures? Listen then.
My sire was Polybus of Corinth, and
My mother Merope, a Dorian;
810   And I was held the foremost citizen,
Till a strange thing befell me, strange indeed,
Yet scarce deserving all the heat it stirred.
A roisterer at some banquet, flown with wine,
Shouted "Thou art not true son of thy sire."
It irked me, but I stomached for the nonce
The insult; on the morrow I sought out
My mother and my sire and questioned them.
They were indignant at the random slur
Cast on my parentage and did their best
820   To comfort me, but still the venomed barb
Rankled, for still the scandal spread and grew.
So privily without their leave I went
To Delphi, and Apollo sent me back
Baulked of the knowledge that I came to seek.
But other grievous things he prophesied,
Woes, lamentations, mourning, portents dire;
To wit I should defile my mother's bed
And raise up seed too loathsome to behold,
And slay the father from whose loins I sprang.
830   Then, lady,—thou shalt hear the very truth—
As I drew near the triple-branching roads,

A herald met me and a man who sat
In a car drawn by colts—as in thy tale—
The man in front and the old man himself
Threatened to thrust me rudely from the path,
Then jostled by the charioteer in wrath
I struck him, and the old man, seeing this,
Watched till I passed and from his car brought down
Full on my head the double-pointed goad.
Yet was I quits with him and more; one stroke   840
Of my good staff sufficed to fling him clean
Out of the chariot seat and laid him prone.
And so I slew them every one. But if
Betwixt this stranger there was aught in common
With Laius, who more miserable than I,
What mortal could you find more god-abhorred?
Wretch whom no sojourner, no citizen
May harbor or address, whom all are bound
To harry from their homes. And this same curse
Was laid on me, and laid by none but me.   850
Yea with these hands all gory I pollute
The bed of him I slew. Say, am I vile?
Am I not utterly unclean, a wretch
Doomed to be banished, and in banishment
Forgo the sight of all my dearest ones,
And never tread again my native earth;
Or else to wed my mother and slay my sire,
Polybus, who begat me and upreared?
If one should say, this is the handiwork
Of some inhuman power, who could blame   860
His judgment? But, ye pure and awful gods,
Forbid, forbid that I should see that day!
May I be blotted out from living men
Ere such a plague spot set on me its brand!

Chorus

We too, O king, are troubled; but till thou
Hast questioned the survivor, still hope on.

Oedipus

My hope is faint, but still enough survives
To bid me bide the coming of this herd.

Jocasta

Suppose him here, what wouldst thou learn of him?

Oedipus

870   I'll tell thee, lady; if his tale agrees
       With thine, I shall have 'scaped calamity.

Jocasta

And what of special import did I say?

Oedipus

In thy report of what the herdsman said
Laius was slain by robbers; now if he
Still speaks of robbers, not a robber, I
Slew him not; "one" with "many" cannot square.
But if he says one lonely wayfarer,
The last link wanting to my guilt is forged.

Jocasta

Well, rest assured, his tale ran thus at first,
880   Nor can he now retract what then he said;
       Not I alone but all our townsfolk heard it.
       E'en should he vary somewhat in his story,
       He cannot make the death of Laius
       In any wise jump with the oracle.
       For Loxias said expressly he was doomed
       To die by my child's hand, but he, poor babe,
       He shed no blood, but perished first himself.
       So much for divination. Henceforth I
       Will look for signs neither to right nor left.

Oedipus

890   Thou reasonest well. Still I would have thee send
       And fetch the bondsman hither. See to it.

Jocasta

That will I straightway. Come, let us within.
I would do nothing that my lord mislikes.

[Exeunt Oedipus and Jocasta.]

Chorus

[strophe 1]

> My lot be still to lead
> The life of innocence and fly
> Irreverence in word or deed,
> To follow still those laws ordained on high
> Whose birthplace is the bright ethereal sky
> No mortal birth they own,
> Olympus their progenitor alone: 900
> Ne'er shall they slumber in oblivion cold,
> The god in them is strong and grows not old.

[antistrophe 1]

> Of insolence is bred
> The tyrant; insolence full blown,
> With empty riches surfeited,
> Scales the precipitous height and grasps the throne.
> Then topples o'er and lies in ruin prone;
> No foothold on that dizzy steep.
> But O may Heaven the true patriot keep
> Who burns with emulous zeal to serve the State.   910
> God is my help and hope, on him I wait.

[strophe 2]

> But the proud sinner, or in word or deed,
> That will not Justice heed,
> Nor reverence the shrine
> Of images divine,
> Perdition seize his vain imaginings,
> If, urged by greed profane,
> He grasps at ill-got gain,
> And lays an impious hand on holiest things.
> Who when such deeds are done   920
> Can hope heaven's bolts to shun?
> If sin like this to honor can aspire,
> Why dance I still and lead the sacred choir?

[antistrophe 2]

900

No more I'll seek earth's central oracle,
Or Abae's hallowed cell,
Nor to Olympia bring
My votive offering.
If before all God's truth be not bade plain.
O Zeus, reveal thy might,

930

King, if thou'rt named aright
Omnipotent, all-seeing, as of old;
For Laius is forgot;
His weird, men heed it not;
Apollo is forsook and faith grows cold.

[Enter Jocasta.]

Jocasta

My lords, ye look amazed to see your queen
With wreaths and gifts of incense in her hands.
I had a mind to visit the high shrines,
For Oedipus is overwrought, alarmed
With terrors manifold. He will not use

940

His past experience, like a man of sense,
To judge the present need, but lends an ear
To any croaker if he augurs ill.
Since then my counsels naught avail, I turn
To thee, our present help in time of trouble,
Apollo, Lord Lycean, and to thee
My prayers and supplications here I bring.
Lighten us, lord, and cleanse us from this curse!
For now we all are cowed like mariners
Who see their helmsman dumbstruck in the storm.

[Enter Corinthian Messenger.]

Messenger

950

My masters, tell me where the palace is
Of Oedipus; or better, where's the king.

Chorus

> Here is the palace and he bides within;
> This is his queen the mother of his children.

Messenger

> All happiness attend her and the house,
> Blessed is her husband and her marriage-bed.

Jocasta

> My greetings to thee, stranger; thy fair words
> Deserve a like response. But tell me why
> Thou comest—what thy need or what thy news.

Messenger

> Good for thy consort and the royal house.

Jocasta

> What may it be? Whose messenger art thou?   960

Messenger

> The Isthmian commons have resolved to make
> Thy husband king—so 'twas reported there.

Jocasta

> What! is not aged Polybus still king?

Messenger

> No, verily; he's dead and in his grave.

Jocasta

> What! is he dead, the sire of Oedipus?

Messenger

> If I speak falsely, may I die myself.

Jocasta

> Quick, maiden, bear these tidings to my lord.

Ye god-sent oracles, where stand ye now!
This is the man whom Oedipus long shunned,
970   In dread to prove his murderer; and now
He dies in nature's course, not by his hand.

[Enter Oedipus.]

Oedipus

My wife, my queen, Jocasta, why hast thou
Summoned me from my palace?

Jocasta

Hear this man,
And as thou hearest judge what has become
Of all those awe-inspiring oracles.

Oedipus

Who is this man, and what his news for me?

Jocasta

He comes from Corinth and his message this:
Thy father Polybus hath passed away.

Oedipus

980   What? let me have it, stranger, from thy mouth.

Messenger

If I must first make plain beyond a doubt
My message, know that Polybus is dead.

Oedipus

By treachery, or by sickness visited?

Messenger

One touch will send an old man to his rest.

Oedipus

So of some malady he died, poor man.

Messenger

> Yes, having measured the full span of years.

Oedipus

> Out on it, lady! why should one regard
> The Pythian hearth or birds that scream i' the air?
> Did they not point at me as doomed to slay
> My father? but he's dead and in his grave   990
> And here am I who ne'er unsheathed a sword;
> Unless the longing for his absent son
> Killed him and so I slew him in a sense.
> But, as they stand, the oracles are dead--
> Dust, ashes, nothing, dead as Polybus.

Jocasta

> Say, did not I foretell this long ago?

Oedipus

> Thou didst: but I was misled by my fear.

Jocasta

> Then let it no more weigh upon thy soul.

Oedipus

> Must I not fear my mother's marriage bed?

Jocasta

> Why should a mortal man, the sport of chance,   1000
> With no assured foreknowledge, be afraid?
> Best live a careless life from hand to mouth.
> This wedlock with thy mother fear not thou.
> How oft it chances that in dreams a man
> Has wed his mother! He who least regards
> Such brainsick phantasies lives most at ease.

Oedipus

> I should have shared in full thy confidence,

Were not my mother living; since she lives
Though half convinced I still must live in dread.

Jocasta

1010

And yet thy sire's death lights out darkness much.

Oedipus

Much, but my fear is touching her who lives.

Messenger

Who may this woman be whom thus you fear?

Oedipus

Merope, stranger, wife of Polybus.

Messenger

And what of her can cause you any fear?

Oedipus

A heaven-sent oracle of dread import.

Messenger

A mystery, or may a stranger hear it?

Oedipus

Aye, 'tis no secret. Loxias once foretold
That I should mate with mine own mother, and shed
With my own hands the blood of my own sire.

1020

Hence Corinth was for many a year to me
A home distant; and I trove abroad,
But missed the sweetest sight, my parents' face.

Messenger

1000

Was this the fear that exiled thee from home?

Oedipus

Yea, and the dread of slaying my own sire.

Messenger

> Why, since I came to give thee pleasure, King,
> Have I not rid thee of this second fear?

Oedipus

> Well, thou shalt have due guerdon for thy pains.

Messenger

> Well, I confess what chiefly made me come
> Was hope to profit by thy coming home.

Oedipus

> Nay, I will ne'er go near my parents more.   1030

Messenger

> My son, 'tis plain, thou know'st not what thou doest.

Oedipus

> How so, old man? For heaven's sake tell me all.

Messenger

> If this is why thou dreadest to return.

Oedipus

> Yea, lest the god's word be fulfilled in me.

Messenger

> Lest through thy parents thou shouldst be accursed?

Oedipus

> This and none other is my constant dread.

Messenger

> Dost thou not know thy fears are baseless all?

Oedipus

> How baseless, if I am their very son?

Messenger

> Since Polybus was naught to thee in blood.

Oedipus

1040

> What say'st thou? was not Polybus my sire?

Messenger

> As much thy sire as I am, and no more.

Oedipus

> My sire no more to me than one who is naught?

Messenger

> Since I begat thee not, no more did he.

Oedipus

> What reason had he then to call me son?

Messenger

> Know that he took thee from my hands, a gift.

Oedipus

> Yet, if no child of his, he loved me well.

Messenger

> A childless man till then, he warmed to thee.

Oedipus

> A foundling or a purchased slave, this child?

Messenger

> I found thee in Cithaeron's wooded glens.

Oedipus

1050

> What led thee to explore those upland glades?

Messenger

> My business was to tend the mountain flocks.

Oedipus

A vagrant shepherd journeying for hire?

Messenger

True, but thy savior in that hour, my son.

Oedipus

My savior? from what harm? what ailed me then?

Messenger

Those ankle joints are evidence enow.

Oedipus

Ah, why remind me of that ancient sore?

Messenger

I loosed the pin that riveted thy feet.

Oedipus

Yes, from my cradle that dread brand I bore.

Messenger

Whence thou deriv'st the name that still is thine.

Oedipus

Who did it? I adjure thee, tell me who   1060
Say, was it father, mother?

Messenger

I know not.
The man from whom I had thee may know more.

Oedipus

What, did another find me, not thyself?

Messenger

Not I; another shepherd gave thee me.

Oedipus

> Who was he? Would'st thou know again the man?

Messenger

> He passed indeed for one of Laius' house.

Oedipus

> The king who ruled the country long ago?

Messenger

> The same: he was a herdsman of the king.

Oedipus

1070
> And is he living still for me to see him?

Messenger

> His fellow-countrymen should best know that.

Oedipus

> Doth any bystander among you know
> The herd he speaks of, or by seeing him
> Afield or in the city? answer straight!
> The hour hath come to clear this business up.

Chorus

> Methinks he means none other than the hind
> Whom thou anon wert fain to see; but that
> Our queen Jocasta best of all could tell.

Oedipus

1080
> Madam, dost know the man we sent to fetch?
> Is the same of whom the stranger speaks?

Jocasta

> Who is the man? What matter? Let it be.
> 'Twere waste of thought to weigh such idle words.

212

Oedipus

> No, with such guiding clues I cannot fail
> To bring to light the secret of my birth.

Jocasta

> Oh, as thou carest for thy life, give o'er
> This quest. Enough the anguish I endure.

Oedipus

> Be of good cheer; though I be proved the son
> Of a bondwoman, aye, through three descents
> Triply a slave, thy honor is unsmirched.

Jocasta

> Yet humor me, I pray thee; do not this.   1090

Oedipus

> I cannot; I must probe this matter home.

Jocasta

> 'Tis for thy sake I advise thee for the best.

Oedipus

> I grow impatient of this best advice.

Jocasta

> Ah mayst thou ne'er discover who thou art!

Oedipus

> Go, fetch me here the herd, and leave yon woman
> To glory in her pride of ancestry.

Jocasta

> O woe is thee, poor wretch! With that last word
> I leave thee, henceforth silent evermore.

[Exit Jocasta.]

Chorus

1100

Why, Oedipus, why stung with passionate grief
Hath the queen thus departed? Much I fear
From this dead calm will burst a storm of woes.

Oedipus

Let the storm burst, my fixed resolve still holds,
To learn my lineage, be it ne'er so low.
It may be she with all a woman's pride
Thinks scorn of my base parentage. But I
Who rank myself as Fortune's favorite child,
The giver of good gifts, shall not be shamed.
She is my mother and the changing moons
My brethren, and with them I wax and wane.

1110

Thus sprung why should I fear to trace my birth?
Nothing can make me other than I am.

Chorus

[strophe]

If my soul prophetic err not,
If my wisdom aught avail,
    Thee, Cithaeron, I shall hail,
As the nurse and foster-mother of our Oedipus shall greet
Ere tomorrow's full moon rises, and exalt thee as is meet.
Dance and song shall hymn thy praises,
Lover of our royal race.
    Phoebus, may my words find grace!

[antistrophe]

1120

Child, who bare thee, nymph or goddess?
Sure thy sire was more than man,
    Haply the hill-roamer Pan.
Or did Loxias beget thee, for he haunts the upland wold;
Or Cyllene's lord, or Bacchus, dweller on the hilltops cold?
Did some Heliconian Oread give him thee, a new-born joy?
Nymphs with whom he love to toy?

Oedipus

> Elders, if I, who never yet before
> Have met the man, may make a guess, methinks
> I see the herdsman who we long have sought;
> His time-worn aspect matches with the years   1130
> Of yonder aged messenger; besides
> I seem to recognize the men who bring him
> As servants of my own. But you, perchance,
> Having in past days known or seen the herd,
> May better by sure knowledge my surmise.

Chorus

> I recognize him; one of Laius' house;
> A simple hind, but true as any man.

[Enter Herdsman.]

Oedipus

> Corinthian stranger, I address thee first,
> Is this the man thou meanest!

Messenger

> This is he.   1140

Oedipus

> And now old man, look up and answer all
> I ask thee. Wast thou once of Laius' house?

Herdsman

> I was, a thrall, not purchased but home-bred.

Oedipus

> What was thy business? how wast thou employed?

Herdsman

> The best part of my life I tended sheep.

Oedipus

What were the pastures thou didst most frequent?

Herdsman

Cithaeron and the neighboring alps.

Oedipus

Then there
Thou must have known yon man, at least by fame?

Herdsman

1150 Yon man? in what way? what man dost thou mean?

Oedipus

The man here, having met him in past times...

Herdsman

Off-hand I cannot call him well to mind.

Messenger

No wonder, master. But I will revive
His blunted memories. Sure he can recall
What time together both we drove our flocks,
He two, I one, on the Cithaeron range,
For three long summers; I his mate from spring
Till rose Arcturus; then in winter time
I led mine home, he his to Laius' folds.
1160 Did these things happen as I say, or no?

Herdsman

'Tis long ago, but all thou say'st is true.

Messenger

Well, thou must then remember giving me
A child to rear as my own foster-son?

Herdsman

Why dost thou ask this question? What of that?

Messenger

Friend, he that stands before thee was that child.

Herdsman

A plague upon thee! Hold thy wanton tongue!

Oedipus

Softly, old man, rebuke him not; thy words
Are more deserving chastisement than his.

Herdsman

O best of masters, what is my offense?

Oedipus

Not answering what he asks about the child. 1170

Herdsman

He speaks at random, babbles like a fool.

Oedipus

If thou lack'st grace to speak, I'll loose thy tongue.

Herdsman

For mercy's sake abuse not an old man.

Oedipus

Arrest the villain, seize and pinion him!

Herdsman

Alack, alack!
What have I done? what wouldst thou further learn?

Oedipus

Didst give this man the child of whom he asks?

Herdsman

I did; and would that I had died that day!

Oedipus

And die thou shalt unless thou tell the truth.

Herdsman

1180

But, if I tell it, I am doubly lost.

Oedipus

The knave methinks will still prevaricate.

Herdsman

Nay, I confessed I gave it long ago.

Oedipus

Whence came it? was it thine, or given to thee?

Herdsman

I had it from another, 'twas not mine.

Oedipus

From whom of these our townsmen, and what house?

Herdsman

Forbear for God's sake, master, ask no more.

Oedipus

If I must question thee again, thou'rt lost.

Herdsman

Well then—it was a child of Laius' house.

Oedipus

Slave-born or one of Laius' own race?

Herdsman

1190

Ah me!
I stand upon the perilous edge of speech.

Oedipus

> And I of hearing, but I still must hear.

Herdsman

> Know then the child was by repute his own,
> But she within, thy consort best could tell.

Oedipus

> What! she, she gave it thee?

Herdsman

> 'Tis so, my king.

Oedipus

> With what intent?

Herdsman

> To make away with it.

Oedipus

> What, she its mother.

Herdsman

> Fearing a dread weird.   1200

Oedipus

> What weird?

Herdsman

> 'Twas told that he should slay his sire.

Oedipus

> What didst thou give it then to this old man?

Herdsman

> Through pity, master, for the babe. I thought
> He'd take it to the country whence he came;

But he preserved it for the worst of woes.
For if thou art in sooth what this man saith,
God pity thee! thou wast to misery born.

Oedipus

1210
Ah me! ah me! all brought to pass, all true!
O light, may I behold thee nevermore!
I stand a wretch, in birth, in wedlock cursed,
A parricide, incestuously, triply cursed!

[Exit Oedipus.]

Chorus

[strophe 1]

Races of mortal man
Whose life is but a span,
I count ye but the shadow of a shade!
For he who most doth know
Of bliss, hath but the show;
A moment, and the visions pale and fade.
Thy fall, O Oedipus, thy piteous fall
1220
Warns me none born of women blest to call.

[antistrophe 1]

For he of marksmen best,
O Zeus, outshot the rest,
And won the prize supreme of wealth and power.
By him the vulture maid
Was quelled, her witchery laid;
1200
He rose our savior and the land's strong tower.
We hailed thee king and from that day adored
Of mighty Thebes the universal lord.

[strophe 2]

1230
O heavy hand of fate!
Who now more desolate,
Whose tale more sad than thine, whose lot more dire?
O Oedipus, discrowned head,

Thy cradle was thy marriage bed;
One harborage sufficed for son and sire.
How could the soil thy father ploughed so long
Endure to bear in silence such a wrong?

[antistrophe 2]

All-seeing Time hath caught
Guilt, and to justice brought
The son and sire commingled in one bed.
O child of Laius' ill-starred race   1240
Would I had ne'er beheld thy face;
I raise for thee a dirge as o'er the dead.
Yet, sooth to say, through thee I drew new breath,
And now through thee I feel a second death.

[Enter Second Messenger.]

Second Messenger

Most grave and reverend senators of Thebes,
What Deeds ye soon must hear, what sights behold
How will ye mourn, if, true-born patriots,
Ye reverence still the race of Labdacus!
Not Ister nor all Phasis' flood, I ween,
Could wash away the blood-stains from this house,   1250
The ills it shrouds or soon will bring to light,
Ills wrought of malice, not unwittingly.
The worst to bear are self-inflicted wounds.

Chorus

Grievous enough for all our tears and groans
Our past calamities; what canst thou add?

Second Messenger

My tale is quickly told and quickly heard.
Our sovereign lady queen Jocasta's dead.

Chorus

Alas, poor queen! how came she by her death?

Second Messenger

By her own hand. And all the horror of it,
1260 Not having seen, yet cannot comprehend.
Nevertheless, as far as my poor memory serves,
I will relate the unhappy lady's woe.
When in her frenzy she had passed inside
The vestibule, she hurried straight to win
The bridal-chamber, clutching at her hair
With both her hands, and, once within the room,
She shut the doors behind her with a crash.
"Laius," she cried, and called her husband dead
Long, long ago; her thought was of that child
1270 By him begot, the son by whom the sire
Was murdered and the mother left to breed
With her own seed, a monstrous progeny.
Then she bewailed the marriage bed whereon
Poor wretch, she had conceived a double brood,
Husband by husband, children by her child.
What happened after that I cannot tell,
Nor how the end befell, for with a shriek
Burst on us Oedipus; all eyes were fixed
On Oedipus, as up and down he strode,
1280 Nor could we mark her agony to the end.
For stalking to and fro "A sword!" he cried,
"Where is the wife, no wife, the teeming womb
That bore a double harvest, me and mine?"
And in his frenzy some supernal power
(No mortal, surely, none of us who watched him)
Guided his footsteps; with a terrible shriek,
As though one beckoned him, he crashed against
The folding doors, and from their staples forced
The wrenched bolts and hurled himself within.
1290 Then we beheld the woman hanging there,
A running noose entwined about her neck.
But when he saw her, with a maddened roar
He loosed the cord; and when her wretched corpse
Lay stretched on earth, what followed—O 'twas dread!
He tore the golden brooches that upheld
Her queenly robes, upraised them high and smote
Full on his eye-balls, uttering words like these:
"No more shall ye behold such sights of woe,

222

Deeds I have suffered and myself have wrought;
Henceforward quenched in darkness shall ye see   1300
Those ye should ne'er have seen; now blind to those
Whom, when I saw, I vainly yearned to know."
Such was the burden of his moan, whereto,
Not once but oft, he struck with his hand uplift
His eyes, and at each stroke the ensanguined orbs
Bedewed his beard, not oozing drop by drop,
But one black gory downpour, thick as hail.
Such evils, issuing from the double source,
Have whelmed them both, confounding man and wife.
Till now the storied fortune of this house   1310
Was fortunate indeed; but from this day
Woe, lamentation, ruin, death, disgrace,
All ills that can be named, all, all are theirs.

Chorus

But hath he still no respite from his pain?

Second Messenger

He cries, "Unbar the doors and let all Thebes
Behold the slayer of his sire, his mother's—"
That shameful word my lips may not repeat.
He vows to fly self-banished from the land,
Nor stay to bring upon his house the curse
Himself had uttered; but he has no strength   1320
Nor one to guide him, and his torture's more
Than man can suffer, as yourselves will see.
For lo, the palace portals are unbarred,
And soon ye shall behold a sight so sad
That he who must abhor would pity it.

[Enter Oedipus blinded.]

Chorus

Woeful sight! more woeful none
These sad eyes have looked upon.
Whence this madness? None can tell
Who did cast on thee his spell,   *1300*

1330

Prowling all thy life around,
Leaping with a demon bound.
Hapless wretch! how can I brook
On thy misery to look?
Though to gaze on thee I yearn,
Much to question, much to learn,
Horror-struck away I turn.

Oedipus

Ah me! ah woe is me!
Ah whither am I borne!
How like a ghost forlorn

1340

My voice flits from me on the air!
On, on the demon goads. The end, ah where?

Chorus

An end too dread to tell, too dark to see.

Oedipus

[strophe 1]

Dark, dark! The horror of darkness, like a shroud,
Wraps me and bears me on through mist and cloud.
Ah me, ah me! What spasms athwart me shoot,
What pangs of agonizing memory?

Chorus

No marvel if in such a plight thou feel'st
The double weight of past and present woes.

Oedipus

[antistrophe 1]

Ah friend, still loyal, constant still and kind,

1350

Thou carest for the blind.
I know thee near, and though bereft of eyes,
Thy voice I recognize.

Chorus

> O doer of dread deeds, how couldst thou mar
> Thy vision thus? What demon goaded thee?

Oedipus

[strophe 2]

> Apollo, friend, Apollo, he it was
> That brought these ills to pass;
> But the right hand that dealt the blow
> Was mine, none other. How,
> How, could I longer see when sight
> Brought no delight?   1360

Chorus

> Alas! 'tis as thou sayest.

Oedipus

> Say, friends, can any look or voice
> Or touch of love henceforth my heart rejoice?
> Haste, friends, no fond delay,
> Take the twice cursed away
> Far from all ken,
> The man abhorred of gods, accursed of men.

Chorus

> O thy despair well suits thy desperate case.
> Would I had never looked upon thy face!

Oedipus

[antistrophe 2]

>   1370
> My curse on him whoe'er unrived
> The waif's fell fetters and my life revived!
> He meant me well, yet had he left me there,
> He had saved my friends and me a world of care.

Chorus

I too had wished it so.

Oedipus

Then had I never come to shed
My father's blood nor climbed my mother's bed;
The monstrous offspring of a womb defiled,
Co-mate of him who gendered me, and child.
Was ever man before afflicted thus,
Like Oedipus.

1380

Chorus

I cannot say that thou hast counseled well,
For thou wert better dead than living blind.

Oedipus

What's done was well done. Thou canst never shake
My firm belief. A truce to argument.
For, had I sight, I know not with what eyes
I could have met my father in the shades,
Or my poor mother, since against the twain
I sinned, a sin no gallows could atone.
Aye, but, ye say, the sight of children joys
A parent's eyes. What, born as mine were born?
No, such a sight could never bring me joy;
Nor this fair city with its battlements,
Its temples and the statues of its gods,
Sights from which I, now wretchedst of all,
Once ranked the foremost Theban in all Thebes,
By my own sentence am cut off, condemned
By my own proclamation 'gainst the wretch,
The miscreant by heaven itself declared
Unclean—and of the race of Laius.
Thus branded as a felon by myself,
How had I dared to look you in the face?
Nay, had I known a way to choke the springs
Of hearing, I had never shrunk to make
A dungeon of this miserable frame,
Cut off from sight and hearing; for 'tis bliss

1390

1400

To bide in regions sorrow cannot reach.
Why didst thou harbor me, Cithaeron, why
Didst thou not take and slay me? Then I never
Had shown to men the secret of my birth.
O Polybus, O Corinth, O my home,   1410
Home of my ancestors (so wast thou called)   .
How fair a nursling then I seemed, how foul
The canker that lay festering in the bud!
Now is the blight revealed of root and fruit.
Ye triple high-roads, and thou hidden glen,
Coppice, and pass where meet the three-branched ways,
Ye drank my blood, the life-blood these hands spilt,   1400
My father's; do ye call to mind perchance
Those deeds of mine ye witnessed and the work
I wrought thereafter when I came to Thebes?   1420
O fatal wedlock, thou didst give me birth,
And, having borne me, sowed again my seed,
Mingling the blood of fathers, brothers, children,
Brides, wives, and mothers, an incestuous brood,
All horrors that are wrought beneath the sun,
Horrors so foul to name them were unmeet.
O, I adjure you, hide me anywhere
Far from this land, or slay me straight, or cast me
Down to the depths of ocean out of sight.
Come hither, deign to touch an abject wretch;   1430
Draw near and fear not; I myself must bear
The load of guilt that none but I can share.

[Enter Creon.]

Chorus

Lo, here is Creon, the one man to grant
Thy prayer by action or advice, for he
Is left the State's sole guardian in thy stead.

Oedipus

Ah me! what words to accost him can I find?
What cause has he to trust me? In the past
I have been proved his rancorous enemy.

Creon

1440
> Not in derision, Oedipus, I come
> Nor to upbraid thee with thy past misdeeds.

[To Bystanders.]

> But shame upon you! if ye feel no sense
> Of human decencies, at least revere
> The Sun whose light beholds and nurtures all.
> Leave not thus nakedly for all to gaze at
> A horror neither earth nor rain from heaven
> Nor light will suffer. Lead him straight within,
> For it is seemly that a kinsman's woes
> Be heard by kin and seen by kin alone.

Oedipus

1450
> O listen, since thy presence comes to me
> A shock of glad surprise—so noble thou,
> And I so vile—O grant me one small boon.
> I ask it not on my behalf, but thine.

Creon

> And what the favor thou wouldst crave of me?

Oedipus

> Forth from thy borders thrust me with all speed;
> Set me within some vasty desert where
> No mortal voice shall greet me any more.

Creon

> This had I done already, but I deemed
> It first behooved me to consult the god.

Oedipus

1460
> His will was set forth fully--to destroy
> The parricide, the scoundrel; and I am he.

Creon

> Yea, so he spake, but in our present plight

'Twere better to consult the god anew.

Oedipus

Dare ye inquire concerning such a wretch?

Creon

Yea, for thyself wouldst credit now his word.

Oedipus

Aye, and on thee in all humility
I lay this charge: let her who lies within
Receive such burial as thou shalt ordain;
Such rites 'tis thine, as brother, to perform.
But for myself, O never let my Thebes,
The city of my sires, be doomed to bear   1470
The burden of my presence while I live.
No, let me be a dweller on the hills,
On yonder mount Cithaeron, famed as mine,
My tomb predestined for me by my sire
And mother, while they lived, that I may die
Slain as they sought to slay me, when alive.
This much I know full surely, nor disease
Shall end my days, nor any common chance;
For I had ne'er been snatched from death, unless
I was predestined to some awful doom.   1480
So be it. I reck not how Fate deals with me
But my unhappy children—for my sons
Be not concerned, O Creon, they are men,
And for themselves, where'er they be, can fend.
But for my daughters twain, poor innocent maids,
Who ever sat beside me at the board
Sharing my viands, drinking of my cup,
For them, I pray thee, care, and, if thou willst,
O might I feel their touch and make my moan.
Hear me, O prince, my noble-hearted prince!   1490
Could I but blindly touch them with my hands
I'd think they still were mine, as when I saw.

[Antigone and Ismene are led in.]

What say I? can it be my pretty ones
Whose sobs I hear? Has Creon pitied me
And sent me my two darlings? Can this be?

Creon

'Tis true; 'twas I procured thee this delight,
Knowing the joy they were to thee of old.

Oedipus

God speed thee! and as meed for bringing them
May Providence deal with thee kindlier
1500   Than it has dealt with me! O children mine,
Where are ye? Let me clasp you with these hands,
A brother's hands, a father's; hands that made
Lack-luster sockets of his once bright eyes;
Hands of a man who blindly, recklessly,
Became your sire by her from whom he sprang.
Though I cannot behold you, I must weep
In thinking of the evil days to come,
The slights and wrongs that men will put upon you.
Where'er ye go to feast or festival,
1510   No merrymaking will it prove for you,
But oft abashed in tears ye will return.
And when ye come to marriageable years,
Where's the bold wooers who will jeopardize
To take unto himself such disrepute
As to my children's children still must cling,
For what of infamy is lacking here?
"Their father slew his father, sowed the seed
Where he himself was gendered, and begat
These maidens at the source wherefrom he sprang."
1500   1520   Such are the gibes that men will cast at you.
Who then will wed you? None, I ween, but ye
Must pine, poor maids, in single barrenness.
O Prince, Menoeceus' son, to thee, I turn,
With thee it rests to father them, for we
Their natural parents, both of us, are lost.
O leave them not to wander poor, unwed,
Thy kin, nor let them share my low estate.

O pity them so young, and but for thee
All destitute. Thy hand upon it, Prince.
To you, my children I had much to say,   1530
Were ye but ripe to hear. Let this suffice:
Pray ye may find some home and live content,
And may your lot prove happier than your sire's.

Creon

Thou hast had enough of weeping; pass within.

Oedipus

I must obey,
Though 'tis grievous.

Creon

Weep not, everything must have its day.

Oedipus

Well I go, but on conditions.

Creon

What thy terms for going, say.

Oedipus

Send me from the land an exile.   1540

Creon

Ask this of the gods, not me.

Oedipus

But I am the gods' abhorrence.

Creon

Then they soon will grant thy plea.

Oedipus

Lead me hence, then, I am willing.

Creon

> Come, but let thy children go.

Oedipus

> Rob me not of these my children!

Creon

> Crave not mastery in all,
> For the mastery that raised thee was thy bane
> And wrought thy fall.

Chorus

1550
> Look ye, countrymen and Thebans,
> This is Oedipus the great,
> He who knew the Sphinx's riddle
> And was mightiest in our state.
> Who of all our townsmen
> Gazed not on his fame with envious eyes?
> Now, in what a sea of troubles
> Sunk and overwhelmed he lies!
> Therefore wait to see life's ending
> Ere thou count one mortal blest;

1560
> Wait till free from pain and sorrow
> He has gained his final rest.

The End

Oedipus at Colonus

TRANSLATED BY F. STORR

Dramatis Personae

OEDIPUS
banished King of Thebes

ANTIGONE
his daughter

ISMENE
his daughter

THESEUS
King of Athens

CREON
brother of Jocasta, now reigning at Thebes

POLYNEICES
elder son of Oedipus

STRANGER
a native of Colonus

MESSENGER
an attendant of Theseus

CHORUS
of the Elders of Colonus

[In front of the grove of the Eumenides. Enter the blind
Oedipus led by his daughter, Antigone.]

Oedipus

    Child of an old blind sire, Antigone,
    What region, say, whose city have we reached?
    Who will provide today with scanted dole
    This wanderer? 'Tis little that he craves,
    And less obtains—that less enough for me;
    For I am taught by suffering to endure,
    And the long years that have grown old with me,
    And last not least, by true nobility.
    My daughter, if thou seest a resting place
    On common ground or by some sacred grove,   10
    Stay me and set me down. Let us discover
    Where we have come, for strangers must inquire
    Of denizens, and do as they are bid.

Antigone

    Long-suffering father, Oedipus, the towers
    That fence the city still are faint and far;
    But where we stand is surely holy ground;
    A wilderness of laurel, olive, vine;
    Within a choir of songster nightingales
    Are warbling. On this native seat of rock
    Rest; for an old man thou hast traveled far.   20

Oedipus

    Guide these dark steps and seat me there secure.

Antigone

    If time can teach, I need not to be told.

Oedipus

    Say, prithee, if thou knowest, where we are.

Antigone

> Athens I recognize, but not the spot.

Oedipus

> That much we heard from every wayfarer.

Antigone

> Shall I go on and ask about the place?

Oedipus

> Yes, daughter, if it be inhabited.

Antigone

> Sure there are habitations; but no need
> To leave thee; yonder is a man hard by.

Oedipus

30

> What, moving hitherward and on his way?

Antigone

> Say rather, here already. Ask him straight
> The needful questions, for the man is here.

[Enter Stranger]

Oedipus

> O stranger, as I learn from her whose eyes
> Must serve both her and me, that thou art here
> Sent by some happy chance to serve our doubts—

Stranger

> First quit that seat, then question me at large:
> The spot thou treadest on is holy ground.

Oedipus

> What is the site, to what god dedicated?

Stranger

> Inviolable, untrod; goddesses,
> Dread brood of Earth and Darkness, here abide.   40

Oedipus

> Tell me the awful name I should invoke?

Stranger

> The Gracious Ones, All-seeing, so our folk
> Call them, but elsewhere other names are rife.

Oedipus

> Then may they show their suppliant grace, for I
> From this your sanctuary will ne'er depart.

Stranger

> What word is this?

Oedipus

> The watchword of my fate.

Stranger

> Nay, 'tis not mine to bid thee hence without
> Due warrant and instruction from the State.

Oedipus

> Now in God's name, O stranger, scorn me not   50
> As a wayfarer; tell me what I crave.

Stranger

> Ask; your request shall not be scorned by me.

Oedipus

> How call you then the place wherein we bide?

Stranger

> Whate'er I know thou too shalt know; the place

Is all to great Poseidon consecrate.
Hard by, the Titan, he who bears the torch,
Prometheus, has his worship; but the spot
Thou treadest, the Brass-footed Threshold named,
Is Athens' bastion, and the neighboring lands
60   Claim as their chief and patron yonder knight
Colonus, and in common bear his name.
Such, stranger, is the spot, to fame unknown,
But dear to us its native worshipers.

Oedipus

Thou sayest there are dwellers in these parts?

Stranger

Surely; they bear the name of yonder god.

Oedipus

Ruled by a king or by the general voice?

Stranger

The lord of Athens is our over-lord.

Oedipus

Who is this monarch, great in word and might?

Stranger

Theseus, the son of Aegeus our late king.

Oedipus

70   Might one be sent from you to summon him?

Stranger

Wherefore? To tell him aught or urge his coming?

Oedipus

Say a slight service may avail him much.

Stranger

How can he profit from a sightless man?

Oedipus

> The blind man's words will be instinct with sight.

Stranger

> Heed then; I fain would see thee out of harm;
> For by the looks, marred though they be by fate,
> I judge thee noble; tarry where thou art,
> While I go seek the burghers—those at hand,
> Not in the city. They will soon decide
> Whether thou art to rest or go thy way.   80

[Exit Stranger]

Oedipus

> Tell me, my daughter, has the stranger gone?

Antigone

> Yes, he has gone; now we are all alone,
> And thou may'st speak, dear father, without fear.

Oedipus

> Stern-visaged queens, since coming to this land
> First in your sanctuary I bent the knee,
> Frown not on me or Phoebus, who, when erst
> He told me all my miseries to come,
> Spake of this respite after many years,
> Some haven in a far-off land, a rest
> Vouchsafed at last by dread divinities.   90
> "There," said he, "shalt thou round thy weary life,
> A blessing to the land wherein thou dwell'st,
> But to the land that cast thee forth, a curse."
> And of my weird he promised signs should come,
> Earthquake, or thunderclap, or lightning flash.
> And now I recognize as yours the sign
> That led my wanderings to this your grove;
> Else had I never lighted on you first,
> A wineless man on your seat of native rock.   *100*
> O goddesses, fulfill Apollo's word,   100

Grant me some consummation of my life,
If haply I appear not all too vile,
A thrall to sorrow worse than any slave.
Hear, gentle daughters of primeval Night,
Hear, namesake of great Pallas; Athens, first
Of cities, pity this dishonored shade,
The ghost of him who once was Oedipus.

Antigone

Hush! for I see some grey-beards on their way,
Their errand to spy out our resting-place.

Oedipus

110

I will be mute, and thou shalt guide my steps
Into the covert from the public road,
Till I have learned their drift. A prudent man
Will ever shape his course by what he learns.

[Enter Chorus]

Chorus

[strophe 1]

Ha! Where is he? Look around!
Every nook and corner scan!
He the all-presumptuous man,
Whither vanished? search the ground!
A wayfarer, I ween,
A wayfarer, no countryman of ours,
120   That old man must have been;
Never had native dared to tempt the Powers,
Or enter their domain,
The Maids in awe of whom each mortal cowers,
Whose name no voice betrays nor cry,
And as we pass them with averted eye,
We move hushed lips in reverent piety.
But now some godless man,
'Tis rumored, here abides;
The precincts through I scan,

Yet wot not where he hides,   130
The wretch profane!
I search and search in vain.

Oedipus

I am that man; I know you near
Ears to the blind, they say, are eyes.

Chorus

O dread to see and dread to hear!

Oedipus

Oh sirs, I am no outlaw under ban.

Chorus

Who can he be—Zeus save us!—this old man?

Oedipus

No favorite of fate,
That ye should envy his estate,
O, Sirs, would any happy mortal, say,   140
Grope by the light of other eyes his way,
Or face the storm upon so frail a stay?

Chorus

[antistrophe 1]

Wast thou then sightless from thy birth?
Evil, methinks, and long
Thy pilgrimage on earth.
Yet add not curse to curse and wrong to wrong.
I warn thee, trespass not
Within this hallowed spot,
Lest thou shouldst find the silent grassy glade
Where offerings are laid,   150
Bowls of spring water mingled with sweet mead.
Thou must not stay,
Come, come away,

Tired wanderer, dost thou heed?
(We are far off, but sure our voice can reach.)
If aught thou wouldst beseech,
Speak where 'tis right; till then refrain from speech.

Oedipus

Daughter, what counsel should we now pursue?

Antigone

We must obey and do as here they do.

Oedipus

160   Thy hand then!

Antigone

Here, O father, is my hand,

Oedipus

O Sirs, if I come forth at your command,
Let me not suffer for my confidence.

Chorus

[strophe 2]

Against thy will no man shall drive thee hence.

Oedipus

Shall I go further?

Chorus

Aye.

Oedipus

What further still?

Chorus

Lead maiden, thou canst guide him where we will.

Antigone

>Follow with blind steps, father, as I lead.

Chorus

>In a strange land strange thou art;   170
>To her will incline thy heart;
>Honor whatso'er the State
>Honors, all she frowns on hate.

Oedipus

>Guide me child, where we may range
>Safe within the paths of right;
>Counsel freely may exchange
>Nor with fate and fortune fight.

Chorus

[antistrophe 2]

>Halt! Go no further than that rocky floor.

Oedipus

>Stay where I now am?

Chorus

>Yes, advance no more.   180

Oedipus

>May I sit down?

Chorus

>Move sideways towards the ledge,
>And sit thee crouching on the scarped edge.

Antigone

>This is my office, father, O incline—   200

Oedipus

>Ah me! ah me!

Antigone

Thy steps to my steps, lean thine aged frame on mine.

Oedipus

Woe on my fate unblest!

Chorus

Wanderer, now thou art at rest,
Tell me of thy birth and home,
From what far country art thou come,
Led on thy weary way, declare!

Oedipus

Strangers, I have no country. O forbear—

Chorus

What is it, old man, that thou wouldst conceal?

Oedipus

Forbear, nor urge me further to reveal—

Chorus

Why this reluctance?

Oedipus

Dread my lineage.

Chorus

Say!

Oedipus

What must I answer, child, ah welladay!

Chorus

Say of what stock thou comest, what man's son—

Oedipus

Ah me, my daughter, now we are undone!

Antigone

> Speak, for thou standest on the slippery verge.

Oedipus

> I will; no plea for silence can I urge.

Chorus

> Will neither speak? Come, Sir, why dally thus!

Oedipus

> Know'st one of Laius—

Chorus

> Ha? Who!

Oedipus

> Seed of Labdacus—

Chorus

> Oh Zeus!

Oedipus

> The hapless Oedipus.

Chorus

> Art he?

Oedipus

> Whate'er I utter, have no fear of me.   210

Chorus

> Begone!

Oedipus

> O wretched me!

Chorus

> Begone!

Oedipus

O daughter, what will hap anon?

Chorus

Forth from our borders speed ye both!

Oedipus

How keep you then your troth?

Chorus

Heaven's justice never smites
Him who ill with ill requites.
But if guile with guile contend,
220   Bane, not blessing, is the end.
Arise, begone and take thee hence straightway,
Lest on our land a heavier curse thou lay.

Antigone

O sirs! ye suffered not my father blind,
Albeit gracious and to ruth inclined,
Knowing the deeds he wrought, not innocent,
But with no ill intent;
Yet heed a maiden's moan
Who pleads for him alone;
My eyes, not reft of sight,
230   Plead with you as a daughter's might
You are our providence,
O make us not go hence!
O with a gracious nod
Grant us the nigh despaired-of boon we crave!
Hear us, O hear,
But all that ye hold dear,
Wife, children, homestead, hearth and God!
Where will you find one, search ye ne'er so well.
Who 'scapes perdition if a god impel!

Chorus

240   Surely we pity thee and him alike
Daughter of Oedipus, for your distress;

But as we reverence the decrees of Heaven
We cannot say aught other than we said.

Oedipus

O what avails renown or fair repute?
Are they not vanity? For, look you, now
Athens is held of States the most devout,
Athens alone gives hospitality
And shelters the vexed stranger, so men say.
Have I found so? I whom ye dislodged
First from my seat of rock and now would drive   250
Forth from your land, dreading my name alone;
For me you surely dread not, nor my deeds,
Deeds of a man more sinned against than sinning,
As I might well convince you, were it meet
To tell my mother's story and my sire's,
The cause of this your fear. Yet am I then
A villain born because in self-defense,
Stricken, I struck the striker back again?
E'en had I known, no villainy 'twould prove:
But all unwitting whither I went, I went—   260
To ruin; my destroyers knew it well,
Wherefore, I pray you, sirs, in Heaven's name,
Even as ye bade me quit my seat, defend me.
O pay not a lip service to the gods
And wrong them of their dues. Bethink ye well,
The eye of Heaven beholds the just of men,
And the unjust, nor ever in this world
Has one sole godless sinner found escape.
Stand then on Heaven's side and never blot
Athens' fair scutcheon by abetting wrong.   270
I came to you a suppliant, and you pledged
Your honor; O preserve me to the end,
O let not this marred visage do me wrong!
A holy and god-fearing man is here
Whose coming purports comfort for your folk.
And when your chief arrives, whoe'er he be,
Then shall ye have my story and know all.
Meanwhile I pray you do me no despite.

Chorus

280

The plea thou urgest, needs must give us pause,
Set forth in weighty argument, but we
Must leave the issue with the ruling powers.

Oedipus

Where is he, strangers, he who sways the realm?

Chorus

In his ancestral seat; a messenger,
The same who sent us here, is gone for him.

Oedipus

300

And think you he will have such care or thought
For the blind stranger as to come himself?

Chorus

Aye, that he will, when once he learns thy name.

Oedipus

But who will bear him word!

Chorus

290

The way is long,
And many travelers pass to speed the news.
Be sure he'll hear and hasten, never fear;
So wide and far thy name is noised abroad,
That, were he ne'er so spent and loth to move,
He would bestir him when he hears of thee.

Oedipus

Well, may he come with blessing to his State
And me! Who serves his neighbor serves himself.

Antigone

Zeus! What is this? What can I say or think?

Oedipus

What now, Antigone?

Antigone

> I see a woman
> Riding upon a colt of Aetna's breed;   300
> She wears for headgear a Thessalian hat
> To shade her from the sun. Who can it be?
> She or a stranger? Do I wake or dream?
> 'Tis she; 'tis not—I cannot tell, alack;
> It is no other! Now her bright'ning glance
> Greets me with recognition, yes, 'tis she,
> Herself, Ismene!

Oedipus

> Ha! what say ye, child?

Antigone

> That I behold thy daughter and my sister,
> And thou wilt know her straightway by her voice.   310

[Enter Ismene]

Ismene

> Father and sister, names to me most sweet,
> How hardly have I found you, hardly now
> When found at last can see you through my tears!

Oedipus

> Art come, my child?

Ismene

> O father, sad thy plight!

Oedipus

> Child, thou art here?

Ismene

> Yes, 'twas a weary way.

Oedipus

> Touch me, my child.

Ismene

    I give a hand to both.

Oedipus

320   O children—sisters!

Ismene

    O disastrous plight!

Oedipus

    Her plight and mine?

Ismene

    Aye, and my own no less.

Oedipus

    What brought thee, daughter?

Ismene

    Father, care for thee.

Oedipus

    A daughter's yearning?

Ismene

    Yes, and I had news
    I would myself deliver, so I came
    With the one thrall who yet is true to me.

Oedipus

330   Thy valiant brothers, where are they at need?

Ismene

    They are—enough, 'tis now their darkest hour.

Oedipus

    Out on the twain! The thoughts and actions all
    Are framed and modeled on Egyptian ways.

For there the men sit at the loom indoors
While the wives slave abroad for daily bread.
So you, my children—those whom I behooved
To bear the burden, stay at home like girls,
While in their stead my daughters moil and drudge,
Lightening their father's misery. The one
Since first she grew from girlish feebleness   340
To womanhood has been the old man's guide
And shared my weary wandering, roaming oft
Hungry and footsore through wild forest ways,
In drenching rains and under scorching suns,
Careless herself of home and ease, if so
Her sire might have her tender ministry.
And thou, my child, formerly thou wentest forth,
Eluding the Cadmeians' vigilance,
To bring thy father all the oracles
Concerning Oedipus, and didst make thyself   350
My faithful lieger, when they banished me.
And now what mission summons thee from home,
What news, Ismene, hast thou for thy father?
This much I know, thou com'st not empty-handed,
Without a warning of some new alarm.

Ismene

The toil and trouble, father, that I bore
To find thy lodging-place and how thou faredst,
I spare thee; surely 'twere a double pain
To suffer, first in act and then in telling;
'Tis the misfortune of thine ill-starred sons   360
I come to tell thee. At the first they willed
To leave the throne to Creon, minded well
Thus to remove the inveterate curse of old,
A canker that infected all thy race.
But now some god and an infatuate soul
Have stirred betwixt them a mad rivalry
To grasp at sovereignty and kingly power.
Today the hot-branded youth, the younger born,
Is keeping Polyneices from the throne,
His elder, and has thrust him from the land.   370
The banished brother (so all Thebes reports)
Fled to the vale of Argos, and by help

Of new alliance there and friends in arms,
Swears he will stablish Argos straight as lord
Of the Cadmeian land, or, if he fail,
Exalt the victor to the stars of heaven.
This is no empty tale, but deadly truth,
My father; and how long thy agony,
Ere the gods pity thee, I cannot tell.

Oedipus

380
Hast thou indeed then entertained a hope
The gods at last will turn and rescue me?

Ismene

Yea, so I read these latest oracles.

Oedipus

What oracles? What hath been uttered, child?

Ismene

Thy country (so it runs) shall yearn in time
To have thee for their weal alive or dead.

Oedipus

And who could gain by such a one as I?

Ismene

On thee, 'tis said, their sovereignty depends.

Oedipus

So, when I cease to be, my worth begins.

Ismene

The gods, who once abased, uplift thee now.

Oedipus

390
Poor help to raise an old man fallen in youth.

Ismene

Howe'er that be, 'tis for this cause alone

254

That Creon comes to thee—and comes anon.

Oedipus

With what intent, my daughter? Tell me plainly.

Ismene

To plant thee near the Theban land, and so
Keep thee within their grasp, yet now allow   *400*
Thy foot to pass beyond their boundaries.

Oedipus

What gain they, if I lay outside?

Oedipus

Thy tomb, if disappointed, brings on them a curse.

Oedipus

It needs no god to tell what's plain to sense.

Ismene

Therefore they fain would have thee close at hand,   400
Not where thou wouldst be master of thyself.

Oedipus

Mean they to shroud my bones in Theban dust?

Ismene

Nay, father, guilt of kinsman's blood forbids.

Oedipus

Then never shall they be my masters, never!

Ismene

Thebes, thou shalt rue this bitterly some day!

Oedipus

When what conjunction comes to pass, my child?

255

Ismene

Thy angry wraith, when at thy tomb they stand.

Oedipus

And who hath told thee what thou tell'st me, child?

Ismene

Envoys who visited the Delphic hearth.

Oedipus

410 Hath Phoebus spoken thus concerning me?

Ismene

So say the envoys who returned to Thebes.

Oedipus

And can a son of mine have heard of this?

Ismene

Yea, both alike, and know its import well.

Oedipus

They knew it, yet the ignoble greed of rule
Outweighed all longing for their sire's return.

Ismene

Grievous thy words, yet I must own them true.

Oedipus

Then may the gods ne'er quench their fatal feud,
And mine be the arbitrament of the fight,
For which they now are arming, spear to spear;
420 That neither he who holds the scepter now
May keep this throne, nor he who fled the realm
Return again. They never raised a hand,
When I their sire was thrust from hearth and home,
When I was banned and banished, what recked they?
Say you 'twas done at my desire, a grace

Which the state, yielding to my wish, allowed?
Not so; for, mark you, on that very day
When in the tempest of my soul I craved
Death, even death by stoning, none appeared
To further that wild longing, but anon,   430
When time had numbed my anguish and I felt
My wrath had all outrun those errors past,
Then, then it was the city went about
By force to oust me, respited for years;
And then my sons, who should as sons have helped,
Did nothing: and, one little word from them
Was all I needed, and they spoke no word,
But let me wander on for evermore,
A banished man, a beggar. These two maids
Their sisters, girls, gave all their sex could give,   440
Food and safe harborage and filial care;
While their two brethren sacrificed their sire
For lust of power and sceptred sovereignty.
No! me they ne'er shall win for an ally,
Nor will this Theban kingship bring them gain;
That know I from this maiden's oracles,
And those old prophecies concerning me,
Which Phoebus now at length has brought to pass.
Come Creon then, come all the mightiest
In Thebes to seek me; for if ye my friends,   450
Championed by those dread Powers indigenous,
Espouse my cause; then for the State ye gain
A great deliverer, for my foemen bane.

Chorus

Our pity, Oedipus, thou needs must move,
Thou and these maidens; and the stronger plea
Thou urgest, as the savior of our land,
Disposes me to counsel for thy weal.

Oedipus

Aid me, kind sirs; I will do all you bid.

Chorus

First make atonement to the deities,
Whose grove by trespass thou didst first profane.   460

Oedipus

> After what manner, stranger? Teach me, pray.

Chorus

> Make a libation first of water fetched
> With undefiled hands from living spring.

Oedipus

> And after I have gotten this pure draught?

Chorus

> Bowls thou wilt find, the carver's handiwork;
> Crown thou the rims and both the handles crown—

Oedipus

> With olive shoots or blocks of wool, or how?

Chorus

> With wool from fleece of yearling freshly shorn.

Oedipus

> What next? how must I end the ritual?

Chorus

470

> Pour thy libation, turning to the dawn.

Oedipus

> Pouring it from the urns whereof ye spake?

Chorus

> Yea, in three streams; and be the last bowl drained
> To the last drop.

Oedipus

> And wherewith shall I fill it,
> Ere in its place I set it? This too tell.

Chorus

> With water and with honey; add no wine.

Oedipus

> And when the embowered earth hath drunk thereof?

Chorus

> Then lay upon it thrice nine olive sprays
> With both thy hands, and offer up this prayer.

Oedipus

> I fain would hear it; that imports the most.   480

Chorus

> That, as we call them Gracious, they would deign
> To grant the suppliant their saving grace.
> So pray thyself or whoso pray for thee,
> In whispered accents, not with lifted voice;
> Then go and look back. Do as I bid,
> And I shall then be bold to stand thy friend;
> Else, stranger, I should have my fears for thee.

Oedipus

> Hear ye, my daughters, what these strangers say?

Antigone

> We listened, and attend thy bidding, father.

Oedipus

> I cannot go, disabled as I am   490
> Doubly, by lack of strength and lack of sight;
> But one of you may do it in my stead;
> For one, I trow, may pay the sacrifice
> Of thousands, if his heart be leal and true.   500
> So to your work with speed, but leave me not
> Untended; for this frame is all too weak
> To move without the help of guiding hand.

Ismene

> Then I will go perform these rites, but where
> To find the spot, this have I yet to learn.

Chorus

500

> Beyond this grove; if thou hast need of aught,
> The guardian of the close will lend his aid.

Ismene

> I go, and thou, Antigone, meanwhile
> Must guard our father. In a parent's cause
> Toil, if there be toil, is of no account.

[Exit Ismene]

Chorus

[strophe 1]

> Ill it is, stranger, to awake
> Pain that long since has ceased to ache,
> And yet I fain would hear—

Oedipus

> What thing?

Chorus

510

> Thy tale of cruel suffering
> For which no cure was found,
> The fate that held thee bound.

Oedipus

> O bid me not (as guest I claim
> This grace) expose my shame.

Chorus

> The tale is spread far and near,
> And echoes still from ear to ear.
> The truth, I fain would hear.

Oedipus

> Ah me!

Chorus

> I prithee yield.

Oedipus

> Ah me!

Chorus

> Grant my request, I granted all to thee. 520

Oedipus

[antistrophe 1]

> Know then I suffered ills most vile, but none
> (So help me Heaven!) from acts in malice done.

Chorus

> Say how.

Oedipus

> The State around
> An all unwitting bridegroom bound
> An impious marriage chain;
> That was my bane.

Chorus

> Didst thou in sooth then share
> A bed incestuous with her that bare—

Oedipus

> It stabs me like a sword, 530
> That two-edged word,
> O stranger, but these maids—my own—

Chorus

> Say on.

Oedipus

> Two daughters, curses twain.

Chorus

Oh God!

Oedipus

Sprang from the wife and mother's travail-pain.

Chorus

[strophe 2]

What, then thy offspring are at once—

Oedipus

Too true. Their father's very sister's too.

Chorus

Oh horror!

Oedipus

540
Horrors from the boundless deep
Back on my soul in refluent surges sweep.

Chorus

Thou hast endured—

Oedipus

Intolerable woe.

Chorus

And sinned—

Oedipus

I sinned not.

Chorus

How so?

Oedipus

I served the State; would I had never won

That graceless grace by which I was undone.

Chorus

[antistrophe 2]

And next, unhappy man, thou hast shed blood?

Oedipus

Must ye hear more? 550

Chorus

A father's?

Oedipus

Flood on flood
Whelms me; that word's a second mortal blow.

Chorus

Murderer!

Oedipus

Yes, a murderer, but know—

Chorus

What canst thou plead?

Oedipus

A plea of justice.

Chorus

How?

Oedipus

I slew who else would me have slain;
I slew without intent, 560
A wretch, but innocent
In the law's eye, I stand, without a stain.

Chorus

> Behold our sovereign, Theseus, Aegeus' son,
> Comes at thy summons to perform his part.

[Enter Theseus]

Theseus

> Oft had I heard of thee in times gone by—
> The bloody mutilation of thine eyes—
> And therefore know thee, son of Laius.
> All that I lately gathered on the way
> Made my conjecture doubly sure; and now
570   Thy garb and that marred visage prove to me
> That thou art he. So pitying thine estate,
> Most ill-starred Oedipus, I fain would know
> What is the suit ye urge on me and Athens,
> Thou and the helpless maiden at thy side.
> Declare it; dire indeed must be the tale
> Whereat I should recoil. I too was reared,
> Like thee, in exile, and in foreign lands
> Wrestled with many perils, no man more.
> Wherefore no alien in adversity
580   Shall seek in vain my succor, nor shalt thou;
> I know myself a mortal, and my share
> In what the morrow brings no more than thine.

Oedipus

> Theseus, thy words so apt, so generous
> So comfortable, need no long reply
> Both who I am and of what lineage sprung,
> And from what land I came, thou hast declared.
> So without prologue I may utter now
> My brief petition, and the tale is told.

Theseus

> Say on, and tell me what I fain would learn.

Oedipus

590   I come to offer thee this woe-worn frame,

A gift not fair to look on; yet its worth
More precious far than any outward show.

Theseus

What profit dost thou proffer to have brought?

Oedipus

Hereafter thou shalt learn, not yet, methinks.

Theseus

When may we hope to reap the benefit?

Oedipus

When I am dead and thou hast buried me.

Theseus

Thou cravest life's last service; all before—
Is it forgotten or of no account?

Oedipus

Yea, the last boon is warrant for the rest.

Theseus

The grace thou cravest then is small indeed.   600

Oedipus

Nay, weigh it well; the issue is not slight.

Theseus

Thou meanest that betwixt thy sons and me?

Oedipus

Prince, they would fain convey me back to Thebes.

Theseus

If there be no compulsion, then methinks
To rest in banishment befits not thee.

265

Oedipus

Nay, when I wished it they would not consent.

Theseus

For shame! such temper misbecomes the faller.

Oedipus

Chide if thou wilt, but first attend my plea.

Theseus

Say on, I wait full knowledge ere I judge.

Oedipus

610

O Theseus, I have suffered wrongs on wrongs.

Theseus

Wouldst tell the old misfortune of thy race?

Oedipus

No, that has grown a byword throughout Greece.

Theseus

What then can be this more than mortal grief?

Oedipus

600

My case stands thus; by my own flesh and blood
I was expelled my country, and can ne'er
Thither return again, a parricide.

Theseus

Why fetch thee home if thou must needs obey?

Oedipus

The sacred oracle compels them to.

Theseus

What are they threatened by the oracle?

266

Oedipus

Destruction that awaits them in this land. 620

Theseus

What can beget ill blood 'twixt them and me?

Oedipus

Dear son of Aegeus, to the gods alone
Is given immunity from eld and death;
But nothing else escapes all-ruinous time.
Earth's might decays, the might of men decays,
Honor grows cold, dishonor flourishes,
There is no constancy 'twixt friend and friend,
Or city and city; be it soon or late,
Sweet turns to bitter, hate once more to love.
If now 'tis sunshine betwixt Thebes and thee 630
And not a cloud, Time in his endless course
Gives birth to endless days and nights, wherein
The merest nothing shall suffice to cut
With serried spears your bonds of amity.
Then shall my slumbering and buried corpse
In its cold grave drink their warm life-blood up,
If Zeus be Zeus and Phoebus still speak true.
No more: 'tis ill to tear aside the veil
Of mysteries; let me cease as I began:
Enough if thou wilt keep thy plighted troth, 640
Then shall thou ne'er complain that Oedipus
Proved an unprofitable and thankless guest,
Except the gods themselves shall play me false.

Chorus

The man, my lord, has from the very first
Declared his power to offer to our land
These and like benefits.

Theseus

Who could reject
The proffered amity of such a friend?
First, he can claim the hospitality
To which by mutual contract we stand pledged: 650

267

Next, coming here, a suppliant to the gods,
He pays full tribute to the State and me;
His favors therefore never will I spurn,
But grant him the full rights of citizen;
And, if it suits the stranger here to bide,
I place him in your charge, or if he please
Rather to come with me—choose, Oedipus,
Which of the two thou wilt. Thy choice is mine.

Oedipus

Zeus, may the blessing fall on men like these!

Theseus

660   What dost thou then decide—to come with me?

Oedipus

Yea, were it lawful—but 'tis rather here—

Theseus

What wouldst thou here? I shall not thwart thy wish.

Oedipus

Here shall I vanquish those who cast me forth.

Theseus

Then were thy presence here a boon indeed.

Oedipus

Such shall it prove, if thou fulfill'st thy pledge.

Theseus

Fear not for me; I shall not play thee false.

Oedipus

No need to back thy promise with an oath.

Theseus

An oath would be no surer than my word.

Oedipus

How wilt thou act then?

Theseus

What is it thou fear'st?   670

Oedipus

My foes will come—

Theseus

Our friends will look to that.

Oedipus

But if thou leave me?

Theseus

Teach me not my duty.

Oedipus

'Tis fear constrains me.

Theseus

My soul knows no fear!

Oedipus

Thou knowest not what threats—

Theseus

I know that none
Shall hale thee hence in my despite. Such threats
Vented in anger oft, are blusterers,   680
An idle breath, forgot when sense returns.
And for thy foemen, though their words were brave,
Boasting to bring thee back, they are like to find
The seas between us wide and hard to sail.
Such my firm purpose, but in any case
Take heart, since Phoebus sent thee here. My name,
Though I be distant, warrants thee from harm.

Chorus

[strophe 1]

690

Thou hast come to a steed-famed land for rest,
O stranger worn with toil,
To a land of all lands the goodliest
Colonus' glistening soil.
'Tis the haunt of the clear-voiced nightingale,
Who hid in her bower, among
The wine-dark ivy that wreathes the vale,
Trilleth her ceaseless song;
And she loves, where the clustering berries nod
O'er a sunless, windless glade,
The spot by no mortal footstep trod,
The pleasance kept for the Bacchic god,

700

Where he holds each night his revels wild
With the nymphs who fostered the lusty child.

[antistrophe 1]

And fed each morn by the pearly dew
The starred narcissi shine,
And a wreath with the crocus' golden hue
For the Mother and Daughter twine.
And never the sleepless fountains cease
That feed Cephisus' stream,
But they swell earth's bosom with quick increase,
And their wave hath a crystal gleam.

710

And the Muses' quire will never disdain
To visit this heaven-favored plain,
Nor the Cyprian queen of the golden rein.

[strophe 2]

And here there grows, unpruned, untamed,
Terror to foemen's spear,
A tree in Asian soil unnamed,
By Pelops' Dorian isle unclaimed,

700

Self-nurtured year by year;
'Tis the grey-leaved olive that feeds our boys;
Nor youth nor withering age destroys

The plant that the Olive Planter tends   720
And the Grey-eyed Goddess herself defends.

[antistrophe 2]

Yet another gift, of all gifts the most
Prized by our fatherland, we boast—
The might of the horse, the might of the sea;
Our fame, Poseidon, we owe to thee,
Son of Kronos, our king divine,
Who in these highways first didst fit
For the mouth of horses the iron bit;
Thou too hast taught us to fashion meet
For the arm of the rower the oar-blade fleet,   730
Swift as the Nereids' hundred feet
As they dance along the brine.

Antigone

Oh land extolled above all lands, 'tis now
For thee to make these glorious titles good.

Oedipus

Why this appeal, my daughter?

Antigone

Father, lo! Creon approaches with his company.

Oedipus

Fear not, it shall be so; if we are old,
This country's vigor has no touch of age.

[Enter Creon with attendants]

Creon

Burghers, my noble friends, ye take alarm
At my approach (I read it in your eyes),   740
Fear nothing and refrain from angry words.
I come with no ill purpose; I am old,
And know the city whither I am come,

Without a peer amongst the powers of Greece.
It was by reason of my years that I
Was chosen to persuade your guest and bring
Him back to Thebes; not the delegate
Of one man, but commissioned by the State,
Since of all Thebans I have most bewailed,
750   Being his kinsman, his most grievous woes.
O listen to me, luckless Oedipus,
Come home! The whole Cadmeian people claim
With right to have thee back, I most of all,
For most of all (else were I vile indeed)
I mourn for thy misfortunes, seeing thee
An aged outcast, wandering on and on,
A beggar with one handmaid for thy stay.
Ah! who had e'er imagined she could fall
To such a depth of misery as this,
760   To tend in penury thy stricken frame,
A virgin ripe for wedlock, but unwed,
A prey for any wanton ravisher?
Seems it not cruel this reproach I cast
On thee and on myself and all the race?
Aye, but an open shame cannot be hid.
Hide it, O hide it, Oedipus, thou canst.
O, by our fathers' gods, consent I pray;
Come back to Thebes, come to thy father's home,
Bid Athens, as is meet, a fond farewell;
770   Thebes thy old foster-mother claims thee first.

Oedipus

O front of brass, thy subtle tongue would twist
To thy advantage every plea of right
Why try thy arts on me, why spread again
Toils where 'twould gall me sorest to be snared?
In old days when by self-wrought woes distraught,
I yearned for exile as a glad release,
Thy will refused the favor then I craved.
But when my frenzied grief had spent its force,
And I was fain to taste the sweets of home,
780   Then thou wouldst thrust me from my country, then
These ties of kindred were by thee ignored;

And now again when thou behold'st this State
And all its kindly people welcome me,
Thou seek'st to part us, wrapping in soft words
Hard thoughts. And yet what pleasure canst thou find
In forcing friendship on unwilling foes?
Suppose a man refused to grant some boon
When you importuned him, and afterwards
When you had got your heart's desire, consented,
Granting a grace from which all grace had fled,   790
Would not such favor seem an empty boon?
Yet such the boon thou profferest now to me,
Fair in appearance, but when tested false.
Yea, I will prove thee false, that these may hear;
Thou art come to take me, not to take me home,
But plant me on thy borders, that thy State
May so escape annoyance from this land.
That thou shalt never gain, but this instead—
My ghost to haunt thy country without end;
And for my sons, this heritage—no more—   800
Just room to die in. Have not I more skill
Than thou to draw the horoscope of Thebes?
Are not my teachers surer guides than thine--
Great Phoebus and the sire of Phoebus, Zeus?
Thou art a messenger suborned, thy tongue
Is sharper than a sword's edge, yet thy speech
Will bring thee more defeats than victories.
Howbeit, I know I waste my words--begone,
And leave me here; whate'er may be my lot,
He lives not ill who lives withal content.   810   *800*

Creon

Which loses in this parley, I o'erthrown
By thee, or thou who overthrow'st thyself?

Oedipus

I shall be well contented if thy suit
Fails with these strangers, as it has with me.

Creon

Unhappy man, will years ne'er make thee wise?
Must thou live on to cast a slur on age?

Oedipus

Thou hast a glib tongue, but no honest man,
Methinks, can argue well on any side.

Creon

'Tis one thing to speak much, another well.

Oedipus

820   Thy words, forsooth, are few and all well aimed!

Creon

Not for a man indeed with wits like thine.

Oedipus

Depart! I bid thee in these burghers' name,
And prowl no longer round me to blockade
My destined harbor.

Creon

        I protest to these,
Not thee, and for thine answer to thy kin,
If e'er I take thee—

Oedipus

Who against their will Could take me?

Creon

Though untaken thou shalt smart.

Oedipus

830   What power hast thou to execute this threat?

Creon

One of thy daughters is already seized,
The other I will carry off anon.

Oedipus

Woe, woe!

Creon

> This is but prelude to thy woes.

Oedipus

> Hast thou my child?

Creon

> And soon shall have the other.

Oedipus

> Ho, friends! ye will not surely play me false?
> Chase this ungodly villain from your land.

Chorus

> Hence, stranger, hence avaunt! Thou doest wrong
> In this, and wrong in all that thou hast done.   840

Creon [to his guards]

> 'Tis time by force to carry off the girl,
> If she refuse of her free will to go.

Antigone

> Ah, woe is me! where shall I fly, where find
> Succor from gods or men?

Chorus

> What would'st thou, stranger?

Creon

> I meddle not with him, but her who is mine.

Oedipus

> O princes of the land!

Chorus

> Sir, thou dost wrong.

Creon

Nay, right.

Chorus

850   How right?

Creon

I take but what is mine.

Oedipus

Help, Athens!

Chorus

What means this, sirrah? quick unhand her, or
We'll fight it out.

Creon

Back!

Chorus

Not till thou forbear.

Creon

'Tis war with Thebes if I am touched or harmed.

Oedipus

Did I not warn thee?

Chorus

Quick, unhand the maid!

Creon

860   Command your minions; I am not your slave.

Chorus

Desist, I bid thee.

Creon [to the Guard]

And I bid thee march!

Chorus

To the rescue, one and all!
Rally, neighbors to my call!
See, the foe is at the gate!
Rally to defend the State.

Antigone

Ah, woe is me, they drag me hence, O friends.

Oedipus

Where art thou, daughter?

Antigone

Haled along by force.

Oedipus

Thy hands, my child!   870

Antigone

They will not let me, father.

Creon

Away with her!

Oedipus

Ah, woe is me, ah woe!

Creon

So those two crutches shall no longer serve thee
For further roaming. Since it pleaseth thee
To triumph o'er thy country and thy friends
Who mandate, though a prince, I here discharge,
Enjoy thy triumph; soon or late thou'lt find
Thou art an enemy to thyself, both now

277

880 And in time past, when in despite of friends
Thou gav'st the rein to passion, still thy bane.

Chorus

Hold there, sir stranger!

Creon

Hands off, have a care.

Chorus

Restore the maidens, else thou goest not.

Creon

Then Thebes will take a dearer surety soon;
I will lay hands on more than these two maids.

Chorus

What canst thou further?

Creon

Carry off this man.

Chorus

Brave words!

Creon

890 And deeds forthwith shall make them good.

Chorus

Unless perchance our sovereign intervene.

Oedipus

O shameless voice! Would'st lay an hand on me?

Creon

Silence, I bid thee!

Oedipus

>Goddesses, allow
>Thy suppliant to utter yet one curse!
>Wretch, now my eyes are gone thou hast torn away
>The helpless maiden who was eyes to me;
>For these to thee and all thy cursed race
>May the great Sun, whose eye is everywhere,
>Grant length of days and old age like to mine. 900

Creon

>Listen, O men of Athens, mark ye this?

Oedipus

>They mark us both and understand that I
>Wronged by the deeds defend myself with words.

Creon

>Nothing shall curb my will; though I be old
>And single-handed, I will have this man.

Oedipus

>O woe is me!

Chorus

>Thou art a bold man, stranger, if thou think'st
>To execute thy purpose.

Creon

>So I do.

Chorus

>Then shall I deem this State no more a State. 910

Creon

>With a just quarrel weakness conquers might.

Oedipus

>Ye hear his words?

Chorus

> Aye words, but not yet deeds,
> Zeus knoweth!

Creon

> Zeus may haply know, not thou.

Chorus

> Insolence!

Creon

> Insolence that thou must bear.

Chorus

> Haste ye princes, sound the alarm!
> Men of Athens, arm ye, arm!
920 > Quickly to the rescue come
> Ere the robbers get them home.

[Enter Theseus]

Theseus

> Why this outcry? What is forward? wherefore was I called aw
> From the altar of Poseidon, lord of your Colonus? Say!
> On what errand have I hurried hither without stop or stay.

Oedipus

> Dear friend—those accents tell me who thou art—
> Yon man but now hath done me a foul wrong.

Theseus

> What is this wrong and who hath wrought it? Speak.

Oedipus

> Creon who stands before thee. He it is
> Hath robbed me of my all, my daughters twain.

Theseus

930 > What means this?

Oedipus

Thou hast heard my tale of wrongs.

Theseus

Ho! hasten to the altars, one of you.
Command my liegemen leave the sacrifice
And hurry, foot and horse, with rein unchecked,   *900*
To where the paths that packmen use diverge,
Lest the two maidens slip away, and I
Become a mockery to this my guest,
As one despoiled by force. Quick, as I bid.
As for this stranger, had I let my rage,
Justly provoked, have play, he had not 'scaped   940
Scathless and uncorrected at my hands.
But now the laws to which himself appealed,
These and none others shall adjudicate.
Thou shalt not quit this land, till thou hast fetched
The maidens and produced them in my sight.
Thou hast offended both against myself
And thine own race and country. Having come
Unto a State that champions right and asks
For every action warranty of law,
Thou hast set aside the custom of the land,   950
And like some freebooter art carrying off
What plunder pleases thee, as if forsooth
Thou thoughtest this a city without men,
Or manned by slaves, and me a thing of naught.
Yet not from Thebes this villainy was learnt;
Thebes is not wont to breed unrighteous sons,
Nor would she praise thee, if she learnt that thou
Wert robbing me—aye and the gods to boot,
Haling by force their suppliants, poor maids.
Were I on Theban soil, to prosecute   960
The justest claim imaginable, I
Would never wrest by violence my own
Without sanction of your State or King;
I should behave as fits an outlander
Living amongst a foreign folk, but thou
Shamest a city that deserves it not,
Even thine own, and plentitude of years

281

Have made of thee an old man and a fool.
Therefore again I charge thee as before,
970   See that the maidens are restored at once,
Unless thou would'st continue here by force
And not by choice a sojourner; so much
I tell thee home and what I say, I mean.

Chorus

Thy case is perilous; though by birth and race
Thou should'st be just, thou plainly doest wrong.

Creon

Not deeming this city void of men
Or counsel, son of Aegeus, as thou say'st
I did what I have done; rather I thought
Your people were not like to set such store
980   By kin of mine and keep them 'gainst my will.
Nor would they harbor, so I stood assured,
A godless parricide, a reprobate
Convicted of incestuous marriage ties.
For on her native hill of Ares here
(I knew your far-famed Areopagus)
Sits Justice, and permits not vagrant folk
To stay within your borders. In that faith
I hunted down my quarry; and e'en then
I had refrained but for the curses dire
990   Wherewith he banned my kinsfolk and myself:
Such wrong, methought, had warrant for my act.
Anger has no old age but only death;
The dead alone can feel no touch of spite.
So thou must work thy will; my cause is just
But weak without allies; yet will I try,
Old as I am, to answer deeds with deeds.

Oedipus

O shameless railer, think'st thou this abuse
Defames my grey hairs rather than thine own?
Murder and incest, deeds of horror, all
1000   Thou blurtest forth against me, all I have borne,
No willing sinner; so it pleased the gods

Wrath haply with my sinful race of old,
Since thou could'st find no sin in me myself
For which in retribution I was doomed
To trespass thus against myself and mine.
Answer me now, if by some oracle
My sire was destined to a bloody end
By a son's hand, can this reflect on me,
Me then unborn, begotten by no sire,
Conceived in no mother's womb? And if   1010
When born to misery, as born I was,
I met my sire, not knowing whom I met or what I did,
And slew him, how canst thou
With justice blame the all-unconscious hand?
And for my mother, wretch, art not ashamed,
Seeing she was thy sister, to extort
From me the story of her marriage, such
A marriage as I straightway will proclaim.
For I will speak; thy lewd and impious speech
Has broken all the bonds of reticence.   1020
She was, ah woe is me! she was my mother;
I knew it not, nor she; and she my mother
Bare children to the son whom she had borne,
A birth of shame. But this at least I know
Wittingly thou aspersest her and me;
But I unwitting wed, unwilling speak.
Nay neither in this marriage or this deed
Which thou art ever casting in my teeth—
A murdered sire—shall I be held to blame.
Come, answer me one question, if thou canst: 1030
If one should presently attempt thy life,
Would'st thou, O man of justice, first inquire
If the assassin was perchance thy sire,
Or turn upon him? As thou lov'st thy life,
On thy aggressor thou would'st turn, no stay
Debating, if the law would bear thee out.
Such was my case, and such the pass whereto
The gods reduced me; and methinks my sire,
Could he come back to life, would not dissent.
Yet thou, for just thou art not, but a man   1040   *1000*
Who sticks at nothing, if it serve his plea,
Reproachest me with this before these men.

It serves thy turn to laud great Theseus' name,
And Athens as a wisely governed State;
Yet in thy flatteries one thing is to seek:
If any land knows how to pay the gods
Their proper rites, 'tis Athens most of all.
This is the land whence thou wast fain to steal
Their aged suppliant and hast carried off
1050   My daughters. Therefore to yon goddesses,
I turn, adjure them and invoke their aid
To champion my cause, that thou mayest learn
What is the breed of men who guard this State.

Chorus

An honest man, my liege, one sore bestead
By fortune, and so worthy of our support.

Theseus

Enough of words; the captors speed amain,
While we the victims stand debating here.

Creon

What would'st thou? What can I, a feeble man?

Theseus

Show us the trail, and I'll attend thee too,
1060   That, if thou hast the maidens hereabouts,
Thou mayest thyself discover them to me;
But if thy guards outstrip us with their spoil,
We may draw rein; for others speed, from whom
They will not 'scape to thank the gods at home.
Lead on, I say, the captor's caught, and fate
Hath ta'en the fowler in the toils he spread;
So soon are lost gains gotten by deceit.
And look not for allies; I know indeed
Such height of insolence was never reached
1070   Without abettors or accomplices;
Thou hast some backer in thy bold essay,
But I will search this matter home and see
One man doth not prevail against the State.

Dost take my drift, or seem these words as vain
As seemed our warnings when the plot was hatched?

Creon

Nothing thou sayest can I here dispute,
But once at home I too shall act my part.

Theseus

Threaten us and—begone! Thou, Oedipus,
Stay here assured that nothing save my death
Will stay my purpose to restore the maids.   1080

Oedipus

Heaven bless thee, Theseus, for thy nobleness
And all thy loving care in my behalf.

[Exeunt Theseus and Creon]

Chorus

[strophe 1]

O when the flying foe,
Turning at last to bay,
Soon will give blow for blow,
Might I behold the fray;
Hear the loud battle roar
Swell, on the Pythian shore,
Or by the torch-lit bay,
Where the dread Queen and Maid   1090
Cherish the mystic rites,
Rites they to none betray,
Ere on his lips is laid
Secrecy's golden key
By their own acolytes,
Priestly Eumolpidae.
There I might chance behold
Theseus our captain bold
Meet with the robber band,
Ere they have fled the land,   1100

285

Rescue by might and main
Maidens, the captives twain.

[antistrophe 1]

Haply on swiftest steed,
Or in the flying car,
Now they approach the glen,
West of white Oea's scaur.
They will be vanquished:
Dread are our warriors, dread
Theseus our chieftain's men.

1110
Flashes each bridle bright,
Charges each gallant knight,
All that our Queen adore,
Pallas their patron, or
Him whose wide floods enring
Earth, the great Ocean-king
Whom Rhea bore.

[strophe 2]

Fight they or now prepare
To fight? a vision rare
Tells me that soon again

1120
I shall behold the twain
Maidens so ill bestead,
By their kin buffeted.
Today, today Zeus worketh some great thing
This day shall victory bring.
O for the wings, the wings of a dove,
To be borne with the speed of the gale,
Up and still upwards to sail
And gaze on the fray from the clouds above.

[antistrophe 2]

All-seeing Zeus, O lord of heaven,

1130
To our guardian host be given
Might triumphant to surprise
Flying foes and win their prize.
Hear us, Zeus, and hear us, child
Of Zeus, Athene undefiled,

Hear, Apollo, hunter, hear,
Huntress, sister of Apollo,
Who the dappled swift-foot deer
O'er the wooded glade dost follow;
Help with your two-fold power
Athens in danger's hour!   1140
O wayfarer, thou wilt not have to tax
The friends who watch for thee with false presage,
For lo, an escort with the maids draws near.

[Enter Antigone and Ismene with Theseus]

Oedipus

Where, where? what sayest thou?

Antigone

O father, father,
Would that some god might grant thee eyes to see   *1100*
This best of men who brings us back again.

Oedipus

My child! and are ye back indeed!

Antigone

Yes, saved by Theseus and his gallant followers.

Oedipus

Come to your father's arms, O let me feel   1150
A child's embrace I never hoped for more.

Antigone

Thou askest what is doubly sweet to give.

Oedipus

Where are ye then?

Antigone

We come together both.

287

Oedipus

> My precious nurslings!

Antigone

> Fathers aye were fond.

Oedipus

> Props of my age!

Antigone

> So sorrow sorrow props.

Oedipus

> I have my darlings, and if death should come,
> Death were not wholly bitter with you near.
> Cling to me, press me close on either side,
> There rest ye from your dreary wayfaring.
> Now tell me of your ventures, but in brief;
> Brief speech suffices for young maids like you.

1160

Antigone

> Here is our savior; thou should'st hear the tale
> From his own lips; so shall my part be brief.

Oedipus

> I pray thee do not wonder if the sight
> Of children, given o'er for lost, has made
> My converse somewhat long and tedious.
> Full well I know the joy I have of them
> Is due to thee, to thee and no man else;
> Thou wast their sole deliverer, none else.
> The gods deal with thee after my desire,
> With thee and with this land! for fear of heaven
> I found above all peoples most with you,
> And righteousness and lips that cannot lie.
> I speak in gratitude of what I know,
> For all I have I owe to thee alone.
> Give me thy hand, O Prince, that I may touch it,
> And if thou wilt permit me, kiss thy cheek.

1170

1180

288

What say I? Can I wish that thou should'st touch
One fallen like me to utter wretchedness,
Corrupt and tainted with a thousand ills?
Oh no, I would not let thee if thou would'st.
They only who have known calamity
Can share it. Let me greet thee where thou art,
And still befriend me as thou hast till now.

Theseus

I marvel not if thou hast dallied long
In converse with thy children and preferred
Their speech to mine; I feel no jealousy,   1190
I would be famous more by deeds than words.
Of this, old friend, thou hast had proof; my oath
I have fulfilled and brought thee back the maids
Alive and nothing harmed for all those threats.
And how the fight was won, 'twere waste of words
To boast—thy daughters here will tell thee all.
But of a matter that has lately chanced
On my way hitherward, I fain would have
Thy counsel—slight 'twould seem, yet worthy thought.
A wise man heeds all matters great or small.   1200

Oedipus

What is it, son of Aegeus? Let me hear.
Of what thou askest I myself know naught.

Theseus

'Tis said a man, no countryman of thine,
But of thy kin, hath taken sanctuary
Beside the altar of Poseidon, where
I was at sacrifice when called away.

Oedipus

What is his country? what the suitor's prayer?

Theseus

I know but one thing; he implores, I am told,
A word with thee—he will not trouble thee.

Oedipus

1210

What seeks he? If a suppliant, something grave.

Theseus

He only waits, they say, to speak with thee,
And then unharmed to go upon his way.

Oedipus

I marvel who is this petitioner.

Theseus

Think if there be not any of thy kin
At Argos who might claim this boon of thee.

Oedipus

Dear friend, forbear, I pray.

Theseus

What ails thee now?

Oedipus

Ask it not of me.

Theseus

Ask not what? explain.

Oedipus

1220

Thy words have told me who the suppliant is.

Theseus

Who can he be that I should frown on him?

Oedipus

My son, O king, my hateful son, whose words
Of all men's most would jar upon my ears.

Theseus

Thou sure mightest listen. If his suit offend,
No need to grant it. Why so loth to hear him?

Oedipus

> That voice, O king, grates on a father's ears;
> I have come to loathe it. Force me not to yield.

Theseus

> But he hath found asylum. O beware,
> And fail not in due reverence to the god.

Antigone

> O heed me, father, though I am young in years.   1230
> Let the prince have his will and pay withal
> What in his eyes is service to the god;
> For our sake also let our brother come.
> If what he urges tend not to thy good
> He cannot surely wrest perforce thy will.
> To hear him then, what harm? By open words
> A scheme of villainy is soon bewrayed.
> Thou art his father, therefore canst not pay
> In kind a son's most impious outrages.
> O listen to him; other men like thee   1240
> Have thankless children and are choleric,
> But yielding to persuasion's gentle spell
> They let their savage mood be exorcised.
> Look thou to the past, forget the present, think
> On all the woe thy sire and mother brought thee;
> Thence wilt thou draw this lesson without fail,
> Of evil passion evil is the end.
> Thou hast, alas, to prick thy memory,
> Stern monitors, these ever-sightless orbs.   *1200*
> O yield to us; just suitors should not need   1250
> To be importunate, nor he that takes
> A favor lack the grace to make return.

Oedipus

> Grievous to me, my child, the boon ye win
> By pleading. Let it be then; have your way
> Only if come he must, I beg thee, friend,
> Let none have power to dispose of me.

Theseus

No need, Sir, to appeal a second time.
It likes me not to boast, but be assured
Thy life is safe while any god saves mine.

[Exit Theseus]

Chorus

[strophe]

1260

Who craves excess of days,
Scorning the common span
Of life, I judge that man
A giddy wight who walks in folly's ways.
For the long years heap up a grievous load,
Scant pleasures, heavier pains,
Till not one joy remains
For him who lingers on life's weary road
And come it slow or fast,
One doom of fate

1270

Doth all await,
For dance and marriage bell,
The dirge and funeral knell.
Death the deliverer freeth all at last.

[antistrophe]

Not to be born at all
Is best, far best that can befall,
Next best, when born, with least delay
To trace the backward way.
For when youth passes with its giddy train,
Troubles on troubles follow, toils on toils,

1280

Pain, pain for ever pain;
And none escapes life's coils.
Envy, sedition, strife,
Carnage and war, make up the tale of life.
Last comes the worst and most abhorred stage
Of unregarded age,
Joyless, companionless and slow,
Of woes the crowning woe.

[epode]

Such ills not I alone,
He too our guest hath known,
E'en as some headland on an iron-bound shore,   1290
Lashed by the wintry blasts and surge's roar,
So is he buffeted on every side
By drear misfortune's whelming tide,
By every wind of heaven o'erborne
Some from the sunset, some from orient morn,
Some from the noonday glow.
Some from Rhipean gloom of everlasting snow.

Antigone

Father, methinks I see the stranger coming,
Alone he comes and weeping plenteous tears.

Oedipus

Who may he be?   1300

Antigone

The same that we surmised.
From the outset—Polyneices. He is here.

[Enter Polyneices]

Polyneices

Ah me, my sisters, shall I first lament
My own afflictions, or my aged sire's,
Whom here I find a castaway, with you,
In a strange land, an ancient beggar clad
In antic tatters, marring all his frame,
While o'er the sightless orbs his unkept locks
Float in the breeze; and, as it were to match,
He bears a wallet against hunger's pinch.   1310
All this too late I learn, wretch that I am,
Alas! I own it, and am proved most vile
In my neglect of thee: I scorn myself.
But as almighty Zeus in all he doth
Hath Mercy for co-partner of this throne,

Let Mercy, father, also sit enthroned
In thy heart likewise. For transgressions past
May be amended, cannot be made worse.

Why silent? Father, speak, nor turn away,
1320   Hast thou no word, wilt thou dismiss me then
In mute disdain, nor tell me why thou art wrath?
O ye his daughters, sisters mine, do ye
This sullen, obstinate silence try to move.
Let him not spurn, without a single word
Of answer, me the suppliant of the god.

Antigone

Tell him thyself, unhappy one, thine errand;
For large discourse may send a thrill of joy,
Or stir a chord of wrath or tenderness,
And to the tongue-tied somehow give a tongue.

Polyneices

1330   Well dost thou counsel, and I will speak out.
First will I call in aid the god himself,
Poseidon, from whose altar I was raised,
With warrant from the monarch of this land,
To parley with you, and depart unscathed.
These pledges, strangers, I would see observed
By you and by my sisters and my sire.
Now, father, let me tell thee why I came.
I have been banished from my native land
Because by right of primogeniture
1340   I claimed possession of thy sovereign throne
Wherefrom Eteocles, my younger brother,
Ousted me, not by weight of precedent,
Nor by the last arbitrament of war,
But by his popular acts; and the prime cause
Of this I deem the curse that rests on thee.
1300   So likewise hold the soothsayers, for when
I came to Argos in the Dorian land
And took the king Adrastus' child to wife,
Under my standard I enlisted all
1350   The foremost captains of the Apian isle,
To levy with their aid that sevenfold host

Of spearmen against Thebes, determining
To oust my foes or die in a just cause.
Why then, thou askest, am I here today?
Father, I come a suppliant to thee
Both for myself and my allies who now
With squadrons seven beneath their seven spears
Beleaguer all the plain that circles Thebes.
Foremost the peerless warrior, peerless seer,
Amphiaraüs with his lightning lance;   1360
Next an Aetolian, Tydeus, Oeneus' son;
Eteoclus of Argive birth the third;
The fourth Hippomedon, sent to the war
By his sire Talaos; Capaneus, the fifth,
Vaunts he will fire and raze the town; the sixth
Parthenopaeus, an Arcadian born
Named of that maid, longtime a maid and late
Espoused, Atalanta's true-born child;
Last I thy son, or thine at least in name,
If but the bastard of an evil fate,   1370
Lead against Thebes the fearless Argive host.
Thus by thy children and thy life, my sire,
We all adjure thee to remit thy wrath
And favor one who seeks a just revenge
Against a brother who has banned and robbed him.
For victory, if oracles speak true,
Will fall to those who have thee for ally.
So, by our fountains and familiar gods
I pray thee, yield and hear; a beggar I
And exile, thou an exile likewise; both   1380
Involved in one misfortune find a home
As pensioners, while he, the lord of Thebes,
O agony! makes a mock of thee and me.
I'll scatter with a breath the upstart's might,
And bring thee home again and stablish thee,
And stablish, having cast him out, myself.
This with thy goodwill I will undertake,
Without it I can scare return alive.

Chorus

For the king's sake who sent him, Oedipus,
Dismiss him not without a meet reply.   1390

295

Oedipus

Nay, worthy seniors, but for Theseus' sake
Who sent him hither to have word of me,
Never again would he have heard my voice;
But now he shall obtain this parting grace,
An answer that will bring him little joy.
O villain, when thou hadst the sovereignty
That now thy brother holdeth in thy stead,
Didst thou not drive me, thine own father, out,
An exile, cityless, and make we wear
1400   This beggar's garb thou weepest to behold,
Now thou art come thyself to my sad plight?
Nothing is here for tears; it must be borne
By me till death, and I shall think of thee
As of my murderer; thou didst thrust me out;
'Tis thou hast made me conversant with woe,
Through thee I beg my bread in a strange land;
And had not these my daughters tended me
I had been dead for aught of aid from thee.
They tend me, they preserve me, they are men
1410   Not women in true service to their sire;
But ye are bastards, and no sons of mine.
Therefore just Heaven hath an eye on thee;
Howbeit not yet with aspect so austere
As thou shalt soon experience, if indeed
These banded hosts are moving against Thebes.
That city thou canst never storm, but first
Shall fall, thou and thy brother, blood-imbrued.
Such curse I lately launched against you twain,
Such curse I now invoke to fight for me,
1420   That ye may learn to honor those who bear thee
Nor flout a sightless father who begat
Degenerate sons—these maidens did not so.
Therefore my curse is stronger than thy "throne,"
Thy "suppliance," if by right of laws eterne
Primeval Justice sits enthroned with Zeus.
Begone, abhorred, disowned, no son of mine,
Thou vilest of the vile! and take with thee
This curse I leave thee as my last bequest:—
Never to win by arms thy native land,

No, nor return to Argos in the Vale,   1430
But by a kinsman's hand to die and slay
Him who expelled thee. So I pray and call
On the ancestral gloom of Tartarus
To snatch thee hence, on these dread goddesses
I call, and Ares who incensed you both
To mortal enmity. Go now proclaim
What thou hast heard to the Cadmeians all,
Thy staunch confederates—this the heritage
That Oedipus divideth to his sons.

Chorus

Thy errand, Polyneices, liked me not   1440
From the beginning; now go back with speed.

Polyneices

Woe worth my journey and my baffled hopes!
Woe worth my comrades! What a desperate end   *1400*
To that glad march from Argos! Woe is me!
I dare not whisper it to my allies
Or turn them back, but mute must meet my doom.
My sisters, ye his daughters, ye have heard
The prayers of our stern father, if his curse
Should come to pass and ye some day return
To Thebes, O then disown me not, I pray,   1450
But grant me burial and due funeral rites.
So shall the praise your filial care now wins
Be doubled for the service wrought for me.

Antigone

One boon, O Polyneices, let me crave.

Polyneices

What would'st thou, sweet Antigone? Say on.

Antigone

Turn back thy host to Argos with all speed,
And ruin not thyself and Thebes as well.

Polyneices

> That cannot be. How could I lead again
> An army that had seen their leader quail?

Antigone

1460
> But, brother, why shouldst thou be wroth again?
> What profit from thy country's ruin comes?

Polyneices

> 'Tis shame to live in exile, and shall I
> The elder bear a younger brother's flouts?

Antigone

> Wilt thou then bring to pass his prophecies
> Who threatens mutual slaughter to you both?

Polyneices

> Aye, so he wishes:—but I must not yield.

Antigone

> O woe is me! but say, will any dare,
> Hearing his prophecy, to follow thee?

Polyneices

> I shall not tell it; a good general
1470
> Reports successes and conceals mishaps.

Antigone

> Misguided youth, thy purpose then stands fast!

Polyneices

> 'Tis so, and stay me not. The road I choose,
> Dogged by my sire and his avenging spirit,
> Leads me to ruin; but for you may Zeus
> Make your path bright if ye fulfill my hest
> When dead; in life ye cannot serve me more.
> Now let me go, farewell, a long farewell!

Ye ne'er shall see my living face again.

Antigone

Ah me!

Polyneices

Bewail me not.   1480

Antigone

Who would not mourn
Thee, brother, hurrying to an open pit!

Polyneices

If I must die, I must.

Antigone

Nay, hear me plead.

Polyneices

It may not be; forbear.

Antigone

Then woe is me, If I must lose thee.

Polyneices

Nay, that rests with fate,
Whether I live or die; but for you both
I pray to heaven ye may escape all ill;
For ye are blameless in the eyes of all.   1490

[Exit Polyneices]

Chorus

[strophe 1]

Ills on ills! no pause or rest!

Come they from our sightless guest?
Or haply now we see fulfilled
What fate long time hath willed?
For ne'er have I proved vain
Aught that the heavenly powers ordain.
Time with never sleeping eye
Watches what is writ on high,
Overthrowing now the great,
1500 Raising now from low estate.
Hark! How the thunder rumbles! Zeus defend us!

Oedipus

Children, my children! will no messenger
Go summon hither Theseus my best friend?

Antigone

And wherefore, father, dost thou summon him?

Oedipus

This winged thunder of the god must bear me
Anon to Hades. Send and tarry not.

Chorus

[antistrophe 1]

Hark! with louder, nearer roar
The bolt of Zeus descends once more.
My spirit quails and cowers: my hair
1510 Bristles for fear. Again that flare!
What doth the lightning-flash portend?
Ever it points to issues grave.
Dread powers of air! Save, Zeus, O save!

Oedipus

Daughters, upon me the predestined end
Has come; no turning from it any more.

Antigone

How knowest thou? What sign convinces thee?

Oedipus

> I know full well. Let some one with all speed
> Go summon hither the Athenian prince.

Chorus

[strophe 2]

> Ha! once more the deafening sound
> Peals yet louder all around   1520
> If thou darkenest our land,
> Lightly, lightly lay thy hand;
> Grace, not anger, let me win,
> If upon a man of sin
> I have looked with pitying eye,
> Zeus, our king, to thee I cry!

Oedipus

> Is the prince coming? Will he when he comes
> Find me yet living and my senses clear!

Antigone

> What solemn charge would'st thou impress on him?

Oedipus

> For all his benefits I would perform   1530
> The promise made when I received them first.

Chorus

[antistrophe 2]

> Hither haste, my son, arise,
> Altar leave and sacrifice,
> If haply to Poseidon now
> In the far glade thou pay'st thy vow.
> For our guest to thee would bring
> And thy folk and offering,
> Thy due guerdon. Haste, O King!

[Enter Theseus]

Theseus

1540

> Wherefore again this general din? at once
> My people call me and the stranger calls.
> Is it a thunderbolt of Zeus or sleet
> Of arrowy hail? a storm so fierce as this
> Would warrant all surmises of mischance.

Oedipus

> Thou com'st much wished for, Prince, and sure some god
> Hath bid good luck attend thee on thy way.

Theseus

> What, son of Laius, hath chanced of new?

Oedipus

> My life hath turned the scale. I would do all
> I promised thee and thine before I die.

Theseus

> What sign assures thee that thine end is near?

Oedipus

1550

> The gods themselves are heralds of my fate;
> Of their appointed warnings nothing fails.

Theseus

> How sayest thou they signify their will?

Oedipus

> This thunder, peal on peal, this lightning hurled
> Flash upon flash, from the unconquered hand.

Theseus

> I must believe thee, having found thee oft
> A prophet true; then speak what must be done.

Oedipus

O son of Aegeus, for this state will I
Unfold a treasure age cannot corrupt.
Myself anon without a guiding hand
Will take thee to the spot where I must end.   1560
This secret ne'er reveal to mortal man,
Neither the spot nor whereabouts it lies,
So shall it ever serve thee for defense
Better than native shields and near allies.
But those dread mysteries speech may not profane
Thyself shalt gather coming there alone;
Since not to any of thy subjects, nor
To my own children, though I love them dearly,
Can I reveal what thou must guard alone,
And whisper to thy chosen heir alone,   1570
So to be handed down from heir to heir.
Thus shalt thou hold this land inviolate
From the dread Dragon's brood. The justest State
By countless wanton neighbors may be wronged,
For the gods, though they tarry, mark for doom
The godless sinner in his mad career.
Far from thee, son of Aegeus, be such fate!
But to the spot—the god within me goads—
Let us set forth no longer hesitate.
Follow me, daughters, this way. Strange that I   1580
Whom you have led so long should lead you now.
Oh, touch me not, but let me all alone
Find out the sepulcher that destiny
Appoints me in this land. Hither, this way,
For this way Hermes leads, the spirit guide,
And Persephassa, empress of the dead.
O light, no light to me, but mine erewhile,
Now the last time I feel thee palpable,
For I am drawing near the final gloom
Of Hades. Blessing on thee, dearest friend,   1590
On thee and on thy land and followers!
Live prosperous and in your happy state
Still for your welfare think on me, the dead.

[Exit Theseus followed by Antigone and Ismene]

Chorus

[strophe]

> If mortal prayers are heard in hell,
> Hear, Goddess dread, invisible!
> Monarch of the regions drear,
> Aidoneus, hear, O hear!
> By a gentle, tearless doom
> Speed this stranger to the gloom,
1600   (Let him enter without pain)
> The all-shrouding Stygian plain.
> Wrongfully in life oppressed,
> Be he now by Justice blessed.

[antistrophe]

> Queen infernal, and thou fell
> Watch-dog of the gates of hell,
> Who, as legends tell, dost glare,
> Gnarling in thy cavernous lair
> At all comers, let him go
> Scathless to the fields below.
1610   For thy master orders thus,
> The son of earth and Tartarus;
> In his den the monster keep,
> Giver of eternal sleep.

[Enter Messenger]

Messenger

> Friends, countrymen, my tidings are in sum
> That Oedipus is gone, but the event
> Was not so brief, nor can the tale be brief.

Chorus

> What, has he gone, the unhappy man?

Messenger

> Know well that he has passed away from life to death.

Chorus

How? By a god-sent, painless doom, poor soul?

Messenger

Thy question hits the marvel of the tale.   1620
How he moved hence, you saw him and must know;
Without a friend to lead the way, himself
Guiding us all. So having reached the abrupt
Earth-rooted Threshold with its brazen stairs,
He paused at one of the converging paths,
Hard by the rocky basin which records
The pact of Theseus and Peirithous.
Betwixt that rift and the Thorician rock,
The hollow pear-tree and the marble tomb,
Midway he sat and loosed his beggar's weeds;   1630
Then calling to his daughters bade them fetch
Of running water, both to wash withal
And make libation; so they clomb the steep;   *1600*
And in brief space brought what their father bade,
Then laved and dressed him with observance due.
But when he had his will in everything,
And no desire was left unsatisfied,
It thundered from the netherworld; the maids
Shivered, and crouching at their father's knees
Wept, beat their breast and uttered a long wail.   1640
He, as he heard their sudden bitter cry,
Folded his arms about them both and said,
"My children, ye will lose your sire today,
For all of me has perished, and no more
Have ye to bear your long, long ministry;
A heavy load, I know, and yet one word
Wipes out all score of tribulations—love.
And love from me ye had—from no man more;
But now must live without me all your days."
So clinging to each other sobbed and wept   1650
Father and daughters both, but when at last
Their mourning had an end and no wail rose,
A moment there was silence; suddenly
A voice that summoned him; with sudden dread
The hair of all stood up and all were 'mazed;

For the call came, now loud, now low, and oft.
"Oedipus, Oedipus, why tarry we?
Too long, too long thy passing is delayed."
But when he heard the summons of the god,
1660   He prayed that Theseus might be brought, and when
The Prince came nearer: "O my friend," he cried,
"Pledge ye my daughters, giving thy right hand—
And, daughters, give him yours—and promise me
Thou never wilt forsake them, but do all
That time and friendship prompt in their behoof."
And he of his nobility repressed
His tears and swore to be their constant friend.
This promise given, Oedipus put forth
Blind hands and laid them on his children, saying,
1670   "O children, prove your true nobility
And hence depart nor seek to witness sights
Unlawful or to hear unlawful words.
Nay, go with speed; let none but Theseus stay,
Our ruler, to behold what next shall hap."
So we all heard him speak, and weeping sore
We companied the maidens on their way.
After brief space we looked again, and lo
The man was gone, vanished from our eyes;
Only the king we saw with upraised hand
1680   Shading his eyes as from some awful sight,
That no man might endure to look upon.
A moment later, and we saw him bend
In prayer to Earth and prayer to Heaven at once.
But by what doom the stranger met his end
No man save Theseus knoweth. For there fell
No fiery bolt that reft him in that hour,
Nor whirlwind from the sea, but he was taken.
It was a messenger from heaven, or else
Some gentle, painless cleaving of earth's base;
1690   For without wailing or disease or pain
He passed away—an end most marvelous.
And if to some my tale seems foolishness
I am content that such could count me fool.

Chorus

Where are the maids and their attendant friends?

Messenger

> They cannot be far off; the approaching sound
> Of lamentation tells they come this way.

[Enter Antigone and Ismene]

Antigone

[strophe 1]

> Woe, woe! on this sad day
> We sisters of one blasted stock
> Must bow beneath the shock,
> Must weep and weep the curse that lay
> On him our sire, for whom
> In life, a life-long world of care
> 'Twas ours to bear,
> In death must face the gloom
> That wraps his tomb.
> What tongue can tell
> That sight ineffable?

1700

Chorus

> What mean ye, maidens?

Antigone

> All is but surmise.

Chorus

> Is he then gone?

1710

Antigone

> Gone as ye most might wish.
> Not in battle or sea storm,
> But reft from sight,
> By hands invisible borne
> To viewless fields of night.
> Ah me! on us too night has come,
> The night of mourning. Wither roam

O'er land or sea in our distress
Eating the bread of bitterness?

Ismene

1720

I know not. O that Death
Might nip my breath,
And let me share my aged father's fate.
I cannot live a life thus desolate.

Chorus

Best of daughters, worthy pair,
What heaven brings ye needs must bear,
Fret no more 'gainst Heaven's will;
Fate hath dealt with you not ill.

Antigone

[antistrophe 1]

Love can turn past pain to bliss,
What seemed bitter now is sweet.

1730

Ah me! that happy toil is sweet.
The guidance of those dear blind feet.

1700

Dear father, wrapt for aye in nether gloom,
E'en in the tomb
Never shalt thou lack of love repine,
Her love and mine.

Chorus

His fate—

Antigone

Is even as he planned.

Chorus

How so?

Antigone

He died, so willed he, in a foreign land.

308

Lapped in kind earth he sleeps his long last sleep,   1740
And o'er his grave friends weep.
How great our lost these streaming eyes can tell,
This sorrow naught can quell.
Thou hadst thy wish 'mid strangers thus to die,
But I, ah me, not by.

Ismene

Alas, my sister, what new fate
Befalls us orphans desolate?

Chorus

His end was blessed; therefore, children, stay
Your sorrow. Man is born to fate a prey.

Antigone

[strophe 2]

Sister, let us back again.   1750

Ismene

Why return?

Antigone

My soul is fain--

Ismene

Is fain?

Antigone

To see the earthy bed.

Ismene

Sayest thou?

Antigone

Where our sire is laid.

Ismene

    Nay, thou can'st not, dost not see--

Antigone

    Sister, wherefore wroth with me?

Ismene

    Know'st not—beside—

Antigone

1760   More must I hear?

Ismene

    Tombless he died, none near.

Antigone

    Lead me thither; slay me there.

Ismene

    How shall I unhappy fare,
    Friendless, helpless, how drag on
    A life of misery alone?

Chorus

[antistrophe 2]

    Fear not, maids—

Antigone

    Ah, whither flee?

Chorus

    Refuge hath been found.

Antigone

    For me?

Chorus

1770   Where thou shalt be safe from harm.

Antigone

> I know it.

Chorus

> Why then this alarm?

Antigone

> How again to get us home
> I know not.

Chorus

> Why then this roam?

Antigone

> Troubles whelm us—

Chorus

> As of yore.

Antigone

> Worse than what was worse before.

Chorus

> Sure ye are driven on the breakers' surge.

Antigone

> Alas! we are.   1780

Chorus

> Alas! 'tis so.

Antigone

> Ah whither turn, O Zeus? No ray
> Of hope to cheer the way
> Whereon the fates our desperate voyage urge.

[Enter Theseus]

Theseus

Dry your tears; when grace is shed
On the quick and on the dead
By dark Powers beneficent,
Over-grief they would resent.

Antigone

Aegeus' child, to thee we pray.

Theseus

1790   What the boon, my children, say.

Antigone

With our own eyes we fain would see
Our father's tomb.

Theseus

That may not be.

Antigone

What say'st thou, King?

Theseus

My children, he
Charged me straitly that no mortal
Should approach the sacred portal,
Or greet with funeral litanies
The hidden tomb wherein he lies;
1800   Saying, "If thou keep'st my hest
Thou shalt hold thy realm at rest."
The God of Oaths this promise heard,
And to Zeus I pledged my word.

Antigone

Well, if he would have it so,
We must yield. Then let us go
Back to Thebes, if yet we may
Heal this mortal feud and stay

312

The self-wrought doom
That drives our brothers to their tomb.

Theseus

Go in peace; nor will I spare   1810
Aught of toil and zealous care,
But on all your needs attend,
Gladdening in his grave my friend.

Chorus

Wail no more, let sorrow rest,
All is ordered for the best.

The End

Antigone

TRANSLATED BY F. STORR

Dramatis Personae

ANTIGONE
daughter of Oedipus and sister of
Polyneices and Eteocles

ISMENE
daughter of Oedipus and sister of
Polyneices and Eteocles

CREON
King of Thebes

EURYDICE
his wife

HAEMON
his son

TEIRESIAS
the blind prophet

A WATCHMAN

A MESSENGER

A SECOND MESSENGER

*[The same as in Oedipus the King, an open space before
the royal palace, once that of Oedipus, at Thebes. The
backscene represents the front of the palace, with three
doors, of which the central and largest is the principal
entrance into the house. The time is at daybreak on the
morning after the fall of the two brothers, Eteocles and
Polyneices, and the flight of the defeated Argives. Antigone
calls Ismene forth from the palace, in order to speak to her
alone.]*

Antigone

 Ismene, sister of my blood and heart,
 See'st thou how Zeus would in our lives fulfill
 The weird of Oedipus, a world of woes!
 For what of pain, affliction, outrage, shame,
 Is lacking in our fortunes, thine and mine?
 And now this proclamation of today
 Made by our Captain-General to the State,
 What can its purport be? Didst hear and heed,
 Or art thou deaf when friends are banned as foes?

Ismene

 To me, Antigone, no word of friends   10
 Has come, or glad or grievous, since we twain
 Were reft of our two brethren in one day
 By double fratricide; and since i' the night
 Our Argive leaguers fled, no later news
 Has reached me, to inspirit or deject.

Antigone

 I know 'twas so, and therefore summoned thee
 Beyond the gates to breathe it in thine ear.

Ismene

 What is it? Some dark secret stirs thy breast.

Antigone

What but the thought of our two brothers dead,
20 The one by Creon graced with funeral rites,
The other disappointed? Eteocles
He hath consigned to earth (as fame reports)
With obsequies that use and wont ordain,
So gracing him among the dead below.
But Polyneices, a dishonored corpse,
(So by report the royal edict runs)
No man may bury him or make lament—
Must leave him tombless and unwept, a feast
For kites to scent afar and swoop upon.
30 Such is the edict (if report speak true)
Of Creon, our most noble Creon, aimed
At thee and me, aye me too; and anon
He will be here to promulgate, for such
As have not heard, his mandate; 'tis in sooth
No passing humor, for the edict says
Whoe'er transgresses shall be stoned to death.
So stands it with us; now 'tis thine to show
If thou art worthy of thy blood or base.

Ismene

But how, my rash, fond sister, in such case
40 Can I do anything to make or mar?

Antigone

Say, wilt thou aid me and abet? Decide.

Ismene

In what bold venture? What is in thy thought?

Antigone

Lend me a hand to bear the corpse away.

Ismene

What, bury him despite the interdict?

Antigone

> My brother, and, though thou deny him, thine
> No man shall say that I betrayed a brother.

Ismene

> Wilt thou persist, though Creon has forbid?

Antigone

> What right has he to keep me from my own?

Ismene

> Bethink thee, sister, of our father's fate,
> Abhorred, dishonored, self-convinced of sin,   50
> Blinded, himself his executioner.
> Think of his mother-wife (ill sorted names)
> Done by a noose herself had twined to death
> And last, our hapless brethren in one day,
> Both in a mutual destiny involved,
> Self-slaughtered, both the slayer and the slain.
> Bethink thee, sister, we are left alone;
> Shall we not perish wretchedest of all,
> If in defiance of the law we cross
> A monarch's will?—weak women, think of that,   60
> Not framed by nature to contend with men.
> Remember this too that the stronger rules;
> We must obey his orders, these or worse.
> Therefore I plead compulsion and entreat
> The dead to pardon. I perforce obey
> The powers that be. 'Tis foolishness, I ween,
> To overstep in aught the golden mean.

Antigone

> I urge no more; nay, wert thou willing still,
> I would not welcome such a fellowship.
> Go thine own way; myself will bury him.   70
> How sweet to die in such employ, to rest,—
> Sister and brother linked in love's embrace—
> A sinless sinner, banned awhile on earth,

But by the dead commended; and with them
I shall abide for ever. As for thee,
Scorn, if thou wilt, the eternal laws of Heaven.

Ismene

I scorn them not, but to defy the State
Or break her ordinance I have no skill.

Antigone

A specious pretext. I will go alone
80   To lap my dearest brother in the grave.

Ismene

My poor, fond sister, how I fear for thee!

Antigone

O waste no fears on me; look to thyself.

Ismene

At least let no man know of thine intent,
But keep it close and secret, as will I.

Antigone

O tell it, sister; I shall hate thee more
If thou proclaim it not to all the town.

Ismene

Thou hast a fiery soul for numbing work.

Antigone

I pleasure those whom I would liefest please.

Ismene

If thou succeed; but thou art doomed to fail.

Antigone

90   When strength shall fail me, yes, but not before.

Ismene

> But, if the venture's hopeless, why essay?

Antigone

> Sister, forbear, or I shall hate thee soon,
> And the dead man will hate thee too, with cause.
> Say I am mad and give my madness rein
> To wreck itself; the worst that can befall
> Is but to die an honorable death.

Ismene

> Have thine own way then; 'tis a mad endeavor,
> Yet to thy lovers thou art dear as ever.

[Exeunt]

Chorus

[Str. 1]

> Sunbeam, of all that ever dawn upon   100
>   Our seven-gated Thebes the brightest ray,
>   O eye of golden day,
> How fair thy light o'er Dirce's fountain shone,
> Speeding upon their headlong homeward course,
> Far quicker than they came, the Argive force;
>   Putting to flight
> The argent shields, the host with scutcheons white.
> Against our land the proud invader came
> To vindicate fell Polyneices' claim.
>   Like to an eagle swooping low,
>   On pinions white as new fall'n snow.   110
> With clanging scream, a horsetail plume his crest,
> The aspiring lord of Argos onward pressed.

[Ant. 1]

> Hovering around our city walls he waits,
> His spearmen raven at our seven gates.
> But ere a torch our crown of towers could burn,

Ere they had tasted of our blood, they turn
Forced by the Dragon; in their rear
The din of Ares panic-struck they hear.
For Zeus who hates the braggart's boast
120 Beheld that gold-bespangled host;
As at the goal the paean they upraise,
He struck them with his forked lightning blaze.

[Str. 2]

To earth from earth rebounding, down he crashed;
The fire-brand from his impious hand was dashed,
As like a Bacchic reveler on he came,
Outbreathing hate and flame,
And tottered. Elsewhere in the field,
Here, there, great Area like a war-horse wheeled;
Beneath his car down thrust
130 Our foemen bit the dust.
Seven captains at our seven gates
Thundered; for each a champion waits,
Each left behind his armor bright,
Trophy for Zeus who turns the fight;
Save two alone, that ill-starred pair
One mother to one father bare,
Who lance in rest, one 'gainst the other
Drave, and both perished, brother slain by brother.

[Ant. 2]

Now Victory to Thebes returns again
140 And smiles upon her chariot-circled plain.

Now let feast and festal shout
Memories of war blot out.
Let us to the temples throng,
Dance and sing the live night long.
God of Thebes, lead thou the round.
Bacchus, shaker of the ground!
Let us end our revels here;
Lo! Creon our new lord draws near,
Crowned by this strange chance, our king.
150 What, I marvel, pondering?

Why this summons? Wherefore call
Us, his elders, one and all,
Bidding us with him debate,
On some grave concern of State?

[Enter Creon]

Creon

Elders, the gods have righted once again
Our storm-tossed ship of state, now safe in port.
But you by special summons I convened
As my most trusted councilors; first, because
I knew you loyal to Laius of old;
Again, when Oedipus restored our State,   160
Both while he ruled and when his rule was o'er,
Ye still were constant to the royal line.
Now that his two sons perished in one day,
Brother by brother murderously slain,
By right of kinship to the Princes dead,
I claim and hold the throne and sovereignty.
Yet 'tis no easy matter to discern
The temper of a man, his mind and will,
Till he be proved by exercise of power;
And in my case, if one who reigns supreme   170
Swerve from the highest policy, tongue-tied
By fear of consequence, that man I hold,
And ever held, the basest of the base.
And I condemn the man who sets his friend
Before his country. For myself, I call
To witness Zeus, whose eyes are everywhere,
If I perceive some mischievous design
To sap the State, I will not hold my tongue;
Nor would I reckon as my private friend
A public foe, well knowing that the State   180
Is the good ship that holds our fortunes all:
Farewell to friendship, if she suffers wreck.
Such is the policy by which I seek
To serve the Commons and conformably
I have proclaimed an edict as concerns
The sons of Oedipus; Eteocles

Who in his country's battle fought and fell,
The foremost champion—duly bury him
With all observances and ceremonies
190 That are the guerdon of the heroic dead.
But for the miscreant exile who returned
Minded in flames and ashes to blot out
His father's city and his father's gods,
And glut his vengeance with his kinsmen's blood,
Or drag them captive at his chariot wheels—
For Polyneices 'tis ordained that none
Shall give him burial or make mourn for him,
But leave his corpse unburied, to be meat
For dogs and carrion crows, a ghastly sight.
200 So am I purposed; never by my will
Shall miscreants take precedence of true men,
But all good patriots, alive or dead,
Shall be by me preferred and honored.

Chorus

Son of Menoeceus, thus thou will'st to deal
With him who loathed and him who loved our State.
Thy word is law; thou canst dispose of us
The living, as thou will'st, as of the dead.

Creon

See then ye execute what I ordain.

Chorus

On younger shoulders lay this grievous charge.

Creon

210 Fear not, I've posted guards to watch the corpse.

Chorus

What further duty would'st thou lay on us?

Creon

Not to connive at disobedience.

Chorus

> No man is mad enough to court his death.

Creon

> The penalty is death: yet hope of gain
> Hath lured men to their ruin oftentimes.

[Enter Guard]

Guard

> My lord, I will not make pretense to pant
> And puff as some light-footed messenger.
> In sooth my soul beneath its pack of thought
> Made many a halt and turned and turned again;
> For conscience plied her spur and curb by turns.   220
> "Why hurry headlong to thy fate, poor fool?"
> She whispered. Then again, "If Creon learn
> This from another, thou wilt rue it worse."
> Thus leisurely I hastened on my road;
> Much thought extends a furlong to a league.
> But in the end the forward voice prevailed,
> To face thee. I will speak though I say nothing.
> For plucking courage from despair methought,
> 'Let the worst hap, thou canst but meet thy fate.'

Creon

> What is thy news? Why this despondency?   230

Guard

> Let me premise a word about myself.
> I neither did the deed nor saw it done,
> Nor were it just that I should come to harm.

Creon

> Thou art good at parry, and canst fence about
> Some matter of grave import, as is plain.

325

Guard

The bearer of dread tidings needs must quake.

Creon

Then, sirrah, shoot thy bolt and get thee gone.

Guard

Well, it must out; the corpse is buried; someone
E'en now besprinkled it with thirsty dust,
240   Performed the proper ritual—and was gone.

Creon

What say'st thou? Who hath dared to do this thing?

Guard

I cannot tell, for there was ne'er a trace
Of pick or mattock—hard unbroken ground,
Without a scratch or rut of chariot wheels,
No sign that human hands had been at work.
When the first sentry of the morning watch
Gave the alarm, we all were terror-stricken.
The corpse had vanished, not interred in earth,
But strewn with dust, as if by one who sought
250   To avert the curse that haunts the unburied dead:
Of hound or ravening jackal, not a sign.
Thereat arose an angry war of words;
Guard railed at guard and blows were like to end it,
For none was there to part us, each in turn
Suspected, but the guilt brought home to none,
From lack of evidence. We challenged each
The ordeal, or to handle red-hot iron,
Or pass through fire, affirming on our oath
Our innocence—we neither did the deed
260   Ourselves, nor know who did or compassed it.
Our quest was at a standstill, when one spake
And bowed us all to earth like quivering reeds,
For there was no gainsaying him nor way
To escape perdition: Ye are bound to tell
The King, ye cannot hide it; so he spake.

And he convinced us all; so lots were cast,
And I, unlucky scapegoat, drew the prize.
So here I am unwilling and withal
Unwelcome; no man cares to hear ill news.

Chorus

I had misgivings from the first, my liege,   270
Of something more than natural at work.

Creon

O cease, you vex me with your babblement;
I am like to think you dote in your old age.
Is it not arrant folly to pretend
That gods would have a thought for this dead man?
Did they forsooth award him special grace,
And as some benefactor bury him,
Who came to fire their hallowed sanctuaries,
To sack their shrines, to desolate their land,
And scout their ordinances? Or perchance   280
The gods bestow their favors on the bad.
No! no! I have long noted malcontents
Who wagged their heads, and kicked against the yoke,
Misliking these my orders, and my rule.
'Tis they, I warrant, who suborned my guards
By bribes. Of evils current upon earth
The worst is money. Money 'tis that sacks
Cities, and drives men forth from hearth and home;
Warps and seduces native innocence,
And breeds a habit of dishonesty.   290
But they who sold themselves shall find their greed   *300*
Out-shot the mark, and rue it soon or late.
Yea, as I still revere the dread of Zeus,
By Zeus I swear, except ye find and bring
Before my presence here the very man
Who carried out this lawless burial,
Death for your punishment shall not suffice.
Hanged on a cross, alive ye first shall make
Confession of this outrage. This will teach you
What practices are like to serve your turn.   300
There are some villainies that bring no gain.

For by dishonesty the few may thrive,
The many come to ruin and disgrace.

Guard

May I not speak, or must I turn and go
Without a word?—

Creon

              Begone! canst thou not see
That e'en this question irks me?

Guard

                    Where, my lord?
Is it thy ears that suffer, or thy heart?

Creon

310   Why seek to probe and find the seat of pain?

Guard

I gall thine ears—this miscreant thy mind.

Creon

What an inveterate babbler! get thee gone!

Guard

Babbler perchance, but innocent of the crime.

Creon

Twice guilty, having sold thy soul for gain.

Guard

Alas! how sad when reasoners reason wrong.

Creon

Go, quibble with thy reason. If thou fail'st
To find these malefactors, thou shalt own
The wages of ill-gotten gains is death.

[Exit Creon]

Guard

> I pray he may be found. But caught or not
> (And fortune must determine that) thou never   320
> Shalt see me here returning; that is sure.
> For past all hope or thought I have escaped,
> And for my safety owe the gods much thanks.

Chorus

[Str. 1]

> Many wonders there be, but naught more wondrous than man;
> Over the surging sea, with a whitening south wind wan,
> Through the foam of the firth, man makes his perilous way;
> And the eldest of deities Earth that knows not toil nor decay
> Ever he furrows and scores, as his team, year in year out,
> With breed of the yoked horse, the ploughshare turneth about.

[Ant. 1]

> The light-witted birds of the air, the beasts of the weald and   330
> the wood
> He traps with his woven snare, and the brood of the briny
> flood.
> Master of cunning he: the savage bull, and the hart
> Who roams the mountain free, are tamed by his infinite art;
> And the shaggy rough-maned steed is broken to bear the bit.

[Str. 2]

> Speech and the wind-swift speed of counsel and civic wit,
> He hath learnt for himself all these; and the arrowy rain to fly
> And the nipping airs that freeze, 'neath the open winter sky.
> He hath provision for all: fell plague he hath learnt to endure; 340
> Safe whate'er may befall: yet for death he hath found no cure.

[Ant. 2]

> Passing the wildest flight thought are the cunning and skill,
> That guide man now to the light, but now to counsels of ill.

If he honors the laws of the land, and reveres the Gods of t|
State
Proudly his city shall stand; but a cityless outcast I rate
Whoso bold in his pride from the path of right doth depart;
Ne'er may I sit by his side, or share the thoughts of his heart|

350

What strange vision meets my eyes,
Fills me with a wild surprise?
Sure I know her, sure 'tis she,
The maid Antigone.
Hapless child of hapless sire,
Didst thou recklessly conspire,
Madly brave the King's decree?
Therefore are they haling thee?

[Enter Guard bringing Antigone]

Guard

> Here is the culprit taken in the act
> Of giving burial. But where's the King?

Chorus

> There from the palace he returns in time.

[Enter Creon]

Creon

360

> Why is my presence timely? What has chanced?

Guard

> No man, my lord, should make a vow, for if
> He ever swears he will not do a thing,
> His afterthoughts belie his first resolve.
> When from the hail-storm of thy threats I fled
> I sware thou wouldst not see me here again;
> But the wild rapture of a glad surprise
> Intoxicates, and so I'm here forsworn.
> And here's my prisoner, caught in the very act,

Decking the grave. No lottery this time;
This prize is mine by right of treasure-trove.   370
So take her, judge her, rack her, if thou wilt.
She's thine, my liege; but I may rightly claim
Hence to depart well quit of all these ills.   *400*

Creon

Say, how didst thou arrest the maid, and where?

Guard

Burying the man. There's nothing more to tell.

Creon

Hast thou thy wits? Or know'st thou what thou say'st?

Guard

I saw this woman burying the corpse
Against thy orders. Is that clear and plain?

Creon

But how was she surprised and caught in the act?

Guard

It happened thus. No sooner had we come,   380
Driven from thy presence by those awful threats,
Than straight we swept away all trace of dust,
And bared the clammy body. Then we sat
High on the ridge to windward of the stench,
While each man kept he fellow alert and rated
Roundly the sluggard if he chanced to nap.
So all night long we watched, until the sun
Stood high in heaven, and his blazing beams
Smote us. A sudden whirlwind then upraised
A cloud of dust that blotted out the sky,   390
And swept the plain, and stripped the woodlands bare,
And shook the firmament. We closed our eyes
And waited till the heaven-sent plague should pass.
At last it ceased, and lo! there stood this maid.

A piercing cry she uttered, sad and shrill,
As when the mother bird beholds her nest
Robbed of its nestlings; even so the maid
Wailed as she saw the body stripped and bare,
And cursed the ruffians who had done this deed.
400   Anon she gathered handfuls of dry dust,
Then, holding high a well-wrought brazen urn,
Thrice on the dead she poured a lustral stream.
We at the sight swooped down on her and seized
Our quarry. Undismayed she stood, and when
We taxed her with the former crime and this,
She disowned nothing. I was glad—and grieved;
For 'tis most sweet to 'scape oneself scot-free,
And yet to bring disaster to a friend
Is grievous. Take it all in all, I deem
410   A man's first duty is to serve himself.

Creon

Speak, girl, with head bent low and downcast eyes,
Does thou plead guilty or deny the deed?

Antigone

Guilty. I did it, I deny it not.

Creon [to Guard]

Sirrah, begone whither thou wilt, and thank
Thy luck that thou hast 'scaped a heavy charge.

[To Antigone]

Now answer this plain question, yes or no,
Wast thou acquainted with the interdict?

Antigone

I knew, all knew; how should I fail to know?

Creon

And yet wert bold enough to break the law?

Antigone

> Yea, for these laws were not ordained of Zeus, 420
> And she who sits enthroned with gods below,
> Justice, enacted not these human laws.
> Nor did I deem that thou, a mortal man,
> Could'st by a breath annul and override
> The immutable unwritten laws of Heaven.
> They were not born today nor yesterday;
> They die not; and none knoweth whence they sprang.
> I was not like, who feared no mortal's frown,
> To disobey these laws and so provoke
> The wrath of Heaven. I knew that I must die, 430
> E'en hadst thou not proclaimed it; and if death
> Is thereby hastened, I shall count it gain.
> For death is gain to him whose life, like mine,
> Is full of misery. Thus my lot appears
> Not sad, but blissful; for had I endured
> To leave my mother's son unburied there,
> I should have grieved with reason, but not now.
> And if in this thou judgest me a fool,
> Methinks the judge of folly's not acquit.

Chorus

> A stubborn daughter of a stubborn sire, 440
> This ill-starred maiden kicks against the pricks.

Creon

> Well, let her know the stubbornest of wills
> Are soonest bended, as the hardest iron,
> O'er-heated in the fire to brittleness,
> Flies soonest into fragments, shivered through.
> A snaffle curbs the fieriest steed, and he
> Who in subjection lives must needs be meek.
> But this proud girl, in insolence well-schooled,
> First overstepped the established law, and then—
> A second and worse act of insolence— 450
> She boasts and glories in her wickedness.
> Now if she thus can flout authority
> Unpunished, I am woman, she the man.

But though she be my sister's child or nearer
Of kin than all who worship at my hearth,
Nor she nor yet her sister shall escape
The utmost penalty, for both I hold,
As arch-conspirators, of equal guilt.
Bring forth the older; even now I saw her
460   Within the palace, frenzied and distraught.
The workings of the mind discover oft
Dark deeds in darkness schemed, before the act.
More hateful still the miscreant who seeks
When caught, to make a virtue of a crime.

Antigone

Would'st thou do more than slay thy prisoner?

Creon

Not I, thy life is mine, and that's enough.

Antigone

Why dally then? To me no word of thine
500   Is pleasant: God forbid it e'er should please;
Nor am I more acceptable to thee.
470   And yet how otherwise had I achieved
A name so glorious as by burying
A brother? so my townsmen all would say,
Where they not gagged by terror, manifold
A king's prerogatives, and not the least
That all his acts and all his words are law.

Creon

Of all these Thebans none so deems but thou.

Antigone

These think as I, but bate their breath to thee.

Creon

Hast thou no shame to differ from all these?

Antigone

> To reverence kith and kin can bring no shame.

Creon

> Was his dead foeman not thy kinsman too? 480

Antigone

> One mother bare them and the self-same sire.

Creon

> Why cast a slur on one by honoring one?

Antigone

> The dead man will not bear thee out in this.

Creon

> Surely, if good and evil fare alive.

Antigone

> The slain man was no villain but a brother.

Creon

> The patriot perished by the outlaw's brand.

Antigone

> Nevertheless the realms below these rites require.

Creon

> Not that the base should fare as do the brave.

Antigone

> Who knows if this world's crimes are virtues there?

Creon

> Not even death can make a foe a friend. 490

Antigone

> My nature is for mutual love, not hate.

Creon

> Die then, and love the dead if thou must;
> No woman shall be the master while I live.

[Enter Ismene]

Chorus

> Lo from out the palace gate,
> Weeping o'er her sister's fate,
> Comes Ismene; see her brow,
> Once serene, beclouded now,
> See her beauteous face o'erspread
> With a flush of angry red.

Creon

500
> Woman, who like a viper unperceived
> Didst harbor in my house and drain my blood,
> Two plagues I nurtured blindly, so it proved,
> To sap my throne. Say, didst thou too abet
> This crime, or dost abjure all privity?

Ismene

> I did the deed, if she will have it so,
> And with my sister claim to share the guilt.

Antigone

> That were unjust. Thou would'st not act with me
> At first, and I refused thy partnership.

Ismene

510
> But now thy bark is stranded, I am bold
> To claim my share as partner in the loss.

Antigone

> Who did the deed the under-world knows well:
> A friend in word is never friend of mine.

Ismene

> O sister, scorn me not, let me but share
> Thy work of piety, and with thee die.

Antigone

> Claim not a work in which thou hadst no hand;
> One death sufficeth. Wherefore should'st thou die?

Ismene

> What would life profit me bereft of thee?

Antigone

> Ask Creon, he's thy kinsman and best friend.

Ismene

> Why taunt me? Find'st thou pleasure in these gibes?

Antigone

> 'Tis a sad mockery, if indeed I mock.

520

Ismene

> O say if I can help thee even now.

Antigone

> No, save thyself; I grudge not thy escape.

Ismene

> Is e'en this boon denied, to share thy lot?

Antigone

> Yea, for thou chosed'st life, and I to die.

Ismene

> Thou canst not say that I did not protest.

Antigone

> Well, some approved thy wisdom, others mine.

Ismene

But now we stand convicted, both alike.

Antigone

Fear not; thou livest, I died long ago
Then when I gave my life to save the dead.

Creon

530 Both maids, methinks, are crazed. One suddenly
Has lost her wits, the other was born mad.

Ismene

Yea, so it falls, sire, when misfortune comes,
The wisest even lose their mother wit.

Creon

I' faith thy wit forsook thee when thou mad'st
Thy choice with evil-doers to do ill.

Ismene

What life for me without my sister here?

Creon

Say not thy sister here: thy sister's dead.

Ismene

What, wilt thou slay thy own son's plighted bride?

Creon

Aye, let him raise him seed from other fields.

Ismene

540 No new espousal can be like the old.

Creon

A plague on trulls who court and woo our sons.

Antigone

O Haemon, how thy sire dishonors thee!

Creon

A plague on thee and thy accursed bride!

Chorus

What, wilt thou rob thine own son of his bride?

Creon

'Tis death that bars this marriage, not his sire.

Chorus

So her death-warrant, it would seem, is sealed.

Creon

By you, as first by me; off with them, guards,
And keep them close. Henceforward let them learn
To live as women use, not roam at large.
For e'en the bravest spirits run away   550
When they perceive death pressing on life's heels.

Chorus

[Str. 1]

Thrice blest are they who never tasted pain!
    If once the curse of Heaven attaint a race,
    The infection lingers on and speeds apace,
Age after age, and each the cup must drain.

So when Etesian blasts from Thrace downpour
    Sweep o'er the blackening main and whirl to land
    From Ocean's cavernous depths his ooze and sand,
Billow on billow thunders on the shore.

[Ant. 1]

On the Labdacidae I see descending   560

Woe upon woe; from days of old some god
Laid on the race a malison, and his rod
Scourges each age with sorrows never ending.

The light that dawned upon its last born son
Is vanished, and the bloody axe of Fate
600   Has felled the goodly tree that blossomed late.
O Oedipus, by reckless pride undone!

[Str. 2]

Thy might, O Zeus, what mortal power can quell?
Not sleep that lays all else beneath its spell,
570   Nor moons that never tire: untouched by Time,
Throned in the dazzling light
That crowns Olympus' height,
Thou reignest King, omnipotent, sublime.

Past, present, and to be,
All bow to thy decree,
All that exceeds the mean by Fate
Is punished, Love or Hate.

[Ant. 2]

Hope flits about never-wearying wings;
Profit to some, to some light loves she brings,
580   But no man knoweth how her gifts may turn,
Till 'neath his feet the treacherous ashes burn.
Sure 'twas a sage inspired that spake this word;
If evil good appear
To any, Fate is near;
And brief the respite from her flaming sword.

Hither comes in angry mood
Haemon, latest of thy brood;
Is it for his bride he's grieved,
Or her marriage-bed deceived,
590   Doth he make his mourn for thee,
Maid forlorn, Antigone?

[Enter Haemon]

Creon

Soon shall we know, better than seer can tell.
Learning ay fixed decree about thy bride,
Thou mean'st not, son, to rave against thy sire?
Know'st not whate'er we do is done in love?

Haemon

O father, I am thine, and I will take
Thy wisdom as the helm to steer withal.
Therefore no wedlock shall by me be held
More precious than thy loving goverance.

Creon

Well spoken: so right-minded sons should feel,   600
In all deferring to a father's will.
For 'tis the hope of parents they may rear
A brood of sons submissive, keen to avenge
Their father's wrongs, and count his friends their own.
But who begets unprofitable sons,
He verily breeds trouble for himself,
And for his foes much laughter. Son, be warned
And let no woman fool away thy wits.
Ill fares the husband mated with a shrew,
And her embraces very soon wax cold.   610
For what can wound so surely to the quick
As a false friend? So spew and cast her off,
Bid her go find a husband with the dead.
For since I caught her openly rebelling,
Of all my subjects the one malcontent,
I will not prove a traitor to the State.
She surely dies. Go, let her, if she will,
Appeal to Zeus the God of Kindred, for
If thus I nurse rebellion in my house,
Shall not I foster mutiny without?   620
For whoso rules his household worthily,
Will prove in civic matters no less wise.
But he who overbears the laws, or thinks
To overrule his rulers, such a one
I never will allow. Whome'er the State
Appoints must be obeyed in everything,

But small and great, just and unjust alike.
I warrant such a one in either case
Would shine, as King or subject; such a man
630 Would in the storm of battle stand his ground,
A comrade leal and true; but Anarchy—
What evils are not wrought by Anarchy!
She ruins States, and overthrows the home,
She dissipates and routs the embattled host;
While discipline preserves the ordered ranks.
Therefore we must maintain authority
And yield to title to a woman's will.
Better, if needs be, men should cast us out
Than hear it said, a woman proved his match.

Chorus

640 To me, unless old age have dulled wits,
Thy words appear both reasonable and wise.

Haemon

Father, the gods implant in mortal men
Reason, the choicest gift bestowed by heaven.
'Tis not for me to say thou errest, nor
Would I arraign thy wisdom, if I could;
And yet wise thoughts may come to other men
And, as thy son, it falls to me to mark
The acts, the words, the comments of the crowd.
The commons stand in terror of thy frown,
650 And dare not utter aught that might offend,
But I can overhear their muttered plaints,
Know how the people mourn this maiden doomed
For noblest deeds to die the worst of deaths.
When her own brother slain in battle lay
Unsepulchered, she suffered not his corpse
To lie for carrion birds and dogs to maul:
Should not her name (they cry) be writ in gold?
700 Such the low murmurings that reach my ear.
O father, nothing is by me more prized
660 Than thy well-being, for what higher good
Can children covet than their sire's fair fame,
As fathers too take pride in glorious sons?

Therefore, my father, cling not to one mood,
And deemed not thou art right, all others wrong.
For whoso thinks that wisdom dwells with him,
That he alone can speak or think aright,
Such oracles are empty breath when tried.
The wisest man will let himself be swayed
By others' wisdom and relax in time.
See how the trees beside a stream in flood   670
Save, if they yield to force, each spray unharmed,
But by resisting perish root and branch.
The mariner who keeps his mainsheet taut,
And will not slacken in the gale, is like
To sail with thwarts reversed, keel uppermost.
Relent then and repent thee of thy wrath;
For, if one young in years may claim some sense,
I'll say 'tis best of all to be endowed
With absolute wisdom; but, if that's denied,
(And nature takes not readily that ply)   680
Next wise is he who lists to sage advice.

Chorus

If he says aught in season, heed him, King.

[To Haemon]

Heed thou thy sire too; both have spoken well.

Creon

What, would you have us at our age be schooled,
Lessoned in prudence by a beardless boy?

Haemon

I plead for justice, father, nothing more.
Weigh me upon my merit, not my years.

Creon

Strange merit this to sanction lawlessness!

Haemon

For evil-doers I would urge no plea.

Creon

690   Is not this maid an arrant law-breaker?

Haemon

The Theban commons with one voice say, No.

Creon

What, shall the mob dictate my policy?

Haemon

'Tis thou, methinks, who speakest like a boy.

Creon

Am I to rule for others, or myself?

Haemon

A State for one man is no State at all.

Creon

The State is his who rules it, so 'tis held.

Haemon

As monarch of a desert thou wouldst shine.

Creon

This boy, methinks, maintains the woman's cause.

Haemon

If thou be'st woman, yes. My thought's for thee.

Creon

700   O reprobate, would'st wrangle with thy sire?

Haemon

Because I see thee wrongfully perverse.

Creon

And am I wrong, if I maintain my rights?

Haemon

> Talk not of rights; thou spurn'st the due of Heaven

Creon

> O heart corrupt, a woman's minion thou!

Haemon

> Slave to dishonor thou wilt never find me.

Creon

> Thy speech at least was all a plea for her.

Haemon

> And thee and me, and for the gods below.

Creon

> Living the maid shall never be thy bride.

Haemon

> So she shall die, but one will die with her.

Creon

> Hast come to such a pass as threaten me?   710

Haemon

> What threat is this, vain counsels to reprove?

Creon

> Vain fool to instruct thy betters; thou shall rue it.

Haemon

> Wert not my father, I had said thou err'st.

Creon

> Play not the spaniel, thou a woman's slave.

Haemon

> When thou dost speak, must no man make reply?

345

Creon

This passes bounds. By heaven, thou shalt not rate
And jeer and flout me with impunity.
Off with the hateful thing that she may die
At once, beside her bridegroom, in his sight.

Haemon

720

Think not that in my sight the maid shall die,
Or by my side; never shalt thou again
Behold my face hereafter. Go, consort
With friends who like a madman for their mate.

[Exit Haemon]

Chorus

Thy son has gone, my liege, in angry haste.
Fell is the wrath of youth beneath a smart.

Creon

Let him go vent his fury like a fiend:
These sisters twain he shall not save from death.

Chorus

Surely, thou meanest not to slay them both?

Creon

730

I stand corrected; only her who touched
The body.

Chorus

And what death is she to die?

Creon

She shall be taken to some desert place
By man untrod, and in a rock-hewn cave,
With food no more than to avoid the taint
That homicide might bring on all the State,

346

Buried alive. There let her call in aid
The King of Death, the one god she reveres,
Or learn too late a lesson learnt at last:
'Tis labor lost, to reverence the dead.

Chorus

[Str.]

Love resistless in fight, all yield at a glance of thine eye,   740
Love who pillowed all night on a maiden's cheek dost lie,
Over the upland holds. Shall mortals not yield to thee?

[Ant.]

Mad are thy subjects all, and even the wisest heart
Straight to folly will fall, at a touch of thy poisoned dart.
Thou didst kindle the strife, this feud of kinsman with kin,
By the eyes of a winsome wife, and the yearning her heart to
win.
For as her consort still, enthroned with Justice above,
Thou bendest man to thy will, O all invincible Love.   800

Lo I myself am borne aside,   750
From Justice, as I view this bride.
(O sight an eye in tears to drown)
    Antigone, so young, so fair,
    Thus hurried down
Death's bower with the dead to share.

Antigone

[Str. 1]

Friends, countrymen, my last farewell I make;
    My journey's done.
One last fond, lingering, longing look I take
    At the bright sun.
For Death who puts to sleep both young and old   760
    Hales my young life,
And beckons me to Acheron's dark fold,
    An unwed wife.

347

No youths have sung the marriage song for me,
    My bridal bed
No maids have strewn with flowers from the lea,
    'Tis Death I wed.

Chorus

    But bethink thee, thou art sped,
    Great and glorious, to the dead.
770   Thou the sword's edge hast not tasted,
    No disease thy frame hath wasted.
    Freely thou alone shalt go
    Living to the dead below.

Antigone

[Ant. 1]

    Nay, but the piteous tale I've heard men tell
      Of Tantalus' doomed child,
    Chained upon Siphylus' high rocky fell,
      That clung like ivy wild,
    Drenched by the pelting rain and whirling snow,
      Left there to pine,
780   While on her frozen breast the tears aye flow—
      Her fate is mine.

Chorus

    She was sprung of gods, divine,
    Mortals we of mortal line.
    Like renown with gods to gain
    Recompenses all thy pain.
    Take this solace to thy tomb
    Hers in life and death thy doom.

Antigone

[Str. 2]

    Alack, alack! Ye mock me. Is it meet
      Thus to insult me living, to my face?
790   Cease, by our country's altars I entreat,

Ye lordly rulers of a lordly race.
O fount of Dirce, wood-embowered plain
  Where Theban chariots to victory speed,
Mark ye the cruel laws that now have wrought my bane,
  The friends who show no pity in my need!
Was ever fate like mine? O monstrous doom,
  Within a rock-built prison sepulchered,
To fade and wither in a living tomb,
  An alien midst the living and the dead.

Chorus

[Str. 3]

In thy boldness over-rash   800
Madly thou thy foot didst dash
'Gainst high Justice' altar stair.
Thou a father's guild dost bear.

Antigone

[Ant. 2]

At this thou touchest my most poignant pain,
  My ill-starred father's piteous disgrace,
The taint of blood, the hereditary stain,
  That clings to all of Labdacus' famed race.
Woe worth the monstrous marriage-bed where lay
  A mother with the son her womb had borne,
Therein I was conceived, woe worth the day,   810
  Fruit of incestuous sheets, a maid forlorn,
And now I pass, accursed and unwed,
  To meet them as an alien there below;
And thee, O brother, in marriage ill-bestead,
  'Twas thy dead hand that dealt me this death-blow.

Chorus

Religion has her chains, 'tis true,
Let rite be paid when rites are due.
Yet is it ill to disobey
The powers who hold by might the sway.

820

Thou hast withstood authority,
A self-willed rebel, thou must die.

Antigone

Unwept, unwed, unfriended, hence I go,
No longer may I see the day's bright eye;
Not one friend left to share my bitter woe,
And o'er my ashes heave one passing sigh.

Creon

If wail and lamentation aught availed
To stave off death, I trow they'd never end.
Away with her, and having walled her up
In a rock-vaulted tomb, as I ordained,

830

Leave her alone at liberty to die,
Or, if she choose, to live in solitude,
The tomb her dwelling. We in either case
Are guiltless as concerns this maiden's blood,
Only on earth no lodging shall she find.

Antigone

O grave, O bridal bower, O prison house
Hewn from the rock, my everlasting home,
Whither I go to join the mighty host
Of kinsfolk, Persephassa's guests long dead,
The last of all, of all more miserable,

840

I pass, my destined span of years cut short.
And yet good hope is mine that I shall find
A welcome from my sire, a welcome too,
From thee, my mother, and my brother dear;

900

From with these hands, I laved and decked your limbs
In death, and poured libations on your grave.
And last, my Polyneices, unto thee
I paid due rites, and this my recompense!
Yet am I justified in wisdom's eyes.
For even had it been some child of mine,

850

Or husband mouldering in death's decay,
I had not wrought this deed despite the State.
What is the law I call in aid? 'Tis thus
I argue. Had it been a husband dead

I might have wed another, and have borne
Another child, to take the dead child's place.
But, now my sire and mother both are dead,
No second brother can be born for me.
Thus by the law of conscience I was led
To honor thee, dear brother, and was judged
By Creon guilty of a heinous crime.   860
And now he drags me like a criminal,
A bride unwed, amerced of marriage-song
And marriage-bed and joys of motherhood,
By friends deserted to a living grave.
What ordinance of heaven have I transgressed?
Hereafter can I look to any god
For succor, call on any man for help?
Alas, my piety is impious deemed.
Well, if such justice is approved of heaven,
I shall be taught by suffering my sin;   870
But if the sin is theirs, O may they suffer
No worse ills than the wrongs they do to me.

Chorus

The same ungovernable will
Drives like a gale the maiden still.

Creon

Therefore, my guards who let her stay
Shall smart full sore for their delay.

Antigone

Ah, woe is me! This word I hear
Brings death most near.

Chorus

I have no comfort. What he saith,
Portends no other thing than death.   880

Antigone

My fatherland, city of Thebes divine,
Ye gods of Thebes whence sprang my line,

351

Look, puissant lords of Thebes, on me;
The last of all your royal house ye see.
Martyred by men of sin, undone.
Such meed my piety hath won.

[Exit Antigone]

Chorus

[Str. 1]

Like to thee that maiden bright,
    Danae, in her brass-bound tower,
Once exchanged the glad sunlight
890   For a cell, her bridal bower.
And yet she sprang of royal line,
    My child, like thine,
    And nursed the seed
    By her conceived
Of Zeus descending in a golden shower.
Strange are the ways of Fate, her power
Nor wealth, nor arms withstand, nor tower;
Nor brass-prowed ships, that breast the sea
    From Fate can flee.

[Ant. 1]

900   Thus Dryas' child, the rash Edonian King,
For words of high disdain
Did Bacchus to a rocky dungeon bring,
To cool the madness of a fevered brain.
    His frenzy passed,
    He learnt at last
'Twas madness gibes against a god to fling.
For once he fain had quenched the Maenad's fire;
And of the tuneful Nine provoked the ire.

[Str. 2]

910   By the Iron Rocks that guard the double main,
    On Bosporus' lone strand,

352

Where stretcheth Salmydessus' plain
   In the wild Thracian land,
There on his borders Ares witnessed
   The vengeance by a jealous step-dame ta'en
The gore that trickled from a spindle red,
   The sightless orbits of her step-sons twain.

[Ant. 2]

Wasting away they mourned their piteous doom,
The blasted issue of their mother's womb.
But she her lineage could trace
   To great Erechtheus' race;   920
Daughter of Boreas in her sire's vast caves
   Reared, where the tempest raves,
Swift as his horses o'er the hills she sped;
A child of gods; yet she, my child, like thee,
   By Destiny
That knows not death nor age—she too was vanquished.

[Enter Teiresias and Boy]

Teiresias

Princes of Thebes, two wayfarers as one,
Having betwixt us eyes for one, we are here.
The blind man cannot move without a guide.

Creon

What tidings, old Teiresias?   930

Teiresias

        I will tell thee;
And when thou hearest thou must heed the seer.

Creon

Thus far I ne'er have disobeyed thy rede.

Teiresias

So hast thou steered the ship of State aright.

Creon

I know it, and I gladly own my debt.

Teiresias

Bethink thee that thou treadest once again
The razor edge of peril.

Creon

What is this?
Thy words inspire a dread presentiment.

Teiresias

940

The divination of my arts shall tell.
Sitting upon my throne of augury,
As is my wont, where every fowl of heaven

1000

Find harborage, upon mine ears was borne
A jargon strange of twitterings, hoots, and screams;
So knew I that each bird at the other tare
With bloody talons, for the whirr of wings
Could signify naught else. Perturbed in soul,
I straight essayed the sacrifice by fire
On blazing altars, but the God of Fire

950

Came not in flame, and from the thigh bones dripped
And sputtered in the ashes a foul ooze;
Gall-bladders cracked and spurted up: the fat
Melted and fell and left the thigh bones bare.
Such are the signs, taught by this lad, I read—
As I guide others, so the boy guides me—
The frustrate signs of oracles grown dumb.
O King, thy willful temper ails the State,
For all our shrines and altars are profaned
By what has filled the maw of dogs and crows,

960

The flesh of Oedipus' unburied son.
Therefore the angry gods abominate
Our litanies and our burnt offerings;
Therefore no birds trill out a happy note,
Gorged with the carnival of human gore.
O ponder this, my son. To err is common
To all men, but the man who having erred

354

Hugs not his errors, but repents and seeks
The cure, is not a wastrel nor unwise.
No fool, the saw goes, like the obstinate fool.
Let death disarm thy vengeance. O forbear   970
To vex the dead. What glory wilt thou win
By slaying twice the slain? I mean thee well;
Counsel's most welcome if I promise gain.

Creon

Old man, ye all let fly at me your shafts
Like anchors at a target; yea, ye set
Your soothsayer on me. Peddlers are ye all
And I the merchandise ye buy and sell.
Go to, and make your profit where ye will,
Silver of Sardis change for gold of Ind;
Ye will not purchase this man's burial,   980
Not though the winged ministers of Zeus
Should bear him in their talons to his throne;
Not e'en in awe of prodigy so dire
Would I permit his burial, for I know
No human soilure can assail the gods;
This too I know, Teiresias, dire's the fall
Of craft and cunning when it tries to gloss
Foul treachery with fair words for filthy gain.

Teiresias

Alas! doth any know and lay to heart—

Creon

Is this the prelude to some hackneyed saw?   990

Teiresias

How far good counsel is the best of goods?

Creon

True, as unwisdom is the worst of ills.

Teiresias

Thou art infected with that ill thyself.

Creon

    I will not bandy insults with thee, seer.

Teiresias

    And yet thou say'st my prophesies are frauds.

Creon

    Prophets are all a money-getting tribe.

Teiresias

    And kings are all a lucre-loving race.

Creon

    Dost know at whom thou glancest, me thy lord?

Teiresias

    Lord of the State and savior, thanks to me.

Creon

1000   Skilled prophet art thou, but to wrong inclined.

Teiresias

    Take heed, thou wilt provoke me to reveal
    The mystery deep hidden in my breast.

Creon

    Say on, but see it be not said for gain.

Teiresias

    Such thou, methinks, till now hast judged my words.

Creon

    Be sure thou wilt not traffic on my wits.

Teiresias

    Know then for sure, the coursers of the sun
    Not many times shall run their race, before

Thou shalt have given the fruit of thine own loins
In quittance of thy murder, life for life;
For that thou hast entombed a living soul, 1010
And sent below a denizen of earth,
And wronged the nether gods by leaving here
A corpse unlaved, unwept, unsepulchered.
Herein thou hast no part, nor e'en the gods
In heaven; and thou usurp'st a power not thine.
For this the avenging spirits of Heaven and Hell
Who dog the steps of sin are on thy trail:
What these have suffered thou shalt suffer too.
And now, consider whether bought by gold
I prophesy. For, yet a little while, 1020
And sound of lamentation shall be heard,
Of men and women through thy desolate halls;
And all thy neighbor States are leagues to avenge
Their mangled warriors who have found a grave
I' the maw of wolf or hound, or winged bird
That flying homewards taints their city's air.
These are the shafts, that like a bowman I
Provoked to anger, loosen at thy breast,
Unerring, and their smart thou shalt not shun.
Boy, lead me home, that he may vent his spleen 1030
On younger men, and learn to curb his tongue
With gentler manners than his present mood.

[Exit Teiresias]

Chorus

My liege, that man hath gone, foretelling woe.
And, O believe me, since these grizzled locks
Were like the raven, never have I known
The prophet's warning to the State to fail.

Creon

I know it too, and it perplexes me.
To yield is grievous, but the obstinate soul
That fights with Fate, is smitten grievously.

Chorus

1040

Son of Menoeceus, list to good advice.

Creon

What should I do. Advise me. I will heed.

Chorus

1100

Go, free the maiden from her rocky cell;
And for the unburied outlaw build a tomb.

Creon

Is that your counsel? You would have me yield?

Chorus

Yea, king, this instant. Vengeance of the gods
Is swift to overtake the impenitent.

Creon

Ah! what a wrench it is to sacrifice
My heart's resolve; but Fate is ill to fight.

Chorus

Go, trust not others. Do it quick thyself.

Creon

1050

I go hot-foot. Bestir ye one and all,
My henchmen! Get ye axes! Speed away
To yonder eminence! I too will go,
For all my resolution this way sways.
'Twas I that bound, I too will set her free.
Almost I am persuaded it is best
To keep through life the law ordained of old.

[Exit Creon]

Chorus

[Str. 1]

358

Thou by many names adored,
    Child of Zeus the God of thunder,
    Of a Theban bride the wonder,
Fair Italia's guardian lord;   1060

In the deep-embosomed glades
    Of the Eleusinian Queen
Haunt of revelers, men and maids,
    Dionysus, thou art seen.

Where Ismenus rolls his waters,
    Where the Dragon's teeth were sown,
Where the Bacchanals thy daughters
    Round thee roam,
    There thy home;
Thebes, O Bacchus, is thine own.   1070

[Ant. 1]

Thee on the two-crested rock
    Lurid-flaming torches see;
Where Corisian maidens flock,
    Thee the springs of Castaly.

By Nysa's bastion ivy-clad,
By shores with clustered vineyards glad,
There to thee the hymn rings out,
And through our streets we Thebans shout,
    All call to thee
    Evoe, Evoe!   1080

[Str. 2]

Oh, as thou lov'st this city best of all,
To thee, and to thy Mother levin-stricken,
In our dire need we call;
Thou see'st with what a plague our townsfolk sicken.
    Thy ready help we crave,
Whether adown Parnassian heights descending,
Or o'er the roaring straits thy swift way wending,
    Save us, O save!

[Ant. 2]

Brightest of all the orbs that breathe forth light,
1090   Authentic son of Zeus, immortal king,
Leader of all the voices of the night,
    Come, and thy train of Thyiads with thee bring,
    Thy maddened rout
Who dance before thee all night long, and shout,
    Thy handmaids we,
    Evoe, Evoe!

[Enter Messenger]

Messenger

Attend all ye who dwell beside the halls
Of Cadmus and Amphion. No man's life
As of one tenor would I praise or blame,
1100 For Fortune with a constant ebb and rise
Casts down and raises high and low alike,
And none can read a mortal's horoscope.
Take Creon; he, methought, if any man,
Was enviable. He had saved this land
Of Cadmus from our enemies and attained
A monarch's powers and ruled the state supreme,
While a right noble issue crowned his bliss.
Now all is gone and wasted, for a life
Without life's joys I count a living death.
1110 You'll tell me he has ample store of wealth,
The pomp and circumstance of kings; but if
These give no pleasure, all the rest I count
The shadow of a shade, nor would I weigh
His wealth and power 'gainst a dram of joy.

Chorus

What fresh woes bring'st thou to the royal house?

Messenger

Both dead, and they who live deserve to die.

Chorus

> Who is the slayer, who the victim? speak.

Messenger

> Haemon; his blood shed by no stranger hand.

Chorus

> What mean ye? by his father's or his own?

Messenger

> His own; in anger for his father's crime.   1120

Chorus

> O prophet, what thou spakest comes to pass.

Messenger

> So stands the case; now 'tis for you to act.

Chorus

> Lo! from the palace gates I see approaching
> Creon's unhappy wife, Eurydice.
> Comes she by chance or learning her son's fate?

[Enter Eurydice]

Eurydice

> Ye men of Thebes, I overheard your talk.
> As I passed out to offer up my prayer
> To Pallas, and was drawing back the bar
> To open wide the door, upon my ears
> There broke a wail that told of household woe   1130
> Stricken with terror in my handmaids' arms
> I fell and fainted. But repeat your tale
> To one not unacquainted with misery.

Messenger

> Dear mistress, I was there and will relate

The perfect truth, omitting not one word.
Why should we gloze and flatter, to be proved
Liars hereafter? Truth is ever best.
Well, in attendance on my liege, your lord,
I crossed the plain to its utmost margin, where
1140 The corpse of Polyneices, gnawn and mauled,
Was lying yet. We offered first a prayer
To Pluto and the goddess of cross-ways,
1200 With contrite hearts, to deprecate their ire.
Then laved with lustral waves the mangled corpse,
Laid it on fresh-lopped branches, lit a pyre,
And to his memory piled a mighty mound
Of mother earth. Then to the caverned rock,
The bridal chamber of the maid and Death,
We sped, about to enter. But a guard
1150 Heard from that godless shrine a far shrill wail,
And ran back to our lord to tell the news.
But as he nearer drew a hollow sound
Of lamentation to the King was borne.
He groaned and uttered then this bitter plaint:
"Am I a prophet? miserable me!
Is this the saddest path I ever trod?
'Tis my son's voice that calls me. On press on,
My henchmen, haste with double speed to the tomb
Where rocks down-torn have made a gap, look in
1160 And tell me if in truth I recognize
The voice of Haemon or am heaven-deceived."
So at the bidding of our distraught lord
We looked, and in the cavern's vaulted gloom
I saw the maiden lying strangled there,
A noose of linen twined about her neck;
And hard beside her, clasping her cold form,
Her lover lay bewailing his dead bride
Death-wedded, and his father's cruelty.
When the King saw him, with a terrible groan
1170 He moved towards him, crying, "O my son
What hast thou done? What ailed thee? What mischance
Has reft thee of thy reason? O come forth,
Come forth, my son; thy father supplicates."
But the son glared at him with tiger eyes,
Spat in his face, and then, without a word,

362

Drew his two-hilted sword and smote, but missed
His father flying backwards. Then the boy,
Wroth with himself, poor wretch, incontinent
Fell on his sword and drove it through his side
Home, but yet breathing clasped in his lax arms   1180
The maid, her pallid cheek incarnadined
With his expiring gasps. So there they lay
Two corpses, one in death. His marriage rites
Are consummated in the halls of Death:
A witness that of ills whate'er befall
Mortals' unwisdom is the worst of all.

[Exit Eurydice]

Chorus

What makest thou of this? The Queen has gone
Without a word importing good or ill.

Messenger

I marvel too, but entertain good hope.
'Tis that she shrinks in public to lament   1190
Her son's sad ending, and in privacy
Would with her maidens mourn a private loss.
Trust me, she is discreet and will not err.

Chorus

I know not, but strained silence, so I deem,
Is no less ominous than excessive grief.

Messenger

Well, let us to the house and solve our doubts,
Whether the tumult of her heart conceals
Some fell design. It may be thou art right:
Unnatural silence signifies no good.

Chorus
                                                         1200
Lo! the King himself appears.
Evidence he with him bears
'Gainst himself (ah me! I quake

363

'Gainst a king such charge to make)
But all must own,
The guilt is his and his alone.

[Enter Creon]

Creon

[Str. 1]

Woe for sin of minds perverse,
Deadly fraught with mortal curse.
Behold us slain and slayers, all akin.
Woe for my counsel dire, conceived in sin.
1210   Alas, my son,
             Life scarce begun,
             Thou wast undone.
The fault was mine, mine only, O my son!

Chorus

Too late thou seemest to perceive the truth.

Creon

[Str. 2]

By sorrow schooled. Heavy the hand of God,
Thorny and rough the paths my feet have trod,
Humbled my pride, my pleasure turned to pain;
Poor mortals, how we labor all in vain!

[Enter Second Messenger]

Second Messenger

Sorrows are thine, my lord, and more to come,
1220   One lying at thy feet, another yet
          More grievous waits thee, when thou comest home.

Creon

What woe is lacking to my tale of woes?

Second Messenger

> Thy wife, the mother of thy dead son here,
> Lies stricken by a fresh inflicted blow.

Creon

[Ant. 1]

> How bottomless the pit!
>   Does claim me too, O Death?
>   What is this word he saith,
> This woeful messenger? Say, is it fit
> To slay anew a man already slain?
>   Is Death at work again,   1230
> Stroke upon stroke, first son, then mother slain?

Chorus

> Look for thyself. She lies for all to view.

Creon

[Ant. 2]

> Alas! another added woe I see.
> What more remains to crown my agony?
> A minute past I clasped a lifeless son,
> And now another victim Death hath won.
> Unhappy mother, most unhappy son!   *1300*

Second Messenger

> Beside the altar on a keen-edged sword
> She fell and closed her eyes in night, but erst
> She mourned for Megareus who nobly died   1240
> Long since, then for her son; with her last breath
> She cursed thee, the slayer of her child.

Creon

[Str. 3]

> I shudder with affright

365

O for a two-edged sword to slay outright
A wretch like me,
Made one with misery.

Second Messenger

'Tis true that thou wert charged by the dead Queen
As author of both deaths, hers and her son's.

Creon

In what wise was her self-destruction wrought?

Second Messenger

1250
Hearing the loud lament above her son
With her own hand she stabbed herself to the heart.

Creon

[Str. 4]

I am the guilty cause. I did the deed,
Thy murderer. Yea, I guilty plead.
My henchmen, lead me hence, away, away,
A cipher, less than nothing; no delay!

Chorus

Well said, if in disaster aught is well
His past endure demand the speediest cure.

Creon

[Ant. 3]

Come, Fate, a friend at need,
Come with all speed!
1260
Come, my best friend,
And speed my end!
Away, away!
Let me not look upon another day!

Chorus

This for the morrow; to us are present needs

That they whom it concerns must take in hand.

Creon

I join your prayer that echoes my desire.

Chorus

O pray not, prayers are idle; from the doom
Of fate for mortals refuge is there none.

Creon

[Ant. 4]

Away with me, a worthless wretch who slew
Unwitting thee, my son, thy mother too.   1270
Whither to turn I know now; every way
      Leads but astray,
And on my head I feel the heavy weight
      Of crushing Fate.

Chorus

Of happiness the chiefest part
      Is a wise heart:
And to defraud the gods is aught
      With peril's fraught.
Swelling words of high-flown might
Mightily the gods do smite.   1280
Chastisement for errors past
Wisdom brings to age at last.

The End

EURIPIDES

Euripides
•
The Trojan Women

Translated by Gilbert Murray

Dramatis Personae

POSEIDON

PALLAS ATHENA

HECUBA
Queen of Troy, wife of Priam,
mother of Hector and Paris.

CASSANDRA
daughter of Hecuba, a prophetess.

ANDROMACHE
wife of Hector, Prince of Troy.

HELEN
wife of Menelaus, King of Sparta;
carried off by Paris, Prince of Troy.

TALTHYBIUS
Herald of the Greeks.

MENELAUS
King of Sparta and, together with his brother
Agamemnon, General of the Greeks.

SOLDIERS
Attendant on Talthybius and Menelaus.

CHORUS
Captive Trojan women, young and old,
maiden and married.

[The scene represents a battlefield, a few days after the bat-
tle. At the back are the walls of Troy, partially ruined. In
front of them, to right and left, are some huts, containing
those of the Captive Women who have been specially set
apart for the chief Greek leaders. At one side some dead
bodies of armed men are visible. In front a tall woman
with white hair is lying on the ground asleep.

It is the dusk of early dawn, before sunrise. The figure of
the god Poseidon is dimly seen before the walls.]

Poseidon

    Up from Aegean caverns, pool by pool
    Of blue salt sea, where feet most beautiful
    Of Nereid maidens weave beneath the foam
    Their long sea-dances, I, their lord, am come,
    Poseidon of the Sea. 'Twas I whose power,
    With great Apollo, builded tower by tower
    These walls of Troy; and still my care doth stand
    True to the ancient People of my hand;
    Which now as smoke is perished, in the shock
    Of Argive spears. Down from Parnassus' rock   10
    The Greek Epeios came, of Phocian seed,
    And wrought by Pallas' mysteries a Steed
    Marvellous, big with arms; and through my wall
    It passed, a death-fraught image magical.
      The groves are empty and the sanctuaries
    Run red with blood. Unburied Priam lies
    By his own hearth, on God's high altar-stair,
    And Phrygian gold goes forth and raiment rare
    To the Argive ships; and weary soldiers roam
    Waiting the wind that blows at last for home,   20
    For wives and children, left long years away,
    Beyond the seed's tenth fullness and decay,
    To work this land's undoing. And for me,
    Since Argive Hera conquereth, and she

Who wrought with Hera to the Phrygians' woe,
Pallas, behold, I bow mine head and go
Forth from great Ilion and mine altars old.
When a still city lieth in the hold
Of Desolation, all God's spirit there
30   Is sick and turns from worship.—Hearken where
The ancient River waileth with a voice
Of many women, portioned by the choice
Of war amid new lords, as the lots leap
For Thessaly, or Argos, or the steep
Of Theseus' Rock. And others yet there are,
High women, chosen from the waste of war
For the great kings, behind these portals hid;
And with them that Laconian Tyndarid,
Helen, like them a prisoner and a prize.
40   And this unhappy one—would any eyes
Gaze now on Hecuba? Here at the Gates
She lies 'mid many tears for many fates
Of wrong. One child beside Achilles' grave
In secret slain, Polyxena the brave,
Lies bleeding. Priam and his sons are gone;
And, lo, Cassandra, she the Chosen One,
Whom Lord Apollo spared to walk her way
A swift and virgin spirit, on this day
Lust hath her, and she goeth garlanded
50   A bride of wrath to Agamemnon's bed.

[He turns to go; and another divine Presence becomes visible in the dusk. It is the goddess, Pallas Athena.]

O happy long ago, farewell, farewell,
Ye shining towers and mine old citadel;
Broken by Pallas, Child of God, or still
Thy roots had held thee true.

Pallas

Is it the will
Of God's high Brother, to whose hand is given
Great power of old, and worship of all Heaven,
To suffer speech from one whose enmities

This day are cast aside?

Poseidon

    His will it is: 60
Kindred and long companionship withal,
Most high Athena, are things magical.

Pallas

    Blest be thy gentle mood!—Methinks I see
A road of comfort here, for thee and me.

Poseidon

    Thou hast some counsel of the Gods, or word
Spoken of Zeus? Or is it tidings heard
From some far Spirit?

Pallas

    For this Ilion's sake,
Whereon we tread, I seek thee, and would make   70
My hand as thine.

Poseidon

    Hath that old hate and deep
Failed, where she lieth in her ashen sleep?
Thou pitiest her?

Pallas

    Speak first; wilt thou be one
In heart with me and hand till all be done?

Poseidon

Yea; but lay bare thy heart. For this land's sake
Thou comest, not for Hellas?

Pallas

    I would make
Mine ancient enemies laugh for joy, and bring
On these Greek ships a bitter homecoming.   80

Poseidon

> Swift is thy spirit's path, and strange withal,
> And hot thy love and hate, where'er they fall.

Pallas

> A deadly wrong they did me, yea within
> Mine holy place: thou knowest?

Poseidon

> I know the sin
> Of Ajax , when he cast Cassandra down....

Pallas

> And no man rose and smote him; not a frown
> Nor word from all the Greeks!

Poseidon

> And 'twas thine hand
> That gave them Troy!

Pallas

> Therefore with thee I stand
> To smite them.

Poseidon

> All thou cravest, even now
> Is ready in mine heart. What seekest thou?

Pallas

> An homecoming that striveth ever more
> And cometh to no home.

Poseidon

> Here on the shore
> Wouldst hold them or amid mine own salt foam?

Pallas

> When the last ship hath bared her sail for home!

90

Zeus shall send rain, long rain and flaw of driven   100
Hail, and a whirling darkness blown from heaven;
To me his levin-light he promiseth
O'er ships and men, for scourging and hot death:
Do thou make wild the roads of the sea, and steep
With war of waves and yawning of the deep,
Till dead men choke Euboea's curling bay.
So Greece shall dread even in an after day
My house, nor scorn the Watchers of strange lands!

Poseidon

I give thy boon unbartered. These mine hands
Shall stir the waste Aegean; reefs that cross   110
The Delian pathways, jag-torn Myconos,
Scyros and Lemnos, yea, and storm-driven
Caphêreus with the bones of drownèd men
Shall glut him.—Go thy ways, and bid the Sire
Yield to thine hand the arrows of his fire.
Then wait thine hour, when the last ship shall wind
Her cable coil for home!

[Exit Pallas.]

How are ye blind,
Ye treaders down of cities, ye that cast
Temples to desolation, and lay waste   120
Tombs, the untrodden sanctuaries where lie
The ancient dead; yourselves so soon to die!

[Exit Poseidon.]

[The day slowly dawns: Hecuba wakes.]

Hecuba

Up from the earth, O weary head!
  This is not Troy, about, above—
  Not Troy, nor we the lords thereof.   *100*
Thou breaking neck, be strengthenèd!
Endure and chafe not. The winds rave
  And falter. Down the world's wide road,

Float, float where streams the breath of God;
130 Nor turn thy prow to breast the wave.
Ah woe!... For what woe lacketh here?
My children lost, my land, my lord.
O thou great wealth of glory, stored
Of old in Ilion, year by year
We watched ... and wert thou nothingness?
What is there that I fear to say?
And yet, what help?... Ah, well-a-day,
This ache of lying, comfortless
And haunted! Ah, my side, my brow
140 And temples! All with changeful pain
My body rocketh, and would fain
Move to the tune of tears that flow:
For tears are music too, and keep
A song unheard in hearts that weep.

[She rises and gazes towards the Greek ships far off on the shore.]

O ships, O crowding faces
Of ships, O hurrying beat
Of oars as of crawling feet,
How found ye our holy places?
Threading the narrows through,
150 Out from the gulfs of the Greek,
Out to the clear dark blue,
With hate ye came and with joy,
And the noise of your music flew,
Clarion and pipe did shriek,
As the coilèd cords ye threw,
Held in the heart of Troy!
What sought ye then that ye came?
A woman, a thing abhorred:
A King's wife that her lord
160 Hateth: and Castor's shame
Is hot for her sake, and the reeds
Of old Eurôtas stir
With the noise of the name of her.
She slew mine ancient King,
The Sower of fifty Seeds,

And cast forth mine and me,
As shipwrecked men, that cling
To a reef in an empty sea.
Who am I that I sit
Here at a Greek king's door,
Yea, in the dust of it?
A slave that men drive before,
A woman that hath no home,
Weeping alone for her dead;
A low and bruisèd head,
And the glory struck therefrom.

*[She starts up from her solitary brooding, and calls to the
other Trojan Women in the huts.]*

O Mothers of the Brazen Spear,
And maidens, maidens, brides of shame,
Troy is a smoke, a dying flame;
Together we will weep for her:
I call ye as a wide-wing'd bird
Calleth the children of her fold,
To cry, ah, not the cry men heard
In Ilion, not the songs of old,
That echoed when my hand was true
On Priam's sceptre, and my feet
Touched on the stone one signal beat,
And out the Dardan music rolled;
And Troy's great Gods gave ear thereto.

*[The door of one of the huts on the right opens, and the
Women steal out severally, startled and afraid.]*

First Woman

[Strophe I.]

How say'st thou? Whither moves thy cry,
    Thy bitter cry? Behind our door
    We heard thy heavy heart outpour
Its sorrow: and there shivered by
    Fear and a quick sob shaken
From prisoned hearts that shall be free no more!

Hecuba

Child, 'tis the ships that stir upon the shore....

Second Woman

The ships, the ships awaken!

Third Woman

Dear God, what would they? Overseas
Bear me afar to strange cities?

Hecuba

200

Nay, child, I know not. Dreams are these,
Fears of the hope-forsaken.

First Woman

Awake, O daughters of affliction, wake
And learn your lots! Even now the Argives break
Their camp for sailing!

Hecuba

Ah, not Cassandra! Wake not her
Whom God hath maddened, lest the foe
Mock at her dreaming. Leave me clear
From that one edge of woe.
O Troy, my Troy, thou diest here

210

Most lonely; and most lonely we
The living wander forth from thee,
And the dead leave thee wailing!

[One of the huts on the left is now open, and the rest of the Chorus come out severally. Their number eventually amounts to fifteen.]

Fourth Woman

[Antistrophe I.]

Out of the tent of the Greek king
I steal, my Queen, with trembling breath:

What means thy call? Not death; not death!
They would not slay so low a thing!

Fifth Woman

O, 'tis the ship-folk crying
To deck the galleys: and we part, we part!

Hecuba

Nay, daughter: take the morning to thine heart.

Fifth Woman

My heart with dread is dying!   220

Sixth Woman

An herald from the Greek hath come!

Fifith Woman

How have they cast me, and to whom
A bondmaid?

Hecuba

Peace, child: wait thy doom.
Our lots are near the trying.

Fourth Woman

Argos, belike, or Phthia shall it be,
Or some lone island of the tossing sea,
    Far, far from Troy?

Hecuba

And I the agèd, where go I,
    A winter-frozen bee, a slave   230
Death-shapen, as the stones that lie
    Hewn on a dead man's grave:
The children of mine enemy
To foster, or keep watch before
The threshold of a master's door,
    I that was Queen in Troy!

A Woman to Another

[Strophe 2.]

And thou, what tears can tell thy doom?

The Other

The shuttle still shall flit and change
Beneath my fingers, but the loom,
  Sister, be strange.

Another (wildly)

Look, my dead child! My child, my love,
The last look....

Another

  Oh, there cometh worse.
A Greek's bed in the dark....

Another

  God curse
That night and all the powers thereof!

Another

Or pitchers to and fro to bear
 To some Pirênê on the hill,
 Where the proud water craveth still
Its broken-hearted minister.

Another

God guide me yet to Theseus' land,
 The gentle land, the famed afar....

Another

But not the hungry foam—Ah, never!—
Of fierce Eurotas, Helen's river,
To bow to Menelaus' hand,
 That wasted Troy with war!

A Woman

[Antistrophe 2.]

    They told us of a land high-born,
      Where glimmers round Olympus' roots
    A lordly river, red with corn
    And burdened fruits.   260

Another

    Aye, that were next in my desire
      To Athens, where good spirits dwell....

Another

    Or Aetna's breast, the deeps of fire
      That front the Tyrian's Citadel:
    First mother, she, of Sicily
      And mighty mountains: fame hath told
      Their crowns of goodness manifold....

Another

    And, close beyond the narrowing sea,
    A sister land, where float enchanted
      Ionian summits, wave on wave,   270
    And Crathis of the burning tresses
    Makes red the happy vale, and blesses
    With gold of fountains spirit-haunted
    Homes of true men and brave!

Leader

    But lo, who cometh: and his lips
      Grave with the weight of dooms unknown:
    A Herald from the Grecian ships.
      Swift comes he, hot-foot to be done
    And finished. Ah, what bringeth he
    Of news or judgment? Slaves are we,   280
      Spoils that the Greek hath won!

[Talthybius, followed by some Soldiers, enters from the left.]

Talthybius

> Thou know'st me, Hecuba. Often have I crossed
> Thy plain with tidings from the Hellene host.
> 'Tis I, Talthybius…. Nay, of ancient use
> Thou know'st me. And I come to bear thee news.

Hecuba

> Ah me, 'tis here, 'tis here,
> Women of Troy, our long embosomed fear!

Talthybius

> The lots are cast, if that it was ye feared.

Hecuba

> What lord, what land…. Ah me,
> Phthia or Thebes, or sea-worn Thessaly?

290

Talthybius

> Each hath her own. Ye go not in one herd.

Hecuba

> Say then what lot hath any? What of joy
> Falls, or can fall on any child of Troy?

Talthybius

> I know: but make thy questions severally.

Hecuba

> My stricken one must be
> Still first. Say how Cassandra's portion lies.

Talthybius

> Chosen from all for Agamemnon's prize!

Hecuba

> How, for his Spartan bride
> A tirewoman? For Helen's sister's pride?

Talthybius

> Nay, nay: a bride herself, for the King's bed.   300

Hecuba

> The sainted of Apollo? And her own
>   Prize that God promised
> Out of the golden clouds, her virgin crown?...

Talthybius

> He loved her for that same strange holiness.

Hecuba

>   Daughter, away, away,
>   Cast all away,
> The haunted Keys, the lonely stole's array
> That kept thy body like a sacred place!

Talthybius

> Is't not rare fortune that the King hath smiled
> On such a maid?   310

Hecuba

>   What of that other child
> Ye reft from me but now?

Talthybius (speaking with some constraint)

> Polyxena? Or what child meanest thou?

Hecuba

> The same. What man now hath her, or what doom?

Talthybius

> She rests apart, to watch Achilles' tomb.

Hecuba

> To watch a tomb? My daughter? What is this?...
> Speak, Friend? What fashion of the laws of Greece?

Talthybius

> Count thy maid happy! She hath naught of ill
> To fear....

Hecuba

320   What meanest thou? She liveth still?

Talthybius

> I mean, she hath one toil that holds her free
> From all toil else.

Hecuba

> What of Andromache,
> Wife of mine iron-hearted Hector, where
> Journeyeth she?

Talthybius

> Pyrrhus, Achilles' son, hath taken her.

Hecuba

> And I, whose slave am I,
> The shaken head, the arm that creepeth by,
> Staff-crutchèd, like to fall?

Talthybius

330   Odysseus, Ithaca's king, hath thee for thrall.

Hecuba

> Beat, beat the crownless head:
> Rend the cheek till the tears run red!
> A lying man and a pitiless
> Shall be lord of me, a heart full-flown
>   With scorn of righteousness:
> O heart of a beast where law is none,
> Where all things change so that lust be fed,
> The oath and the deed, the right and the wrong,
> Even the hate of the forked tongue:

386

Even the hate turns and is cold, 340
False as the love that was false of old!
O Women of Troy, weep for me!
Yea, I am gone: I am gone my ways.
Mine is the crown of misery,
The bitterest day of all our days.

Leader

Thy fate thou knowest, Queen: but I know not
What lord of South or North has won my lot.

Talthybius

Go, seek Cassandra, men! Make your best speed,
That I may leave her with the King, and lead
These others to their diverse lords…. Ha, there! 350
What means that sudden light? Is it the flare
Of torches?

*[Light is seen shining through the crevices of the second hut
on the right. He moves towards it.]*

    Would they fire their prison rooms,
Or how, these dames of Troy?—'Fore God, the dooms *300*
Are known, and now they burn themselves and die
Rather than sail with us! How savagely
In days like these a free neck chafes beneath
Its burden!… Open! Open quick! Such death
Were bliss to them, it may be: but 'twill bring
Much wrath, and leave me shamed before the King! 360

Hecuba

There is no fire, no peril: 'tis my child,
Cassandra, by the breath of God made wild.

*[The door opens from within and Cassandra enters, white-
robed and wreathed like a Priestess, a great torch in her
hand. She is singing softly to herself and does not see the
Herald or the scene before her.]*

387

Cassandra

[Strophe.]

Lift, lift it high:
  Give it to mine hand!
  Lo, I bear a flame
  Unto God! I praise his name.
I light with a burning brand
This sanctuary.
Blessèd is he that shall wed,
370   And blessèd, blessèd am I
  In Argos: a bride to lie
With a king in a king's bed.
  Hail, O Hymen red,
  O Torch that makest one!
  Weepest thou, Mother mine own?
Surely thy cheek is pale
With tears, tears that wail
For a land and a father dead.
But I go garlanded:
380   I am the Bride of Desire:
  Therefore my torch is borne—
Lo, the lifting of morn,
Lo, the leaping of fire!—
For thee, O Hymen bright,
For thee, O Moon of the Deep,
So Law hath charged, for the light
Of a maid's last sleep.

[Antistrophe.]

Awake, O my feet, awake:
  Our father's hope is won!
390   Dance as the dancing skies
  Over him, where he lies
  Happy beneath the sun!...
  Lo, the Ring that I make....

[She makes a circle round her with a torch, and visions appear to her.]

Apollo!... Ah, is it thou?
O shrine in the laurels cold,
I bear thee still, as of old,
Mine incense! Be near to me now.

[She waves the torch as though bearing incense.]

O Hymen, Hymen fleet:
Quick torch that makest one!...
How? Am I still alone?   400
Laugh as I laugh, and twine
In the dance, O Mother mine:
Dear feet, be near my feet!
Come, greet ye Hymen, greet
Hymen with songs of pride:
Sing to him loud and long,
Cry, cry, when the song
Faileth, for joy of the bride!
O Damsels girt in the gold
Of Ilion, cry, cry ye,   410
For him that is doomed of old
To be lord of me!

Leader

O hold the damsel, lest her trancèd feet
Lift her afar, Queen, toward the Hellene fleet!

Hecuba

O Fire, Fire, where men make marriages
Surely thou hast thy lot; but what are these
Thou bringest flashing? Torches savage-wild
And far from mine old dreams.—Alas, my child,
How little dreamed I then of wars or red
Spears of the Greek to lay thy bridal bed!   420
Give me thy brand; it hath no holy blaze
Thus in thy frenzy flung. Nor all thy days
Nor all thy griefs have changed them yet, nor learned
Wisdom.—Ye women, bear the pine half burned
To the chamber back; and let your drownèd eyes
Answer the music of these bridal cries!

[She takes the torch and gives it to one of the women.]

Cassandra

O Mother, fill mine hair with happy flowers,
And speed me forth. Yea, if my spirit cowers,
Drive me with wrath! So liveth Loxias,
430   A bloodier bride than ever Helen was
Go I to Agamemnon, Lord most high
Of Hellas!... I shall kill him, mother; I
Shall kill him, and lay waste his house with fire
As he laid ours. My brethren and my sire
Shall win again....
    [Checking herself] But part I must let be,
And speak not. Not the axe that craveth me,
And more than me; not the dark wanderings
Of mother-murder that my bridal brings,
440   And all the House of Atreus down, down, down....
    Nay, I will show thee. Even now this town
Is happier than the Greeks. I know the power
Of God is on me: but this little hour,
Wilt thou but listen, I will hold him back!
    One love, one woman's beauty, o'er the track
Of hunted Helen, made their myriads fall.
And this their King so wise, who ruleth all,
What wrought he? Cast out Love that Hate might feed:
Gave to his brother his own child, his seed
450   Of gladness, that a woman fled, and fain
To fly for ever, should be turned again!
So the days waned, and armies on the shore
Of Simois stood and strove and died. Wherefore?
No man had moved their landmarks; none had shook
Their wallèd towns.—And they whom Ares took,
Had never seen their children: no wife came
With gentle arms to shroud the limbs of them
For burial, in a strange and angry earth
Laid dead. And there at home, the same long dearth:
460   Women that lonely died, and aged men
Waiting for sons that ne'er should turn again,
Nor know their graves, nor pour drink-offerings,
To still the unslakèd dust. These be the things
The conquering Greek hath won!
        But we—what pride,
What praise of men were sweeter?—fighting died

To save our people. And when war was red
Around us, friends upbore the gentle dead
Home, and dear women's heads about them wound
White shrouds, and here they sleep in the old ground   470
Belovèd. And the rest long days fought on,
Dwelling with wives and children, not alone
And joyless, like these Greeks. And Hector's woe,
What is it? He is gone, and all men know
His glory, and how true a heart he bore.
It is the gift the Greek hath brought! Of yore
Men saw him not, nor knew him. Yea, and even
Paris hath loved withal a child of heaven:
Else had his love but been as others are.
   Would ye be wise, ye Cities, fly from war!   480
Yet if war come, there is a crown in death
For her that striveth well and perisheth
Unstained: to die in evil were the stain!
Therefore, O Mother, pity not thy slain,
Nor Troy, nor me, the bride. Thy direst foe   *400*
And mine by this my wooing is brought low.

Talthybius [at last breaking through the spell that has held him]

I swear, had not Apollo made thee mad,
Not lightly hadst thou flung this shower of bad
Bodings, to speed my General o'er the seas!
   'Fore God, the wisdoms and the greatnesses   490
Of seeming, are they hollow all, as things
Of naught? This son of Atreus, of all kings
Most mighty, hath so bowed him to the love
Of this mad maid, and chooseth her above
All women! By the Gods, rude though I be,
I would not touch her hand! Look thou; I see
Thy lips are blind, and whatso words they speak,
Praises of Troy or shamings of the Greek,
I cast to the four winds! Walk at my side
In peace!... And heaven content him of his bride!   500

*[He moves as though to go, but turns to Hecuba, and
speaks more gently.]*

And thou shalt follow to Odysseus' host

391

When the word comes. 'Tis a wise queen thou go'st
To serve, and gentle: so the Ithacans say.

Cassandra [seeing for the first time the Herald and all the scene]

How fierce a slave!... O Heralds, Heralds! Yea,
Voices of Death ; and mists are over them
Of dead men's anguish, like a diadem,
These weak abhorred things that serve the hate
Of kings and peoples!... To Odysseus' gate
My mother goeth, say'st thou? Is God's word
510   As naught, to me in silence ministered,
That in this place she dies? ...
        [To herself] No more; no more!
Why should I speak the shame of them, before
They come?... Little he knows, that hard-beset
Spirit, what deeps of woe await him yet;
Till all these tears of ours and harrowings
Of Troy, by his, shall be as golden things.
Ten years behind ten years athwart his way
Waiting: and home, lost and unfriended.... Nay:
520   Why should Odysseus' labours vex my breath?
On; hasten; guide me to the house of Death,
To lie beside my bridegroom!... Thou Greek King,
Who deem'st thy fortune now so high a thing,
Thou dust of the earth, a lowlier bed I see,
In darkness, not in light, awaiting thee:
And with thee, with thee ... there, where yawneth plain
A rift of the hills, raging with winter rain,
Dead ... and out-cast ... and naked.... It is I
Beside my bridegroom: and the wild beasts cry,
530   And ravin on God's chosen!

[She clasps her hands to her brow and feels the wreaths.]

    O, ye wreaths!
Ye garlands of my God, whose love yet breathes
About me, shapes of joyance mystical,
Begone! I have forgot the festival,
Forgot the joy. Begone! I tear ye, so,
From off me!... Out on the swift winds they go.
With flesh still clean I give them back to thee,

Still white, O God, O light that leadest me!

[Turning upon the Herald.]

Where lies the galley? Whither shall I tread?
See that your watch be set, your sail be spread   540
The wind comes quick ! Three Powers—mark me, thou!—
There be in Hell, and one walks with thee now!
Mother, farewell, and weep not! O my sweet
City, my earth-clad brethren, and thou great
Sire that begat us, but a space, ye Dead,
And I am with you, yea, with crowned head
I come, and shining from the fires that feed
On these that slay us now, and all their seed!

*[She goes out, followed by Talthybius and the Soldiers.
Hecuba, after waiting for an instant motionless, falls to
the ground.]*

Leader of Chorus

The Queen, ye Watchers! See, she falls, she falls,
Rigid without a word! O sorry thralls,   550
Too late! And will ye leave her downstricken,
A woman, and so old? Raise her again!

*[Some women go to Hecuba, but she refuses their aid and
speaks without rising.]*

Hecuba

Let lie … the love we seek not is no love….
This ruined body! Is the fall thereof
Too deep for all that now is over me
Of anguish, and hath been, and yet shall be?
Ye Gods…. Alas! Why call on things so weak
For aid? Yet there is something that doth seek,
Crying, for God, when one of us hath woe.
O, I will think of things gone long ago   560
And weave them to a song, like one more tear
In the heart of misery…. All kings we were;

393

And I must wed a king. And sons I brought
My lord King, many sons ... nay, that were naught;
But high strong princes, of all Troy the best.
Hellas nor Troäs nor the garnered East
Held such a mother! And all these things beneath
The Argive spear I saw cast down in death,
And shore these tresses at the dead men's feet.
570 Yea, and the gardener of my garden great,
It was not any noise of him nor tale
I wept for; these eyes saw him, when the pale
Was broke, and there at the altar Priam fell
Murdered, and round him all his citadel
Sacked. And my daughters, virgins of the fold,
Meet to be brides of mighty kings, behold,
'Twas for the Greek I bred them! All are gone;
And no hope left, that I shall look upon
Their faces any more, nor they on mine.
580 And now my feet tread on the utmost line:
An old, old slave-woman, I pass below
Mine enemies' gates; and whatso task they know
For this age basest, shall be mine; the door,
Bowing, to shut and open.... I that bore
Hector!... and meal to grind, and this racked head
Bend to the stones after a royal bed;
Torn rags about me, aye, and under them
Torn flesh; 'twill make a woman sick for shame!
Woe's me; and all that one man's arms might hold
590 One woman, what long seas have o'er me rolled
500 And roll for ever!... O my child, whose white
Soul laughed amid the laughter of God's light,
Cassandra, what hands and how strange a day
Have loosed thy zone! And thou, Polyxena,
Where art thou? And my sons? Not any seed
Of man nor woman now shall help my need.
Why raise me any more? What hope have I
To hold me? Take this slave that once trod high
In Ilion; cast her on her bed of clay
600 Rock-pillowed, to lie down, and pass away
Wasted with tears. And whatso man they call
Happy, believe not ere the last day fall!

Chorus

[Strophe.]

    O Muse, be near me now, and make
    A strange song for Ilion's sake,
Till a tone of tears be about mine ears
    And out of my lips a music break
    For Troy, Troy, and the end of the years:
      When the wheels of the Greek above me pressed,
      And the mighty horse-hoofs beat my breast;
      And all around were the Argive spears   610
A towering Steed of golden rein—
    O gold without, dark steel within!—
Ramped in our gates; and all the plain
    Lay silent where the Greeks had been.
And a cry broke from all the folk
Gathered above on Ilion's rock:
    "Up, up, O fear is over now!
    To Pallas, who hath saved us living,
To Pallas bear this victory-vow!"
Then rose the old man from his room,   620
The merry damsel left her loom,
And each bound death about his brow
    With minstrelsy and high thanksgiving!

[Antistrophe.]

    O, swift were all in Troy that day,
    And girt them to the portal-way,
Marvelling at that mountain Thing
    Smooth-carven, where the Argives lay,
    And wrath, and Ilion's vanquishing:
      Meet gift for her that spareth not,
      Heaven's yokeless Rider. Up they brought   630
Through the steep gates her offering:
    Like some dark ship that climbs the shore
    On straining cables, up, where stood
Her marble throne, her hallowed floor,
    Who lusted for her people's blood.
A very weariness of joy
Fell with the evening over Troy:

And lutes of Afric mingled there
With Phrygian songs: and many a maiden,
640   With white feet glancing light as air,
Made happy music through the gloom:
And fires on many an inward room
All night broad-flashing, flung their glare
On laughing eyes and slumber-laden.

A Maiden

I was among the dancers there
To Artemis, and glorying sang
Her of the Hills, the Maid most fair,
Daughter of Zeus: and, lo, there rang
A shout out of the dark, and fell
650   Deathlike from street to street, and made
A silence in the citadel:
And a child cried, as if afraid,
And hid him in his mother's veil.
Then stalked the Slayer from his den,
The hand of Pallas served her well!
O blood, blood of Troy was deep
About the streets and altars then:
And in the wedded rooms of sleep,
Lo, the desolate dark alone,
660   And headless things, men stumbled on.
And forth, lo, the women go,
The crown of War, the crown of Woe,
To bear the children of the foe
And weep, weep, for Ilion!

*[As the song ceases a chariot is seen approaching from the
town, laden with spoils. On it sits a mourning Woman
with a child in her arms.]*

Leader

Lo, yonder on the heapèd crest
Of a Greek wain, Andromache,
As one that o'er an unknown sea
Tosseth; and on her wave-borne breast
Her loved one clingeth, Hector's child,

Astyanax…. O most forlorn   670
Of women, whither go'st thou, borne
'Mid Hector's bronzen arms, and piled
Spoils of the dead, and pageantry
    Of them that hunted Ilion down?
    Aye, richly thy new lord shall crown
The mountain shrines of Thessaly!

Andromache

[Strophe I.]

    Forth to the Greek I go,
        Driven as a beast is driven.

Hecuba

    Woe, woe!

Andromache

    Nay, mine is woe: 680
    Woe to none other given,
    And the song and the crown therefore!

Hecuba

    O Zeus!

Andromeche

    He hates thee sore!

Hecuba

    Children!

Andromache

    No more, no more
    To aid thee: their strife is striven!

Hecuba

[Antistrophe I.]

    Troy, Troy is gone!

Andromache

> Yea, and her treasure parted.

Hecuba

690

> Gone, gone, mine own
> Children, the noble-hearted!

Andromache

> Sing sorrow....

Hecuba

> For me, for me!

Andromache

> Sing for the Great City,
> That falleth, falleth to be
> A shadow, a fire departed.

[Strophe 2.]

> Come to me, O my lover!

Hecuba

> The dark shroudeth him over,
> My flesh, woman, not thine, not thine!

Andromache

700

> Make of thine arms my cover!

Hecuba

[Antistrophe 2.]

> O thou whose wound was deepest,
> Thou that my children keepest,
> Priam, Priam, O age-worn King,
> Gather me where thou sleepest.

Andromache [her hands upon her heart]

[Strophe 3.]

    O here is the deep of desire,

Hecuba

    (How? And is this not woe?)

Andromache

    For a city burned with fire;

Hecuba

    (It beateth, blow on blow.)

Andromache

    God's wrath for Paris, thy son, that he died not long ago: 710
      Who sold for his evil love
    Troy and the towers thereof:
    Therefore the dead men lie
    Naked, beneath the eye
    Of Pallas, and vultures croak
      And flap for joy:
    So Love hath laid his yoke   *600*
      On the neck of Troy!

Hecuba

[Antistrophe 3.]

    O mine own land, my home,

Andromache

    (I weep for thee, left forlorn,)

Hecuba

    See'st thou what end is come?   720

Andromache

(And the house where my babes were born.)

Hecuba

A desolate Mother we leave, O children, a City of scorn:
    Even as the sound of a song
    Left by the way, but long
    Remembered, a tune of tears
    Falling where no man hears,
    In the old house, as rain,
     For things loved of yore:
    But the dead hath lost his pain
730   And weeps no more.

Leader

How sweet are tears to them in bitter stress,
And sorrow, and all the songs of heaviness.

Andromache

Mother of him of old, whose mighty spear
Smote Greeks like chaff, see'st thou what things are here?

Hecuba

I see God's hand, that buildeth a great crown
For littleness, and hath cast the mighty down.

Andromache

I and my babe are driven among the droves
Of plundered cattle. O, when fortune moves
So swift, the high heart like a slave beats low.

Hecuba

740   'Tis fearful to be helpless. Men but now
Have taken Cassandra, and I strove in vain.

Andromache

Ah, woe is me; hath Ajax come again?
But other evil yet is at thy gate.

400

Hecuba

> Nay, Daughter, beyond number, beyond weight
> My evils are! Doom raceth against doom.

Andromache

> Polyxena across Achilles' tomb
> Lies slain, a gift flung to the dreamless dead.

Hecuba

> My sorrow!... 'Tis but what Talthybius said:
> So plain a riddle, and I read it not.

Andromache

> I saw her lie, and stayed this chariot;   750
> And raiment wrapt on her dead limbs, and beat
> My breast for her.

Hecuba [to herself]

> O the foul sin of it!
> The wickedness! My child. My child! Again
> I cry to thee. How cruelly art thou slain!

Andromache

> She hath died her death, and howso dark it be,
> Her death is sweeter than my misery.

Hecuba

> Death cannot be what Life is, Child; the cup
> Of Death is empty, and Life hath always hope.

Andromache

> O Mother, having ears, hear thou this word   760
> Fear-conquering, till thy heart as mine be stirred
> With joy. To die is only not to be;
> And better to be dead than grievously
> Living. They have no pain, they ponder not
> Their own wrong. But the living that is brought
> From joy to heaviness, his soul doth roam,

As in a desert, lost, from its old home.
Thy daughter lieth now as one unborn,
Dead, and naught knowing of the lust and scorn
770   That slew her. And I ... long since I drew my bow
Straight at the heart of good fame; and I know
My shaft hit; and for that am I the more
Fallen from peace. All that men praise us for,
I loved for Hector's sake, and sought to win.
I knew that alway, be there hurt therein
Or utter innocence, to roam abroad
Hath ill report for women; so I trod
Down the desire thereof, and walked my way
In mine own garden. And light words and gay
780   Parley of women never passed my door.
The thoughts of mine own heart ... I craved no more....
    Spoke with me, and I was happy. Constantly
I brought fair silence and a tranquil eye
For Hector's greeting, and watched well the way
Of living, where to guide and where obey.
    And, lo! some rumour of this peace, being gone
Forth to the Greek, hath cursed me. Achilles' son,
So soon as I was taken, for his thrall
Chose me. I shall do service in the hall
790   Of them that slew.... How? Shall I thrust aside
Hector's beloved face, and open wide
My heart to this new lord? Oh, I should stand
A traitor to the dead! And if my hand
And flesh shrink from him ... lo, wrath and despite
O'er all the house, and I a slave! One night,
One night ... aye, men have said it ... maketh tame
A woman in a man's arms.... O shame, shame!
What woman's lips can so forswear her dead,
And give strange kisses in another's bed?
800   Why, not a dumb beast, not a colt will run
In the yoke untroubled, when her mate is gone—
A thing not in God's image, dull, unmoved
Of reason. O my Hector! best beloved,
That, being mine, wast all in all to me,
My prince, my wise one, O my majesty
Of valiance! No man's touch had ever come

Near me, when thou from out my father's home
Didst lead me and make me thine.... And thou art dead,
And I war-flung to slavery and the bread
Of shame in Hellas, over bitter seas!   810
  What knoweth she of evils like to these,
That dead Polyxena, thou weepest for?
There liveth not in my life any more
The hope that others have. Nor will I tell
The lie to mine own heart, that aught is well
Or shall be well.... Yet, O, to dream were sweet!

Leader

Thy feet have trod the pathway of my feet,
And thy clear sorrow teacheth me mine own.

Hecuba

Lo, yonder ships: I ne'er set foot on one,
But tales and pictures tell, when over them   820
Breaketh a storm not all too strong to stem,
Each man strives hard, the tiller gripped, the mast
Manned, the hull baled, to face it: till at last
Too strong breaks the o'erwhelming sea: lo, then
They cease, and yield them up as broken men
To fate and the wild waters. Even so
I in my many sorrows bear me low,
Nor curse, nor strive that other things may be.
The great wave rolled from God hath conquered me.
  But, O, let Hector and the fates that fell   830
On Hector, sleep. Weep for him ne'er so well,
Thy weeping shall not wake him. Honour thou
The new lord that is set above thee now,
And make of thine own gentle piety   *700*
A prize to lure his heart. So shalt thou be
A strength to them that love us, and—God knows,
It may be—rear this babe among his foes,
My Hector's child, to manhood and great aid
For Ilion. So her stones may yet be laid
One on another, if God will, and wrought   840
Again to a city! Ah, how thought to thought

Still beckons!... But what minion of the Greek
Is this that cometh, with new words to speak?

[Enter Talthybius with a band of Soldiers. He comes for-
ward slowly and with evident disquiet.]

Talthybius

Spouse of the noblest heart that beat in Troy,
Andromache, hate me not! 'Tis not in joy
I tell thee. But the people and the Kings
Have with one voice....

Andromache

What is it? Evil things
Are on thy lips!

Talthybius

850 'Tis ordered, this child.... Oh,
How can I tell her of it?

Andromache

Doth he not go
With me, to the same master?

Talthybius

There is none
In Greece, shall e'er be master of thy son.

Andromache

How? Will they leave him here to build again
The wreck?...

Talthybius

I know not how to tell thee plain!

Andromache

Thou hast a gentle heart ... if it be ill,

And not good, news thou hidest! 860

Talthybius

> 'Tis their will
> Thy son shall die.... The whole vile thing is said
> Now!

Andromache

> Oh, I could have borne mine enemy's bed!

Talthybius

> And speaking in the council of the host
> Odysseus hath prevailed—

Andromache

> O lost! lost! lost!...
> Forgive me! It is not easy....

Talthybius

> ... That the son
> Of one so perilous be not fostered on 870
> To manhood—

Andromache

> God; may his own counsel fall
> On his own sons!

Talthybius

> ... But from this crested wall
> Of Troy be dashed, and die.... Nay, let the thing
> Be done. Thou shalt be wiser so. Nor cling
> So fiercely to him. Suffer as a brave
> Woman in bitter pain; nor think to have
> Strength which thou hast not. Look about thee here!
> Canst thou see help, or refuge anywhere? 880
> Thy land is fallen and thy lord, and thou
> A prisoner and alone, one woman; how
> Canst battle against us? For thine own good

405

I would not have thee strive, nor make ill blood
And shame about thee.... Ah, nor move thy lips
In silence there, to cast upon the ships
Thy curse! One word of evil to the host,
This babe shall have no burial, but be tossed
Naked.... Ah, peace! And bear as best thou may,
War's fortune. So thou shalt not go thy way
Leaving this child unburied; nor the Greek
Be stern against thee, if thy heart be meek!

Andromache [to the child]

Go, die, my best-beloved, my cherished one,
In fierce men's hands, leaving me here alone.
Thy father was too valiant; that is why
They slay thee! Other children, like to die,
Might have been spared for that. But on thy head
His good is turned to evil. O thou bed
And bridal; O the joining of the hand,
That led me long ago to Hector's land
To bear, O not a lamb for Grecian swords
To slaughter, but a Prince o'er all the hordes
Enthroned of wide-flung Asia.... Weepest thou?
Nay, why, my little one? Thou canst not know.
And Father will not come; he will not come;
Not once, the great spear flashing, and the tomb
Riven to set thee free! Not one of all
His brethren, nor the might of Ilion's wall.
How shall it be? One horrible spring ... deep, deep
Down. And thy neck.... Ah God, so cometh sleep!...
And none to pity thee!... Thou little thing
That curlest in my arms, what sweet scents cling
All round thy neck! Belovèd; can it be
All nothing, that this bosom cradled thee
And fostered; all the weary nights, wherethrough
I watched upon thy sickness, till I grew
Wasted with watching? Kiss me. This one time;
Not ever again. Put up thine arms, and climb
About my neck: now, kiss me, lips to lips....
O, ye have found an anguish that outstrips
All tortures of the East, ye gentle Greeks!
Why will ye slay this innocent, that seeks

890

900

910

920

No wrong?... O Helen, Helen, thou ill tree
That Tyndareus planted, who shall deem of thee
As child of Zeus? O, thou hast drawn thy breath
From many fathers, Madness, Hate, red Death,
And every rotting poison of the sky!
Zeus knows thee not, thou vampire, draining dry.
Greece and the world! God hate thee and destroy,
That with those beautiful eyes hast blasted Troy,   930
And made the far-famed plains a waste withal.
Quick! take him: drag him: cast him from the wall,
If cast ye will! Tear him, ye beasts, be swift!
God hath undone me, and I cannot lift
One hand, one hand, to save my child from death....
O, hide my head for shame: fling me beneath
Your galleys' benches!...

[She swoons: then half-rising.]

    Quick: I must begone
To the bridal.... I have lost my child, my own!

[The Soldiers close round her.]

Leader

    O Troy ill-starred; for one strange woman, one   940
Abhorrèd kiss, how are thine hosts undone!

Talthybius [bending over Andromache and gradually taking the Child from her]

Come, Child: let be that clasp of love
  Outwearied! Walk thy ways with me,
Up to the crested tower, above
  Thy father's wall.... Where they decree
Thy soul shall perish.—Hold him: hold!—
  Would God some other man might ply
These charges, one of duller mould,
  And nearer to the iron than I!

Hecuba

    O Child, they rob us of our own,   950
  Child of my Mighty One outworn:

Ours, ours thou art!—Can aught be done
Of deeds, can aught of pain be borne,
To aid thee?—Lo, this beaten head,
This bleeding bosom! These I spread
As gifts to thee. I can thus much.
Woe, woe for Troy, and woe for thee!
What fall yet lacketh, ere we touch
The last dead deep of misery?

*[The Child, who has started back from Talthybius, is
taken up by one of the Soldiers and borne back towards
the city, while Andromache is set again on the Chariot
and driven off towards the ships. Talthybius goes with the
Child.]*

Chorus

[Strophe I.]

960

In Salamis, filled with the foaming
Of billows and murmur of bees,
Old Telamon stayed from his roaming,
800   Long ago, on a throne of the seas;
Looking out on the hills olive-laden,
Enchanted, where first from the earth
The grey-gleaming fruit of the Maiden
Athena had birth;
A soft grey crown for a city
Belovèd a City of Light:
970   Yet he rested not there, nor had pity,
But went forth in his might,
Where Heracles wandered, the lonely
Bow-bearer, and lent him his hands
For the wrecking of one land only,
Of Ilion, Ilion only,
Most hated of lands!

[Antistrophe I.]

Of the bravest of Hellas he made him
A ship-folk, in wrath for the Steeds,

And sailed the wide waters, and stayed him
　At last amid Simoïs' reeds;　　　　　　　　　　980
And the oars beat slow in the river,
　And the long ropes held in the strand,
And he felt for his bow and his quiver,
　The wrath of his hand.
And the old king died; and the towers
　That Phoebus had builded did fall,
And his wrath, as a flame that devours,
　Ran red over all;
And the fields and the woodlands lay blasted,
　Long ago. Yea, twice hath the Sire　　　　　990
Uplifted his hand and downcast it
On the wall of the Dardan, downcast it
　As a sword and as fire.

[Strophe 2.]

In vain, all in vain,
　O thou 'mid the wine-jars golden
　　That movest in delicate joy,
　　Ganymêdês, child of Troy,
The lips of the Highest drain
　The cup in thine hand upholden:
And thy mother, thy mother that bore thee,　　1000
　Is wasted with fire and torn;
　　And the voice of her shores is heard,
　　Wild, as the voice of a bird,
For lovers and children before thee
　Crying, and mothers outworn.
And the pools of thy bathing are perished,
　And the wind-strewn ways of thy feet:
Yet thy face as aforetime is cherished
Of Zeus, and the breath of it sweet;
Yea, the beauty of Calm is upon it　　　　　1010
In houses at rest and afar.
But thy land, He hath wrecked and o'erthrown it
In the wailing of war.

[Antistrophe 2.]

O Love, ancient Love,

409

Of old to the Dardan given;
Love of the Lords of the Sky;
How didst thou lift us high
In Ilion, yea, and above
All cities, as wed with heaven!
1020   For Zeus—O leave it unspoken:
But alas for the love of the Morn;
Morn of the milk-white wing,
The gentle, the earth-loving,
That shineth on battlements broken
In Troy, and a people forlorn!
And, lo, in her bowers Tithônus,
Our brother, yet sleeps as of old:
O, she too hath loved us and known us,
And the Steeds of her star, flashing gold,
1030   Stooped hither and bore him above us;
Then blessed we the Gods in our joy.
But all that made them to love us
Hath perished from Troy.

*[As the song ceases, the King Menelaus enters, richly armed
and followed by a bodyguard of Soldiers. He is a prey to
violent and conflicting emotions.]*

Menelaus

How bright the face of heaven, and how sweet
The air this day, that layeth at my feet
The woman that I.... Nay: 'twas not for her
I came. 'Twas for the man, the cozener
And thief, that ate with me and stole away
My bride. But Paris lieth, this long day,
1040   By God's grace, under the horse-hoofs of the Greek,
And round him all his land. And now I seek....
Curse her! I scarce can speak the name she bears,
That was my wife. Here with the prisoners
They keep her, in these huts, among the hordes
Of numbered slaves.—The host whose labouring swords
Won her, have given her up to me, to fill
My pleasure; perchance kill her, or not kill,
But lead her home.—Methinks I have foregone

410

The slaying of Helen here in Ilion....
Over the long seas I will bear her back,   1050
And there, there, cast her out to whatsoever wrack
Of angry death they may devise, who know
Their dearest dead for her in Ilion.—Ho!
Ye soldiers! Up into the chambers where
She croucheth! Grip the long blood-reeking hair,
And drag her to mine eyes ...
    [Controlling himself] And when there come
Fair breezes, my long ships shall bear her home.

*[The Soldiers go to force open the door of the second hut
on the left.]*

Hecuba

Thou deep Base of the World , and thou high Throne
Above the World, whoe'er thou art, unknown   1060
And hard of surmise, Chain of Things that be,
Or Reason of our Reason; God, to thee
I lift my praise, seeing the silent road
That bringeth justice ere the end be trod
To all that breathes and dies.

Menelaus [turning]

Ha! who is there
That prayeth heaven, and in so strange a prayer?

Hecuba

I bless thee, Menelaus, I bless thee,
If thou wilt slay her! Only fear to see
Her visage, lest she snare thee and thou fall!   1070
She snareth strong men's eyes; she snareth tall
Cities; and fire from out her eateth up
Houses. Such magic hath she, as a cup
Of death!... Do I not know her? Yea, and thou,
And these that lie around, do they not know?

*[The Soldiers return from the hut and stand aside to let
Helen pass between them. She comes through them, gentle
and unafraid; there is no disorder in her raiment.]*

Helen

King Menelaus, thy first deed might make
A woman fear. Into my chamber brake
Thine armèd men, and lead me wrathfully.
Methinks, almost, I know thou hatest me.
Yet I would ask thee, what decree is gone
Forth for my life or death?

Menelaus [struggling with his emotion]

There was not one
That scrupled for thee. All, all with one will
Gave thee to me, whom thou hast wronged, to kill!

Helen

And is it granted that I speak, or no,
In answer to them ere I die, to show
I die most wronged and innocent?

Menelaus

I seek
To kill thee, woman; not to hear thee speak!

Hecuba

O hear her! She must never die unheard,
King Menelaus! And give me the word
To speak in answer! All the wrong she wrought
Away from thee, in Troy, thou knowest not.
The whole tale set together is a death
Too sure; she shall not 'scape thee!

Menelaus.

'Tis but breath
And time. For thy sake, Hecuba, if she need
To speak, I grant the prayer. I have no heed
Nor mercy—let her know it well—for her!

Helen

It may be that, how false or true soe'er
Thou deem me, I shall win no word from thee.

412

So sore thou holdest me thine enemy.
Yet I will take what words I think thy heart
Holdeth of anger: and in even part
Set my wrong and thy wrong, and all that fell.

[Pointing to Hecuba]

She cometh first, who bare the seed and well
Of springing sorrow, when to life she brought
Paris: and that old King, who quenched not
Quick in the spark, ere yet he woke to slay,
The fire-brand's image.—But enough: a day   1110
Came, and this Paris judged beneath the trees
Three Crowns of Life, three diverse Goddesses.
The gift of Pallas was of War, to lead
His East in conquering battles, and make bleed
The hearths of Hellas. Hera held a Throne—
If majesties he craved—to reign alone
From Phrygia to the last realm of the West.
And Cypris, if he deemed her loveliest,
Beyond all heaven, made dreams about my face
And for her grace gave me. And, lo! her grace   1120
Was judged the fairest, and she stood above
Those twain.—Thus was I loved, and thus my love
Hath helped Hellas. No fierce Eastern crown
Is o'er your lands, no spear hath cast them down.
O, it was well for Hellas! But for me
Most ill; caught up and sold across the sea
For this my beauty; yea, dishonourèd
For that which else had been about my head
A crown of honour.... Ah, I see thy thought;
The first plain deed, 'tis that I answer not,   1130
How in the dark out of thy house I fled....
There came the Seed of Fire, this woman's seed;
Came—O, a Goddess great walked with him then—
This Alexander, Breaker-down-of-Men,
This Paris, Strength-is-with-him; whom thou, whom—
O false and light of heart—thou in thy room
Didst leave, and spreadest sail for Cretan seas,
Far, far from me!... And yet, how strange it is!
I ask not thee; I ask my own sad thought,
What was there in my heart, that I forgot   1140

413

My home and land and all I loved, to fly
With a strange man? Surely it was not I,
But Cypris, there! Lay thou thy rod on her,
And be more high than Zeus and bitterer,
Who o'er all other spirits hath his throne,
But knows her chain must bind him. My wrong done
Hath its own pardon.... One word yet thou hast,
Methinks, of righteous seeming. When at last
The earth for Paris oped and all was o'er,
And her strange magic bound my feet no more,
Why kept I still his house, why fled not I
To the Argive ships?... Ah, how I strove to fly!
The old Gate-Warden could have told thee all,
My husband, and the watchers from the wall;
It was not once they took me, with the rope
Tied, and this body swung in the air, to grope
Its way toward thee, from that dim battlement.
Ah, husband still, how shall thy hand be bent
To slay me? Nay, if Right be come at last,
What shalt thou bring but comfort for pains past,
And harbour for a woman storm-driven:
A woman borne away by violent men:
And this one birthright of my beauty, this
That might have been my glory, lo, it is
A stamp that God hath burned, of slavery!
Alas! and if thou cravest still to be
As one set above gods, inviolate,
'Tis but a fruitless longing holds thee yet.

Leader

O Queen, think of thy children and thy land,
And break her spell! The sweet soft speech, the hand
And heart so fell: it maketh me afraid.

Hecuba

Meseems her goddesses first cry mine aid
Against these lying lips!... Not Hera, nay,
Nor virgin Pallas deem I such low clay,
To barter their own folk, Argos and brave
Athens, to be trod down, the Phrygian's slave,
All for vain glory and a shepherd's prize

414

On Ida! Wherefore should great Hera's eyes
So hunger to be fair? She doth not use
To seek for other loves, being wed with Zeus.   1180
And maiden Pallas ... did some strange god's face
Beguile her, that she craved for loveliness,
Who chose from God one virgin gift above
All gifts, and fleeth from the lips of love?
   Ah, deck not out thine own heart's evil springs
By making spirits of heaven as brutish things
And cruel. The wise may hear thee, and guess all!
   And Cypris must take ship-fantastical!
Sail with my son and enter at the gate
To seek thee! Had she willed it, she had sate   1190
At peace in heaven, and wafted thee, and all
Amyclae with thee, under Ilion's wall.
   My son was passing beautiful, beyond
His peers; and thine own heart, that saw and conned
His face, became a spirit enchanting thee.
For all wild things that in mortality
   Have being, are Aphroditê; and the name
She bears in heaven is born and writ of them.
   Thou sawest him in gold and orient vest
Shining, and lo, a fire about thy breast   1200
Leapt! Thou hadst fed upon such little things,
Pacing thy ways in Argos. But now wings
Were come! Once free from Sparta, and there rolled
The Ilian glory, like broad streams of gold,
To steep thine arms and splash the towers! How small,
How cold that day was Menelaus' hall!
   Enough of that. It was by force my son
Took thee, thou sayst, and striving.... Yet not one
In Sparta knew! No cry, no sudden prayer   *1000*
Rang from thy rooms that night.... Castor was there   1210
To hear thee, and his brother: both true men,
Not yet among the stars! And after, when
Thou camest here to Troy, and in thy track
Argos and all its anguish and the rack
Of war—Ah God!—perchance men told thee 'Now
The Greek prevails in battle': then wouldst thou
Praise Menelaus, that my son might smart,
Striving with that old image in a heart

Uncertain still. Then Troy had victories:
1220 And this Greek was as naught! Alway thine eyes
Watched Fortune's eyes, to follow hot where she
Led first. Thou wouldst not follow Honesty.
  Thy secret ropes, thy body swung to fall
Far, like a desperate prisoner, from the wall!
Who found thee so? When wast thou taken? Nay,
Hadst thou no surer rope, no sudden way
Of the sword, that any woman honest-souled
Had sought long since, loving her lord of old?
  Often and often did I charge thee; 'Go,
1230 My daughter; go thy ways. My sons will know
New loves. I will give aid, and steal thee past
The Argive watch. O give us peace at last,
Us and our foes!' But out thy spirit cried
As at a bitter word. Thou hadst thy pride
In Alexander's house, and O, 'twas sweet
To hold proud Easterns bowing at thy feet.
They were great things to thee!... And comest thou now
Forth, and hast decked thy bosom and thy brow,
And breathest with thy lord the same blue air,
1240 Thou evil heart? Low, low, with ravaged hair,
Rent raiment, and flesh shuddering, and within—
O shame at last, not glory for thy sin;
So face him if thou canst!... Lo, I have done.
Be true, O King; let Hellas bear her crown
Of Justice. Slay this woman, and upraise
The law for evermore: she that betrays
Her husband's bed, let her be judged and die.

Leader

Be strong, O King; give judgment worthily
For thee and thy great house. Shake off thy long
1250 Reproach; not weak, but iron against the wrong!

Menelaus

Thy thought doth walk with mine in one intent.
'Tis sure; her heart was willing, when she went
Forth to a stranger's bed. And all her fair
Tale of enchantment, 'tis a thing of air!...

[Turning furiously upon Helen.]

> Out, woman! There be those that seek thee yet
> With stones! Go, meet them. So shall thy long debt
> Be paid at last. And ere this night is o'er
> Thy dead face shall dishonour me no more!

Helen [kneeling before him and embracing him]

> Behold, mine arms are wreathed about thy knees;   1260
> Lay not upon my head the phantasies
> Of Heaven. Remember all, and slay me not!

Hecuba

> Remember them she murdered, them that fought
> Beside thee, and their children! Hear that prayer!

Menelaus

> Peace, agèd woman, peace! 'Tis not for her;
> She is as naught to me.
> *[To the Soldiers]* ... March on before,
> Ye ministers, and tend her to the shore ...
> And have some chambered galley set for her,
> Where she may sail the seas.

Hecuba

> If thou be there,   1270
> I charge thee, let not her set foot therein!

Menelaus

> How? Shall the ship go heavier for her sin?

Hecuba

> A lover once, will alway love again.

Menelaus

> If that he loved be evil, he will fain
> Hate it!... Howbeit, thy pleasure shall be done.
> Some other ship shall bear her, not mine own....

417

Thou counsellest very well.... And when we come
To Argos, then ... O then some pitiless doom
Well-earned, black as her heart! One that shall bind
Once for all time the law on womankind
Of faithfulness!... 'Twill be no easy thing,
God knoweth. But the thought thereof shall fling
A chill on the dreams of women, though they be
Wilder of wing and loathèd more than she!

1280

[Exit, following Helen, who is escorted by the Soldiers.]

Chorus [Some Women.]

[Strophe I.]

And hast thou turned from the Altar of frankincense,
And given to the Greek thy temple of Ilion?
The flame of the cakes of corn, is it gone from hence,
The myrrh on the air and the wreathèd towers gone?
And Ida, dark Ida, where the wild ivy grows,
The glens that run as rivers from the summer-broken snows,
And the Rock, is it forgotten, where the first sunbeam glows,
The lit house most holy of the Dawn?

1290

Others

[Antistrophe I.]

The sacrifice is gone and the sound of joy,
The dancing under the stars and the night-long prayer:
The Golden Images and the Moons of Troy,
The twelve Moons and the mighty names they bear:
My heart, my heart crieth, O Lord Zeus on high,
Were they all to thee as nothing, thou thronèd in the sky,
Thronèd in the fire-cloud, where a City, near to die,
Passeth in the wind and the flare?

1300

A Woman

[Strophe 2.]

Dear one, O husband mine,

Thou in the dim dominions
Driftest with waterless lips,
Unburied; and me the ships
Shall bear o'er the bitter brine,
  Storm-birds upon angry pinions,
Where the towers of the Giants shine
O'er Argos cloudily,
And the riders ride by the sea.

Others

And children still in the Gate   1310
  Crowd and cry,
A multitude desolate,
Voices that float and wait
  As the tears run dry:
'Mother, alone on the shore
  They drive me, far from thee:
Lo, the dip of the oar,
  The black hull on the sea!
Is it the Isle Immortal,
  Salamis, waits for me?   1320
Is it the Rock that broods
Over the sundered floods
Of Corinth, the ancient portal
  Of Pelops' sovranty?'

A Woman

[Antistrophe 2.]

Out in the waste of foam,   *1100*
  Where rideth dark Menelaus,
Come to us there, O white
And jagged, with wild sea-light
And crashing of oar-blades, come,
  O thunder of God, and slay us: 1330
While our tears are wet for home,
While out in the storm go we,
Slaves of our enemy!

Others

And, God, may Helen be there,

419

With mirror of gold,
Decking her face so fair,
Girl-like; and hear, and stare,
And turn death-cold:
Never, ah, never more
1340   The hearth of her home to see,
Nor sand of the Spartan shore,
     Nor tombs where her fathers be,
     Nor Athena's bronzen Dwelling,
     Nor the towers of Pitanê
For her face was a dark desire
Upon Greece, and shame like fire,
And her dead are welling, welling,
From red Simoïs to the sea!

*[Talthybius, followed by one or two Soldiers and bearing
the child Astyanax dead, is seen approaching.]*

Leader

Ah, change on change! Yet each one racks
1350   This land with evil manifold;
     Unhappy wives of Troy, behold,
They bear the dead Astyanax,
Our prince, whom bitter Greeks this hour
Have hurled to death from Ilion's tower.

Talthybius

One galley, Hecuba, there lingereth yet,
Lapping the wave, to gather the last freight
Of Pyrrhus' spoils for Thessaly. The chief
Himself long since hath parted, much in grief
For Pêleus' sake, his grandsire, whom, men say,
1360 Acastus, Pelias' son, in war array
Hath driven to exile. Loath enough before
Was he to linger, and now goes the more
In haste, bearing Andromache, his prize.
'Tis she hath charmed these tears into mine eyes,
Weeping her fatherland, as o'er the wave
She gazed, and speaking words to Hector's grave.
Howbeit, she prayed us that due rites be done

For burial of this babe, thine Hector's son,
That now from Ilion's tower is fallen and dead.
And, lo! this great bronze-fronted shield, the dread 1370
Of many a Greek, that Hector held in fray,
O never in God's name—so did she pray—
Be this borne forth to hang in Pêleus' hall
Or that dark bridal chamber, that the wall
May hurt her eyes; but here, in Troy o'erthrown,
Instead of cedar wood and vaulted stone,
Be this her child's last house.... And in thine hands
She bade me lay him, to be swathed in bands
Of death and garments, such as rest to thee
In these thy fallen fortunes; seeing that she 1380
Hath gone her ways, and, for her master's haste,
May no more fold the babe unto his rest.
  Howbeit, so soon as he is garlanded
And robed, we will heap earth above his head
And lift our sails.... See all be swiftly done,
As thou art bidden. I have saved thee one
Labour. For as I passed Scamander's stream
Hard by, I let the waters run on him,
And cleansed his wounds.—See, I will go forth now
And break the hard earth for his grave: so thou 1390
And I will haste together, to set free
Our oars at last to beat the homeward sea!

*[He goes out with his Soldiers, leaving the body of the
Child in Hecuba's arms.]*

Hecuba

Set the great orb of Hector's shield to lie
Here on the ground. 'Tis bitter that mine eye
Should see it.... O ye Argives, was your spear
Keen, and your hearts so low and cold, to fear
This babe? 'Twas a strange murder for brave men!
For fear this babe some day might raise again
His fallen land! Had ye so little pride?
While Hector fought, and thousands at his side, 1400
Ye smote us, and we perished; and now, now,
When all are dead and Ilion lieth low,

Ye dread this innocent! I deem it not
Wisdom, that rage of fear that hath no thought....
  Ah, what a death hath found thee, little one!
Hadst thou but fallen fighting, hadst thou known
Strong youth and love and all the majesty
Of godlike kings, then had we spoken of thee
As of one blessed ... could in any wise

1410 These days know blessedness. But now thine eyes
Have seen, thy lips have tasted, but thy soul
No knowledge had nor usage of the whole
Rich life that lapt thee round.... Poor little child!
Was it our ancient wall, the circuit piled
By loving Gods, so savagely hath rent
Thy curls, these little flowers innocent
That were thy mother's garden, where she laid
Her kisses; here, just where the bone-edge frayed
Grins white above—Ah heaven, I will not see!

1420   Ye tender arms, the same dear mould have ye
As his; how from the shoulder loose ye drop
And weak! And dear proud lips, so full of hope
And closed for ever! What false words ye said
At daybreak, when he crept into my bed,
Called me kind names, and promised: 'Grandmother,
When thou art dead, I will cut close my hair
And lead out all the captains to ride by
Thy tomb.' Why didst thou cheat me so? 'Tis I,
Old, homeless, childless, that for thee must shed

1430 Cold tears, so young, so miserably dead.
  Dear God, the pattering welcomes of thy feet,
The nursing in my lap; and O, the sweet
Falling asleep together! All is gone.
How should a poet carve the funeral stone
To tell thy story true? 'There lieth here
A babe whom the Greeks feared, and in their fear
Slew him.' Aye, Greece will bless the tale it tells!
Child, they have left thee beggared of all else
In Hector's house; but one thing shalt thou keep,

1440 This war-shield bronzen-barred, wherein to sleep.
Alas, thou guardian true of Hector's fair
Left arm, how art thou masterless! And there

I see his handgrip printed on thy hold;
And deep stains of the precious sweat, that rolled
In battle from the brows and beard of him,
Drop after drop, are writ about thy rim.
  Go, bring them—such poor garments hazardous   *1200*
As these days leave. God hath not granted us
Wherewith to make much pride. But all I can,
I give thee, Child of Troy.—O vain is man,   1450
Who glorieth in his joy and hath no fears:
While to and fro the chances of the years
Dance like an idiot in the wind! And none
By any strength hath his own fortune won.

[During these lines several Women are seen approaching
with garlands and raiment in their hands.]

Leader

Lo these, who bear thee raiment harvested
From Ilion's slain, to fold upon the dead.

[During the following scene Hecuba gradually takes the
garments and wraps them about the Child.]

Hecuba

O not in pride for speeding of the car
Beyond thy peers, not for the shaft of war
True aimed, as Phrygians use; not any prize
Of joy for thee, nor splendour in men's eyes,   1460
Thy father's mother lays these offerings
About thee, from the many fragrant things
That were all thine of old. But now no more.
One woman, loathed of God, hath broke the door
And robbed thy treasure-house, and thy warm breath
Made cold, and trod thy people down to death!

Chorus [Some Women]

Deep in the heart of me
  I feel thine hand,

423

Mother: and is it he
1470   Dead here, our prince to be,
And lord of the land?

Hecuba

Glory of Phrygian raiment, which my thought
Kept for thy bridal day with some far-sought
Queen of the East, folds thee for evermore.
And thou, grey Mother, Mother-Shield that bore
A thousand days of glory, thy last crown
Is here.... Dear Hector's shield! Thou shalt lie down
Undying with the dead, and lordlier there
Than all the gold Odysseus' breast can bear,
1480   The evil and the strong!

Chorus [Some Women]

Child of the Shield-bearer,
Alas, Hector's child!
Great Earth, the All-mother,
Taketh thee unto her
With wailing wild!

Others

Mother of misery,
Give Death his song!
(*Hec.* Woe!) Aye and bitterly
(*Hec.* Woe!) We too weep for thee,
1490   And the infinite wrong!

*[During these lines Hecuba, kneeling by the body, has been
performing a funeral rite, symbolically staunching the dead
Child's wounds.]*

Hecuba

I make thee whole;
I bind thy wounds, O little vanished soul.
This wound and this I heal with linen white:
O emptiness of aid!... Yet let the rite

424

Be spoken. This and…. Nay, not I, but he,
Thy father far away shall comfort thee!

*[She bows her head to the ground and remains motionless
and unseeing.]*

Chorus

Beat, beat thine head:
  Beat with the wailing chime
  Of hands lifted in time:
Beat and bleed for the dead.   1500
Woe is me for the dead!

Hecuba

O Women! Ye, mine own….

[She rises bewildered, as though she had seen a vision.]

Leader

  Hecuba, speak!
Oh, ere thy bosom break….

Hecuba

Lo, I have seen the open hand of God;
And in it nothing, nothing, save the rod
Of mine affliction, and the eternal hate,
Beyond all lands, chosen and lifted great
For Troy! Vain, vain were prayer and incense-swell
And bulls' blood on the altars!… All is well.   1510
Had He not turned us in His hand, and thrust
Our high things low and shook our hills as dust,
We had not been this splendour, and our wrong
An everlasting music for the song
Of earth and heaven!
    Go, women: lay our dead
In his low sepulchre. He hath his meed
Of robing. And, methinks, but little care
Toucheth the tomb, if they that moulder there

1520

Have rich honours. 'Tis we, 'tis we,
That dream, we living and our vanity!

*[The Women bear out the dead Child upon the shield,
singing, when presently flames of fire and dim forms are
seen among the ruins of the City.]*

Chorus [Some Women]

Woe for the mother that bare thee, child,
Thread so frail of a hope so high,
That Time hath broken: and all men smiled
About thy cradle, and, passing by,
Spoke of thy father's majesty.
Low, low, thou liest!

Others

Ha! Who be these on the crested rock?
Fiery hands in the dusk, and a shock

1530

Of torches flung! What lingereth still,
O wounded City, of unknown ill,
Ere yet thou diest?

Talthybius [coming out through the ruined Wall]

Ye Captains that have charge to wreck this keep
Of Priam's City, let your torches sleep
No more! Up, fling the fire into her heart!
Then have we done with Ilion, and may part
In joy to Hellas from this evil land.
And ye—so hath one word two faces—stand,
Daughters of Troy, till on your ruined wall

1540

The echo of my master's trumpet call
In signal breaks: then, forward to the sea,
Where the long ships lie waiting. And for thee,
O ancient woman most unfortunate,
Follow: Odysseus' men be here, and wait
To guide thee…. 'Tis to him thou go'st for thrall.

Hecuba

Ah, me! and is it come, the end of all,

426

The very crest and summit of my days?
I go forth from my land, and all its ways
Are filled with fire! Bear me, O aged feet,
A little nearer: I must gaze, and greet   1550
My poor town ere she fall. Farewell, farewell!
O thou whose breath was mighty on the swell
Of orient winds, my Troy! Even thy name
Shall soon be taken from thee. Lo, the flame
Hath thee, and we, thy children, pass away
To slavery…. God! O God of mercy! Nay:
Why call I on the Gods? They know, they know,
My prayers, and would not hear them long ago.
Quick, to the flames! O, in thine agony,
My Troy, mine own, take me to die with thee!   1560

*[She springs toward the flames, but is seized and held by
the Soldiers.]*

Talthybius

Back! Thou art drunken with thy miseries,
Poor woman!—Hold her fast, men, till it please
Odysseus that she come. She was his lot
Chosen from all and portioned. Lose her not!

*[He goes to watch over the burning of the City. The dusk
deepens.]*

Chorus [Diverse Women]

    Woe, woe, woe!
Thou of the Ages, O wherefore fleest thou,
  Lord of the Phrygian, Father that made us?
  'Tis we, thy children; shall no man aid us?
  'Tis we, thy children! Seest thou, seest thou?

Others

He seeth, only his heart is pitiless;   1570
    And the land dies: yea, she,
She of the Mighty Cities perisheth citiless!

427

Troy shall no more be!

Others

> Woe, woe, woe!
> Ilion shineth afar!
> Fire in the deeps thereof,
> Fire in the heights above,
> And crested walls of War!

Others

1580
> As smoke on the wing of heaven
> Climbeth and scattereth,
> Torn of the spear and driven,
> The land crieth for death:
1300
> O stormy battlements that red fire hath riven,
> And the sword's angry breath!

[A new thought comes to Hecuba; she kneels and beats the earth with her hands.]

Hecuba

[Strophe.]

> O Earth, Earth of my children; hearken! and O mine own,
> Ye have hearts and forget not, ye in the darkness lying!

Leader

> Now hast thou found thy prayer, crying to them that are gone

Hecuba

> Surely my knees are weary, but I kneel above your head;
> Hearken, O ye so silent! My hands beat your bed!

Leader

1590
> I, I am near thee;
> I kneel to thy dead to hear thee,
> Kneel to mine own in the darkness;
> O husband, hear my crying!

Hecuba

Even as the beasts they drive, even as the loads they bear,

Leader

(Pain; O pain!)

Hecuba

We go to the house of bondage. Hear, ye dead, O hear!

Leader

(Go, and come not again!)

Hecuba

Priam, mine own Priam,
  Lying so lowly,
Thou in thy nothingness,   1600
Shelterless, comfortless,
See'st thou the thing I am?
Know'st thou my bitter stress?

Leader

Nay, thou art naught to him!
Out of the strife there came,
Out of the noise and shame,
Making his eyelids dim,
  Death, the Most Holy!

[The fire and smoke rise constantly higher.]

Hecuba

[Antistrophe.]

O high houses of Gods, beloved streets of my birth,
  Ye have found the way of the sword, the fiery and   1610
    blood-red river!

Leader

Fall, and men shall forget you! Ye shall lie in the gentle earth.

429

Hecuba.

> The dust as smoke riseth; it spreadeth wide its wing;
> It maketh me as a shadow, and my City a vanished thing!

Leader

> Out on the smoke she goeth,
> And her name no man knoweth;
> And the cloud is northward, southward; Troy is gone
> for ever!

[A great crash is heard, and the Wall is lost in smoke and darkness.]

Hecuba

> Ha! Marked ye? Heard ye? The crash of the towers that fall!

Leader

1620
> All is gone!

Hecuba

> Wrath in the earth and quaking and a flood that sweepeth all

Leader

> And passeth on!

[The Greek trumpet sounds.]

Hecuba

> Farewell!—O spirit grey,
>   Whatso is coming,
> Fail not from under me.
> Weak limbs, why tremble ye?
> Forth where the new long day
> Dawneth to slavery!

Chorus

> Farewell from parting lips,

Farewell!—Come, I and thou,   1630
Whatso may wait us now,
Forth to the long Greek ships
  And the sea's foaming.

[The trumpet sounds again, and the Women go out in the darkness.]

Euripides
•
The Medea

Translated by Theodore Alois Buckley

Dramatis Personae

NURSE

TUTOR

MEDEA

CHORUS
of Corinthian women

CREON

JASON

ÆGEUS

MESSENGER

SONS OF MEDEA

[The Scene lies in the vestibule of the palace of Jason at Corinth.

The Argument

Jason, having come to Corinth, and bringing with him Medea, espouses Glauce, the daughter of Creon, king of Corinth. But Medea, on the point of being banished from Corinth by Creon, having asked to remain one day, and having obtained her wish, sends to Glauce, by the hands of her sons, presents, as an acknowledgment for the favor, a robe and a golden chaplet, which she puts on and perishes; Creon also having embraced his daughter is destroyed. But Medea, when she had slain her children, escapes to Athens, in a chariot drawn by winged dragons, which she received from the Sun, and there marries Ægeus son of Pandion.]

Nurse of Medea.

Would that the hull of Argo had not winged her way to the Colchian land through the Cyanean Symplegades, and that the pine felled in the forests of Pelion had never fallen, nor had caused the hands of the chiefs to row, who went in search of the golden fleece for Pelias; for neither then would my mistress Medea have sailed to the towers of the Iolcian land, deeply smitten in her mind with the love of Jason; nor having persuaded the daughters of Pelias to slay their father would she have inhabited this country of Corinth with her husband and her children, pleasing indeed by her flight the citizens to whose land she came, and herself concurring in every respect with Jason; which is the surest support of conjugal happiness, when the wife is not estranged from the husband. But now every thing is at variance, and the dearest ties are weakened. For having betrayed his own children, and my mistress, Jason reposes in royal wedlock, having married the daughter of Creon, who is prince of this land. But Medea the unhappy, dishonored, calls on his oaths, and recalls the hands they plighted, the greatest pledge of fidelity, and invokes the gods to witness what return she meets with from Jason. And she lies

10

without tasting food, having sunk her body in grief, dissolving all her tedious time in tears, after she had once known that she had been injured by her husband, neither raising her eye, nor lifting her countenance from the ground; but as the rock, or the wave of the sea, does she listen to her friends when advised. Save that sometimes having turned her snow-white neck she to herself bewails her dear father, and her country, and her house, having betrayed which she hath come hither with a man who has now dishonored her. And she wretched hath discovered from affliction what it is not to forsake one's paternal country. But she hates her children, nor is she delighted at beholding them: but I fear her, lest she form some new design: for violent is her mind, nor will it endure to suffer ills. I know her, and I fear her, lest she should force the sharpened sword through her heart, or even should murder the princess and him who married her, and after that receive some greater ill. For she is violent; he who engages with her in enmity will not with ease at least sing the song of victory. But these her children are coming hither having ceased from their exercises, nothing mindful of their mother's ills, for the mind of youth is not wont to grieve.

[Tutor, with the sons of Medea, nurse.]

Tutor

O thou ancient possession of my mistress's house, why dost thou stand at the gates preserving thus thy solitude, bewailing to thyself our misfortunes? How doth Medea wish to be left alone without thee?

Nurse

O aged man, attendant on the children of Jason, to faithful servants the affairs of their masters turning out ill are a calamity, and lay hold upon their feelings. For I have arrived at such a height of grief that desire hath stolen on me to come forth hence and tell the misfortunes of Medea to the earth and heaven.

Tutor

Does not she wretched yet receive any respite from her grief?

Nurse

I envy thy ignorance; her woe is at its rise, and not even yet at its height.

Tutor

O unwise woman, if it is allowable to say this of one's lords, since she knows nothing of later ills.

Nurse

But what is this, O aged man? grudge not to tell me.

Tutor

Nothing: I have repented even of what was said before. 50

Nurse

Do not, I beseech you by your beard, conceal it from your fellow-servant; for I will preserve silence, if it be necessary, on these subjects.

Tutor

I heard from some one who was saying, not appearing to listen, having approached the places where dice is played, where the elders sit, around the hallowed font of Pirene, that the king of this land, Creon, intends to banish from the Corinthian country these children, together with their mother; whether this report be true, however, I know not; but I wish this may not be the case.

Nurse

And will Jason endure to see his children suffer this, even although he is at enmity with their mother? 60

Tutor

Ancient alliances are deserted for new, and he is no friend to this family.

Nurse

We perish then, if to the old we shall add a new ill, before the former be exhausted.

Tutor

But do thou, for it is not seasonable that my mistress should know this, restrain your tongue, and be silent on this report.

Nurse

O my children, do you hear what your father is toward you? Yet may he not perish, for he is my master, yet he is found to be treacherous toward his friends.

Tutor

70 And what man is not? dost thou only now know this, that every one loves himself dearer than his neighbor, some indeed with justice, but others even for the sake of gain, unless it be that their father loves not these at least on account of new nuptials.

Nurse

100 Go within the house, my children, for all will be well. But do thou keep these as much as possible out of the way, and let them not approach their mother, deranged through grief. For but now I saw her looking with wildness in her eyes on these, as about to execute some design, nor will she cease from her fury, I well know, before she overwhelm some one with it; upon her enemies however, and not her friends, may she do 80 some (ill.)

Medea.

(within) Wretch that I am, and miserable on account of my misfortunes, alas me! would I might perish!

Nurse

Thus it is, my children; your mother excites her heart, excites her fury.

Hasten as quick as possible within the house, and come not near her sight, nor approach her, but guard against the fierce temper and violent nature of her self-willed mind. Go now, go as quick as possible within. But it is evident that the cloud of grief raised up from the beginning will quickly burst forth with greater fury; what I pray will her soul, great in rage, implacable, irritated by ills, perform!

Medea

Alas! alas! I wretched have suffered, have suffered treatment worthy of great lamentation. O ye accursed children of a hated mother, may ye perish with your father, and may the whole house fall.

Nurse

Alas! alas! me miserable! but why should your children share their father's error? Why dost thou hate these! Alas me, my children, how be- 90 yond measure do I grieve lest ye suffer any evil! Dreadful are the disposi- tions of tyrants, and somehow in few things controlled, in most absolute, they with difficulty lay aside their passion. The being accustomed then to live in mediocrity of life is the better: may it be my lot then to grow old if not in splendor, at least in security. For, in the first place, even to 100 mention the name of moderation carries with it superiority, but to use it is by far the best conduct for men; but excess of fortune brings more power to men than is convenient; and has brought greater woes upon families, when the Deity be enraged.

[*Nurse, Chorus.*]

Chorus

I heard the voice, I heard the cry of the unhappy Colchian; is not she yet appeased? but, O aged matron, tell me; for within the apartment with double doors, I heard her cry; nor am I delighted, O woman, with the griefs of the family, since it is friendly to me.

Nurse

The family is not; these things are gone already: for he possesses the bed 110 of royalty; but she, my mistress, is melting away her life in her chamber, in no way soothing her mind by the advice of any one of her friends.

Medea

Alas! alas! may the flame of heaven rush through my head, what profit for me to live any longer. Alas! alas! may I rest myself in death, having left a hated life.

Chorus

Dost thou hear, O Jove, and earth, and light, the cry which the wretched bride utters? why I pray should this insatiable love of the marriage-bed hasten thee, O vain woman, to death? Pray not for this. But if thy husband courts a new bed, be not thus enraged with him. Jove will avenge
120 these wrongs for thee: waste not thyself so, bewailing thy husband.

Medea

O great Themis and revered Diana, do ye behold what I suffer, having bound my accursed husband by powerful oaths? Whom may I at some time see and his bride torn piecemeal with their very houses, who dare to injure me first. O my father, O my city, whom I basely abandoned, having slain my brother.

Nurse

Do ye hear what she says, and how she invokes Themis hearing the vow, and Jove who is considered the dispenser of oaths to mortals? It is not possible that my mistress will lull her rage to rest on any trivial circumstance.

Chorus

130 By what means could she come into our sight, and hear the voice of our discourse, if she would by any means remit her fierce anger and her fury of mind. Let not my zeal however be wanting ever to my friends. But go and conduct her hither from without the house, my friend, and tell her this, hasten, before she injure in any way those within, for this grief of hers is increased to a great height.

Nurse

I will do it, but I fear that I shall not persuade my mistress; neverthe-less I will give you this favor of my labor. And yet with the aspect of a lioness that has just brought forth does she look sternly on her atten-dants when any one approaches near attempting to address her. But thou wouldest not err in calling men of old foolish and nothing wise, who   140
invented songs, for festivals, for banquets, and for suppers, the delights of life that charm the ear; but no mortal has discovered how to soothe with music and with varied strains those bitter pangs, from which death and dreadful misfortunes overthrow families. And yet for men to assuage   200
these griefs with music were gain; but where the plenteous banquet is furnished, why raise they the song in vain? for the present bounty of the feast brings pleasure of itself to men.

Chorus

I heard the dismal sound of groans, and in a shrill voice she vents her bitter anguish on the traitor to her bed, her faithless husband—and suffering wrongs she calls upon the Goddess Themis, arbitress of oaths,   150
daughter of Jove, who conducted her to the opposite coast of Greece, across the sea by night, over the salt straits of the boundless ocean.

[Medea, Chorus.]

Medea

Ye Corinthian dames, I have come from out my palace; do not in any wise blame me; for I have known many men who have been renowned, some who have lived far from public notice, and others in the world; but those of a retired turn have gained for themselves a character of infa-my and indolence. For justice dwells not in the eyes of man, whoever, before he can well discover the disposition of a man, hates him at sight, in no way wronged by him. But it is necessary for a stranger exactly to   160
conform himself to the state, nor would I praise the native, whoever becoming self-willed is insolent to his fellow-citizens through ignorance. But this unexpected event that hath fallen upon me hath destroyed my spirit: I am going, and having given up the pleasure of life I am desirous to meet death, my friends. For he on whom my all rested, as you well know, my husband, has turned out the basest of men. But of all things

as many as have life and intellect, we women are the most wretched race. Who indeed first must purchase a husband with excess of money, and receive him a lord of our persons; for this is a still greater ill than the former. And in this is the greatest risk, whether we receive a bad one or a good one; for divorces bring not good fame to women, nor is it possible to repudiate one's husband. But on passing to new tempers and new laws, one need be a prophetess, as one can not learn of one's self, what sort of consort one shall most likely experience. And if with us carefully performing these things a husband shall dwell not imposing on us a yoke with severity, enviable is our life; if not, to die is better. But a man, when he is displeased living with those at home, having gone abroad is wont to relieve his heart of uneasiness, having recourse either to some friend or compeer. But we must look but to one person. But they say of us that we live a life of ease at home, but they are fighting with the spear; judging ill, since I would rather thrice stand in arms, than once suffer the pangs of child-birth. But, for the same argument comes not home to you and me, this is thy city, and thy father's house, thine are both the luxuries of life, and the society of friends; but I being destitute, cityless, am wronged by my husband, brought as a prize from a foreign land, having neither mother, nor brother, nor relation to afford me shelter from this calamity. So much then I wish to obtain from you, if any plan or contrivance be devised by me to repay with justice these injuries on my husband, and on him who gave his daughter, and on her to whom he was married, that you would be silent; for a woman in other respects is full of fear, and timid to look upon deeds of courage and the sword; but when she is injured in her bed, no other disposition is more blood-thirsty.

Chorus

I will do this; for with justice, Medea, wilt thou avenge thyself on thy husband, and I do not wonder that you lament your misfortunes. But I see Creon monarch of this land advancing, the messenger of new counsels.

[Creon, Medea, Chorus.]

Creon

Thee of gloomy countenance, and enraged with thy husband, Medea, I command to depart in exile from out of this land, taking with thee thy two children, and not to delay in any way, since I am the arbiter of this edict, and I will not return back to my palace, until I shall drive thee beyond the boundaries of this realm.

Medea

Alas! alas! I wretched am utterly destroyed, for my enemies stretch out every cable against me; nor is there any easy escape from this evil, but I will speak, although suffering injurious treatment; for what, Creon, dost thou drive me from this land?

Creon

I fear thee (there is no need for me to wrap my words in obscurity) lest thou do my child some irremediable mischief, And many circumstances are in unison with this dread. Thou art wise, and skilled in many evil sciences, and thou art exasperated, deprived of thy husband's bed. And I hear that thou threatenest, as they tell me, to wreak some deed of vengeance on the betrother, and the espouser and the espoused; against this then, before I suffer, will I guard. Better is it for me now to incur enmity from you, than softened by your words afterward greatly to lament it.

Medea

Alas! alas! not now for the first time, but often, Creon, hath this opinion injured me, and worked me much woe. But whatever man is prudent, let him never educate his children too deep in wisdom. For, independent of the other charges of idleness which they meet with, they find hostile envy from their fellow-citizens. For holding out to fools some new-discovered wisdom, thou wilt seem to be useless and not wise. And being judged superior to others who seem to have some varied knowledge, thou wilt appear offensive in the city. But even I myself share this fortune; for being wise, to some I am an object of envy, but to others, unsuited; but I am not very wise. Thou then fearest me, lest thou suffer some grievous mischief. My affairs are not in a state, fear me not, Creon, so as to offend against princes. For in what hast thou injured me? Thou hast given thy daughter to whom thy mind led thee; but I hate my husband: but thou, I think, didst these things in prudence. And now I envy not that thy affairs are prospering; make your alliances, be successful; but suffer me to dwell in this land, for although injured will I keep silence, overcome by my superiors.

Creon

Thou speakest soft words to the ear, but within my mind I have my fears, lest thou meditate some evil intent. And so much the less do I trust thee than before. For a woman that is quick to anger, and a man likewise, is easier to guard against, than one that is crafty and keeps silence. But begone as quick as possible, make no more words; since this is decreed, and thou hast no art, by which thou wilt stay with us, being hostile to me.

Medea

No I beseech you by your knees, and your newly-married daughter.

Creon

240   Thou wastest words; for thou wilt never persuade me.

Medea

Wilt thou then banish me, nor reverence my prayers?

Creon

For I do not love thee better than my own family.

Medea

O my country, how I remember thee now!

Creon

For next to my children it is much the dearest thing to me.

Medea

Alas! alas! how great an ill is love to man!

Creon

That is, I think, as fortune also shall attend it.

Medea

Jove, let it not escape thine eye, who is the cause of these misfortunes.

Creon

Begone, fond woman, and free me from these cares.

Medea

Care indeed; and do not I experience cares?

Creon

Quickly shalt thou be driven hence by force by the hands of my do-　250
mestics.

Medea

No, I pray not this at least; but I implore thee, Creon.

Creon

Thou wilt give trouble, woman, it seems.

Medea

I will go; I dare not ask to obtain this of you.

Creon

Why then dost thou resist, and wilt not depart from these realms?

Medea

Permit me to remain here this one day, and to bring my purpose to a
conclusion, in what way we shall fly, and to make provision for my sons,
since their father in no way regards providing for his children; but pity

260 them, for thou also art the father of children; and it is probable that thou hast tenderness: for of myself I have no care whether I may suffer banishment, but I weep for them experiencing this calamity.

Creon

My disposition is least of all imperious, and through feeling pity in many cases have I injured myself. And now I see that I am doing wrong, O lady, but nevertheless thou shalt obtain thy request; but this I warn thee, if to-morrow's light of the God of day shall behold thee and thy children within the confines of these realms, thou shalt die: this word is spoken in truth. But now if thou must stay, remain here yet one day, for thou wilt not do any horrid deed of which I have dread.

[Medea, Chorus.]

Chorus

270 Unhappy woman! alas wretched on account of thy griefs! whither wilt thou turn? what hospitality, or house, or country wilt thou find a refuge for these ills? how the Deity hath led thee, Medea, into a pathless tide of woes!

Medea

Ill hath it been done on every side. Who will gainsay it? but these things are not in this way, do not yet think it. Still is there a contest for those lately married, and to those allied to them no small affliction. For dost thou think I ever would have fawned upon this man, if I were not to gain something, or form some plan? I would not even have addressed him. I would not even have touched him with my hands. But he hath arrived at such a height of folly, as that, when it was in his power to 280 have crushed my plans, by banishing me from this land, he hath granted me to stay this day in which three of mine enemies will I put to death, the father, the bride, and my husband. But having in my power many resources of destruction against them, I know not, my friends, which I shall first attempt. Whether shall I consume the bridal house with fire, or force the sharpened sword through her heart having entered the chamber by stealth where the couch is spread? But one thing is against me;

if I should be caught entering the house and prosecuting my plans, by my death I shall afford laughter for my foes. Best then is it to pursue the straight path, in which I am most skilled, to take them off by poison. Let it be so. And suppose them dead: what city will receive me? What hospi- 290 table stranger affording a land of safety and a faithful home will protect my person? There is none. Waiting then yet a little time, if any tower of safety shall appear to us, I will proceed to this murder in treachery and silence. But if ill fortune that leaves me without resource force me, I myself having grasped the sword, although I should die, will kill them, and will rush to the extreme height of daring. For never, I swear by my mistress whom I revere most of all, and have chosen for my assistant, Hecate, who dwells in the inmost recesses of my house, shall any one of them wring my heart with grief with impunity. Bitter and mournful to them will I make these nuptials, and bitter this alliance, and my flight 300 400 from this land. But come, spare none of these sciences in which thou art skilled, Medea, deliberating and plotting. Proceed to the deed of terror: now is the time of resolution: seest thou what thou art suffering? Ill doth it become thee to incur ridicule from the race of Sisyphus, and from the nuptials of Jason, who art sprung from a noble father, and from the sun. And thou art skilled. Besides also we women are, by nature, to good actions of the least capacity, but the most cunning inventors of every ill.

Chorus

The waters of the hallowed streams flow upward to their sources, and justice and every thing is reversed. The counsels of men are treacherous, 310 and no longer is the faith of heaven firm. But fame changes, so that my sex may have the glory. Honor cometh to the female race; no longer shall opprobrious fame oppress the women. But the Muses shall cease from their ancient strains, from celebrating our perfidy. For Phœbus, leader of the choir, gave not to our minds the heavenly music of the lyre, since they would in turn have raised a strain against the race of men. But time of old hath much to say both of our life and the life of men. But thou hast sailed from thy father's house with maddened heart, having passed through the double rocks of the ocean, and thou dwellest in a foreign land, having lost the shelter of thy widowed bed, wretched woman, and 320 art driven dishonored an exile from this land. The reverence of oaths is gone, nor does shame any longer dwell in mighty Greece, but hath fled away through the air. But thou helpless woman hast neither father's house to afford you haven from your woes, and another more powerful queen of the nuptial bed rules over the house.

[Jason, Medea, Chorus.]

Jason

Not now for the first time, but often have I perceived that fierce anger is an irremediable ill. For though it was in your power to inhabit this land and this house, bearing with gentleness the determination of thy superiors, by thy rash words thou shalt be banished from this land. And to me indeed it is of no importance; never cease from saying that Jason is the worst of men. But for what has been said by thee against the royal family, think it the greatest good fortune that thou art punished by banishment only. I indeed was always employed in diminishing the anger of the enraged princes, and was willing that thou shouldest remain. But thou remittest not of thy folly, always reviling the ruling powers; wherefore thou shalt be banished from the land. But nevertheless even after this am I come, not wearied with my friends, providing for thee, O woman, that thou mightest not be banished with thy children, either without money, or in want of any thing. Banishment draws many misfortunes with it. For although thou hatest me, I never could wish thee evil.

Medea

O thou vilest of men (for this is the greatest reproach I have in my power with my tongue to tell thee, for thy unmanly cowardice), hast thou come to us, hast thou come, who art most hateful? This is not fortitude, or confidence, to look in the face of friends whom thou hast injured, but the worst of all diseases among men, impudence. But thou hast done well in coming. For both I shall be lightened in my heart while reviling thee, and thou wilt be pained at hearing me. But I will first begin to speak from the first circumstances. I preserved thee (as those Greeks well know as many as embarked with thee on board the same ship Argo) when sent to master the fire-breathing bulls with the yoke, and to sow the fatal seed: and having slain the dragon who watching around the golden fleece guarded it with spiry folds, a sleepless guard, I raised up to thee a light of safety. But I myself having betrayed my father, and my house, came to the Peliotic Iolcos with thee, with more readiness than prudence. And I slew Pelias by a death which it is most miserable to die, by the hands of his own children, and I freed thee from every fear. And having experienced these services from me, thou vilest of men, thou hast betrayed me and hast procured for thyself a new bed, children being born to thee, for if thou wert still childless it would be pardonable in thee to be enamored of this alliance. But the faith of oaths is vanished: nor can I discover whether thou thinkest that the former Gods are not still in power, or whether new laws are now laid down for men, since thou art at least conscious of being perjured toward me. Alas! this right hand which thou hast often touched, and these knees, since in vain have I been polluted by a wicked husband, and have failed in my hopes. Come (for I will converse with thee as with a friend, not expecting to receive any benefit from thee at least, but nevertheless I will; for when questioned thou wilt appear more base), now whither shall I turn? Whether to my father's house, which I betrayed for thee, and my country, and came hither? or to the miserable daughters of Pelias? friendly would they indeed receive me in their house, whose father I slew. For thus it is: I am in enmity with my friends at home; but those whom I ought not to injure, by obliging thee, I make my enemies. On which account in return for this thou hast made me to be called happy by many dames through Greece, and in thee I, wretch that I am, have an admirable and faithful husband, if cast out at least I shall fly this land, deserted by my friends, lonely with thy lonely children. Fair renown indeed to the new married bridegroom, that his children are wandering in poverty, and I also who preserved thee. O Jove, why I pray hast thou given to men certain proofs of the gold which is adulterate, but no mark is set by nature on the person of men by which one may distinguish the bad man.

Chorus

Dreadful is that anger and irremediable, when friends with friends kindle strife.

Jason

It befits me, it seems, not to be weak in argument, but as the prudent pilot of a vessel, with all the sail that can be hoisted, to run from out of thy violent abuse, O woman. But I, since thou thus much vauntest thy favors, think that Venus alone both of Gods and men was the protectress of my voyage. But thou hast a fickle mind, but it is an invidious account to go through, how love compelled thee with his inevitable arrows

390 to preserve my life. But I will not follow up arguments with too great accuracy, for where thou hast assisted me it is well. Moreover thou hast received more at least from my safety than thou gavest, as I will explain to thee. First of all thou dwellest in Greece instead of a foreign land, and thou learnest what justice is, and to enjoy laws, not to be directed by mere force. And all the Grecians have seen that thou art wise, and thou hast renown; but if thou wert dwelling in the extreme confines of that land, there would not have been fame of thee. But may neither gold in my house be my lot, nor to attune the strain more sweet than Orpheus,

400 if my fortune be not conspicuous. So much then have I said of my toils; for thou first broughtest forward this contest of words. But with regard to those reproaches which thou heapest on me for my royal marriage, in this will I show first that I have been wise, in the next place moderate, thirdly a great friend to thee, and my children: but be silent. After I had come hither from the Iolcian land bringing with me many grievous calamities, what measure more fortunate than this could I have invented, than, an exile as I was, to marry the daughter of the monarch? not, by which thou art grated, loathing thy bed, nor smitten with desire of a new bride, nor having emulation of a numerous offspring, for those born

410 to me are sufficient, nor do I find fault with that; but that (which is of the greatest consequence) we might live honorably, and might not be in want, knowing well that every friend flies out of the way of a poor man; and that I might bring up my children worthy of my house, and that having begotten brothers to those children sprung from thee, I might place them on the same footing, and having united the family, I might flourish; for both thou hast some need of children, and to me it were advantageous to advance my present progeny by means of the children which might arise; have I determined ill? not even thou couldest say so, if thy bed did not gall thee. But thus far have you come, that your bed

420 being safe, you women think that you have every thing. But if any misfortune befall that, the most excellent and fairest objects you make the most hateful. It were well then that men should generate children from some other source, and that the female race should not exist, and thus there would not have been any evil among men.

Chorus

Jason, thou hast well adorned these arguments of thine, but nevertheless to me, although I speak reluctantly, thou appearest, in betraying thy wife, to act unjustly.

Medea

Surely I am in many things different from many mortals, for in my judgment, whatever man being unjust, is deeply skilled in argument, merits the severest punishment. For vaunting that with his tongue he can well gloze over injustice, he dares to work deceit, but he is not over-wise. Thus do not thou also be now plausible to me, nor skilled in speaking, for one word will overthrow thee: it behooved thee, if thou wert not a bad man, to have contracted this marriage having persuaded me, and not without the knowledge of thy friends.

430

Jason

Well wouldest thou have lent assistance to this report, if I had mentioned the marriage to thee, who not even now endurest to lay aside this unabated rage of heart.

Medea

This did not move thee, but a foreign bed would lead in its result to an old age without honor.

Jason

Be well assured of this, that I did not form this alliance with the princess, which I now hold, for the sake of the woman, but, as I said before also, wishing to preserve thee, and to beget royal children brothers to my sons, a support to our house.

440

Medea

Let not a splendid life of bitterness be my lot, nor wealth, which rends my heart.

Jason

Dost thou know how to alter thy prayers, and appear wiser? Let not good things ever seem to you bitter, nor when in prosperity seem to be in adversity.

600

451

Medea

Insult me, since thou hast refuge, but I destitute shall fly this land.

Jason

450   Thou chosest this thyself, blame no one else.

Medea

By doing what? by marrying and betraying thee?

Jason

By imprecating unhallowed curses on the royal family.

Medea

From thy house at least am I laden with curses.

Jason

I will not dispute more of this with thee. But if thou wishest to receive either for thyself or children any part of my wealth as an assistant on thy flight, speak, since I am ready to give with an unsparing hand, and to send tokens of hospitality to my friends, who will treat you well; and refusing these thou wilt be foolish, woman, but ceasing from thine anger, thou wilt gain better treatment.

Medea

460   I will neither use thy friends, nor will I receive aught; do not give to me, for the gifts of a bad man bring no assistance.

Jason

Then I call the Gods to witness, that I wish to assist thee and thy children in every thing; but good things please thee not, but thou rejectest thy friends with audacity, wherefore shalt thou grieve the more.

Medea

Begone, for thou art captured by desire of thy new bride, tarrying so long without the palace; wed her, for perhaps, but with the assistance of the God shall it be said, thou wilt make such a marriage alliance, as thou wilt hereafter wish to renounce.

Chorus

The loves, when they come too impetuously, have given neither good report nor virtue among men, but if Venus come with moderation, no other Goddess is so benign. Never, O my mistress, mayest thou send forth against me from thy golden bow thy inevitable shaft, having steeped it in desire. But may temperance preserve me, the noblest gift of heaven; never may dreaded Venus, having smitten my mind for another's bed, heap upon me jealous passions and unabated quarrels, but approving the peaceful union, may she quick of perception sit in judgment on the bed of women. O my country, and my house, never may I be an outcast of my city, having a life scarce to be endured through poverty, the most lamentable of all woes. By death, by death, may I before that be subdued, having lived to accomplish that day; but no greater misfortune is there than to be deprived of one's paternal country. We have seen it, nor have we to speak from others' accounts; for thee, neither city nor friend hath pitied, though suffering the most dreadful anguish. Thankless may he perish who desires not to assist his friends, having unlocked the pure treasures of his mind; never shall he be friend to me.

[Ægeus, Medea, Chorus.]

Ægeus

Medea, hail! for no one hath known a more honorable salutation to address to friends than this.

Medea

Hail thou also, son of the wise Pandion, Ægeus, coming from what

490   quarter dost thou tread the plain of this land?

Ægeus

Having left the ancient oracle of Phœbus.

Medea

But wherefore wert thou sent to the prophetic centre of the earth?

Ægeus

Inquiring of the God how offspring may arise to me.

Medea

By the Gods, tell me, dost thou live this life hitherto childless?

Ægeus

Childless I am, by the disposal of some deity.

Medea

Hast thou a wife, or knowest thou not the marriage-bed!

Ægeus

I am not destitute of the connubial bed.

Medea

What then did Apollo tell thee respecting thy offspring?

Ægeus

Words deeper than a man can form opinion of.

Medea

    Is it allowable for me to know the oracle of the God?   500

Ægeus

    Certainly, inasmuch as it needs also a deep-skilled mind.

Medea

    What then did he say? Speak, if I may hear.

Ægeus

    That I was not to loose the projecting foot of the vessel—

Medea

    Before thou didst what, or came to what land?

Ægeus

    Before I revisit my paternal hearth.

Medea

    Then as desiring what dost thou direct thy voyage to this land?

Ægeus

    There is one Pittheus, king of the country of Trazene.

Medea

    The most pious son, as report says, of Pelops.

Ægeus

    To him I wish to communicate the oracle of the God.

Medea

510   For he is a wise man, and versed in such matters.

Ægeus

And to me at least the dearest of all my friends in war.

Medea

Mayest thou prosper, and obtain what thou desirest.

Ægeus

But why is thine eye and thy color thus faded?

Medea

Ægeus, my husband is the worst of all men.

Ægeus

What sayest thou? tell me all thy troubles.

Medea

Jason wrongs me, having never suffered wrong from me.

Ægeus

Having done what? tell me more clearly.

Medea

He hath here a wife besides me, mistress of the house.

Ægeus

Hath he dared to commit this disgraceful action?

Medea

Be assured he has; but we his former friends are dishonored. 520

Egeus

Enamored of her, or hating thy bed?

Medea

(Smitten with) violent love indeed, he was faithless to his friends.

Egeus

Let him perish then, since, as you say, he is a bad man.

Medea

He was charmed to receive an alliance with princes. 700

Egeus

And who gives the bride to him? finish the account, I beg.

Medea

Creon, who is monarch of this Corinthian land.

Egeus

Pardonable was it then that thou art grieved, O lady.

Medea

I perish, and in addition to this am I banished from this land.

Egeus

By whom? thou art mentioning another fresh misfortune.

Medea

530   Creon drives me an exile out of this land of Corinth.

Ægeus

And does Jason suffer it? I praise not this.

Medea

By his words he does not, but at heart he wishes [to endure my banishment:] but by this thy beard I entreat thee, and by these thy knees, and I become thy suppliant, pity me, pity this unfortunate woman, nor behold me going forth in exile abandoned, but receive me at thy hearth in thy country and thy house. Thus by the Gods shall thy desire of children be accomplished to thee, and thou thyself shalt die in happiness. But thou knowest not what this fortune is that thou hast found; but I will free thee from being childless, and I will cause thee to raise up offspring, such
540   charms I know.

Ægeus

On many accounts, O lady, am I willing to confer this favor on thee, first on account of the Gods, then of the children, whose birth thou holdest forth; for on this point else I am totally sunk in despair. But thus am I determined: if thou comest to my country, I will endeavor to receive thee with hospitality, being a just man; so much however I beforehand apprise thee of, O lady, I shall not be willing to lead thee with me from this land; but if thou comest thyself to my house, thou shalt stay there in safety, and to no one will I give thee up. But do thou of thyself withdraw thy foot from this country, for I wish to be without blame even
550   among strangers.

Medea

It shall be so, but if there was a pledge of this given to me, I should have all things from thee in a noble manner.

Ægeus

Dost thou not trust me? what is thy difficulty?

Medea

I trust thee; but the house of Pelias is mine enemy, and Creon too; to these then, wert thou bound by oaths, thou wouldest not give me up from the country, should they attempt to drag me thence. But having agreed by words alone, and without calling the Gods to witness, thou mightest be their friend, and perhaps be persuaded by an embassy; for weak is my state, but theirs are riches, and a royal house.

Egeus

Thou hast spoken much prudence, O lady. But if it seems fit to thee   560
that I should do this, I refuse not. For to me also this seems the safest plan, that I should have some pretext to show to your enemies, and thy safety is better secured; propose the Gods that I am to invoke.

Medea

Swear by the earth, and by the sun the father of my father, and join the whole race of Gods.

Egeus

That I will do what thing, or what not do? speak.

Medea

That thou wilt neither thyself ever cast me forth from out of thy country, nor, if any one of my enemies desire to drag me thence, that thou wilt, while living, give me up willingly.

Egeus

I swear by the earth, and the hallowed majesty of the sun, and by all   570
the Gods, to abide by what I hear from thee.

Medea

It is sufficient: but what wilt thou endure shouldest thou not abide by this oath?

Ægeus

That which befalls impious men.

Medea

Go with blessings; for every thing is well. And I will come as quick as possible to thy city, having performed what I intend, and having obtained what I desire.

Chorus

580　But may the son of Maia the king, the guide, conduct thee safely to thy house, and the plans of those things, which thou anxiously keepest in thy mind, mayest thou bring to completion, since, Ægeus, thou hast appeared to us to be a noble man.

[Medea, Chorus.]

Medea

O Jove, and thou vengeance of Jove, and thou light of the sun, now, my friends, shall I obtain a splendid victory over my enemies, and I have struck into the path. Now is there hope that my enemies will suffer punishment. For this man, where I was most at a loss, hath appeared a harbor to my plans. From him will I make fast my cable from the stern, having come to the town and citadel of Pallas. But now will I communicate all my plans to thee; but receive my words not as attuned to pleasure.

590　Having sent one of my domestics, I will ask Jason to come into my presence; and when he is come, I will address gentle words to him, as that it appears to me that these his actions are both honorable, and are advantageous and well determined on. And I will entreat him that my sons may stay; not that I would leave my children in a hostile country for my enemies to insult, but that by deceit I may slay the king's daughter. For I will send them bearing presents in their hands, both a fine-wrought robe, and a golden-twined wreath. And if she take the ornaments and place them round her person, she shall perish miserably, and every one who shall touch the damsel; with such charms will I anoint the presents. Here however I finish this account; but I bewail the deed such as must next be 600 done by me; for I shall slay my children; there is no one who shall rescue them from me; and having heaped in ruins the whole house of Jason, I will go from out this land, flying the murder of my dearest children, and having dared a deed most unhallowed. For it is not to be borne, my friends, to be derided by one's enemies. Let things take their course; what gain is it to me to live longer? I have neither country, nor house, nor ref- uge from my ills. Then erred I, when I left my father's house, persuaded *800* by the words of a Grecian man, who with the will of the Gods shall suffer punishment from me. For neither shall he ever hereafter behold the children he had by me alive, nor shall he raise a child by his new 610 wedded wife, since it is fated that the wretch should wretchedly perish by my spells. Let no one think me mean-spirited and weak, nor of a gentle temper, but of a contrary disposition to my foes relentless, and to my friends kind: for the lives of such sort are most glorious.

Chorus

Since thou hast communicated this plan to me, desirous both of do- ing good to thee, and assisting the laws of mortals, I dissuade thee from doing this.

Medea

It can not be otherwise, but it is pardonable in thee to say this, not suffering the cruel treatment that I do.

Chorus

But wilt thou dare to slay thy two sons, O lady? 620

Medea

For in this way will my husband be most afflicted.

Chorus

But thou at least wilt be the most wretched woman.

Medea

Be that as it may: all intervening words are superfluous; but go, hasten, and bring Jason hither; for I make use of thee in all matters of trust. And thou wilt mention nothing of the plans determined on by me, if at least thou meanest well to thy mistress, and art a woman.

Chorus

The Athenians happy of old, and the descendants of the blessed Gods, feeding on the most exalted wisdom of a country sacred and unconquered, always tripping elegantly through the purest atmosphere, 630 where they say that of old the golden-haired Harmonia gave birth to the chaste nine Pierian Muses. And they report also that Venus drawing in her breath from the stream of the fair-flowing Cephisus, breathed over their country gentle sweetly-breathing gales of air; and always entwining in her hair the fragrant wreath of roses, sends the loves as assessors to wisdom; the assistants of every virtue. How then will the city of hallowed rivers, or the country which conducts thee to friends, receive the murderer of her children, the unholy one? Consider in conjunction with others of the slaughter of thy children, consider what a murder thou wilt undertake. Do not by thy knees, by every plea, by every prayer, we entreat 640 you, do not murder your children; but how wilt thou acquire confidence either of mind or hand or in heart against thy children, attempting a dreadful deed of boldness? But how, having darted thine eyes upon thy children, wilt thou endure the perpetration of the murder without tears? Thou wilt not be able, when thy children fall suppliant at thy feet, to imbrue thy savage hand in their wretched life-blood.

[Jason, Medea, Chorus.]

Jason

I am come, by thee requested; for although thou art enraged, thou shalt not be deprived of this at least; but I will hear what new service thou dost desire of me, lady.

Medea

650 Jason, I entreat you to be forgiving of what has been said, but right

is it that you should bear with my anger, since many friendly acts have been done by us two. But I reasoned with myself and rebuked myself; wayward woman, why am I maddened and am enraged with those who consult well for me? and why am I in enmity with the princes of the land and with my husband, who is acting in the most advantageous manner for us, having married a princess, and begetting brothers to my children? Shall I not cease from my rage? What injury do I suffer, the Gods providing well for me? Have I not children? And I know that I am flying the country, and am in want of friends. Revolving this in my mind I perceive that I had much imprudence, and was enraged without reason. Now then I approve of this, and thou appearest to me to be prudent, having added this alliance to us; but I was foolish, who ought to share in these plans, and to join in adorning and to stand by the bed, and to delight with thee that thy bride was enamored of thee; but we women are as we are, I will not speak evil of the sex; wherefore it is not right that you should put yourself on an equality with the evil, nor repay folly for folly. I give up, and say that then I erred in judgment, but now I have determined on these things better. O my children, my children, come forth, leave the house, come forth, salute, and address your father with me, and be reconciled to your friends from your former hatred together with your mother. For there is amity between us, and my rage hath ceased. Take his right hand. Alas! my misfortunes; how I feel some hidden ill in my mind! Will ye, my children, in this manner, and for a long time enjoying life, stretch out your dear hands? Wretch that I am! how near am I to weeping and full of fear!—But at last canceling this dispute with your father, I have filled thus my tender sight with tears.

660

670

900

Chorus

In my eyes also the moist tear is arisen; and may not the evil advance to a greater height than it is at present.

Jason

I approve of this, lady, nor do I blame the past; for it is reasonable that the female sex be enraged with a husband who barters them for another union.—But thy heart has changed to the more proper side, and thou hast discovered, but after some time, the better counsel: these are the actions of a wise woman. But for you, my sons, your father not without thought hath formed many provident plans, with the assistance of the

680

Gods. For I think that you will be yet the first in this Corinthian country, together with your brothers. But advance and prosper: and the rest your father, and whatever God is propitious, will effect. And may I behold you blooming arrive at the prime of youth, superior to my enemies. And thou, why dost thou bedew thine eyes with the moist tear, having turned aside thy white cheek, and why dost thou not receive these words from me with pleasure?

Medea

It is nothing. I was thinking of my sons.

Jason

Be of good courage; for I will arange well for them.

Medea

I will be so, I will not mistrust thy words; but a woman is of soft mould, and was born to tears.

Jason

Why, I pray, dost thou so grieve for thy children?

Medea

I brought them into the world, and when thou wert praying that thy children might live, a feeling of pity came upon me if that would be. But for what cause thou hast come to a conference with me, partly hath been explained, but the other reasons I will mention. Since it appeareth fit to the royal family to send me from this country, for me also this appears best, I know it well, that I might not dwell here, a check either to thee or to the princes of the land; for I seem to be an object of enmity to the house; I indeed will set out from this land in flight; but to the end that the children may be brought up by thy hand, entreat Creon that they may not leave this land.

690

700

Jason

I know not whether I shall persuade him; but it is right to try.

Medea

But do thou then exhort thy bride to ask her father, that my children may not leave this country.

Jason

Certainly I will, and I think at least that she will persuade him, if indeed   710
she be one of the female sex.

Medea

I also will assist you in this task, for I will send to her presents which (I well know) far surpass in beauty any now among men, both a fine-wrought robe, and a golden-twined chaplet, my sons carrying them. But as quick as possible let one of my attendants bring hither these ornaments. Thy bride shall be blessed not in one instance, but in many, having met with you at least the best of husbands, and possessing ornaments which the sun my father's father once gave to his descendants. Take these nuptial presents, my sons, in your hands, and bear and present them to the blessed royal bride; she shall receive gifts not indeed to be despised.   720

Jason

Why, O fond woman, dost thou rob thy hands of these; thinkest thou that the royal palace is in want of vests? in want of gold? keep these presents, give them not away; for if the lady esteems me of any value, she will prefer pleasing me to riches, I know full well.

Medea

But do not oppose me; gifts, they say, persuade even the Gods, and gold is more powerful than a thousand arguments to men. Hers is fortune, her substance the God now increases, she in youth governs all. But the sentence of banishment on my children I would buy off with my life,

730 not with gold alone. But my children, enter you the wealthy palace, to the new bride of your father, and my mistress, entreat her, beseech her, that you may not leave the land, presenting these ornaments; but this is of the greatest consequence, that, she receive these gifts in her own hand. Go as quick as possible, and may you be bearers of good tidings to your mother in what she desires to obtain, having succeeded favorably.

Chorus

Now no longer have I any hope of life for the children, no longer is there hope; for already are they going to death. The bride shall receive the destructive present of the golden chaplet, she wretched shall receive them, and around her golden tresses shall she place the attire of death, having received the presents in her hands. The beauty and the divine 740 glitter of the robe will persuade her to place around her head the golden-wrought chaplet. Already with the dead shall the bride be adorned; into such a net will she fall, and such a destiny will she, hapless woman, meet with; nor will she escape her fate. But thou, oh unhappy man! oh wretched bridegroom! son-in-law of princes, unknowingly thou bringest on thy children destruction, and on thy wife a bitter death; hapless man, how much art thou fallen from thy state! But I lament for thy grief, O 1000 wretch, mother of these children, who wilt murder thy sons on account of a bridal-bed; deserting which, in defiance of thee, thy husband dwells 750 with another wife.

[Tutor, Medea, Chorus.]

Tutor

Thy sons, my mistress, are reprieved from banishment, and the royal bride received thy presents in her hands with pleasure, and hence is peace to thy children.

Medea

Ah!

Tutor

Why dost thou stand in confusion, when thou art fortunate?

Medea

Alas! alas!

Tutor

This behavior is not consonant with the message I have brought thee.

Medea

Alas! again.

Tutor

Have I reported any ill fortune unknowingly, and have I failed in my   760
hope of being the messenger of good?

Medea

Thou hast said what thou hast said, I blame not thee.

Tutor

Why then dost thou bend down thine eye, and shed tears?

Medea

Strong necessity compels me, O aged man, for this the Gods and I
deliberating ill have contrived.

Tutor

Be of good courage; thou also wilt return home yet through thy chil-
dren.

Medea

Others first will I send to their home, O wretched me!

Tutor

770 Thou art not the only one who art separated from thy children; it behooves a mortal to bear calamities with meekness.

Medea

I will do so; but go within the house, and prepare for the children what is needful for the day. O my sons, my sons, you have indeed a city, and a house, in which having forsaken me miserable, you shall dwell, ever deprived of a mother. But I am now going an exile into a foreign land, before I could have delight in you, and see you flourishing, before I could adorn your marriage, and wife, and nuptial-bed, and hold up the torch. O unfortunate woman that I am, on account of my wayward temper. In vain then, my children, have I brought you up, in vain have I toiled, and been consumed with cares, suffering the strong agonies of child-bearing.

780 Surely once there was a time when I hapless woman had many hopes in you, that you would both tend me in my age, and when dead would with your hands decently compose my limbs, a thing desired by men. But now this pleasing thought hath indeed perished; for deprived of you I shall pass a life of misery, and bitter to myself. But you will no longer behold your mother with your dear eyes, having passed into another state of life. Alas! alas! why do you look upon me with your eyes, my children? Why do ye smile that last smile? Alas! alas! what shall I do? for my heart is sinking. Ye females, when I behold the cheerful look of my children, I have no power. Farewell my counsels: I will take my children with me

790 from this land. What does it avail me grieving their father with the ills of these, to acquire twice as much pain for myself? never will I at least do this. Farewell my counsels. And yet what do I suffer? do I wish to incur ridicule, having left my foes unpunished? This must be dared. But the bringing forward words of tenderness in my mind arises also from my cowardice. Go, my children, into the house; and he for whom it is not lawful to be present at my sacrifice, let him take care himself to keep away. But I will not stain my hand. Alas! alas! do not thou then, my soul, do not thou at least perpetrate this. Let them escape, thou wretch, spare thy sons. There shall they live with us and delight thee. No, I swear by the

infernal deities who dwell with Pluto, never shall this be, that I will give   800
up my children to be insulted by my enemies. [At all events they must die,
and since they must, I who brought them into the world will perpetrate
the deed.] This is fully determined by fate, and shall not pass away. And
now the chaplet is on her head, and the bride is perishing in the robes; of
this I am well assured. But, since I am now going a most dismal path, and
these will I send by one still more dismal, I desire to address my children:
give, my sons, give thy right hand for thy mother to kiss. O most dear
hand, and those lips dearest to me, and that form and noble countenance
of my children, be ye blessed, but there; for every thing here your father
hath taken away. O the sweet embrace, and that soft skin, and that most   810
fragrant breath of my children. Go, go; no longer am I able to look upon
you, but am overcome by my ills. I know indeed the ills that I am about
to dare, but my rage is master of my counsels, which is indeed the cause
of the greatest calamities to men.

Chorus

Already have I often gone through more refined reasonings, and have
come to greater arguments than suits the female mind to investigate; for
we also have a muse, which dwelleth with us, for the sake of teaching
wisdom; but not with all, for haply thou wilt find but a small number of
the race of women out of many not ungifted with the muse.

And I say that those men who are entirely free from wedlock, and have   820
not begotten children, surpass in happiness those who have families;
those indeed who are childless, through inexperience whether children
are born a joy or anguish to men, not having them themselves, are ex-
empt from much misery. But those who have a sweet blooming offspring
of children in their house, I behold worn with care the whole time; first   *1100*
of all how they shall bring them up honorably, and how they shall leave
means of sustenance for their children. And still after this, whether they
are toiling for bad or good sons, this is still in darkness. But one ill to
mortals, the last of all, I now will mention. For suppose they have both
found sufficient store, and the bodies of their children have arrived at   830
manhood, and that they are good; but if this fortune shall happen to
them, death, bearing away their sons, vanishes with them to the shades of
darkness. How then does it profit that the Gods heap on mortals yet this
grief in addition to others, the most bitter of all, for the sake of children?

[Medea, Messenger, Chorus.]

Medea

For a long time waiting for the event, my friends, I am anxiously expecting what will be the result thence. And I see indeed one of the domestics of Jason coming hither, and his quickened breath shows that he will be the messenger of some new ill.

Messenger

840   O thou, that hast impiously perpetrated a deed of terror, Medea, fly, fly, leaving neither the ocean chariot, nor the car whirling o'er the plain.

Medea

But what is done that requires this flight?

Messenger

The princess is just dead, and Creon her father destroyed by thy charms.

Medea

Thou hast spoken most glad tidings: and hereafter from this time shalt thou be among my benefactors and friends.

Messenger

What sayest thou? Art thou in thy senses, and not mad, lady? who having destroyed the king and family, rejoicest at hearing it, and fearest not such things?

Medea

850   I also have something to say to these words of thine at least; but be not hasty, my friend; but tell me how they perished, for twice as much

delight wilt thou give me if they died miserably.

Messenger

    As soon as thy two sons were come with their father, and had entered the bridal house, we servants, who were grieved at thy misfortunes, were delighted; and immediately there was much conversation in our ears, that thy husband and thou had brought the former quarrel to a friendly termination. One kissed the hand, another the auburn head of thy sons, and I also myself followed with them to the women's apartments through joy. But my mistress, whom we now reverence instead of thee, before she saw thy two sons enter, held her cheerful eyes fixed on Jason; afterward however she covered her eyes, and turned aside her white cheek, disgusted at the entrance of thy sons; but thy husband quelled the anger and rage of the young bride, saying this: Be not angry with thy friends, but cease from thy rage, and turn again thy face, esteeming those as friends, whom thy husband does. But receive the gifts, and ask thy father to give up the sentence of banishment against these children for my sake. But when she saw the ornaments, she refused not, but promised her husband every thing; and before thy sons and their father were gone far from the house, she took and put on the variegated robes, and having placed the golden chaplet around her tresses she arranges her hair in the radiant mirror, smiling at the lifeless image of her person. And after, having risen from her seat, she goes across the chamber, elegantly tripping with snow-white foot; rejoicing greatly in the presents, looking much and oftentimes with her eyes on her outstretched neck. After that however there was a sight of horror to behold. For having changed color, she goes staggering back trembling in her limbs, and is scarce in time to prevent herself from falling on the ground, by sinking into a chair. And some aged female attendant, when she thought that the wrath either of Pan or some other Deity had visited her, offered up the invocation, before at least she sees the white foam bursting from her mouth, and her mistress rolling her eyeballs from their sockets, and the blood no longer in the flesh; then she sent forth a loud shriek of far different sound from the strain of supplication; and straightway one rushed to the apartments of her father, but another to her newly-married husband, to tell the calamity befallen the bride, and all the house was filled with frequent hurryings to and fro. And by this time a swift runner, exerting his limbs, might have reached the goal of the course of six plethra; but she, wretched woman, from being speechless, and from a closed eye having groaned deeply writhed

860

870

880

890

in agony; for a double pest was warring against her. The golden chaplet indeed placed on her head was sending forth a stream of all-devouring fire wonderful to behold, but the fine-wrought robes, the presents of thy sons, were devouring the white flesh of the hapless woman. But she having started from her seat flies, all on fire, tossing her hair and head on this side and that side, desirous of shaking off the chaplet; but the golden wreath firmly kept its hold; but the fire, when she shook her hair, blazed out with double fury, and she sinks upon the ground overcome by her sufferings, difficult for any one except her father to recognize. For neither was the expression of her eyes clear, nor her noble countenance; but the blood was dropping from the top of her head mixed with fire.

1200

But her flesh was dropping off her bones, as the tear from the pine-tree, by the hidden fangs of the poison; a sight of horror. But all feared to touch the body, for we had her fate to warn us. But the hapless father, through ignorance of her suffering, having come with haste into the apartment, falls on the corpse, and groans immediately; and having folded his arms round her, kisses her, saying these words: O miserable child, what Deity hath thus cruelly destroyed thee? who makes an aged father bowing to the tomb bereaved of thee? Alas me! let me die with thee, my child. But after he had ceased from his lamentations and cries, desiring to raise his aged body, he was held, as the ivy by the boughs of the laurel,

910

by the fine-wrought robes; and dreadful was the struggle, for he wished to raise his knee, but she held him back; but if he drew himself away by force he tore the aged flesh from his bones. But at length the wretched man swooned away, and gave up his life; for no longer was he able to endure the agony. But they lie corpses, the daughter and aged father near one another; a calamity that demands tears. And let thy affairs indeed be not matter for my words; for thou thyself wilt know a refuge from punishment. But the affairs of mortals not now for the first time I deem a shadow, and I would venture to say that those persons who seem to be wise and are researchers of arguments, these I say, run into the greatest

920

folly. For no mortal man is happy; but wealth pouring in, one man may be more fortunate than another, but happy he can not be.

Chorus

The Deity, it seems, will in this day justly heap on Jason a variety of ills. O hapless lady, how we pity thy sufferings, daughter of Creon, who art gone to the house of darkness, through thy marriage with Jason.

Medea

The deed is determined on by me, my friends, to slay my children as soon as possible, and to hasten from this land; and not by delaying to give my sons for another hand more hostile to murder. But come, be armed, my heart; why do we delay to do dreadful but necessary deeds? Come, O wretched hand of mine, grasp the sword, grasp it, advance to the bitter 930 goal of life, and be not cowardly, nor remember thy children how dear they are, how thou broughtest them into the world; but for this short day at least forget thy children; hereafter lament. For although thou slayest them, nevertheless they at least were dear, but I a wretched woman.

Chorus

O thou earth, and thou all-illuming beam of the sun, look down upon, behold this abandoned woman, before she move her blood-stained hand itself about to inflict the blow against her children; for from thy golden race they sprung; but fearful is it for the blood of Gods to fall by the hand of man. But do thou, O heaven-born light, restrain her, stop her, remove from this house this blood-stained and miserable Erinnys 940 agitated by the Furies. The care of thy children perishes in vain, and in vain hast thou produced a dear race, O thou who didst leave the most inhospitable entrance of the Cyanean rocks, the Symplegades. Hapless woman, why does such grievous rage settle on thy mind; and hostile slaughter ensue? For kindred pollutions are difficult of purification to mortals; correspondent calamities falling from the Gods to the earth upon the houses of the murderers.

First Son [within]

Alas! what shall I do? whither shall I fly from my mother's hand?

Second Son

I know not, dearest brother, for we perish. 950

Chorus

Hearest thou the cry? hearest thou the children? O wretch, O ill-fated woman! Shall I enter the house? It seems right to me to ward off the murderous blow from the children.

Sons

Nay, by the Gods assist us, for it is in needful time; since now at least are we near the destruction of the sword.

Chorus

960

Miserable woman, art thou then a rock, or iron, who cuttest down with death by thine own hand the fair crop of children which thou producedst thyself? one indeed I hear of, one woman of those of old, who laid violent hands on her children, Ino, maddened by the Gods when the wife of Jove sent her in banishment from her home; and she miserable woman falls into the sea through the impious murder of her children, directing her foot over the sea-shore, and dying with her two sons, there she perished! what then I pray can be more dreadful than this? O thou bed of woman, fruitful in ills, how many evils hast thou already brought to men!

[Jason, Chorus.]

Jason

970

1300

Ye females, who stand near this mansion, is she who hath done these deeds of horror, Medea, in this house; or hath she withdrawn herself in flight? For now it is necessary for her either to be hidden beneath the earth, or to raise her winged body into the vast expanse of air, if she would not suffer vengeance from the king's house. Does she trust that after having slain the princes of this land, she shall herself escape from this house with impunity?—But I have not such care for her as for my children; for they whom she has injured will punish her. But I came to preserve my children's life, lest (Creon's) relations by birth do any injury, avenging the impious murder perpetrated by their mother.

Chorus

Unhappy man! thou knowest not at what misery thou hast arrived,

Jason, or else thou wouldest not have uttered these words.

Jason

What is this, did she wish to slay me also?

Chorus

Thy children are dead by their mother's hand. 980

Jason

Alas me! What wilt thou say? how hast thou killed me, woman!

Chorus

Think now of thy sons as no longer living.

Jason

Where did she slay them, within or without the house?

Chorus

Open those doors, and thou wilt see the slaughter of thy sons.

Jason

Undo the bars, as quick as possible, attendants; unloose the hinges, that I may see this double evil, my sons slain, and may punish her.

Medea

Why dost thou shake and unbolt these gates, seeking the dead and me who did the deed. Cease from this labor; but if thou wantest aught with me, speak if thou wishest any thing; but never shall thou touch me with thy hands; such a chariot the sun my father's father gives me, a defense 990 from the hostile hand.

Jason

O thou abomination! thou most detested woman, both by the Gods and by me, and by all the race of man; who hast dared to plunge the sword in thine own children, thou who bore them, and hast destroyed me childless. And having done this thou beholdest both the sun and the earth, having dared a most impious deed. Mayest thou perish! but I am now wise, not being so then when I brought thee from thy house and from a foreign land to a Grecian habitation, a great pest, traitress to thy father and the land that nurtured thee. But the Gods have sent thy evil 1000 genius on me. For having slain thy brother at the altar, thou embarkedst on board the gallant vessel Argo. Thou begannest indeed with such deeds as these; and being wedded to me, and bearing me children, thou hast destroyed them on account of another bed and marriage. There is not one Grecian woman who would have dared a deed like this, in preference to whom at least, I thought worthy to wed thee, an alliance hateful and destructive to me, a lioness, no woman, having a nature more savage than the Tuscan Scylla. But I can not gall thy heart with ten thousand reproaches, such shameless confidence is implanted in thee. Go, thou worker of ill, and stained with the blood of thy children. But for me it 1010 remains to bewail my fate, who shall neither enjoy my new nuptials, nor shall I have it in my power to address while alive my sons whom I begot and educated, but I have lost them.

Medea

Surely I could make long reply to these words, if the Sire Jupiter did not know what treatment thou receivedst from me, and what thou didst in return; but you were mistaken, when you expected, having dishonored my bed, to lead a life of pleasure, mocking me, and so was the princess, and so was Creon, who proposed the match to thee, when he expected to drive me from this land with impunity. Wherefore, if thou wilt, call me lioness, and Scylla who dwelt in the Tuscan plain. For thy heart, as is 1020 right, I have wounded.

Jason

And thou thyself grievest at least, and art a sharer in these ills.

Medea

Be assured of that; but this lessens the grief, that thou canst not mock me.

Jason

My children, what a wicked mother have ye found!

Medea

My sons, how did ye perish by your father's fault!

Jason

Nevertheless my hand slew them not.

Medea

But injury, and thy new nuptials.

Jason

And on account of thy bed didst thou think fit to slay them?

Medea

Dost thou deem this a slight evil to a woman?

Jason

Whoever at least is modest; but in thee is every ill.   1030

Medea

These are no longer living, for this will gall thee.

Jason

These are living, alas me! avenging furies on thy head.

Medea

The Gods know who began the injury.

Jason

They know indeed thy execrable mind.

Medea

Thou art hateful to me, and I detest thy bitter speech.

Jason

And I in sooth thine; the separation at least is without pain.

Medea

How then? what shall I do? for I also am very desirous.

Jason

Suffer me, I beg, to bury and mourn over these dead bodies.

Medea

1040   Never indeed; since I will bury them with this hand bearing them to the shrine of Juno, the Goddess guardian of the citadel, that no one of my enemies may insult them, tearing up their graves. But in this land of Sisyphus will I institute in addition to this a solemn festival and sacrifices hereafter to expiate this unhallowed murder. But I myself will go to the land of Erectheus, to dwell with Ægeus son of Pandion. But thou, wretch, as is fit, shalt die wretchedly, struck on thy head with a relic of thy ship Argo, having seen the bitter end of my marriage.

Jason

But may the Fury of the children, and Justice the avenger of murder, destroy thee.

Medea

But what God or Deity hears thee, thou perjured man, and traitor to the rights of hospitality? 1050

Jason

Ah! thou abominable woman, and murderer of thy children.

Medea

Go to thy home, and bury thy wife.

Jason

I go, even deprived of both my children.

Medea

Thou dost not yet mourn enough: stay and grow old.

Jason

Oh my dearest sons!

Medea

To their mother at least, but not to thee.

Jason

And yet thou slewest them.

Medea

> To grieve thee.

Jason

1400

> Alas, alas! I hapless man long to kiss the dear mouths of my children.

Medea

1060

> Now them addressest, now salutest them, formerly rejecting them with scorn.

Jason

> Grant me, by the Gods, to touch the soft skin of my sons.

Medea

> It is not possible. Thy words are thrown away in vain.

Jason

> Dost thou hear this, O Jove, how I am rejected, and what I suffer from this accursed and child-destroying lioness? But as much indeed as is in my power and I am able, I lament and mourn over these; calling the Gods to witness, that having slain my children, thou preventest me from touching them with my hands, and from burying the bodies, whom, oh that I had never begotten, and seen them thus destroyed by thee.

Chorus

1070

> Jove is the dispenser of various fates in heaven, and the Gods perform many things contrary to our expectations, and those things which we looked for are not accomplished; but the God hath brought to pass things unthought of. In such manner hath this affair ended.

The End.

ARISTOPHANES

Aristophanes
•
The Frogs

TRANSLATED BY E. D. A. MORSHEAD

Dramatis Personae

DIONYSUS

XANTHIUS
servant of Dionysus

HERACLES

A CORPSE

CHARON

AEACUS

A MAID SERVANT
of Persephone

HOSTESS
Keeper of Cook-Shop

PLATHANE
her servant

EURIPIDES

AESCHYLUS

PLUTO

CHORUS
of Frogs

CHORUS
of Blessed Mystics

[The scene shows the house of Heracles in the background. There enter two travellers: Dionysus on foot, in his customary yellow robe and buskins but also with the club and lion's skin of Heracles, and his servant Xanthius on a donkey, carrying the luggage on a pole over his shoulder.]

Xanthius

> Shall I crack any of those old jokes, master,
> At which the audience never fail to laugh?

Dionysus

> Aye, what you will, except "I'm getting crushed":
> Fight shy of that: I'm sick of that already.

Xanthius

> Nothing else smart?

Dionysus

> Aye, save "my shoulder's aching."

Xanthius

> Come now, that comical joke?

Dionysus

> With all my heart.
> Only be careful not to shift your pole,
> And-

Xanthius

> What?

Dionysus

> And vow that you've a belly-ache.

Xanthius

> May I not say I'm overburdened so
> That if none ease me, I must ease myself?

Dionysus

> For mercy's sake, not till I'm going to vomit.

Xanthius

> What! must I bear these burdens, and not make
> One of the jokes Ameipsias and Lycis
> And Phrynichus, in every play they write,
> Put in the mouths of their burden-bearers?

Dionysus

20
> Don't make them; no! I tell you when I see
> Their plays, and hear those jokes, I come away
> More than a twelvemonth older than I went.

Xanthius

> O thrice unlucky neck of mine, which now
> Is getting crushed, yet must not crack its joke!

Dionysus

> Now is not this fine pampered insolence
> When I myself, Dionysus, son of Pipkin,
> Toil on afoot, and let this fellow ride,
> Taking no trouble, and no burden bearing?

Xanthius

> What, don't I bear?

Dionysus

30
> How can you when you're riding?

Xanthius

> Why, I bear these.

Dionysus

How?

Xanthius

Most unwillingly.

Dionysus

Does not the donkey bear the load you're bearing?

Xanthius

Not what I bear myself: by Zeus, not he.

Dionysus

How can you bear, when you are borne yourself?

Xanthius

Don't know: but anyhow my shoulder's aching.

Dionysus

Then since you say the donkey helps you not,
You lift him up and carry him in turn.

Xanthius

O hang it all! why didn't I fight at sea?   40
You should have smarted bitterly for this.

Dionysus

Get down, you rascal; I've been trudging on
Till now I've reached the portal, where I'm going
First to turn in. Boy! Boy! I say there, Boy!

[Enter Heracles from house.]

Heracles

Who banged the door? How like prancing Centaur
He drove against it! Mercy o' me, what's this?

Dionysus

>Boy.

Xanthius

>Yes.

Dionysus

>Did you observe?

Xanthius

50

>What?

Dionysus

>How alarmed he is.

Xanthius

>Aye truly, lest you've lost your wits.

Heracles

>O by Demeter, I can't choose but laugh.
>Biting my lips won't stop me. Ha! ha! ha!

Dionysus

>Pray you, come hither, I have need of you.

Heracles

>I vow I can't help laughing, I can't help it.
>A lion's hide upon a yellow silk,
>A club and buskin! What's it all about?
>Where were you going?

Dionysus

60

>I was serving lately.

Heracles

>And fought?

Dionysus

> Aboard the Cleisthenes,
> And sank more than a dozen of the enemy's ships.

Heracles

> You two?

Dionysus

> We two.

Heracles

> And then I awoke, and lo!

Dionysus

> There as, on deck, I'm reading to myself
> The Andromeda, a sudden pang of longing.
> Shoots through my heart, you can't conceive how keenly.

Heracles

> How big a pang?   70

Dionysus

> A small one, Molon's size.

Heracles

> Caused by a woman?

Dionysus

> No.

Heracles

> A boy?

Dionysus

> No, no.

Heracles

> A man?

Dionysus

> Ah! ah!

Heracles

> Was it for Cleisthenes?

Dionysus

80
> Don't mock me, brother: on my life I am
> In a bad way: such fierce desire consumes me.

Heracles

> Aye, little brother? how?

Dionysus

> I can't describe it.
> But yet I'll tell you in a riddling way.
> Have you e'er felt a sudden lust for soup?

Heracles

> Soup! Zeus-a-mercy, yes, ten thousand times.

Dionysus

> Is the thing clear, or must I speak again?

Heracles

> Not of the soup: I'm clear about the soup.

Dionysus

> Well, just that sort of pang devours my heart
> For lost Euripides.

Heracles

90
> A dead man too.

Dionysus

> And no one shall persuade me not to go
> After the man.

Heracles

> Do you mean below, to Hades?

Dionysus

> And lower still, if there's a lower still.

Heracles

> What on earth for?

Dionysus

> I want a genuine poet,
> "For some are not, and those that are, are bad."

Heracles

> What! does not Iophon live?

Dionysus

> Well, he's the sole
> Good thing remaining, if even he is good.   100
> For even of that I'm not exactly certain.

Heracles

> If go you must, there's Sophocles—he comes
> Before Euripides—why not take him?

Dionysus

> Not till I've tried if Iophon's coin rings true
> When he's alone, apart from Sophocles.
> Besides, Euripides, the crafty rogue,
> Will find a thousand shifts to get away,
> But he was easy here, is easy there.

Heracles

> But Agathon, where is he?

Dionysus

> He has gone and left us.   110
> A genial poet, by his friends much missed.

Heracles

Gone where?

Dionysus

To join the blessed in their banquets.

Heracles

But what of Xenocles?

Dionysus

O he be hanged!

Heracles

Pythangelus?

Xanthius

But never a word of me,
Not though my shoulder's chafed so terribly.

Heracles

But have you not a shoal of little songsters,
120   Tragedians by the myriad, who can chatter
A furlong faster than Euripides?

Dionysus

Those be mere vintage-leavings, jabberers, choirs
Of swallow-broods, degraders of their art,
Who get one chorus, and are seen no more,
The Muses' love once gained. But O, my friend,
Search where you will, you'll never find a true
Creative genius, uttering startling things.

Heracles

Creative? how do you mean?

Dionysus

I mean a man
130   Who'll dare some novel venturesome conceit,

"Air, Zeus's chamber," or
"Time's foot," or this,
"'Twas not my mind that swore:
My tongue committed
A little perjury on its own account."

Heracles

You like that style?

Dionysus

Like it? I dote upon it.

Heracles

I vow its ribald nonsense, and you know it.

Dionysus

"Rule not my mind": you've got a house to mind.

Heracles

Really and truly though 'tis paltry stuff.   140

Dionysus

Teach me to dine!

Xanthius

But never a word of me.

Dionysus

But tell me truly—'twas for this I came
Dressed up to mimic you—what friends received
And entertained you when you went below
To bring back Cerberus, in case I need them.
And tell me too the havens, fountains, shops,
Roads, resting-places, stews, refreshment-rooms,
Towns, lodgings, hostesses, with whom were found
The fewest bugs.   150

Xanthius

But never a word of me.

495

Heracles

> You are really game to go?

Dionysus

> O drop that, can't you?
> And tell me this: of all the roads you know
> Which is the quickest way to get to Hades?
> I want one not too warm, nor yet too cold.

Heracles

> Which shall I tell you first? which shall it be?
> There's one by rope and bench: you launch away
> And hang yourself.

Dionysus

160

> No thank you: that's too stifling.

Heracles

> Then there's a track, a short and beaten cut,
> By pestle and mortar.

Dionysus

> Hemlock, do you mean?

Heracles

> Just so.

Dionysus

> No, that's too deathly cold a way;
> You have hardly started ere your shins get numbed.

Heracles

> Well, would you like a steep and swift descent?

Dionysus

> Aye, that's the style: my walking powers are small.

Heracles

Go down to the Cerameicus.

Dionysus

And do what?   170

Heracles

Climb to the tower's top pinnacle—

Dionysus

And then?

Heracles

Observe the torch-race started, and when all
The multitude is shouting "Let them go,"
Let yourself go.

Dionysus

Go! whither?

Heracles

To the ground.

Dionysus

And lose, forsooth, two envelopes of brain.
I'll not try that.

Heracles

Which will you try?   180

Dionysus

The way
You went yourself.

Heracles

A perilous voyage that,
For first you'll come to an enormous lake

Of fathomless depth.

Dionysus

And how am I to cross?

Heracles

An ancient mariner will row you over
In a wee boat, so big. The fare's two obols.

Dionysus

Fie! The power two obols have, the whole world through!
How came they thither!

Heracles

Theseus took them down.
And next you'll see great snakes and savage monsters
In tens of thousands.

Dionysus

You needn't try to scare me,
I'm going to go.

Heracles

Then weltering seas of filth
And ever-rippling dung: and plunged therein,
Whoso has wronged the stranger here on earth,
Or robbed his boylove of the promised pay,
Or swinged his mother, or profanely smitten
His father's check, or sworn an oath forsworn,
Or copied out a speech of Morsimus.

Dionysus

There too, perdie, should he be plunged, whoe'er
Has danced the sword-dance of Cinesias.

Heracles

And next the breath of flutes will float around you,
And glorious sunshine, such as ours, you'll see,

And myrtle groves, and happy bands who clap
Their hands in triumph, men and women too.

Dionysus

And who are they?

Heracles

The happy mystic bands. . .   210

Xanthius

And I'm the donkey in the mystery show.
But I'll not stand it, not one instant longer.

Heracles

. . . Who'll tell you everything you want to know.
You'll find them dwelling close beside the road
You are going to travel, just at Pluto's gate.
And fare thee well, my brother.

Dionysus

And to you, Good cheer.

[Exit Heracles.]

Now sirrah, pick you up the traps.

Xanthius

Before I've put them down?

Dionysus

And quickly too.   220

Xanthius

No, prithee, no: but hire a body, one
They're carrying out, on purpose for the trip.

Dionysus

If I can't find one?

Xanthius

Then I'll take them.

Dionysus

Good.
And see they are carrying out a body now.

[Here a Corpse, wrapped in its grave-clothes, and lying on a bier, is carried across the stage.]

Hallo! you there, you deadman, are you willing
To carry down our little traps to Hades?

Corpse

What are they?

Dionysus

230   These.

Corpse

Two drachmas for the job?

Dionysus

Nay, that's too much.

Corpse

Out of the pathway, you!

Dionysus

Beshrew thee, stop: maybe we'll strike a bargain.

Corpse

Pay me two drachmas, or it's no use talking.

Dionysus

One and a half.

Corpse

I'd liefer live again!

Xanthius

> How absolute the knave is! He be hanged!
> I'll go myself.

Dionysus

> You're the right sort, my man.   240
> Now to the ferry.

[Enter Charon.]

Charon

> Yoh, up! lay her to.

Xanthius

> Whatever's that?

Dionysus

> Why, that's the lake, by Zeus,
> Whereof he spake, and yon's the ferry-boat.

Xanthius

> Poseidon, yes, and that old fellow's Charon.

Dionysus

> Charon! O welcome, Charon! welcome, Charon!

Charon

> Who's for the Rest from every pain and ill?
> Who's for the Lethe's plain? the Donkey-shearings?
> Who's for Cerberia? Taenarum? or the Ravens?   250

Dionysus

> I.

Charon

> Hurry in.

Dionysus

> But where are you going really?
> In truth to the Ravens?

Charon

> Aye, for your behoof. Step in.

Dionysus [to Xanthius]

> Now, lad.

Charon

> A slave? I take no slave,
> Unless he has fought for his bodyrights at sea.

Xanthius

> I couldn't go. I'd got the eye-disease.

Charon

260

> Then fetch a circuit round about the lake.

Xanthius

> Where must I wait?

Charon

> Beside the Withering stone, Hard by the Rest.

Dionysus

> You understand?

Xanthius

> Too well.
> O, what ill omen crossed me as I started!

[Exit.]

Charon [to Dionysus]

> Sit to the oar. *[calling]* Who else for the boat? Be quick. *[to*

Dionysus] Hi! what are you doing?

Dionysus

> What am I doing? Sitting
> On to the oar. You told me to, yourself.

Charon

> Now sit you there, you little Potgut.   270

Dionysus

> So?

Charon

> Now stretch your arms full length before you.

Dionysus

> So?

Charon

> Come, don't keep fooling; plant your feet, and now
> Pull with a will.

Dionysus

> Why, how am I to pull?
> I'm not an oarsman, seaman, Salaminian. I can't.

Charon

> You can. Just dip your oar in once,
> You'll hear the loveliest timing songs.

Dionysus

> What from?   280

Charon

> Frog-swans, most wonderful.

Dionysus

> Then give the word.

Charon

Heave ahoy! heave ahoy!

Frogs [off stage]

Brekekekex, ko-ax, ko-ax,
Brekekekex, ko-ax, ko-ax!
We children of the fountain and the lake
Let us wake
Our full choir-shout, as the flutes are ringing out,
Our symphony of clear-voiced song.
290   The song we used to love in the Marshland up above,
In praise of Dionysus to produce,
Of Nysaean Dionysus, son of Zeus,
When the revel-tipsy throng, all crapulous and gay,
To our precinct reeled along on the holy Pitcher day,
Brekekekex, ko-ax, ko-ax.

Dionysus

O, dear! O, dear! now I declare
I've got a bump upon my rump,

Frogs

Brekekekex, ko-ax, ko-ax.

Dionysus

But you, perchance, don't care.

Frogs

300   Brekekekex, ko-ax, ko-ax.

Dionysus

Hang you, and your ko-axing too!
There's nothing but ko-ax with you.

Frogs

That is right, Mr. Busybody, right!
For the Muses of the lyre love us well;
And hornfoot Pan who plays on the pipe his jocund lays;

And Apollo, Harper bright, in our Chorus takes delight;
For the strong reed's sake which I grow within my lake
To be girdled in his lyre's deep shell.
Brekekekex, ko-ax, ko-ax.

Dionysus

> My hands are blistered very sore; 310
> My stern below is sweltering so,
> 'Twill soon, I know, upturn and roar
> Brekekekex, ko-ax, ko-ax.
> O tuneful race, O pray give o'er,
> O sing no more.

Frogs

> Ah, no! ah, no!
> Loud and louder our chant must flow.
> Sing if ever ye sang of yore,
> When in sunny and glorious days
> Through the rushes and marsh-flags springing 320
> On we swept, in the joy of singing
> Myriad divine roundelays.
> Or when fleeing the storm, we went
> Down to the depths, and our choral song
> Wildly raised to a loud and long
> Bubble-bursting accompaniment.

Frogs and Dionysus

> Brekekekex, ko-ax, ko-ax.

Dionysus

> This timing song I take from you.

Frogs

> That's a dreadful thing to do.

Dionysus

> Much more dreadful, if I row 330
> Till I burst myself, I trow.

Frogs and Dionysus

> Brekekekex, ko-ax, ko-ax.

Dionysus

> Go, hang yourselves; for what care I?

Frogs

> All the same we'll shout and cry,
> Stretching all our throats with song,
> Shouting, crying, all day long,

Frogs and Dionysus

> Brekekekex, ko-ax, ko-ax.

Dionysus

> In this you'll never, never win.

Frogs

> This you shall not beat us in.

Dionysus

340
> No, nor ye prevail o'er me.
> Never! never! I'll my song,
> Shout, if need be, all day long,
> Until I've learned to master your ko-ax.
> Brekekekex, ko-ax, ko-ax.
> I thought I'd put a stop to your ko-ax.

Charon

> Stop! Easy! Take the oar and push her to.
> Now pay your fare and go.

Dionysus

> Here' tis: two obols.
> Xanthius! where's Xanthius? Is it Xanthius there?

Xanthius [off stage]

350
> Hoi, hoi!

Dionysus

> Come hither.

Xanthius [Entering]

> Glad to meet you, master.

Dionysus

> What have you there?

Xanthius

> Nothing but filth and darkness.

Dionysus

> But tell me, did you see the parricides
> And perjured folk he mentioned?

Xanthius

> Didn't you?

Dionysus

> Poseidon, yes. Why look!
> *[pointing to the audience]* I see them now.
> What's the next step?

360

Xanthius

> We'd best be moving on.
> This is the spot where Heracles declared
> Those savage monsters dwell.

Dionysus

> O hang the fellow.
> That's all his bluff: he thought to scare me off,
> The jealous dog, knowing my plucky ways.
> There's no such swaggerer lives as Heracles.
> Why, I'd like nothing better than to achieve
> Some bold adventure, worthy of our trip.

Xanthius

> I know you would. Hallo! I hear a noise.

370

Dionysus

>Where? what?

Xanthius

>Behind us, there.

Dionysus

>Get you behind.

Xanthius

>No, it's in front.

Dionysus

>Get you in front directly.

Xanthius

>And now I see the most ferocious monster.

Dionysus

>O, what's it like?

Xanthius

>Like everything by turns.
>Now it's a bull: now it's a mule: and now
380   The loveliest girl.

Dionysus

>O, where? I'll go and meet her.

Xanthius

>It's ceased to be a girl: it's a dog now.

Dionysus

>It is Empusa!

Xanthius

>Well, its face is all

Ablaze with fire.

Dionysus

Has it a copper leg?

Xanthius

A copper leg? yes, one; and one of cow dung.

Dionysus

O, whither shall I flee?

Xanthius

O, whither I?

Dionysus

My priest, protect me, and we'll sup together.   390

Xanthius

King Heracles, we're done for.

Dionysus

O, forbear, Good fellow, call me anything but that.

Xanthius

Well then, Dionysus.

Dionysus

O, that's worse again,

Xanthius [to the Spectre]

Aye, go thy way. O master, here, come here.

Dionysus

O, what's up now?

Xanthius

Take courage; all's serene.

And, like Hegelochus, we now may say
"Out of the storm there comes a new weather."
400   Empusa's gone.

Dionysus

Swear it.

Xanthius

By Zeus she is.

Dionysus

Swear it again.

Xanthius

By Zeus.

Dionysus

Again.

Xanthius

By Zeus.
O dear, O dear, how pale I grew to see her,
But he, from fright has yellowed me all over.

Dionysus

Ah me, whence fall these evils on my head?
410   Who is the god to blame for my destruction?
Air, Zeus's chamber, or the Foot of Time?

[A flute is played behind the scenes.]

Dionysus

Hist!

Xanthius

What's the matter?

Dionysus

    Didn't you hear it?

Xanthius

    What?

Dionysus

    The breath of flutes.

Xanthius

    Aye, and a whiff of torches
    Breathed o'er me too; a very mystic whiff.

Dionysus

    Then crouch we down, and mark what's going on.

Chorus [in the distance]

    O Iacchus! O Iacchus! O Iacchus!   420

Xanthius

    I have it, master: 'tis those blessed Mystics,
    Of whom he told us, sporting hereabouts.
    They sing the Iacchus which Diagoras made.

Dionysus

    I think so too: we had better both keep quiet
    And so find out exactly what it is.

[Enter Chorus, who had chanted the songs of the Frogs, as initiates.]

Chorus

    O Iacchus! power excelling,
    Here in stately temples dwelling.
    O Iacchus! O Iacchus!
    Come to tread this verdant level,
    Come to dance in mystic revel,   430

Come whilst round thy forehead hurtles
Many a wreath of fruitful myrtles,
Come with wild and saucy paces
Mingling in our joyous dance,
Pure and holy, which embraces
All the charms of all the Graces,
When the mystic choirs advance.

Xanthius

Holy and sacred queen, Demeter's daughter,
O, what a jolly whiff of pork breathed o'er me!

Dionysus

440   Hist! and perchance you'll get some tripe yourself.

Chorus

Come, arise, from sleep awaking,
Come the fiery torches shaking,
O Iacchus! O Iacchus!
Morning Star that shinest nightly.
Lo, the mead is blazing brightly,
Age forgets its years and sadness,
Aged knees curvet for gladness,
Lift thy flashing torches o'er us,
Marshal all thy blameless train,
450   Lead, O lead the way before us;
Lead the lovely youthful Chorus
To the marshy flowery plain.
All evil thoughts and profane be still:
Far hence, far hence from our choirs depart,
Who knows not well what the Mystics tell,
Or is not holy and pure of heart;
Who ne'er has the noble revelry learned,
Or danced the dance of the Muses high;
Or shared in the Bacchic rites which old
460   Bull-eating Cratinus's words supply;
Who vulgar coarse buffoonery loves,
Though all untimely the jests they make;
Or lives not easy and kind with all,
Or kindling faction forbears to slake,

But fans the fire, from a base desire
Some pitiful gain for himself to reap;
Or takes, in office, his gifts and bribes,
While the city is tossed on the stormy deep;
Who fort or fleet to the foe betrays;
Or, a vile Thorycion, ships away   470
Forbidden stores from Aegina's shores,
To Epidaurus across the Bay
Transmitting oar-pads and sails and tar,
That curst collector of five per cents;
The knave who tries to procure supplies
For the use of the enemy's armaments;
The Cyclian singer who dares befoul
The Lady Hecate's wayside shrine;
The public speaker who once lampooned
In our Bacchic feasts would, with heart malign,   480
Keep nibbling away the Comedians' pay;—
To these I utter my warning cry,
I charge them once, I charge them twice,
I charge them thrice, that they draw not nigh
To the sacred dance of the Mystic choir.
But ye, my comrades, awake the song,
The night-long revels of joy and mirth
Which ever of right to our feast belong.

Advance, true hearts, advance!
On to the gladsome bowers,   490
On to the sward, with flowers
Embosomed bright!
March on with jest, and jeer, and dance,
Full well ye've supped to-night.

March, chanting loud your lays,
Your hearts and voices raising,
The Saviour goddess praising
Who vows she'll still
Our city save to endless days,
Whate'er Thorycion's will.   500

Break off the measure, and change the time;
And now with chanting and hymns adorn

Demeter, goddess mighty and high,
The harvest-queen, the giver of corn.

O Lady, over our rites presiding,
Preserve and succour thy choral throng,
And grant us all, in thy help confiding,
To dance and revel the whole day long;
And much in earnest, and much in jest,
510   Worthy thy feast, may we speak therein.
And when we have bantered and laughed our best,
The victor's wreath be it ours to win.

Call we now the youthful god,
Call him hither without delay,
Him who travels amongst his chorus,
Dancing along on the Sacred Way.

O, come with the joy of thy festival song,
O, come to the goddess, O, mix with our throng
Untired, though the journey be never so long.
520   O Lord of the frolic and dance,
Iacchus, beside me advance!
For fun, and for cheapness, our dress thou hast rent,
Through thee we may dance to the top of our bent,
Reviling, and jeering, and none will resent.
O Lord of the frolic and dance,
Iacchus, beside me advance!
A sweet pretty girl I observed in the show,
Her robe had been torn in the scuffle, and lo,
There peeped through the tatters a bosom of snow.
530   O Lord of the frolic and dance,
Iacchus, beside me advance!

Dionysus

Wouldn't I like to follow on, and try
A little sport and dancing?

Xanthius

Wouldn't I?

Chorus

>Shall we all a merry joke
>At Archedemus poke,
>Who has not cut his guildsmen yet, though seven years old;
>Yet up among the dead
>He is demagogue and head
>And contrives the topmost place of the rascaldom to hold? 540
>And Cleisthenes, they say,
>Is among the tombs all day,
>Bewailing for his lover with a lamentable whine.
>And Callias, I'm told,
>Has become a sailor bold,
>And casts a lion's hide o'er his members feminine.

Dionysus

>Can any of you tell
>Where Pluto here may dwell,
>For we, sirs, are two strangers who were never here before?

Chorus

>O, then no further stray, 550
>Nor again inquire the way,
>For know that ye have journeyed to his very entrance-door.

Dionysus

>Take up the wraps, my lad.

Xanthius

>Now is not this too bad?
>Like "Zeus's Corinth," he "the wraps" keeps saying o'er and
>o'er.

Chorus

>Now wheel your sacred dances
>Through the glade with flowers bedight,
>All ye who are partakers
>Of the holy festal rite; 560
>And I will with the women
>And the holy maidens go

Where they keep the nightly vigil,
An auspicious light to show.

Now haste we to the roses,
And the meadows full of posies,
Now haste we to the meadows
In our own old way,
In choral dances blending,
570   In dances never ending,
Which only for the holy
The Destinies array.
O, happy mystic chorus,
The blessed sunshine o'er us
On us alone is smiling,
In its soft sweet light:
On us who strove forever
With holy, pure endeavour,
Alike by friend and stranger
580   To guide our steps aright.

Dionysus

What's the right way to knock? I wonder how
The natives here are wont to knock at doors.

Xanthius

No dawdling: taste the door. You've got, remember,
The lion-hide and pride of Heracles.

Dionysus [knocking]

Boy! boy!

[The door opens. Aeacus appears.]

Aeacus

Who's there?

Dionysus

I, Heracles the strong!

Aeacus

> O, you most shameless desperate ruffian, you
> O, villain, villain, arrant vilest villain!
> Who seized our Cerberus by the throat, and fled,   590
> And ran, and rushed, and bolted, haling of
> The dog, my charge! But now I've got thee fast.
> So close the Styx's inky-hearted rock,
> The blood-bedabbled peak of Acheron
> Shall hem thee in: the hell-hounds of Cocytus
> Prowl round thee; whilst the hundred-headed Asp
> Shall rive thy heart-strings: the Tartesian Lamprey
> Prey on thy lungs: and those Tithrasian Gorgons
> Mangle and tear thy kidneys, mauling them,
> Entrails and all, into one bloody mash.   600
> I'll speed a running foot to fetch them hither.

[Exit Aeacus.]

Xanthius

> Hallo! what now?

Dionysus

> I've done it: call the god.

Xanthius

> Get up, you laughing-stock; get up directly,
> Before you're seen.

Dionysus

> What, I get up? I'm fainting.
> Please dab a sponge of water on my heart.

Xanthius

> Here!

Dionysus

> Dab it, you.

Xanthius

610

Where? O, ye golden gods,
Lies your heart there?

Dionysus

It got so terrified
It fluttered down into my stomach's pit.

Xanthius

Cowardliest of gods and men!

Dionysus

The cowardliest? I?
What I, who asked you for a sponge, a thing
A coward never would have done!

Xanthius

What then?

Dionysus

620

A coward would have lain there wallowing;
But I stood up, and wiped myself withal.

Xanthius

Poseidon! quite heroic.

Dionysus

'Deed I think so.
But weren't you frightened at those dreadful threats
And shoutings?

Xanthius

Frightened? Not a bit. I cared not.

Dionysus

Come then, if you're so very brave a man,
Will you be I, and take the hero's club

And lion's skin, since you're so monstrous plucky?
And I'll be now the slave, and bear the luggage.

Xanthius

Hand them across. I cannot choose but take them.   630
And now observe the Xanthio-Heracles
If I'm a coward and a sneak like you.

Dionysus

Nay, you're the rogue from Melite's own self.
And I'll pick up and carry on the traps.

[Enter a Maid-Servant of Persephone, from the door.]

Maid

O welcome, Heracles! come in, sweetheart.
My Lidy, when they told her, set to work,
Baked mighty loaves, boiled two or three tureens
Of lentil soup, roasted a prime ox whole,
Made rolls and honey-cakes. So come along.

Xanthius [declining]
                                              640
You are too kind.

Maid

I will not let you go.
I will not let you! Why, she's stewing slices
Of juicy bird's-flesh, and she's making comfits,
And tempering down her richest wine. Come, dear,
Come along in.

Xanthius [still declining]

Pray thank her.

Maid

O you're jesting,
I shall not let you off: there's such a lovely
Flute-girl all ready, and we've two or three

650 Dancing-girls also.

Xanthius

Eh! what! Dancing-girls?

Maid

Young budding virgins, freshly tired and trimmed.
Come, dear, come in. The cook was dishing up
The cutlets, and they are bringing in the tables.

Xanthius

Then go you in, and tell those dancing-girls
Of whom you spake, I'm coming in Myself.

[Exit Maid.]

Pick up the traps, my lad, and follow me.

Dionysus

Hi! stop! you're not in earnest, just because
I dressed you up, in fun, as Heracles?
660 Come, don't keep fooling, Xanthius, but lift
And carry in the traps yourself.

Xanthius

You are never going to strip me of these togs
You gave me!

Dionysus

Going to? No, I'm doing it now. Off with that lion-skin.

Xanthius

Bear witness all,
The gods shall judge between us.

Dionysus

Gods, indeed!
Why, how could you (the vain and foolish thought!)
A slave, a mortal, act Alemena's son?

Xanthius

All right then, take them; maybe, if God will,   670
You'll soon require my services again.

Chorus

This is the part of a dexterous clever
Man with his wits about him ever,
One who has travelled the world to see;
Always to shift, and to keep through all
Close to the sunny side of the wall;
Not like a pictured block to be,
Standing always in one position;
Nay but to veer, with expedition,
And ever to catch the favouring breeze,   680
This is the part of a shrewd tactician,
This is to be a Theramenes!

Dionysus

Truly an exquisite joke 'twould be,
Him with a dancing-girl to see,
Lolling at ease on Milesian rugs;
Me, like a slave, beside him standing,
Aught that he wants to his lordship handing;
Then as the damsel fair he hugs,
Seeing me all on fire to embrace her,
He would perchance (for there's no man baser),   690
Turning him round like a lazy lout,
Straight on my mouth deliver a facer,
Knocking my ivory choirmen out.

[Enter Hostess and Plathane.]

Hostess.

O Plathane! Plathane! that naughty man,
That's he who got into our tavern once,
And ate up sixteen loaves.

Plathane

O, so he is! The very man.

Xanthius

Bad luck for somebody!

Hostess

O and, besides, those twenty bits of stew,
Half-obol pieces.

Xanthius

Somebody's going to catch it!

Hostess

That garlic too.

Dionysus

Woman, you're talking nonsense.
You don't know what you're saying.

Hostess

O, you thought
I shouldn't know you with your buskins on!
Ah, and I've not yet mentioned all that fish,
No, nor the new-made cheese: he gulped it down,
Baskets and all, unlucky that we were.
And when I just alluded to the price,
He looked so fierce, and bellowed like a bull.

Xanthius

Yes, that's his way: that's what he always does.

Hostess

O, and he drew his sword, and seemed quite mad.

Plathane

O, that he did.

Hostess

And terrified us so
We sprang up to the cockloft, she and I.

Then out he hurled, decamping with the rugs.

Xanthius

That's his way too; something must be done.

Hostess

Quick, run and call my patron Cleon here.

Plathane

O, if you meet him, call Hyperbolus!   720
We'll pay you out to-day.

Hostess

O filthy throat,
O how I'd like to take a stone, and hack
Those grinders out with which you chawed my wares.

Plathane

I'd like to pitch you in the deadman's pit.

Hostess

I'd like to get a reaping-hook and scoop
That gullet out with which you gorged my tripe.
But I'll to Cleon: he'll soon serve his writs;
He'll twist it out of you to-day, he will.

[Exeunt Hostess and Plathane.]

Dionysus

Perdition seize me, if I don't love Xanthius.   730

Xanthius

Aye, aye, I know your drift: stop, stop that talking
I won't be Heracles.

Dionysus

O, don't say so,
Dear, darling Xanthius.

Xanthius

> Why, how can I,
> A slave, a mortal, act Alemena's son!

Dionysus

> Aye, aye, I know you are vexed, and I deserve it
> And if you pummel me, I won't complain.
> But if I strip you of these togs again,
> Perdition seize myself, my wife, my children,
> And, most of all, that blear-eyed Archedemus.

740

Xanthius

> That oath contents me: on those terms I take them.

Chorus

> Now that at last you appear once more,
> Wearing the garb that at first you wore,
> Wielding the club and the tawny skin,
> Now it is yours to be up and doing,
> Glaring like mad, and your youth renewing,
> Mindful of him whose guise you are in.
> If, when caught in a bit of a scrape, you
> Suffer a word of alarm to escape you,
> Showing yourself but a feckless knave,
> Then will your master at once undrape you,
> Then you'll again be the toiling slave.

750

Xanthius

> There, I admit, you have given to me a
> Capital hint, and the like idea,
> Friends, had occurred to myself before.
> Truly if anything good befell
> He would be wanting, I know full well,
> Wanting to take to the togs once more.
> Nevertheless, while in these I'm vested,
> Ne'er shall you find me craven-crested,
> No, for a dittany look I'll wear,
> Aye and methinks it will soon be tested,
> Hark! how the portals are rustling there.

760

[Re-enter Aeacus with assistants.]

Aeacus

> Seize the dog-stealer, bind him, pinion him,
> Drag him to justice.

Dionysus

> Somebody's going to catch it.

Xanthius [striking out]

> Hands off! away! stand back!

Aeacus

> Eh? You're for fighting.
> Ho! Ditylas, Sceblyas, and Pardocas,   770
> Come hither, quick; fight me this sturdy knave.

Dionysus

> Now isn't it a shame the man should strike
> And he a thief besides?

Aeacus

> A monstrous shame!

Dionysus

> A regular burning shame!

Xanthius

> By the Lord Zeus,
> If ever I was here before, if ever
> I stole one hair's-worth from you, let me die!
> And now I'll make you a right noble offer,
> Arrest my lad: torture him as you will,   780
> And if you find I'm guilty, take and kill me.

Aeacus

> Torture him, how?

Xanthius

In any mode you please.
Pile bricks upon him: stuff his nose with acid:
Flay, rack him, hoist him; flog him with a scourge
Of prickly bristles: only not with this,
A soft-leaved onion, or a tender leek.

Aeacus

A fair proposal. If I strike too hard
And maim the boy, I'll make you compensation.

Xanthius

790   I shan't require it. Take him out and flog him.

Aeacus

Nay, but I'll do it here before your eyes.
Now then, put down the traps, and mind you speak
The truth, young fellow.

Dionysus [in agony]

Man, don't torture me!
I am a god. You'll blame yourself hereafter
If you touch me.

Aeacus

Hillo! What's that you are saying?

Dionysus

I say I'm Bacchus, son of Zeus, a god,
And he's the slave.

Aeacus

800   You hear him?

Xanthius

Hear him? Yes.
All the more reason you should flog him well.
For if he is a god, he won't perceive it.

526

Dionysus

> Well, but you say that you're a god yourself.
> So why not you be flogged as well as I?

Xanthius

> A fair proposal. And be this the test,
> Whichever of us two you first behold
> Flinching or crying out-he's not the god.

Aeacus

> Upon my word you're quite the gentleman,
> You're all for right and justice. Strip then, both. 810

Xanthius

> How can you test us fairly?

Aeacus

> Easily. I'll give you blow for blow.

Xanthius

> A good idea. We're ready now!
> *[Aeacus strikes him]* See if you catch me flinching.

Aeacus

> I struck you.

Xanthius [incredulously]

> No!

Aeacus

> Well, it seems "no" indeed.
> Now then I'll strike the other.

[Strikes Dionysus.]

Dionysus

> Tell me when?

Aeacus

820

I struck you.

Dionysus

Struck me? Then why didn't I sneeze?

Aeacus

Don't know, I'm sure. I'll try the other again.

Xanthius

And quickly too. Good gracious!

Aeacus

Why "good gracious"?
Not hurt you, did I?

Xanthius

No, I merely thought of
The Diomeian feast of Heracles.

Aeacus

A holy man! 'Tis now the other's turn.

Dionysus

Hi! Hi!

Aeacus

830

Hallo!

Dionysus

Look at those horsemen, look!

Aeacus

But why these tears?

Dionysus

There's such a smell of onions.

Aeacus

Then you don't mind it?

Dionysus [cheerfully]

Mind it? Not a bit.

Aeacus

Well, I must go to the other one again.

Xanthius

O! O!

Aeacus

Hallo!

Xanthius

Do pray pull out this thorn.

Aeacus

What does it mean? 'Tis this one's turn again.   840

Dionysus [shrieking]

Apollo! Lord!
[*calmly*] of Delos and of Pytho.

Xanthius

He flinched! You heard him?

Dionysus

Not at all; a jolly Verse of Hipponax flashed across my
mind.

Xanthius

You don't half do it: cut his flanks to pieces.

Aeacus

By Zeus, well thought on. Turn your belly here.

529

Dionysus [screaming]

Poseidon!

Xanthius

There! he's flinching.

Dionysus [singing]

850   Who dost reign
Amongst the Aegean peaks and creeks
And o'er the deep blue main.

Aeacus

No, by Demeter, still I can't find out
Which is the god, but come ye both indoors;
My lord himself and Persephassa there,
Being gods themselves, will soon find out the truth.

Dionysus

Right! right! I only wish you had thought of that
Before you gave me those tremendous whacks.

[Exeunt Dionysus, Xanthius, Aeacus, and attendants.]

Chorus

Come, Muse, to our Mystical Chorus,
860   O come to the joy of my song,
O see on the benches before us
That countless and wonderful throng,
Where wits by the thousand abide,
With more than a Cleophon's pride—
On the lips of that foreigner base,
Of Athens the bane and disgrace,
There is shrieking, his kinsman by race,
The garrulous swallow of Thrace;
From that perch of exotic descent,
870   Rejoicing her sorrow to vent,
She pours to her spirit's content,
A nightingale's woful lament,

That e'en though the voting be equal,
His ruin will soon be the sequel.

Well it suits the holy Chorus
Evermore with counsel wise
To exhort and teach the city;
This we therefore now advise—
End the townsmen's apprehensions;
Equalize the rights of all;   880
If by Phrynichus's wrestlings
Some perchance sustained a fall,
Yet to these 'tis surely open,
Having put away their sin,
For their slips and vacillations
Pardon at your hands to win.
Give your brethren back their franchise.
Sin and shame it were that slaves,
Who have once with stern devotion
Fought your battle on the waves,   890
Should be straightway lords and masters,
Yea Plataeans fully blown—
Not that this deserves our censure;
There I praise you; there alone
Has the city, in her anguish,
Policy and wisdom shown-
Nay but these, of old accustomed
On our ships to fight and win,
(They, their fathers too before them),
These our very kith and kin,   900
You should likewise, when they ask you,
Pardon for their single sin.
O by nature best and wisest,
O relax your jealous ire,
Let us all the world as kinsfolk
And as citizens acquire,
All who on our ships will battle
Well and bravely by our side.
If we cocker up our city,
Narrowing her with senseless pride,   910
Now when she is rocked and reeling
In the cradles of the sea,

531

Here again will after ages
Deem we acted brainlessly.

And O if I'm able to scan
The habits and life of a man
Who shall rue his iniquities soon!
Not long shall that little baboon,
That Cleigenes shifty and small,
920 The wickedest bathman of all
Who are lords of the earth—which is brought
From the isle of Cimolus, and wrought
With nitre and lye into soap—
Not long shall he vex us, I hope.
And this the unlucky one knows,
Yet ventures a peace to oppose,
And being addicted to blows
He carries a stick as he goes,
Lest while he is tipsy and reeling,
930 Some robber his cloak should be stealing.
Often has it crossed my fancy,
That the city loves to deal
With the very best and noblest
Members of her commonweal,
Just as with our ancient coinage,
And the newly-minted gold.
Yea for these, our sterling pieces,
All of pure Athenian mould,
All of perfect die and metal,
940 All the fairest of the fair,
All of workmanship unequalled,
Proved and valued everywhere

Both amongst our own Hellenes
Snd Barbarians far away,
These we use not: but the worthles
Pinchbeck coins of yesterday,
Vilest die and basest metal,
Now we always use instead.
Even so, our sterling townsmen,
950 Nobly born and nobly bred,
Men of worth and rank and mettle,

Men of honourable fame,
Trained in every liberal science,
Choral dance and manly game,
These we treat with scorn and insult,
But the strangers newliest come,
Worthless sons of worthless fathers,
Pinchbeck townsmen, yellowy scum,
Whom in earlier days the city
Hardly would have stooped to use   960
Even for her scapegoat victims,
These for every task we choose.
O unwise and foolish people,
Yet to mend your ways begin;
Use again the good and useful:
So hereafter, if ye win
'Twill be due to this your wisdom:
If ye fall, at least 'twill be
Not a fall that brings dishonour,
Falling from a worthy tree.   970

[Enter Aeacus, Xanthius and two attendants.]

Aeacus

By Zeus the Saviour, quite the gentleman
Your master is.

Xanthius

Gentleman? I believe you.
He's all for wine and women, is my master.

Aeacus

But not to have flogged you, when the truth came out
That you, the slave, were passing off as master!

Xanthius

He'd get the worst of that.

Aeacus

Bravo! that's spoken

Like a true slave: that's what I love myself.

Xanthius

You love it, do you?

Aeacus

Love it? I'm entranced
When I can curse my lord behind his back.

Xanthius

How about grumbling, when you have felt the stick,
And scurry out of doors?

Aeacus

That's jolly too.

Xanthius

How about prying?

Aeacus

That beats everything,

Xanthius

Great Kin-god Zeus! And what of overhearing
Your master's secrets?

Aeacus

What? I'm mad with joy.

Xanthius

And blabbing them abroad?

Aeacus

O heaven and earth!
When I do that, I can't contain myself.

Xanthius

Phoebus Apollo! clap your hand in mine,

Kiss and be kissed: and prithee tell me this,
Tell me by Zeus, our rascaldom's own god,
What's all that noise within? What means this hubbub
And row?

Aeacus

That's Aeschylus and Euripides.

Xanthius

Eh?   1000

Aeacus

Wonderful, wonderful things are going on.
The dead are rioting, taking different sides.

Xanthius

Why, what's the matter?

Aeacus

There's a custom here
With all the crafts, the good and noble crafts,
That the chief master of art in each
Shall have his dinner in the assembly hall,
And sit by Pluto's side.

Xanthius

I understand.

Aeacus

Until another comes, more wise than he   1010
In the same art: then must the first give way.

Xanthius

And how has this disturbed our Aeschylus?

Aeacus

'Twas he that occupied the tragic chair,
As, in his craft, the noblest.

Xanthius

Who does now?

Aeacus

But when Euripides came down, he kept
Flourishing off before the highwaymen,
Thieves, burglars, parricides—these form our mob
In Hades—till with listening to his twists
And turns, and pleas and counterpleas, they went
Mad on the man, and hailed him first and wisest:
Elate with this, he claimed the tragic chair
Where Aeschylus was seated.

Xanthius

Wasn't he pelted?

Aeacus

Not he: the populace clamoured out to try
Which of the twain was wiser in his art.

Xanthius

You mean the rascals?

Aeacus

Aye, as high as heaven!

Xanthius

But were there none to side with Aeschylus?

Aeacus

Scanty and sparse the good, *[regards the audience]* the same as
here.

Xanthius

And what does Pluto now propose to do?

Aeacus

He means to hold a tournament, and bring

536

Their tragedies to the proof.

Xanthius

But Sophocles,
How came not he to claim the tragic chair?

Aeacus

Claim it? Not he! When he came down, he kissed
With reverence Aeschylus, and clasped his hand,
And yielded willingly the chair to him.
But now he's going, says Cleidemides,   1040
To sit third-man: and then if Aeschylus win,
He'll stay content: if not, for his art's sake,
He'll fight to the death against Euripides.

Xanthius

Will it come off?

Aeacus

O yes, by Zeus, directly.
And then, I hear, will wonderful things be done,
The art poetic will be weighed in scales.

Xanthius

What! weigh out tragedy, like butcher's meat?

Aeacus

Levels they'll bring, and measuring-tapes for words,
And moulded oblongs,   1050

Xanthius

Is it bricks they are making?

Aeacus

Wedges and compasses: for Euripides
Vows that he'll test the dramas, word by word.

Xanthius

Aeschylus chafes at this, I fancy.

Aeacus

Well, he lowered his brows, upglaring like a bull.

Xanthius

And who's to be the judge?

Aeacus

There came the rub.
Skilled men were hard to find: for with the Athenians
Aeschylus, somehow, did not hit it off.

Xanthius

1060

Too many burglars, I expect, he thought.

Aeacus

And all the rest, he said, were trash and nonsense
To judge poetic wits. So then at last
They chose your lord, an expert in the art.
But we go in for when our lords are bent
On urgent business, that means blows for us.

Chorus

O surely with terrible wrath
Will the thunder-voiced monarch be filled,
When he sees his opponent beside him,
The tonguester, the artifice-skilled,
1070
Stand, whetting his tusks for the fight!
O surely, his eyes rolling-fell
Will with terrible madness be fraught!
O then will be charging of plume-waving
Words with their wild-floating mane,
And then will be whirling of splinters,
And phrases smoothed down with the plane,
When the man would the grand-stepping maxims,
The language gigantic, repel
Of the hero-creator of thought.
1080
There will his shaggy-born crest
Upbristle for anger and woe,

Horribly frowning and growling,
His fury will launch at the foe
Huge-clamped masses of words,
With exertion Titanic up-tearing
Great ship-timber planks for the fray.
But here will the tongue be at work,
Uncoiling, word-testing, refining,
Sophist-creator of phrases,
Dissecting, detracting, maligning,   1090
Shaking the envious bits,
And with subtle analysis paring
The lung's large labour away.

*[Here apparently there is a complete change of scene, to
the Hall of Pluto, with himself sitting on his throne, and
Dionysus, Aeschylus, Euripides, and the foreground.]*

Euripides

Don't talk to me; I won't give up the chair,
I say I am better in the art than he.

Dionysus

You hear him, Aeschylus: why don't you speak?

Euripides

He'll do the grand at first, the juggling trick
He used to play in all his tragedies.

Dionysus

Come, my fine fellow, pray don't talk too big.

Euripides

I know the man, I've scanned him through and through,   1100
A savage-creating stubborn-pulling fellow,
Uncurbed, unfettered, uncontrolled of speech,
Unperiphrastic, bombastiloquent.

Aeschylus

Hah! sayest thou so, child of the garden quean
And this to me, thou chattery-babble-collector,
Thou pauper-creating rags-and-patches-stitcher?
Thou shalt abye it dearly!

Dionysus

Pray, be still;
Nor heat thy soul to fury, Aeschylus.

Aeschylus

1110

Not till I've made you see the sort of man
This cripple-maker is who crows so loudly.

Dionysus

Bring out an ewe, a black-fleeced ewe, my boys:
Here's a typhoon about to burst upon us.

Aeschylus

Thou picker-up of Cretan monodies,
Foisting thy tales of incest on the stage—

Dionysus

Forbear, forbear, most honoured Aeschylus;
And you, my poor Euripides, begone
If you are wise, out of this pitiless hail,
Lest with some heady word he crack your scull
1120   And batter out your brain-less Telephus.
And not with passion, Aeschylus, but calmly
Test and be tested. 'Tis not meet for poets
To scold each other, like two baking-girls.
But you go roaring like an oak on fire.

Euripides

I'm ready, I don't draw back one bit.
I'll lash or, if he will, let him lash first
The talk, the lays, the sinews of a play:
Aye and my Peleus, aye and Aeolus.

And Meleager, aye and Telephus.

Dionysus

And what do you propose? Speak, Aeschylus.   1130

Aeschylus

I could have wished to meet him otherwhere.
We fight not here on equal terms.

Dionysus

Why not?

Aeschylus

My poetry survived me: his died with him:
He's got it here, all handy to recite.
Howbeit, if so you wish it, so we'll have it.

Dionysus

O bring me fire, and bring me frankincense.
I'll pray, or e'er the clash of wits begin,
To judge the strife with high poetic skill.
Meanwhile *[to the Chorus]* invoke the Muses with a song.   1140

Chorus

O Muses, the daughters divine
Of Zeus, the immaculate Nine,
Who gaze from your mansions serene
On intellects subtle and keen,
When down to the tournament lists,
In bright-polished wit they descend,
With wrestling and turnings and twists
In the battle of words to contend,
O come and behold what the two
Antagonist poets can do,   1150
Whose mouths are the swiftest to teach
Grand language and filings of speech:
For now of their wits is the sternest
Encounter commencing in earnest.

541

Dionysus

> Ye two, put up your prayers before ye start.

Aeschylus

> Demeter, mistress, nourisher of my soul,
> O make me worthy of thy mystic rites!

Dionysus [to Euripides]

> Now put on incense, you.

Euripides

> Excuse me, no;
> My vows are paid to other gods than these.

Dionysus

> What, a new coinage of your own?

Euripides

> Precisely.

Dionysus

> Pray then to them, those private gods of yours.

Euripides

> Ether, my pasture, volubly-rolling tongue,
> Intelligent wit and critic nostrils keen,
> O well and neatly may I trounce his plays!

Chorus

> We also are yearning from these to be learning
> Some stately measure, some majestic grand
> Movement telling of conflicts nigh.
> Now for battle arrayed they stand,
> Tongues embittered, and anger high.
> Each has got a venturesome will,
> Each an eager and nimble mind;
> One will wield, with artistic skill,

Clearcut phrases, and wit refined;
Then the other, with words defiant,
Stern and strong, like an angry giant
Laying on with uprooted trees,
Soon will scatter a world of these
Superscholastic subtleties.   1180

Dionysus

Now then, commence your arguments,
And mind you both display
True wit, not metaphors,
Nor things which any fool could say.

Euripides

As for myself, good people all,
I'll tell you by-and-by
My own poetic worth and claims;
But first of all I'll try
To show how this portentous quack
Beguiled the silly fools   1190
Whose tastes were nurtured, ere he came,
In Phrynichus's schools.
He'd bring some single mourner on,
Seated and veiled, 'twould be
Achilles, say, or Niobe—
The face you could not see—
An empty show of tragic woe,
Who uttered not one thing.

Dionysus

'Tis true.

Euripides

Then in the Chorus came, and rattled off a string   1200
Of four continuous lyric odes: the mourner never stirred.

Dionysus

I liked it too. I sometimes think that I those mutes preferred
To all your chatterers now-a-days.

Euripides

Because, if you must know,
You were an ass.

Dionysus

An ass, no doubt; what made him do it though?

Euripides

That was his quackery, don't you see,
To set the audience guessing
When Niobe would speak;
1210   Meanwhile, the drama was progressing.

Dionysus

The rascal, how he took me in!
'Twas shameful, was it not?

[To Aeschylus]

What makes you stamp and fidget so?

Euripides

He's catching it so hot.
So when he had humbugged thus awhile,
and now his wretched play
Was halfway through, a dozen words,
great wild-bull words, he'd say,
Fierce Bugaboos, with bristling crests,
1220   and shaggy eyebrows too,
Which not a soul could understand.

Aeschylus

O heavens!

Dionysus

Be quiet, do.

Euripides

But not one single word was clear.

544

Dionysus

St! don't your teeth be gnashing.

Euripides

'Twas all Scamanders, moated camps,
And griffin-eagles flashing
In burnished copper on the shields, chivalric-precipice-high
Expressions, hard to comprehend.

Dionysus

Aye, by the Powers, and I   1230
Full many a sleepless night have spent
In anxious thought, because
I'd find the tawny cock-horse out,
What sort of bird it was!

Aeschylus

It was a sign, you stupid dolt,
Engraved the ships upon.

Dionysus

Eryxis I supposed it was,
Philoxenus's son.

Euripides

Now really should a cock be brought into a tragic play?

Aeschylus

You enemy gods and men, what was your practice, pray?   1240

Euripides

No cock-horse in my plays, by Zeus,
No goat-stag there you'll see,
Such figures as are blazoned forth
In Median tapestry.
When first I took the art from you,
Bloated and swoln, poor thing,
With turgid gasconading words

545

And heavy dieting,
First I reduced and toned her down,
1250 And made her slim and neat
With wordlets and with exercise
And poultices of beet,
And next a dose of chatterjuice,
Distilled from books, I gave her,
And monodies she took, with sharp
Cephisophon for flavour.
I never used haphazard words,
Or plunged abruptly in;
Who entered first explained at large
1260 The drama's origin
And source.

Dionysus

Its source, I really trust, was better than your own.

Euripides

Then from the very opening lines no idleness was shown;
The mistress talked with all her might, the servant talked as much,
The master talked, the maiden talked, the beldame talked.

Aeschylus

For such an outrage was not death your due?

Euripides

No, by Apollo, no:
That was my democratic way.

Dionysus

1270 Ah, let that topic go.
Your record is not there, my friend, particularly good.

Euripides

Then next I taught all these to speak.

Aeschylus

> You did so, and I would
> That ere such mischief you had wrought, your very lungs
> had split.

Euripides

> Canons of verse I introduced, and neatly chiselled wit;
> To look, to scan: to plot, to plan: to twist, to turn, to woo:
> On all to spy; in all to pry.

Aeschylus

> You did: I say so too.

Euripides

> I showed them scenes of common life,   1280
> The things we know and see,
> Where any blunder would at once by all detected be.
> I never blustered on, or took their breath and wits away
> By Cycnuses or Memnons clad in terrible array,
> With bells upon their horses' heads, the audience to dismay.
> Look at his pupils, look at mine: and there the contrast view.
> Uncouth Megaenetus is his, and rough Phormisius too;
> Great long-beard-lance-and-trumpet-men, flesh-tearers with
> the pine:
> But natty smart Theramenes, and Cleitophon are mine.   1290

Dionysus

> Theramenes? a clever man and wonderfully sly:
> Immerse him in a flood of ills, he'll soon be high and dry,
> "A Kian with a kappa, sir, not Chian with a chi."

Euripides

> I taught them all these knowing ways
> By chopping logic in my plays,
> And making all my speakers try
> To reason out the How and Why.
> So now the people trace the springs,
> The sources and the roots of things,
> And manage all their households too   1300

Far better than they used to do,
Scanning and searching "What's amiss?"
And, "Why was that?" And, "How is this?"

Dionysus

Ay, truly, never now a man
Comes home, but he begins to scan;
And to his household loudly cries,
"Why, where's my pitcher? What's the matter?
'Tis dead and gone my last year's platter.
Who gnawed these olives? Bless the sprat,
Who nibbled off the head of that?
And where's the garlic vanished, pray,
I purchased only yesterday?"
—Whereas, of old, our stupid youths
Would sit, with open mouths and eyes,
Like any dull-brained Mammacouths.

Chorus

"All this thou beholdest, Achilles our boldest."
And what wilt thou reply? Draw tight the rein
Lest that fiery soul of thine
Whirl thee out of the listed plain,
Past the olives, and o'er the line.
Dire and grievous the charge he brings.
See thou answer him, noble heart,
Not with passionate bickerings.
Shape thy course with a sailor's art,
Reef the canvas, shorten the sails,
Shift them edgewise to shun the gales.
When the breezes are soft and low,
Then, well under control, you'll go
Quick and quicker to strike the foe.

O first of all the Hellenic bards
High loftily-towering verse to rear,
And tragic phrase from the dust to raise,
Pour forth thy fountain with right good cheer.

1310

1320

1330

Aeschylus

> My wrath is hot at this vile mischance,
> And my spirit revolts at the thought that I
> Must bandy words with a fellow like him:
> But lest he should vaunt that I can't reply—
> Come, tell me what are the points for which
> A noble poet our praise obtains.

Euripides

> For his ready wit, and his counsels sage,　　　　　　1340
> And because the citizen folk he trains
> To be better townsmen and worthier men.

Aeschylus

> If then you have done the very reverse,
> Found noble-hearted and virtuous men,
> And altered them, each and all, for the worse,
> Pray what is the meed you deserve to get?

Dionysus

> Nay, ask not him. He deserves to die.

Aeschylus

> For just consider what style of men he received from me, great
> six-foot-high
> Heroical souls, who never would blench from a townsman's　　1350
> duties in peace or war;
> Not idle loafers, or low buffoons, or rascally scamps such as
> now they are.
> But men who were breathing spears and helms, and the snow-
> white plume in its crested pride,
> The greave, and the dart, and the warrior's heart in its seven-
> fold casing of tough bull-hide.

Dionysus

> He'll stun me, I know, with his armoury-work; this business is
> going from bad to worse.

Euripides

1360   And how did you manage to make them so grand,
exalted, and brave with your wonderful verse?

Dionysus

Come, Aeschylus, answer, and don't stand mute in your
self-willed pride and arrogant spleen.

Aeschylus

A drama I wrote with the War-god filled.

Dionysus

Its name?

Aeschylus

'Tis the "Seven against Thebes" that I mean.
Which whoso beheld, with eagerness swelled to rush to the
battlefield there and then.

Dionysus

O that was a scandalous thing you did!
1370   You have made the Thebans mightier men,
More eager by far for the business of war.
Now, therefore, receive this punch on the head.

Aeschylus

Ah, ye might have practised the same yourselves,
but ye turned to other pursuits instead.
Then next the "Persians" I wrote, in praise of the noblest d
that the world can show,
And each man longed for the victor's wreath, to fight and t
vanquish his country's foe.

Dionysus

I was pleased, I own, when I heard their moan
1380   For old Darius, their great king, dead;
When they smote together their hands, like this,
And "Evir alake" the Chorus said.

Aeschylus

> Aye, such are the poet's appropriate works:
> And just consider how all along
> From the very first they have wrought you good,
> The noble bards, the masters of song.
> First, Orpheus taught you religious rites,
> And from bloody murder to stay your hands:
> Musaeus healing and oracle lore;
> And Hesiod all the culture of lands, 1390
> The time to gather, the time to plough.
> And gat not Homer his glory divine
> By singing of valour, and honour, and right,
> And the sheen of the battle-extended line,
> The ranging of troops and the arming of men?

Dionysus

> O ay, but he didn't teach that, I opine,
> To Pantacles; when he was leading the show
> I couldn't imagine what he was at,
> He had fastened his helm on the top of his head,
> He was trying to fasten his plume upon that. 1400

Aeschylus

> But others, many and brave, he taught,
> Of whom was Lamachus, hero true;
> And thence my spirit the impress took,
> And many a lion-heart chief I drew,
> Patrocluses, Teucers, illustrious names;
> For I fain the citizen-folk would spur
> To stretch themselves to their measure and height,
> Whenever the trumpet of war they hear.
> But Phaedras and Stheneboeas? No!
> No harlotry business deformed my plays. 1410
> And none can say that ever I drew
> A love-sick woman in all my days.

Euripides

> For you no lot or portion had got in Queen Aphrodite.

Aeschylus

Thank Heaven for that.
But ever on you and yours, my friend, the mighty goddess
mightily sat;
Yourself she cast to the ground at last.

Dionysus

O ay, that came uncommonly pat.
You showed how cuckolds are made, and lo, you were struck
yourself by the very same fate.

Euripides

But say, you cross-grained censor of mine, how my
Stheneboeas could harm the state.

Aeschylus

Full many a noble dame, the wife of a noble citizen, hemlock
took,
And died, unable the shame and sin of your Bellerophon
scenes to brook.

Euripides

Was then, I wonder, the tale I told of Phaedra's passionate lo
untrue?

Aeschylus

Not so: but tales of incestuous vice the sacred poet should
hide from view,
Nor ever exhibit and blazon forth on the public stage to the
public ken.
For boys a teacher at school is found, but we, the poets, are
teachers of men.
We are hound things honest and pure to speak.

Euripides

And to speak great Lycabettuses, pray,
And massive blocks of Parnassian rocks,
Is that things honest and pure to say?

In human fashion we ought to speak.

Aeschylus

> Alas, poor witling, and can't you see   1440
> That for mighty thoughts and heroic aims, the words
> themselves must appropriate be?
> And grander belike on the ear should strike the speech of
> heroes and godlike powers,
> Since even the robes that invest their limbs are statelier,
> grander robes than ours.
> Such was my plan: but when you began, you spoilt and
> degraded it all.

Aeschylus

> Your kings in tatters and rags you dressed,
> And brought them on, a beggarly show,   1450
> To move, forsooth, our pity and ruth.

Euripides

> And what was the harm, I should like to know.

Aeschylus

> No more will a wealthy citizen now equip for the state a galley
> of war.
> He wraps his limbs in tatters and rags, and whines he is "poor,
> too poor by far."

Dionysus

> But under his rags he is wearing a vest, as woolly and soft
> as a man could wish.
> Let him gull the state, and he's off to the mart; an eager,
> extravagant buyer of fish.   1460

Aeschylus

> Moreover to prate, to harangue, to debate,
> Is now the ambition of all in the state.
> Each exercise-ground is in consequence found
> Deserted and empty: to evil repute
> Your lessons have brought our youngsters, and taught

Our sailors to challenge, discuss, and refute
The orders they get from their captains and yet,
When I was alive, I protest that the knaves
Knew nothing at all, save for rations to call,
1470   And to sing "Rhyppapae" as they pulled through the waves.

Dionysus

And bedad to let fly from their sterns in the eye
Of the fellow who tugged at the undermost oar,
And a jolly young messmate with filth to besmirch,
And to land for a filching adventure ashore;
But now they harangue, and dispute, and won't row
And idly and aimlessly float to and fro.

Aeschylus

Of what ills is he not the creator and cause?
Consider the scandalous scenes that he draws,
His bawds, and his panders, his women who give
1480   Give birth in the sacredest shrine,
Whilst others with brothers are wedded and bedded,
And others opine
That "not to be living" is truly "to live."
And therefore our city is swarming to-day
With clerks and with demagogue-monkeys, who play
Their jackanape tricks at all times, in all places,
Deluding the people of Athens; but none
Has training enough in athletics to run
With the torch in his hand at the races.

Dionysus

1490   By the Powers, you are right! At the Panathenaea
I laughed till I felt like a potsherd to see a
Pale, paunchy young gentleman pounding along,
With his head butting forward, the last of the throng,
In the direst of straits;
And behold at the gates,
The Ceramites flapped him, and smacked him,
And slapped him,
In the ribs, and the loin,
And the flank, and the groin,

And still, as they spanked him, he puffed and he panted,   1500
Till at one mighty cuff,
He discharged such a puff
That he blew out his torch and levanted.

Chorus

Dread the battle, and stout the combat,
Mighty and manifold looms the war.
Hard to decide is the fight they're waging,
One like a stormy tempest raging,
One alert in the rally and skirmish,
clever to parry and foin and spar.
Nay but don't be content to sit   1510
Always in one position only:
many the fields for your keen-edged wit.
On then, wrangle in every way,
Argue, battle, be flayed and flay,
Old and new from your stores display,
Yea, and strive with venturesome
daring something subtle and neat to say.

Fear ye this, that to-day's spectators
lack the grace of artistic lore,
Lack the knowledge they need for taking   1520
All the points ye will soon be making?
Fear it not: the alarm is groundless:
that, be sure, is the case no more.
All have fought the campaign ere this:
Each a book of the words is holding;
never a single point they'll miss.
Bright their natures, and now, I ween,
Newly whetted, and sharp, and keen.
Dread not any defect of wit,
Battle away without misgiving,   1530
sure that the audience, at least, are fit.

Euripides

Well then I'll turn me to your prologues now,
Beginning first to test the first beginning
Of this fine poet's plays. Why he's obscure

Even in the enunciation of the facts.

Dionysus

Which of them will you test?

Euripides

Many: but first give us that famous one from the Oresteia.

Dionysus

St! Silence all! Now, Aeschylus, begin.

Aeschylus

1540
"Grave Hermes, witnessing a father's power,
Be thou my saviour and mine aid to-day,
For here I come and hither I return."

Dionysus

Any fault there?

Euripides

A dozen faults and more.

Dionysus

Eh! why the lines are only three in all.

Euripides

But every one contains a score of faults.

Dionysus

Now Aeschylus, keep silent; if you don't
You won't get off with three iambic lines.

Aeschylus

Silent for him!

Dionysus

If my advice you'll take.

Euripides

> Why, at first starting here's a fault skyhigh.   1550

Aeschylus [to Dionysus]

> You see your folly?

Dionysus

> Have your way; I care not.

Aeschylus [to Euripides]

> What is my fault?

Euripides

> Begin the lines again.

Aeschylus

> "Grave Hermes, witnessing a father's power—"

Euripides

> And this beside his murdered father's grave
> Orestes speaks?

Aeschylus

> I say not otherwise.

Euripides

> Then does he mean that when his father fell
> By craft and violence at a woman's hand,   1560
> The god of craft was witnessing the deed?

Aeschylus

> It was not he: it was the Helper Hermes
> He called the grave: and this he showed by adding
> It was his sire's prerogative he held.

Euripides

> Why this is worse than all. If from his father

He held this office grave, why then—

Dionysus

He was a graveyard rifler on his father's side.

Aeschylus

Bacchus, the wine you drink is stale and fusty.

Dionysus

Give him another:
1570   *[to Euripides]* you, look out for faults.

Aeschylus

"Be thou my saviour and mine aid to-day,
For here I come, and hither I return."

Euripides

The same thing twice says clever Aeschylus.

Dionysus

How twice?

Euripides

Why, just consider: I'll explain.
"I come," says he; and "I return," says he:
It's the same thing, to "come" and to "return."

Dionysus

Aye, just as if you said, "Good fellow, lend me
A kneading trough: likewise, a trough to knead in."

Aeschylus

1580   It is not so, you everlasting talker,
They're not the same, the words are right enough.

Dionysus

How so? inform me how you use the words.

Aeschylus

> A man, not banished from his home, may "come"
> To any land, with no especial chance.
> A home-bound exile both "returns" and "comes."

Dionysus

> O good, by Apollo!
> What do you say, Euripides, to that?

Euripides

> I say Orestes never did "return."
> He came in secret: nobody recalled him.

Dionysus

> O good, by Hermes!   1590
> [*Aside*] I've not the least suspicion what he means.

Euripides

> Repeat another line.

Dionysus

> Ay, Aeschylus,
> Repeat one instantly: you, mark what's wrong.

Aeschylus

> "Now on this funeral mound I call my father
> To hear, to hearken.

Euripides

> There he is again.
> To "hear," to "hearken"; the same thing, exactly.

Dionysus

> Aye, but he's speaking to the dead, you knave,
> Who cannot hear us though we call them thrice.   1600

Aeschylus

> And how do you make your prologues?

Euripides

> You shall hear;
> And if you find one single thing said twice,
> Or any useless padding, spit upon me.

Dionysus

> Well, fire away: I'm all agog to hear
> Your very accurate and faultless prologues.

Euripides

> "A happy man was Oedipus at first—

Aeschylus

> Not so, by Zeus; a most unhappy man.
> Who, not yet born nor yet conceived, Apollo
> Foretold would be his father's murderer.
> How could he be a happy man at first?

Euripides

> "Then he became the wretchedest of men."

Aeschylus

> Not so, by Zeus; he never ceased to be.
> No sooner born, than they exposed the babe,
> (And that in winter), in an earthen crock,
> Lest he should grow a man, and slay his father.
> Then with both ankles pierced and swoln, he limped
> Away to Polybus: still young, he married
> An ancient crone, and her his mother too.
> Then scratched out both his eyes.

Dionysus

> Happy indeed had he been Erasinides's colleague!

Euripides

> Nonsense; I say my prologues are first rate.

Aeschylus

> Nay then, by Zeus, no longer line by line

1610

1620

I'll maul your phrases: but with heaven to aid
I'll smash your prologues with a bottle of oil.

Euripides

You mine with a bottle of oil?

Aeschylus

With only one.
You frame your prologues so that each and all
Fit in with a "bottle of oil," or "coverlet-skin,"
Or "reticule-bag." I'll prove it here, and now.   1630

Euripides

You'll prove it? You?

Aeschylus

I will.

Dionysus

Well then, begin.

Euripides

"Aegyptus, sailing with his fifty sons,
As ancient legends mostly tell the tale,
Touching at Argos—"

Aeschylus

Lost his bottle of oil.

Euripides

Hang it, what's that? Confound that bottle of oil!

Dionysus

Give him another: let him try again.

Euripides

"Bacchus, who, clad in fawnskins, leaps and bounds torch and   1640 thyrsus in the choral dance along Parnassus—"

Aeschylus

Lost his bottle of oil.

Dionysus

Ah me, we are stricken with that bottle again!

Euripides

Pooh, pooh, that's nothing. I've a prologue here.
He'll never tack his bottle of oil to this:
"No man is blest in every single thing.
One is of noble birth, but lacking means.
Another, baseborn."

Aeschylus

Lost his bottle of oil.

Dionysus

1650   Euripides!

Euripides

Well?

Dionysus

Lower your sails, my boy;
This bottle of oil is going to blow a gale.

Euripides

O, by Demeter, I don't care one bit;
Now from his hands I'll strike that bottle of oil.

Dionysus

Go on then, go: but ware the bottle of oil.

Euripides

"Once Cadmus, quitting the Sidonian town, Agenor's offspring

Aeschylus

Lost his bottle of oil.

Dionysus

O pray, my man, buy off that bottle of oil,
Or else he'll smash our prologues all to bits.   1660

Euripides

I buy of him?

Dionysus

If my advice you'll take.

Euripides

No, no, I've many a prologue yet to say,
To which he can't tack on his bottle of oil.
"Pelops, the son of Tantalus, while driving
His mares to Pisa—"

Aeschylus

Lost his bottle of oil.

Dionysus

There! he tacked on the bottle of oil again.
O for heaven's sake, pay him its price, dear boy;
You'll get it for an obol, spick and span.   1670

Euripides

Not yet, by Zeus; I've plenty of prologues left.
"Oeneus once reaping—"

Aeschylus

Lost his bottle of oil.

Euripides

Pray let me finish one entire line first.
"Oeneus once reaping an abundant harvest,

Offering the firstfruits—"

Aeschylus

Lost his bottle of oil.

Dionysus

What, in the act of offering? Fie! Who stole it?

Euripides

1680
O don't keep bothering! Let him try with
"Zeus, as by Truth's own voice the tale is told—"

Dionysus

No, he'll cut in with "Lost his bottle of oil!"
Those bottles of oil on all your prologues seem
To gather and grow, like styes upon the eye.
Turn to his melodies now for goodness' sake.

Euripides

O I can easily show that he's a poor
Melody-maker; he makes them all alike.

Chorus

What, O what will be done!
Strange to think that he dare
Blame the bard who has won,
1690
More than all in our days,
Fame and praise for his lays,
Lays so many and fair.
Much I marvel to hear
What the charge he will bring
'Gainst our tragedy king;
Yea for himself do I fear.

Euripides

Wonderful lays! O yes, you'll see directly.
I'll cut down all his metrical strains to one.

Dionysus

And I, I'll take some pebbles, and keep count.

*[A slight pause, during which the music of a flute is heard.
The music continues as an accompaniment to the recita-
tive.]*

Euripides

Lord of Phthia, Achilles, "why hearing the voice of the   1700
hero-dividing. Hah! smiting! approachest thou not
to the rescue?"
We, by the lake who "abide, are adoring our ancestor Hermes.
Hah! smiting! approachest thou not to the rescue?"

Dionysus

O Aeschylus, twice art thou smitten!

Euripides

Hearken to me, great king; yea, hearken
"Atreides, thou noblest of the Achaeans.
Hah! smiting! approachest thou not to the rescue?"

Dionysus

Thrice, Aeschylus, thrice art thou smitten!

Euripides

Hush! the bee-wardens are here: 1710
they "will quickly the Temple of Artemis open.
Hah! smiting! approachest thou not to the rescue?"
I will expound (for "I know it) the omen the chieftains
encountered.
Hah! smiting! approachest thou not to the rescue?"

Dionysus

O Zeus and King, the terrible lot of smittings!
I'll to the bath: I'm very sure my kidneys
Are quite inflamed and swoln with all these smitings.

Euripides

> Wait till you've heard another batch of lays
> 1720   Culled from his lyre-accompanied melodies.

Dionysus

> Go on then, go: but no more smitings, please.

Euripides

> "How the twin-throned powers of Achaea,
> the lords of the mighty Hellenes.
> O phlattothrattophlattothrat!
> Sendeth the Sphinx, the unchancy,
> the chieftainness bloodhound.
> O phlattothrattophlattothratt!
> Launcheth fierce with brand and hand
> the avengers the terrible eagle.
> O phlattothrattophlattothrat!
> So for the swift-winged hounds of the air
> he provided a booty.
> O phlattothrattophlattothrat!
> The throng down-bearing on Aias.
> O phlattothrattophlattothrat!"

Dionysus

> Whence comes that phlattothrat?
> From Marathon, or where picked you up
> these cable-twister's strains?

Aeschylus

> From noblest source for noblest ends I brought them,
> 1740   Unwilling in the Muses' holy field
> The self-same flowers as Phrynichus to cull.
> But he from all things rotten draws his lays,
> From Carian flutings, catches of Meletus,
> Dance-music, dirges. You shall hear directly.
> Bring me the lyre. Yet wherefore need a lyre
> For songs like these? Where's she that bangs and jangles
> Her castanets? Euripides's Muse,
> Present yourself: fit goddess for fit verse.

Dionysus

> The Muse herself can't be a wanton? No!

Aeschylus

> Halycons, who by the ever-rippling   1750
> Waves of the sea are babbling,
> Dewing your plumes with the drops that fall
> From wings in the salt spray dabbling.
>
> Spiders, ever with twir-r-r-r-rling fingers
> Weaving the warp and the woof,
> Little, brittle, network, fretwork,
> Under the coigns of the roof.
>
> The minstrel shuttle's care.
> Where in the front of the dark-prowed ships
> Quickly the flute-loving dolphin skips.   1760
> Races here and oracles there.
>
> And the joy of the young vines smiling,
> And the tendril of grapes, care-beguiling.
> O embrace me, my child, O embrace me.
> *[To Dionysus]* You see this foot?

Dionysus

> I do.

Aeschylus

> And this?

Dionysus

> And that one too.

Aeschylus [to Euripides]

> You, such stuff who compile,
> Dare my songs to upbraid;   1770
> You, whose songs in the style
> Of Cyrene's embraces are made.
> So much for them: but still I'd like to show

567

The way in which your monodies are framed
"O darkly-light mysterious Night,
What may this Vision mean,
Sent from the world unseen
With baleful omens rife;
A thing of lifeless life,
1780   A child of sable night,
A ghastly curdling sight,
In black funereal veils,
With murder, murder in its eyes,
And great enormous nails?
Light ye the lanterns, my maidens,
And dipping your jugs in the stream,
Draw me the dew of the water,
And heat it to boiling and steam;
So will I wash me away the ill effects of my dream.

1790   God of the sea!
My dream's come true.
Ho, lodgers, ho,
This portent view.
Glyce has vanished, carrying off my cock,
My cock that crew!
O Mania, help! O reads of the rock
Pursue! pursue!
For I, poor girl, was working within,
Holding my distaff heavy and full,
1800   Twir-r-r-r-rling my hand as the threads I spin,
Weaving an excellent bobbin of wool;
Thinking 'To-morrow I'll go to the fair,
In the dusk of the morn, and be selling it there.'
But he to the blue upflew, upflew,
On the lightliest tips of his wings outspread;
To me he bequeathed but woe, but woe,
And tears, sad tears, from my eyes o'erflow,
Which I, the bereaved, must shed, must shed.
O children of Ida, sons of Crete,
1810   Grasping your bows to the rescue come;
Twinkle about on your restless feet,
Stand in a circle around her home.
O Artemis, thou maid divine,

Dictynna, huntress, fair to see,
O bring that keen-nosed pack of thine,
And hunt through all the house with me.
O Hecate, with flameful brands,
O Zeus's daughter, arm thine hands,
Those swiftliest hands, both right and left;
Thy rays on Glyce's cottage throw   1820
That I serenely there may go,
And search by moonlight for the theft."

Dionysus

Enough of both your odes.

Aeschylus

Enough for me.
Now would I bring the fellow to the scales.
That, that alone, shall test our poetry now,
And prove whose words are weightiest, his or mine.

Dionysus

Then both come hither, since I needs must weigh
The art poetic like a pound of cheese.

*[Here a large balance is brought out and placed upon the
stage.]*

Chorus

O the labour these wits go throug!   1830
O the wild, extravagant, new,
Wonderful things they are going to do!
Who but they would ever have thought of it?
Why, if a man had happened to meet me
Out in the street, and intelligence brought of it,
I should have thought he was trying to cheat me;
Thought that his story was false and deceiving.
That were a tale I could never believe in.

Dionysus

Each of you stand beside his scale.

Aeschylus and Euripides

1840   We're here.

Dionysus

And grasp it firmly whilst ye speak your lines,
And don't let go until I cry "Cuckoo."

*[Each holds his own scale steady while he speaks his line
into it.]*

Aeschylus and Euripides

Ready!

Dionysus

Now speak your lines into the scale.

Euripides

"O that the Argo had not winged her way—"

Aeschylus

"River Spercheius, cattle-grazing haunts—"

Dionysus

Cuckoo! let go. O look, by far the lowest
His scale sinks down.

Euripides

Why, how came that about?

Dionysus

1850   He threw a river in, like some wool-seller
Wetting his wool, to make it weigh the more.
But you threw in a light and winged word.

Euripides

Come, let him match another verse with mine.

Dionysus

>Each to his scale.

Aeschylus and Euripides

>We're ready.

Dionysus

>Speak your lines.

Euripides

>"Persuasion's only shrine is eloquent speech."

Aeschylus

>"Death loves not gifts, alone amongst the gods."

Dionysus

>Let go, let go. Down goes his scale again.
>He threw in Death, the heaviest ill of all.   1860

Euripides

>And I Persuasion, the most lovely word.

Dionysus

>A vain and empty sound, devoid of sense.
>Think of some heavier-weighted line of yours,
>To drag your scale down: something strong and big.

Euripides

>Where have I got one? Where? Let's see.

Dionysus

>I'll tell you.
>"Achilles threw two singles and a four."
>Come, speak your lines: this is your last set-to.

Euripides

>"In his right hand he grasped an iron-clamped mace."

Aeschylus

"Chariot on chariot, corpse on corpse was hurled."

Dionysus

There now! again he has done you.

Euripides

Done me? How?

Dionysus

He threw two chariots and two corpses in;
Five-score Egyptians could not lift that weight.

Aeschylus

No more of "line for line"; let him—himself,
His children, wife, Cephisophon—get in,
With all his books collected in his arms,
Two lines of mine shall overweigh the lot.

Dionysus

Both are my friends; I can't decide between them:
I don't desire to be at odds with either:
One is so clever, one delights me so.

Pluto [coming forward]

Then you'll effect nothing for which you came?

Dionysus

And how, if I decide?

Pluto

Then take the winner;
So will your journey not be made in vain.

Dionysus

Heaven bless your Highness!
Listen, I came down after a poet.

Euripides

>To what end?

Dionysus

>That so the city, saved, may keep her choral games.
>Now then, whichever of you two shall best   1890
>Advise the city, he shall come with me.
>And first of Alcibiades, let each
>Say what he thinks; the city travails sore.

Euripides

>What does she think herself about him?

Dionysus

>She loves, and hates, and longs to have him back.
>But give me your advice about the man.

Euripides

>I loathe a townsman who is slow to aid,
>And swift to hurt, his town: who ways and means
>Finds for himself, but finds not for the state.

Dionysus

>Poseidon, but that's smart!   1900
>*[to Aeschylus]* And what say you?

Aeschylus

>'Twere best to rear no lion in the state:
>But having reared, 'tis best to humour him.

Dionysus

>By Zeus the Saviour, still I can't decide.
>One is so clever, and so clear the other.
>But once again. Let each in turn declare
>What plan of safety for the state ye've got.

Euripides

>First with Cinesias wing Cleocritus,

Then zephyrs waft them o'er the watery plain.

Dionysus

1910

A funny sight, I own: but where's the sense?

Euripides

If, when the fleets engage, they holding cruets
Should rain down vinegar in the foemen's eyes,
I know, and I can tell you.

Dionysus

Tell away.

Euripides

When things, mistrusted now, shall trusted be,
And trusted things, mistrusted.

Dionysus

How! I don't quite comprehend. Be clear, and not so clever.

Euripides

If we mistrust those citizens of ours
Whom now we trust, and those employ whom now
1920
We don't employ, the city will be saved.
If on our present tack we fail, we surely
Shall find salvation in the opposite course.

Dionysus

Good, O Palamedes! Good, you genius you.
[Aside] Is this your cleverness or Cephisophon's?

Euripides

This is my own: the cruet-plan was his.

Dionysus [to Aeschylus]

Now, you.

Aeschylus

But tell me whom the city uses.
The good and useful?

Dionysus

What are you dreaming of?
She hates and loathes them.   1930

Aeschylus

Does she love the bad?

Dionysus

Not love them, no: she uses them perforce.

Aeschylus

How can one save a city such as this,
Whom neither frieze nor woollen tunic suits?

Dionysus

O, if to earth you rise, find out some way.

Aeschylus

There will I speak: I cannot answer here.

Dionysus

Nay, nay; send up your guerdon from below.

Aeschylus

When they shall count the enemy's soil their own
And theirs the enemy's: when they know that ships
Are their true wealth, their so-called wealth delusion.   1940

Dionysus

Aye, but the justices suck that down, you know.

Pluto

Now then, decide.

Dionysus

    I will; and thus I'll do it.
    I'll choose the man in whom my soul delights.

Euripides

    O, recollect the gods by whom you swore
    You'd take me home again; and choose your friends.

Dionysus

    'Twas my tongue swore; my choice is—
    Aeschylus.

Euripides

    Hah! what have you done?

Dionysus

1950

    Done? Given the victor's prize
    To Aeschylus; why not?

Euripides

    And do you dare
    Look in my face, after that shameful deed?

Dionysus

    What's shameful, if the audience think not so?

Euripides

    Have you no heart? Wretch, would you leave me dead?

Dionysus

    Who knows if death be life, and life be death,
    And breath be mutton broth, and sleep a sheepskin?

Pluto

    Now, Dionysus, come ye in,

Dionysus

>What for?

Pluto

>And sup before ye go.   1960

Dionysus

>A bright idea.
>I'faith, I'm nowise indisposed for that.

[Exeunt Aeschylus, Euripides, Pluto, and Dionysus.]

Chorus

>Blest the man who possesses a
>Keen intelligent mind.
>This full often we find.
>He, the bard of renown,
>Now to earth reascends,
>Goes, a joy to his town,
>Goes, a joy to his friends,
>Just because he possesses a   1970
>Keen intelligent mind.
>Right it is and befitting,
>Not, by Socrates sitting,
>Idle talk to pursue,
>Stripping tragedy-art of
>All things noble and true.
>Surely the mind to school
>Fine-drawn quibbles to seek,
>Fine-set phrases to speak,
>Is but the part of a fool   1980

[Re-enter Pluto and Aeschylus.]

Pluto

>Farewell then Aeschylus, great and wise,
>Go, save our state by the maxims rare
>Of thy noble thought; and the fools chastise,

For many a fool dwells there.

And this *[handing him a rope]* to Cleophon give, my friend,
And this to the revenue-raising crew,
Nichomachus, Myrmex, next I send,
And this to Archenomus too.
And bid them all that without delay,
To my realm of the dead they hasten away.
For if they loiter above, I swear
I'll come myself and arrest them there.
And branded and fettered the slaves shall
With the vilest rascal in all the town,
Adeimantus, son of Leucolophus, down,
Down, down to the darkness below.

Aeschylus

I take the mission. This chair of mine
Meanwhile to Sophocles here commit,
(For I count him next in our craft divine,)
Till I come once more by thy side to sit.
But as for that rascally scoundrel there,
That low buffoon, that worker of ill,
O let him not sit in my vacant chair,
Not even against his will.

Pluto [to the Chorus]

Escort him up with your mystic throngs,
While the holy torches quiver and blaze.
Escort him up with his own sweet gongs,
And his noble festival lays.

Chorus

First, as the poet triumphant
Is passing away to the light,
Grant him success on his journey,
Ye powers that are ruling below.
Grant that he find for the city
Good counsels to guide her aright;
So we at last shall be freed
From the anguish, the fear, and the woe,

Freed from the onsets of war.
Let Cleophon now and his band
Battle, if battle they must,
Far away in their own fatherland.   2020

The End

SAPPHO

Poems of Sappho

Translated by Edwin Marion Cox

- Hymn to Aphrodite -

Shimmering-throned immortal Aphrodite,
Daughter of Zeus, Enchantress, I implore thee,
Spare me, O queen, this agony and anguish,
Crush not my spirit.

Whenever before thou hast hearkened to me—
To my voice calling to thee in the distance,
And heeding, thou hast come, leaving thy father's
Golden dominions,

With chariot yoked to thy fleet-winged coursers,
Fluttering swift pinions over earth's darkness,
And bringing thee through the infinite, gliding
Downwards from heaven,

Then, soon they arrived and thou, blessed goddess,
With divine countenance smiling, didst ask me
What new woe had befallen me now and why,
Thus I had called thee.

What in my mad heart was my greatest desire,
Who was it now that must feel my allurements,
Who was the fair one that must be persuaded,
Who wronged thee Sappho?

For if now she flees, quickly she shall follow
And if she spurns gifts, soon shall she offer them
Yea, if she knows not love, soon shall she feel it
Even reluctant.

Come then, I pray, grant me surcease from sorrow,
Drive away care, I beseech thee, O goddess
Fulfil for me what I yearn to accomplish,
Be thou my ally.

- Second Poem -

Peer of the gods, the happiest man I seem
Sitting before thee, rapt at thy sight, hearing
Thy soft laughter and thy voice most gentle,
Speaking so sweetly.

Then in my bosom my heart wildly flutters,
And, when on thee I gaze never so little,
Bereft am I of all power of utterance,
My tongue is useless.

There rushes at once through my flesh tingling fire,
My eyes are deprived of all power of vision,
My ears hear nothing but sounds of winds roaring,
And all is blackness.

Down courses in streams the sweat of emotion,
A dread trembling o'erwhelms me, paler am I
Than dried grass in autumn, and in my madness
Dead I seem almost.

- Third Poem -

A troop of horse, the serried ranks of marchers,
A noble fleet, some think these of all on earth
Most beautiful. For me naught else regarding
Is my beloved.

To understand this is for all most simple,
For thus gazing much on mortal perfection

And knowing already what life could give her,
Him chose fair Helen,

Him the betrayer of Ilium's honour.
Then recked she not of adored child or parent,
But yielded to love, and forced by her passion,
Dared Fate in exile.

Thus quickly is bent the will of that woman
To whom things near and dear seem to be nothing.
So mightest thou fail, My Anactoria,
If she were with you.

She whose gentle footfall and radiant face
Hold the power to charm more than a vision
Of chariots and the mail-clad battalions
Of Lydia's army.

So must we learn in a world made as this one
Man can never attain his greatest desire,
But must pray for what good fortune Fate holdeth,
Never unmindful.

- Fourth Poem -

The gleaming stars all about the shining moon
Hide their bright faces, when full-orbed and splendid
In the sky she floats, flooding the shadowed earth
With clear silver light.

- Fifth Poem -

By the cool water the breeze murmurs, rustling
Through apple branches, while from quivering leaves
Streams down deep slumber.

- Invocation to Aphrodite -

Come hither foam-born Cyprian goddess, come,
And in golden goblets pour richest nectar
All mixed in most ethereal perfection,
Thus to delight us.

PINDAR

Odes of Pindar

Translated and notes by Ernest Myers

- Fifth Nemean Ode -

For Pytheas Of Aigina,

Winner In The Boys' Pankration.

[The date of this ode is uncertain. The winner's brother Phylakidas, gained the two victories, also in the pankration, which are celebrated in the fourth and fifth Isthmians.]

No statuary I, that I should fashion images to rest idly on their pedestals, nay but by every trading-ship and plying boat forth from Aigina fare, sweet song of mine, and bear abroad the news, how that Lampon's son, the strong-limbed Pytheas, hath won at Nemea the pankratiast's crown, while on his cheeks he showeth not as yet the vine-bloom's mother, mellowing midsummer.

So to the warrior heroes sprung from Kronos and Zeus and from the golden nymphs, even to the Aiakidai, hath he done honour, and to the mother-city, a friendly field to strangers. That she should have issue of goodly men and should be famous in her ships, this prayed they of old, standing beside the altar of their grandsire, Zeus Hellenios, and together stretched forth their hands toward heaven, even the glorious sons of Endais and the royal strength of Phokos, the goddess-born, whom on the sea-beach Psamatheia bare. Of their deed portentous and unjustly dared I am loth to tell, and how they left that famous isle, and of the fate that drove the valiant heroes from Oinone. I will make pause: not for every perfect truth is it best that it discover its face: silence is oft man's wisest thought.

But if the praise of good hap or of strength of hand or of steel-clad war be my resolve, let one mark me a line for a long leap hence: in my knees I have a nimble spring: even beyond the sea the eagles wing their way.

With goodwill too for the Aiakidai in Pelion sang the Muses' choir most fair, and in the midst Apollo playing with golden quill upon his seven-toned lyre led them in ever-changing strains. They first of all from Zeus beginning sang of holy Thetis and of Peleus, and how that Kretheus' dainty daughter Hippolyte would fain have caught him by her wile, and persuaded his friend the king of the Magnetes her husband by counsels of deceit, for she forged a lying tale thereto devised, how that he essayed to go in unto her in Akastos' bridal bed. But the truth was wholly contrary thereto, for often and with all her soul she had besought him with beguiling speech; but her bold words vexed his spirit; and forthwith he refused the bride, fearing the wrath of the Father who guardeth host and guest. And he, the cloud-compelling Zeus in heaven, the immortal's king, was aware thereof, and he promised him that with all speed he would find him a sea-bride from among the Nereids of golden distaffs, having persuaded thereto Poseidon, their kinsman by his marriage, who from Aigai to the famous Dorian Isthmus cometh oftentimes, where happy troops with the reed-flute's noise welcome the god, and in bold strength of limb men strive.

The fate that is born with a man is arbiter of all his acts. Thou, Euthymenes , at Aigina falling into the goddess victory's arms didst win thee hymns of subtle strain: yea and now too to thee, O Pytheas, who art his kinsman of the same stock and followest in his footsteps, doth thy mother's brother honour. Nemea is favourable unto him, and the month of his country that Apollo loveth: the youth that came to strive with him he overcame, both at home and by Nisos' hill of pleasant glades. I have joy that the whole state striveth for glory. Know that through Menander's aid thou hast attained unto sweet recompense of toils. And meet it is that from Athens a fashioner of athletes come.

But if thou comest to Themistios, to sing of him, away with chill reserve, shout aloud, hoist to the top-yard of the mast the sail, and tell how in the boxing and the pankration at Epidauros he won a double prize of valour, and to the portals of Aiakos bare fresh wreaths of flowers, led by the Graces of the yellow hair.

- Tenth Pythian Ode -

For Hippokleas Of Thessaly,

Winner In The Two-Stadion Foot-Race Of Boys.

[The only reason we know for the digression about Perseus which occupies a great part of this ode seems to be that Thorax, who engaged Pindar to write it for Hippokleas, and perhaps Hippokleas himself, belonged to the family of the Aleuadai, who were descended through Herakles from Perseus.]

[This ode is the earliest entire poem of Pindar's which survives. He wrote it when he was twenty years old. The simplicity of the style and manner of composition are significant of this. But there can scarcely be said to be traces here of Pindar's early tendency in dealing with mythological allusions to 'sow not with the hand but with the whole sack,' which Korinna advised him to correct, and which is conspicuous in a fragment remaining to us of one of his Hymns.]

Happy is Lakedaimon, blessed is Thessaly: in both there reigneth a race sprung from one sire, from Herakles bravest in the fight. What vaunt is this unseasonable? Nay, now, but Pytho calleth me, and Pelinnaion, and the sons of Aleuas who would fain lead forth the loud voices of a choir of men in honour of Hippokleas.

For now hath he tasted the joy of games, and to the host of the dwellers round about hath the valley beneath Parnassos proclaimed him best among the boys who ran the double race.

O Apollo, sweet is the end when men attain thereto, and the beginning availed more when it is speeded of a god. Surely of thy devising were his deeds: and this his inborn valour hath trodden in the footsteps of his father twice victor at Olympia in panoply of war-affronting arms: moreover the games in the deep meadow beneath Kirrha's cliff gave victory to the fleet feet of Phrikias.

May good luck follow them, so that even in after days the splendour of their wealth shall bloom. Of the pleasant things of Hellas they have no scanty portion to their lot; may they happen on no envious repentings of the gods. A god's heart, it may be, is painless ever; but happy and a theme of poet's song is that man who for his valiance of hands or feet the chiefest prizes hath by strength and courage won, and in his life-time seen his young son by good hap attaining to the Pythian crown. Never indeed shall he climb the brazen heaven, but whatsoever splendours we of mortal race may reach, through such he hath free course even to the utmost harbourage. But neither by taking ship, neither by any travel on foot, to the Hyperborean folk shalt thou find the wondrous way.

Yet of old the chieftain Perseus entered into their houses and feasted among them, when that he had lighted on them as they were sacrificing ample hecatombs of asses to their god. For ever in their feasts and hymns hath Apollo especial joy, and laugheth to see the braying ramp of the strange beasts. Nor is the Muse a stranger to their lives, but everywhere are stirring to and fro dances of maidens and shrill noise of pipes: and binding golden bay-leaves in their hair they make them merry cheer. Nor pestilence nor wasting eld approach that hallowed race: they toil not neither do they fight, and dwell unharmed of cruel Nemesis.

In the eagerness of his valiant heart went of old the son of Danaë, for that Athene led him on his way, unto the company of that blessed folk. Also he slew the Gorgon and bare home her head with serpent tresses decked, to the island folk a stony death. I ween there is no marvel impossible if gods have wrought thereto.

Let go the oar, and quickly drive into the earth an anchor from the prow, to save us from the rocky reef, for the glory of my song of praise flitteth like a honey-bee from tale to tale.

I have hope that when the folk of Ephyra pour forth my sweet strains by Peneus' side, yet more glorious shall I make their Hippokleas for his crowns and by my songs among his fellows and his elders, and I will make him possess the minds of the young maidens.

For various longings stir secretly the minds of various men; yet each if he attain to the thing he striveth for will hold his eager desire for the time present to him, but what a year shall bring forth, none shall foreknow by any sign.

My trust is in the kindly courtesy of my host Thorax, of him who to speed my fortune hath yoked this four-horse car of the Pierides, as friend for friend, and willing guide for guide.

As gold to him that trieth it by a touch-stone, so is a true soul known.

His noble brethren also will we praise, for that they exalt and make great the Thessalians' commonwealth. For in the hands of good men lieth the good piloting of the cities wherein their fathers ruled.

- First Olympian Ode -

For Hieron Of Syracuse,

Winner In The Horse-Race.

[This ode seems to owe its position at the head of Pindar's extant works to Aristophanes the grammarian, who placed it there on account of its being specially occupied with the glorification of the Olympic games in comparison with others, and with the story of Pelops, who was their founder.]

[Hieron won this race B.C. 472, while at the height of his power at Syracuse. Probably the ode was sung at Syracuse, perhaps, as has been suggested, at a banquet.]

Best is Water of all, and Gold as a flaming fire in the night shineth eminent amid lordly wealth; but if of prizes in the games thou art fain, O my soul, to tell, then, as for no bright star more quickening than the sun must thou search in the void firmament by day, so neither shall we find any games greater than the Olympic whereof to utter our voice: for hence cometh the glorious hymn and entereth into the minds of the skilled in song, so that they celebrate the son of Kronos, when to the rich and happy hearth of Hieron they are come; for he wieldeth the sceptre of justice in Sicily of many flocks, culling the choice fruits of all kinds of excellence: and with the flower of music is he made splendid, even such strains as we sing blithely at the table of a friend.

Take from the peg the Dorian lute, if in any wise the glory of Phereni-kos at Pisa hath swayed thy soul unto glad thoughts, when by the banks of Alpheos he ran, and gave his body ungoaded in the course, and brought victory to his master, the Syracusans' king, who delighteth in horses.

Bright is his fame in Lydian Pelops' colony, inhabited of a goodly race, whose founder mighty earth-enfolding Poseidon loved, what time from the vessel of purifying Klotho took him with the bright ivory furnishment of his shoulder.

Verily many things are wondrous, and haply tales decked out with cunning fables beyond the truth make false men's speech concerning them. For Charis, who maketh all sweet things for mortal men, by lending honour unto such maketh oft the unbelievable thing to be believed; but the days that follow after are the wisest witnesses.

Meet is it for a man that concerning gods he speak honourably; for the reproach is less. Of thee, son of Tantalos, I will speak contrariwise to them who have gone before me, and I will tell how when thy father had bidden thee to that most seemly feast at his beloved Sipylos, repaying to the gods their banquet, then did he of the Bright Trident, his heart vanquished by love, snatch thee and bear thee behind his golden steeds to the house of august Zeus in the highest, whither again on a like errand came Ganymede in the after time.

But when thou hadst vanished, and the men who sought thee long brought thee not to thy mother, some one of the envious neighbours said secretly that over water heated to boiling they had hewn asunder with a knife thy limbs, and at the tables had shared among them and eaten sodden fragments of thy flesh. But to me it is impossible to call one of the blessed gods cannibal; I keep aloof; in telling ill tales is often little gain.

Now if any man ever had honour of the guardians of Olympus, Tantalos was that man; but his high fortune he could not digest, and by excess thereof won him an overwhelming woe, in that the Father hath hung above him a mighty stone that he would fain ward from his head, and therewithal he is fallen from joy.

This hopeless life of endless misery he endureth with other three, for that he stole from the immortals and gave to his fellows at a feast the nectar and ambrosia, whereby the gods had made him incorruptible. But if a man thinketh that in doing aught he shall be hidden from God, he erreth.

Therefore also the immortals sent back again his son to be once more counted with the short-lived race of men. And he when toward the bloom of his sweet youth the down began to shade his darkening cheek, took counsel with himself speedily to take to him for his wife the noble Hippodameia from her Pisan father's hand.

And he came and stood upon the margin of the hoary sea, alone in the darkness of the night, and called aloud on the deep-voiced Wielder of the Trident; and he appeared unto him nigh at his foot.

Then he said unto him: 'Lo now, O Poseidon, if the kind gifts of the Cyprian goddess are anywise pleasant in thine eyes, restrain Oinomaos' bronze spear, and send me unto Elis upon a chariot exceeding swift, and give the victory to my hands. Thirteen lovers already hath Oinomaos slain, and still delayeth to give his daughter in marriage. Now a great peril alloweth not of a coward: and forasmuch as men must die, wherefore should one sit vainly in the dark through a dull and nameless age, and without lot in noble deeds? Not so, but I will dare this strife: do thou give the issue I desire.'

Thus spake he, nor were his words in vain: for the god made him a glorious gift of a golden car and winged untiring steeds: so he overcame Oinomaos and won the maiden for his bride.

And he begat six sons, chieftains, whose thoughts were ever of brave deeds: and now hath he part in honour of blood-offerings in his grave beside Alpheos' stream, and hath a frequented tomb, whereto many strangers resort: and from afar off he beholdeth the glory of the Olympian games in the courses called of Pelops, where is striving of swift feet and of strong bodies brave to labour; but he that overcometh hath for the sake of those games a sweet tranquillity throughout his life for evermore.

Now the good that cometh of to-day is ever sovereign unto every man. My part it is to crown Hieron with an equestrian strain in Aeolian mood: and sure am I that no host among men that now are shall I ever glorify in sounding labyrinths of song more learned in the learning of honour and withal with more might to work thereto. A god hath guard over thy hopes, O Hieron, and taketh care for them with a peculiar care: and if he fail thee not, I trust that I shall again proclaim in song a sweeter glory yet, and find thereto in words a ready way, when to the fair-shining hill of Kronos I am come. Her strongest-wingèd dart my Muse hath yet in store.

Of many kinds is the greatness of men; but the highest is to be achieved by kings. Look not thou for more than this. May it be thine to walk loftily all thy life, and mine to be the friend of winners in the games, winning honour for my art among Hellenes everywhere.

- First Isthmian Ode -

For Herodotos of Thebes,

Winner In The Chariot-Race.

[The date of this ode is unknown. We gather from the first strophe that Pindar was engaged at the time to write an ode in honour of the Delian Apollo to be sung at Keos, but that he put this off in order first to write the present ode in honour of a victory won for his own native state of Thebes.]

O mother, Thebe of the golden shield, thy service will I set even above the matter that was in my hand. May rocky Delos, whereto I am vowed, be not therefore wroth with me. Is there aught dearer to the good than noble parents?

Give place O Apollonian isle: these twain fair offices, by the grace of God, will I join together in their end, and to Phoibos of the unshorn hair in island Keos with men of her sea-race will I make my choral song, and therewithal this other for the sea-prisoning cliffs of Isthmos.

For six crowns hath Isthmos given from her games to the people of Kadmos, a fair glory of triumph for my country, for the land wherein Alkmene bare her dauntless son, before whom trembled aforetime the fierce hounds of Geryon.

But I for Herodotos' praise am fain to do honour unto his four-horsed car, and to marry to the strain of Kastoreian or Iolaic song the fame that he hath earned, handling his reins in his own and no helping hand.

For these Kastor and Iolaos were of all heroes the mightiest chari-oteers, the one to Lakedaimon, the other born to Thebes. And at the games they entered oftenest for the strife, and with tripods and caldrons and cups of gold they made fair their houses, attaining unto victorious crowns: clear shineth their prowess in the foot-race, run naked or with the heavy clattering shield; and when they hurled the javelin and the quoit: for then was there no five-fold game, but for each several feat there was a prize. Oft did they bind about their hair a crowd of crowns, and showed themselves unto the waters of Dirke or on Eurotas' banks, the son of Iphikles a fellow-townsman of the Spartoi's race, the son of Tyndareus inhabiting the upland dwelling-place of Therapna among the Achaians.

So hail ye and farewell: I on Poseidon and holy Isthmos, and on the lake-shores of Onchestos will throw the mantle of my song, and will among the glories of this man make glorious also the story of his father Asopodoros' fate, and his new country Orchomenos, which, when he drave ashore on a wrecked ship, harboured him amid his dismal hap. But now once more hath the fortune of his house raised him up to see the fair days of the old time: and he who hath suffered pain beareth forethought within his soul.

If a man's desire be wholly after valour, and he give thereto both wealth and toil, meet is it that to such as attain unto it we offer with ungrudging heart high meed of praise. For an easy gift it is for a son of wisdom, by a good word spoken in recompense for labour manifold to set on high the public fame.

For diverse meeds for diverse works are sweet to men, to the shepherd and to the ploughman, to the fowler and to him whom the sea feedeth— howbeit all those strive but to keep fierce famine from their bellies; but whoso in the games or in war hath won delightful fame, receiveth the highest of rewards in fair words of citizens and of strangers.

Us it beseemeth to requite the earth-shaking son of Kronos, who is also neighbour unto us, and to sound his praise as our well-doer, who hath given speed to the horses of our car, and to call upon thy sons, Amphitryon, and the inland dwelling of Minyas, and the famous grove of Demeter, even Eleusis, and Euboia with her curving race-course. And thy holy place, Protesilas, add I unto these, built thee at Phylake by Achaian men.

But to tell over all that Hermes lord of games hath given to Herodotos by his horses, the short space of my hymn alloweth not. Yea and full oft doth the keeping of silence bring forth a larger joy.

Now may Herodotos, up-borne upon the sweet-voiced Muse's shining wings, yet again with wreaths from Pytho and choice wreaths from Alpheos from the Olympian games entwine his hand, and bring honour unto seven-gated Thebes.

Now if one at home store hidden wealth, and fall upon other men to mock them, this man considereth not that he shall give up his soul to death having known no good report.

THEOCRITUS

Idylls of Theocritus

Translated by C.S. Calverley

- IDYLL I. -

The Death of Daphnis

[Thyrsis. A Goatherd.]

Thyrsis.

Sweet are the whispers of yon pine that makes
Low music o'er the spring, and, Goatherd, sweet
  Thy piping; second thou to Pan alone.
Is his the horned ram? then thine the goat.
Is his the goat? to thee shall fall the kid;
  And toothsome is the flesh of unmilked kids.

Goatherd.

Shepherd, thy lay is as the noise of streams
Falling and falling aye from yon tall crag.
  If for their meed the Muses claim the ewe,
Be thine the stall-fed lamb; or if they choose
The lamb, take thou the scarce less-valued ewe.

Thyrsis.

Pray, by the Nymphs, pray, Goatherd, seat thee here
Against this hill-slope in the tamarisk shade,
  And pipe me somewhat, while I guard thy goats.

Goatherd.

I durst not, Shepherd, O I durst not pipe
At noontide; fearing Pan, who at that hour
  Rests from the toils of hunting. Harsh is he;
  Wrath at his nostrils aye sits sentinel.

But, Thyrsis, thou canst sing of Daphnis' woes;
High is thy name for woodland minstrelsy:
Then rest we in the shadow of the elm
Fronting Priapus and the Fountain-nymphs.
There, where the oaks are and the Shepherd's seat,
Sing as thou sang'st erewhile, when matched with him
Of Libya, Chromis; and I'll give thee, first,
To milk, ay thrice, a goat—she suckles twins,
Yet ne'ertheless can fill two milkpails full;—
Next, a deep drinking-cup, with sweet wax scoured,
Two-handled, newly-carven, smacking yet
On the chisel. Ivy reaches up and climbs
About its lip, gilt here and there with sprays
Of woodbine, that enwreathed about it flaunts
Her saffron fruitage. Framed therein appears
A damsel ('tis a miracle of art)
In robe and snood: and suitors at her side
With locks fair-flowing, on her right and left,
Battle with words, that fail to reach her heart.
She, laughing, glances now on this, flings now
Her chance regards on that: they, all for love
Wearied and eye-swoln, find their labour lost.
Carven elsewhere an ancient fisher stands
On the rough rocks: thereto the old man with pains
Drags his great casting-net, as one that toils
Full stoutly: every fibre of his frame
Seems fishing; so about the gray-beard's neck
(In might a youngster yet) the sinews swell.
Hard by that wave-beat sire a vineyard bends
Beneath its graceful load of burnished grapes;
A boy sits on the rude fence watching them.
Near him two foxes: down the rows of grapes
One ranging steals the ripest; one assails
With wiles the poor lad's scrip, to leave him soon
Stranded and supperless. He plaits meanwhile
With ears of corn a right fine cricket-trap,
And fits it on a rush: for vines, for scrip,
Little he cares, enamoured of his toy.
The cup is hung all round with lissom briar,
Triumph of Æolian art, a wondrous sight.
It was a ferryman's of Calydon:

A goat it cost me, and a great white cheese.
Ne'er yet my lips came near it, virgin still
It stands. And welcome to such boon art thou,
If for my sake thou'lt sing that lay of lays.
I jest not: up, lad, sing: no songs thou'lt own
In the dim land where all things are forgot.

Thyrsis *[sings].*

Begin, sweet Maids, begin the woodland song.
The voice of Thyrsis. Ætna's Thyrsis I.
Where were ye, Nymphs, oh where, while Daphnis pined?
In fair Penëus' or in Pindus' glens?
For great Anapus' stream was not your haunt,
Nor Ætna's cliff, nor Acis' sacred rill.
Begin, sweet Maids, begin the woodland song.
O'er him the wolves, the jackals howled o'er him;
The lion in the oak-copse mourned his death.
Begin, sweet Maids, begin the woodland song.
The kine and oxen stood around his feet,
The heifers and the calves wailed all for him.
Begin, sweet Maids, begin the woodland song.
First from the mountain Hermes came, and said,
"Daphnis, who frets thee? Lad, whom lov'st thou so?"
Begin, sweet Maids, begin the woodland song.
Came herdsmen, shepherds came, and goatherds came;
All asked what ailed the lad. Priapus came
And said, "Why pine, poor Daphnis? while the maid
Foots it round every pool and every grove,
(Begin, sweet Maids, begin the woodland song)
"O lack-love and perverse, in quest of thee;
Herdsman in name, but goatherd rightlier called.
With eyes that yearn the goatherd marks his kids
Run riot, for he fain would frisk as they:
(Begin, sweet Maids, begin the woodland song):
"With eyes that yearn dost thou too mark the laugh
Of maidens, for thou may'st not share their glee."
Still naught the herdsman said: he drained alone
His bitter portion, till the fatal end.
Begin, sweet Maids, begin the woodland song.
Came Aphroditè, smiles on her sweet face,
False smiles, for heavy was her heart, and spake:

601

"So, Daphnis, thou must try a fall with Love!
But stalwart Love hath won the fall of thee."
Begin, sweet Maids, begin the woodland song.
Then "Ruthless Aphroditè," Daphnis said,
"Accursed Aphroditè, foe to man!
Say'st thou mine hour is come, my sun hath set?
Dead as alive, shall Daphnis work Love woe."
Begin, sweet Maids, begin the woodland song.
"Fly to Mount Ida, where the swain (men say)
And Aphroditè—to Anchises fly:
There are oak-forests; here but galingale,
And bees that make a music round the hives.
Begin, sweet Maids, begin the woodland song.
"Adonis owed his bloom to tending flocks
And smiting hares, and bringing wild beasts down.
Begin, sweet Maids, begin the woodland song.
"Face once more Diomed: tell him 'I have slain
The herdsman Daphnis; now I challenge thee.'
Begin, sweet Maids, begin the woodland song.
"Farewell, wolf, jackal, mountain-prisoned bear!
Ye'll see no more by grove or glade or glen
Your herdsman Daphnis! Arethuse, farewell,
And the bright streams that pour down Thymbris' side.
Begin, sweet Maids, begin the woodland song.
"I am that Daphnis, who lead here my kine,
Bring here to drink my oxen and my calves.
Begin, sweet Maids, begin the woodland song.
"Pan, Pan, oh whether great Lyceum's crags
Thou haunt'st to-day, or mightier Mænalus,
Come to the Sicel isle! Abandon now
Rhium and Helicè, and the mountain-cairn
(That e'en gods cherish) of Lycaon's son!
Forget, sweet Maids, forget your woodland song.
"Come, king of song, o'er this my pipe, compact
With wax and honey-breathing, arch thy lip:
For surely I am torn from life by Love.
Forget, sweet Maids, forget your woodland song.
"From thicket now and thorn let violets spring,
Now let white lilies drape the juniper,
And pines grow figs, and nature all go wrong:
For Daphnis dies. Let deer pursue the hounds,

And mountain-owls outsing the nightingale.
Forget, sweet Maids, forget your woodland song."

So spake he, and he never spake again.
Fain Aphroditè would have raised his head;
But all his thread was spun. So down the stream
Went Daphnis: closed the waters o'er a head
Dear to the Nine, of nymphs not unbeloved.
Now give me goat and cup; that I may milk
The one, and pour the other to the Muse.
Fare ye well, Muses, o'er and o'er farewell!
I'll sing strains lovelier yet in days to be.

Goatherd.

Thyrsis, let honey and the honeycomb
Fill thy sweet mouth, and figs of Ægilus:
For ne'er cicala trilled so sweet a song.
Here is the cup: mark, friend, how sweet it smells:
The Hours, thou'lt say, have washed it in their well.
Hither, Cissætha! Thou, go milk her! Kids,
Be steady, or your pranks will rouse the ram.

- Idyll VI -

The Drawn Battle

[Daphnis. Damoetas.]

Daphnis the herdsman and Damoetas once
Had driven, Aratus, to the selfsame glen.
One chin was yellowing, one shewed half a beard.
And by a brookside on a summer noon
The pair sat down and sang; but Daphnis led
The song, for Daphnis was the challenger.

Daphnis.

"See! Galatea pelts thy flock with fruit,
And calls their master 'Lack-love,' Polypheme.

603

Thou mark'st her not, blind, blind, but pipest aye
Thy wood-notes. See again, she smites thy dog:
Sea-ward the fleeced flocks' sentinel peers and barks,
And, through the clear wave visible to her still,
Careers along the gently babbling beach.
Look that he leap not on the maid new-risen
From her sea-bath and rend her dainty limbs.
She fools thee, near or far, like thistle-waifs
In hot sweet summer: flies from thee when wooed,
Unwooed pursues thee: risks all moves to win;
For, Polypheme, things foul seem fair to Love."

And then, due prelude made, Damoetas sang.

Damoetas.
"I marked her pelt my dog, I was not blind,
By Pan, by this my one my precious eye
That bounds my vision now and evermore!
But Telemus the Seer, be his the woe,
His and his children's, that he promised me!
Yet do I too tease her; I pass her by,
Pretend to woo another:—and she hears
(Heaven help me!) and is faint with jealousy;
And hurrying from the sea-wave as if stung,
Scans with keen glance my grotto and my flock.
'Twas I hissed on the dog to bark at her;
For, when I loved her, he would whine and lay
His muzzle in her lap. These things she'll note
Mayhap, and message send on message soon:
But I will bar my door until she swear
To make me on this isle fair bridal-bed.
And I am less unlovely than men say.
I looked into the mere (the mere was calm),
And goodly seemed my beard, and goodly seemed
My solitary eye, and, half-revealed,
My teeth gleamed whiter than the Parian marl.
Thrice for good luck I spat upon my robe:
That learned I of the hag Cottytaris—her
Who fluted lately with Hippocoön's mowers."

Damoetas then kissed Daphnis lovingly:
One gave a pipe and one a goodly flute.
Straight to the shepherd's flute and herdsman's pipe
The younglings bounded in the soft green grass:
And neither was o'ermatched, but matchless both.

- Idyll VII -

Harvest-Home

Once on a time did Eucritus and I
(With us Amyntas) to the riverside
Steal from the city. For Lycopeus' sons
Were that day busy with the harvest-home,
Antigenes and Phrasidemus, sprung
(If aught thou holdest by the good old names)
By Clytia from great Chalcon—him who erst
Planted one stalwart knee against the rock,
And lo, beneath his foot Burinè's rill
Brake forth, and at its side poplar and elm
Shewed aisles of pleasant shadow, greenly roofed
By tufted leaves. Scarce midway were we now,
Nor yet descried the tomb of Brasilas:
When, thanks be to the Muses, there drew near
A wayfarer from Crete, young Lycidas.
The horned herd was his care: a glance might tell
So much: for every inch a herdsman he.
Slung o'er his shoulder was a ruddy hide
Torn from a he-goat, shaggy, tangle-haired,
That reeked of rennet yet: a broad belt clasped
A patched cloak round his breast, and for a staff
A gnarled wild-olive bough his right hand bore.
Soon with a quiet smile he spoke—his eye
Twinkled, and laughter sat upon his lip:
"And whither ploddest thou thy weary way
Beneath the noontide sun, Simichidas?
For now the lizard sleeps upon the wall,
The crested lark folds now his wandering wing.
Dost speed, a bidden guest, to some reveller's board?

Or townward to the treading of the grape?
For lo! recoiling from thy hurrying feet
The pavement-stones ring out right merrily."
Then I: "Friend Lycid, all men say that none
Of haymakers or herdsmen is thy match
At piping: and my soul is glad thereat.
Yet, to speak sooth, I think to rival thee.
Now look, this road holds holiday to-day:
For banded brethren solemnise a feast
To richly-dight Demeter, thanking her
For her good gifts: since with no grudging hand
Hath the boon goddess filled the wheaten floors.
So come: the way, the day, is thine as mine:
Try we our woodcraft—each may learn from each.
I am, as thou, a clarion-voice of song;
All hail me chief of minstrels. But I am not,
Heaven knows, o'ercredulous: no, I scarce can yet
(I think) outvie Philetas, nor the bard
Of Samos, champion of Sicilian song.
They are as cicadas challenged by a frog."

I spake to gain mine ends; and laughing light
He said: "Accept this club, as thou'rt indeed
A born truth-teller, shaped by heaven's own hand!
I hate your builders who would rear a house
High as Oromedon's mountain-pinnacle:
I hate your song-birds too, whose cuckoo-cry
Struggles (in vain) to match the Chian bard.
But come, we'll sing forthwith, Simichidas,
Our woodland music: and for my part I—
List, comrade, if you like the simple air
I forged among the uplands yesterday.

[Sings] Safe be my true-love convoyed o'er the main
To Mitylenè—though the southern blast
Chase the lithe waves, while westward slant the Kids,
Or low above the verge Orion stand—
If from Love's furnace she will rescue me,
For Lycidas is parched with hot desire.
Let halcyons lay the sea-waves and the winds,
Northwind and Westwind, that in shores far-off

Flutters the seaweed—halcyons, of all birds
Whose prey is on the waters, held most dear
By the green Nereids: yea let all things smile
    On her to Mitylenè voyaging,
And in fair harbour may she ride at last.
I on that day, a chaplet woven of dill
Or rose or simple violet on my brow,
Will draw the wine of Pteleas from the cask
Stretched by the ingle. They shall roast me beans,
    And elbow-deep in thyme and asphodel
And quaintly-curling parsley shall be piled
    My bed of rushes, where in royal ease
    I sit and, thinking of my darling, drain
With stedfast lip the liquor to the dregs.
I'll have a pair of pipers, shepherds both,
    This from Acharnæ, from Lycopè that;
And Tityrus shall be near me and shall sing
How the swain Daphnis loved the stranger-maid;
And how he ranged the fells, and how the oaks
(Such oaks as Himera's banks are green withal)
    Sang dirges o'er him waning fast away
Like snow on Athos, or on Hæmus high,
    Or Rhodopè, or utmost Caucasus.
And he shall sing me how the big chest held
(All through the maniac malice of his lord)
A living goatherd: how the round-faced bees,
Lured from their meadow by the cedar-smell,
Fed him with daintiest flowers, because the Muse
Had made his throat a well-spring of sweet song.
Happy Cometas, this sweet lot was thine!
Thee the chest prisoned, for thee the honey-bees
Toiled, as thou slavedst out the mellowing year:
And oh hadst thou been numbered with the quick
    In my day! I had led thy pretty goats
About the hill-side, listening to thy voice:
While thou hadst lain thee down 'neath oak or pine,
    Divine Cometas, warbling pleasantly."

He spake and paused; and thereupon spake I.
    "I too, friend Lycid, as I ranged the fells,
Have learned much lore and pleasant from the Nymphs,

Whose fame mayhap hath reached the throne of Zeus.
But this wherewith I'll grace thee ranks the first:
Thou listen, since the Muses like thee well.

[Sings] On me the young Loves sneezed: for hapless I
Am fain of Myrto as the goats of Spring.
But my best friend Aratus inly pines
For one who loves him not. Aristis saw—
(A wondrous seer is he, whose lute and lay
Shrinèd Apollo's self would scarce disdain)—
How love had scorched Aratus to the bone.
O Pan, who hauntest Homolè's fair champaign,
Bring the soft charmer, whosoe'er it be,
Unbid to his sweet arms—so, gracious Pan,
May ne'er thy ribs and shoulderblades be lashed
With squills by young Arcadians, whensoe'er
They are scant of supper! But should this my prayer
Mislike thee, then on nettles mayest thou sleep,
Dinted and sore all over from their claws!
Then mayest thou lodge amid Edonian hills
By Hebrus, in midwinter; there subsist,
The Bear thy neighbour: and, in summer, range
With the far Æthiops 'neath the Blemmyan rocks
Where Nile is no more seen! But O ye Loves,
Whose cheeks are like pink apples, quit your homes
By Hyetis, or Byblis' pleasant rill,
Or fair Dionè's rocky pedestal,
And strike that fair one with your arrows, strike
The ill-starred damsel who disdains my friend.
And lo, what is she but an o'er-ripe pear?
The girls all cry 'Her bloom is on the wane.'
We'll watch, Aratus, at that porch no more,
Nor waste shoe-leather: let the morning cock
Crow to wake others up to numb despair!
Let Molon, and none else, that ordeal brave:
While we make ease our study, and secure
Some witch, to charm all evil from our door."

I ceased. He smiling sweetly as before,
Gave me the staff, 'the Muses' parting gift,'
And leftward sloped toward Pyxa. We the while,

Bent us to Phrasydeme's, Eucritus and I,
And baby-faced Amyntas: there we lay
Half-buried in a couch of fragrant reed
And fresh-cut vineleaves, who so glad as we?
A wealth of elm and poplar shook o'erhead;
Hard by, a sacred spring flowed gurgling on
From the Nymphs' grot, and in the sombre boughs
The sweet cicada chirped laboriously.
Hid in the thick thorn-bushes far away
The treefrog's note was heard; the crested lark
Sang with the goldfinch; turtles made their moan,
And o'er the fountain hung the gilded bee.
All of rich summer smacked, of autumn all:
Pears at our feet, and apples at our side
Rolled in luxuriance; branches on the ground
Sprawled, overweighed with damsons; while we brushed
From the cask's head the crust of four long years.
Say, ye who dwell upon Parnassian peaks,
Nymphs of Castalia, did old Chiron e'er
Set before Heracles a cup so brave
In Pholus' cavern—did as nectarous draughts
Cause that Anapian shepherd, in whose hand
Rocks were as pebbles, Polypheme the strong,
Featly to foot it o'er the cottage lawns:—
As, ladies, ye bid flow that day for us
All by Demeter's shrine at harvest-home?
Beside whose cornstacks may I oft again
Plant my broad fan: while she stands by and smiles,
Poppies and cornsheaves on each laden arm.

- Idyll XI -

A Giant's Wooing

Methinks all nature hath no cure for Love,
Plaster or unguent, Nicias, saving one;
And this is light and pleasant to a man,
Yet hard withal to compass—minstrelsy.
As well thou wottest, being thyself a leech,
And a prime favourite of those Sisters nine.

'Twas thus our Giant lived a life of ease,
Old Polyphemus, when, the down scarce seen
On lip and chin, he wooed his ocean nymph:
No curlypated rose-and-apple wooer,
But a fell madman, blind to all but love.
Oft from the green grass foldward fared his sheep
Unbid: while he upon the windy beach,
Singing his Galatea, sat and pined
From dawn to dusk, an ulcer at his heart:
Great Aphrodite's shaft had fixed it there.
Yet found he that one cure: he sate him down
On the tall cliff, and seaward looked, and sang:—

"White Galatea, why disdain thy love?
White as a pressed cheese, delicate as the lamb,
Wild as the heifer, soft as summer grapes!
If sweet sleep chain me, here thou walk'st at large;
If sweet sleep loose me, straightway thou art gone,
Scared like a sheep that sees the grey wolf near.
I loved thee, maiden, when thou cam'st long since,
To pluck the hyacinth-blossom on the fell,
Thou and my mother, piloted by me.
I saw thee, see thee still, from that day forth
For ever; but 'tis naught, ay naught, to thee.
I know, sweet maiden, why thou art so coy:
Shaggy and huge, a single eyebrow spans
From ear to ear my forehead, whence one eye
Gleams, and an o'erbroad nostril tops my lip.
Yet I, this monster, feed a thousand sheep
That yield me sweetest draughts at milking-tide:
In summer, autumn, or midwinter, still
Fails not my cheese; my milkpail aye o'erflows.
Then I can pipe as ne'er did Giant yet,
Singing our loves—ours, honey, thine and mine—
At dead of night: and hinds I rear eleven
(Each with her fawn) and bearcubs four, for thee.
Oh come to me—thou shalt not rue the day—
And let the mad seas beat against the shore!
'Twere sweet to haunt my cave the livelong night:
Laurel, and cypress tall, and ivy dun,
And vines of sumptuous fruitage, all are there:

And a cold spring that pine-clad Ætna flings
Down from, the white snow's midst, a draught for gods!
Who would not change for this the ocean-waves?

"But thou mislik'st my hair? Well, oaken logs
Are here, and embers yet aglow with fire.
Burn (if thou wilt) my heart out, and mine eye,
Mine only eye wherein is my delight.
Oh why was I not born a finny thing,
To float unto thy side and kiss thy hand,
Denied thy lips—and bring thee lilies white
And crimson-petalled poppies' dainty bloom!
Nay—summer hath his flowers and autumn his;
I could not bring all these the selfsame day.
Lo, should some mariner hither oar his road,
Sweet, he shall teach me straightway how to swim,
That haply I may learn what bliss ye find
In your sea-homes. O Galatea, come
Forth from yon waves, and coming forth forget
(As I do, sitting here) to get thee home:
And feed my flocks and milk them, nothing loth,
And pour the rennet in to fix my cheese!

"The blame's my mother's; she is false to me;
Spake thee ne'er yet one sweet word for my sake,
Though day by day she sees me pine and pine.
I'll feign strange throbbings in my head and feet
To anguish her—as I am anguished now."

O Cyclops, Cyclops, where are flown thy wits?
Go plait rush-baskets, lop the olive-boughs
To feed thy lambkins—'twere the shrewder part.
Chase not the recreant, milk the willing ewe:
The world hath Galateas fairer yet.

"—Many a fair damsel bids me sport with her
The livelong night, and smiles if I give ear.
On land at least I still am somebody."

Thus did the Giant feed his love on song,
And gained more ease than may be bought with gold.

HESIOD

Hesiod's Works and Days

Tranlated by H.G. Evelyn-White

- Hymn to Zeus -

[1] Muses of Pieria who give glory through song, come hither, tell of Zeus your father and chant his praise. Through him mortal men are famed or unfamed, sung or unsung alike, as great Zeus wills. For easily he makes strong, and easily he brings the strong man low; easily he humbles the proud and raises the obscure, and easily he straightens the crooked and blasts the proud—Zeus who thunders aloft and has his dwelling most high. Attend thou with eye and ear, and make judgements straight with righteousness. And I, Perses, would tell of true things.

- Two Kinds of Strife –

[11] So, after all, there was not one kind of Strife alone, but all over the earth there are two. As for the one, a man would praise her when he came to understand her; but the other is blameworthy: and they are wholly different in nature. For one fosters evil war and battle, being cruel: her no man loves; but perforce, through the will of the deathless gods, men pay harsh Strife her honour due. But the other is the elder daughter of dark Night, and the son of Cronos who sits above and dwells in the aether, set her in the roots of the earth: and she is far kinder to men. She stirs up even the shiftless to toil; for a man grows eager to work when he considers his neighbour, a rich man who hastens to plough and plant and put his house in good order; and neighbour vies with his neighbour as he hurries after wealth. This Strife is wholesome for men. And potter is angry with potter, and craftsman with craftsman, and beggar is jealous of beggar, and minstrel of minstrel.

[25] Perses, lay up these things in your heart, and do not let that Strife who delights in mischief hold your heart back from work, while you peep and peer and listen to the wrangles of the court-house. Little concern has he with quarrels and courts who has not a year's victuals laid up betimes, even that which the earth bears, Demeter's grain. When you

have got plenty of that, you can raise disputes and strive to get another's goods. But you shall have no second chance to deal so again: nay, let us settle our dispute here with true judgement divided our inheritance, but you seized the greater share and carried it off, greatly swelling the glory of our bribe-swallowing lords who love to judge such a cause as this. Fools! They know not how much more the half is than the whole, nor what great advantage there is in mallow and asphodel [poor man's fare].

- Pandora and the Jar -

[42] For the gods keep hidden from men the means of life. Else you would easily do work enough in a day to supply you for a full year even without working; soon would you put away your rudder over the smoke, and the fields worked by ox and sturdy mule would run to waste. But Zeus in the anger of his heart hid it, because Prometheus the crafty deceived him; therefore he planned sorrow and mischief against men. He hid fire; but that the noble son of Iapetus stole again for men from Zeus the counsellor in a hollow fennel-stalk, so that Zeus who delights in thunder did not see it. But afterwards Zeus who gathers the clouds said to him in anger:

[54] Son of Iapetus, surpassing all in cunning, you are glad that you have outwitted me and stolen fire—a great plague to you yourself and to men that shall be. But I will give men as the price for fire an evil thing in which they may all be glad of heart while they embrace their own destruction.'

[60] So said the father of men and gods, and laughed aloud. And he bade famous Hephaestus make haste and mix earth with water and to put in it the voice and strength of human kind, and fashion a sweet, lovely maiden-shape, like to the immortal goddesses in face; and Athene to teach her needlework and the weaving of the varied web; and golden Aphrodite to shed grace upon her head and cruel longing and cares that weary the limbs. And he charged Hermes the guide, the Slayer of Argus, to put in her a shameless mind and a deceitful nature.

[69] So he ordered. And they obeyed the lord Zeus the son of Cronos. Forthwith the famous Lame God moulded clay in the likeness of a modest maid, as the son of Cronos purposed. And the goddess bright-eyed Athene girded and clothed her, and the divine Graces and queenly Persuasion put necklaces of gold upon her, and the rich-haired Hours

crowned her head with spring flowers. And Pallas Athene bedecked her form with all manners of finery. Also the Guide, the Slayer of Argus, contrived within her lies and crafty words and a deceitful nature at the will of loud thundering Zeus, and the Herald of the gods put speech in her. And he called this woman Pandora (All Endowed), because all they who dwelt on Olympus gave each a gift, a plague to men who eat bread.

[83] But when he had finished the sheer, hopeless snare, the Father sent glorious Argus-Slayer, the swift messenger of the gods, to take it to Epimetheus as a gift. And Epimetheus did not think on what Prometheus had said to him, bidding him never take a gift of Olympian Zeus, but to send it back for fear it might prove to be something harmful to men. But he took the gift, and afterwards, when the evil thing was already his, he understood.

[90] For ere this the tribes of men lived on earth remote and free from ills and hard toil and heavy sickness which bring the Fates upon men; for in misery men grow old quickly. But the woman took off the great lid of the jar with her hands and scattered all these and her thought caused sorrow and mischief to men. Only Hope remained there in an unbreakable home within under the rim of the great jar, and did not fly out at the door; for ere that, the lid of the jar stopped her, by the will of Aegis-holding Zeus who gathers the clouds. But the rest, countless plagues, wander amongst men; for earth is full of evils and the sea is full. Of themselves diseases come upon men continually by day and by night, bringing mischief to mortals silently; for wise Zeus took away speech from them. So is there no way to escape the will of Zeus.

- The Ages of Man -

[106] Or if you will, I will sum you up another tale well and skilfully— and do you lay it up in your heart—how the gods and mortal men sprang from one source.

[109] First of all the deathless gods who dwell on Olympus made a golden race of mortal men who lived in the time of Cronos when he was reigning in heaven. And they lived like gods without sorrow of heart, remote and free from toil and grief: miserable age rested not on them; but with legs and arms never failing they made merry with feasting beyond the reach of all evils. When they died, it was as though they were overcome with sleep, and they had all good things; for the fruitful earth

615

unforced bare them fruit abundantly and without stint. They dwelt in ease and peace upon their lands with many good things, rich in flocks and loved by the blessed gods.

[121] But after earth had covered this generation—they are called pure spirits dwelling on the earth, and are kindly, delivering from harm, and guardians of mortal men; for they roam everywhere over the earth, clothed in mist and keep watch on judgements and cruel deeds, givers of wealth; for this royal right also they received—then they who dwell on Olympus made a second generation which was of silver and less noble by far. It was like the golden race neither in body nor in spirit. A child was brought up at his good mother's side an hundred years, an utter simpleton, playing childishly in his own home. But when they were full grown and were come to the full measure of their prime, they lived only a little time in sorrow because of their foolishness, for they could not keep from sinning and from wronging one another, nor would they serve the immortals, nor sacrifice on the holy altars of the blessed ones as it is right for men to do wherever they dwell. Then Zeus the son of Cronos was angry and put them away, because they would not give honour to the blessed gods who live on Olympus.

[140] But when earth had covered this generation also—they are called blessed spirits of the underworld by men, and, though they are of second order, yet honour attends them also—Zeus the Father made a third generation of mortal men, a brazen race, sprung from ash-trees; and it was in no way equal to the silver age, but was terrible and strong. They loved the lamentable works of Ares and deeds of violence; they ate no bread, but were hard of heart like adamant, fearful men. Great was their strength and unconquerable the arms which grew from their shoulders on their strong limbs. Their armour was of bronze, and their houses of bronze, and of bronze were their implements: there was no black iron. These were destroyed by their own hands and passed to the dank house of chill Hades, and left no name: terrible though they were, black Death seized them, and they left the bright light of the sun.

[156] But when earth had covered this generation also, Zeus the son of Cronos made yet another, the fourth, upon the fruitful earth, which was nobler and more righteous, a god-like race of hero-men who are called demi-gods, the race before our own, throughout the boundless earth. Grim war and dread battle destroyed a part of them, some in the

land of Cadmus at seven-gated Thebe when they fought for the flocks of Oedipus, and some, when it had brought them in ships over the great sea gulf to Troy for rich-haired Helen's sake: there death's end enshrouded a part of them. But to the others father Zeus the son of Cronos gave a living and an abode apart from men, and made them dwell at the ends of earth. And they live untouched by sorrow in the islands of the blessed along the shore of deep swirling Ocean, happy heroes for whom the grain-giving earth bears honey-sweet fruit flourishing thrice a year, far from the deathless gods, and Cronos rules over them; for the father of men and gods released him from his bonds. And these last equally have honour and glory.

[169c] And again far-seeing Zeus made yet another generation, the fifth, of men who are upon the bounteous earth.

[170] Thereafter, would that I were not among the men of the fifth generation, but either had died before or been born afterwards. For now truly is a race of iron, and men never rest from labour and sorrow by day, and from perishing by night; and the gods shall lay sore trouble upon them. But, notwithstanding, even these shall have some good mingled with their evils. And Zeus will destroy this race of mortal men also when they come to have grey hair on the temples at their birth. The father will not agree with his children, nor the children with their father, nor guest with his host, nor comrade with comrade; nor will brother be dear to brother as aforetime. Men will dishonour their parents as they grow quickly old, and will carp at them, chiding them with bitter words, hard-hearted they, not knowing the fear of the gods. They will not repay their aged parents the cost their nurture, for might shall be their right: and one man will sack another's city. There will be no favour for the man who keeps his oath or for the just or for the good; but rather men will praise the evil-doer and his violent dealing. Strength will be right and reverence will cease to be; and the wicked will hurt the worthy man, speaking false words against him, and will swear an oath upon them. Envy, foul-mouthed, delighting in evil, with scowling face, will go along with wretched men one and all. And then Aidos and Nemesis [shame of wrongdoing and indignation against the wrongdoer], with their sweet forms wrapped in white robes, will go from the wide-pathed earth and forsake mankind to join the company of the deathless gods: and bitter sorrows will be left for mortal men, and there will be no help against evil.

- The Hawk and Nightingale -

[202] And now I will tell a fable for princes who themselves understand. Thus said the hawk to the nightingale with speckled neck, while he carried her high up among the clouds, gripped fast in his talons, and she, pierced by his crooked talons, cried pitifully. To her he spoke disdainfully: Miserable thing, why do you cry out? One far stronger than you now holds you fast, and you must go wherever I take you, songstress as you are. And if I please I will make my meal of you, or let you go. He is a fool who tries to withstand the stronger, for he does not get the mastery and suffers pain besides his shame.' So said the swiftly flying hawk, the long-winged bird.

- Acting Justly -

[212] But you, Perses, listen to right and do not foster violence; for violence is bad for a poor man. Even the prosperous cannot easily bear its burden, but is weighed down under it when he has fallen into delusion. The better path is to go by on the other side towards justice; for Justice beats Outrage when she comes at length to the end of the race. But only when he has suffered does the fool learn this. For Oath keeps pace with wrong judgements. There is a noise when Justice is being dragged in the way where those who devour bribes and give sentence with crooked judgements, take her. And she, wrapped in mist, follows to the city and haunts of the people, weeping, and bringing mischief to men, even to such as have driven her forth in that they did not deal straightly with her.

[225] But they who give straight judgements to strangers and to the men of the land, and go not aside from what is just, their city flourishes, and the people prosper in it: Peace, the nurse of children, is abroad in their land, and all-seeing Zeus never decrees cruel war against them. Neither famine nor disaster ever haunt men who do true justice; but light-heartedly they tend the fields which are all their care. The earth bears them victual in plenty, and on the mountains the oak bears acorns upon the top and bees in the midst. Their woolly sheep are laden with fleeces; their women bear children like their parents. They flourish continually with good things, and do not travel on ships, for the grain-giving earth bears them fruit.

[238] But for those who practice violence and cruel deeds far-seeing

Zeus, the son of Cronos, ordains a punishment. Often even a whole city suffers for a bad man who sins and devises presumptuous deeds, and the son of Cronos lays great trouble upon the people, famine and plague together, so that the men perish away, and their women do not bear children, and their houses become few, through the contriving of Olympian Zeus. And again, at another time, the son of Cronos either destroys their wide army, or their walls, or else makes an end of their ships on the sea.

[248] You princes, mark well this punishment you also; for the deathless gods are near among men and mark all those who oppress their fellows with crooked judgements, and reck not the anger of the gods. For upon the bounteous earth Zeus has thrice ten thousand spirits, watchers of mortal men, and these keep watch on judgements and deeds of wrong as they roam, clothed in mist, all over the earth. And there is virgin Justice, the daughter of Zeus, who is honoured and reverenced among the gods who dwell on Olympus, and whenever anyone hurts her with lying slander, she sits beside her father, Zeus the son of Cronos, and tells him of men's wicked heart, until the people pay for the mad folly of their princes who, evilly minded, pervert judgement and give sentence crookedly. Keep watch against this, you princes, and make straight your judgements, you who devour bribes; put crooked judgements altogether from your thoughts.

[265] He does mischief to himself who does mischief to another, and evil planned harms the plotter most.

[267] The eye of Zeus, seeing all and understanding all, beholds these things too, if so he will, and fails not to mark what sort of justice is this that the city keeps within it. Now, therefore, may neither I myself be righteous among men, nor my son—for then it is a bad thing to be righteous—if indeed the unrighteous shall have the greater right. But I think that all-wise Zeus will not yet bring that to pass.

[274] But you, Perses, lay up these things within you heart and listen now to right, ceasing altogether to think of violence. For the son of Cronos has ordained this law for men, that fishes and beasts and winged fowls should devour one another, for right is not in them; but to mankind he gave right which proves far the best. For whoever knows the right and is ready to speak it, far-seeing Zeus gives him prosperity; but whoever deliberately lies in his witness and forswears himself, and so hurts Justice and sins beyond repair, that man's generation is left obscure thereafter.

But the generation of the man who swears truly is better thenceforward.

[286] To you, foolish Perses, I will speak good sense. Badness can be got easily and in shoals: the road to her is smooth, and she lives very near us. But between us and Goodness the gods have placed the sweat of our brows: long and steep is the path that leads to her, and it is rough at the first; but when a man has reached the top, then is she easy to reach, though before that she was hard.

[293] That man is altogether best who considers all things himself and marks what will be better afterwards and at the end; and he, again, is good who listens to a good adviser; but whoever neither thinks for himself nor keeps in mind what another tells him, he is an unprofitable man. But do you at any rate, always remembering my charge, work, high-born Perses, that Hunger may hate you, and venerable Demeter richly crowned may love you and fill your barn with food; for Hunger is altogether a meet comrade for the sluggard. Both gods and men are angry with a man who lives idle, for in nature he is like the stingless drones who waste the labour of the bees, eating without working; but let it be your care to order your work properly, that in the right season your barns may be full of victual. Through work men grow rich in flocks and substance, and working they are much better loved by the immortals. Work is no disgrace: it is idleness which is a disgrace. But if you work, the idle will soon envy you as you grow rich, for fame and renown attend on wealth. And whatever be your lot, work is best for you, if you turn your misguided mind away from other men's property to your work and attend to your livelihood as I bid you. An evil shame is the needy man's companion, shame which both greatly harms and prospers men: shame is with poverty, but confidence with wealth.

[320] Wealth should not be seized: god-given wealth is much better; for if a man take great wealth violently and perforce, or if he steal it through his tongue, as often happens when gain deceives men's sense and dishonour tramples down honour, the gods soon blot him out and make that man's house low, and wealth attends him only for a little time. Alike with him who does wrong to a suppliant or a guest, or who goes up to his brother's bed and commits unnatural sin in lying with his wife, or who infatuately offends against fatherless children, or who abuses his old father at the cheerless threshold of old age and attacks him with harsh words, truly Zeus himself is angry, and at the last lays on him a heavy requittal for his evil doing. But do you turn your foolish heart alto-

gether away from these things, and, as far as you are able, sacrifice to the deathless gods purely and cleanly, and burn rich meats also, and at other times propitiate them with libations and incense, both when you go to bed and when the holy light has come back, that they may be gracious to you in heart and spirit, and so you may buy another's holding and not another yours.

[342] Call your friend to a feast; but leave your enemy alone; and especially call him who lives near you: for if any mischief happen in the place, neighbours come ungirt, but kinsmen stay to gird themselves. A bad neighbour is as great a plague as a good one is a great blessing; he who enjoys a good neighbour has a precious possession. Not even an ox would die but for a bad neighbour. Take fair measure from your neighbour and pay him back fairly with the same measure, or better, if you can; so that if you are in need afterwards, you may find him sure.

[352] Do not get base gain: base gain is as bad as ruin. Be friends with the friendly, and visit him who visits you. Give to one who gives, but do not give to one who does not give. A man gives to the free-handed, but no one gives to the close-fisted. Give is a good girl, but Take is bad and she brings death. For the man who gives willingly, even though he gives a great thing, rejoices in his gift and is glad in heart; but whoever gives way to shamelessness and takes something himself, even though it be a small thing, it freezes his heart. He who adds to what he has, will keep off bright-eyed hunger; for it you add only a little to a little and do this often, soon that little will become great. What a man has by him at home does not trouble him: it is better to have your stuff at home, for whatever is abroad may mean loss. It is a good thing to draw on what you have; but it grieves your heart to need something and not to have it, and I bid you mark this. Take your fill when the cask is first opened and when it is nearly spent, but midways be sparing: it is poor saving when you come to the lees.

[370] Let the wage promised to a friend be fixed; even with your brother smile—and get a witness; for trust and mistrust, alike ruin men.

[373] Do not let a flaunting woman coax and cozen and deceive you: she is after your barn. The man who trusts womankind trust deceivers.

[376] There should be an only son, to feed his father's house, for so wealth will increase in the home; but if you leave a second son you should

die old. Yet Zeus can easily give great wealth to a greater number. More hands mean more work and more increase.

[381] If your heart within you desires wealth, do these things and work with work upon work.

- The Agrarian Calendar -

[383] When the Pleiades, daughters of Atlas, are rising [in early May] begin your harvest, and your ploughing when they are going to set [in November]. Forty nights and days they are hidden and appear again as the year moves round, when first you sharpen your sickle. This is the law of the plains, and of those who live near the sea, and who inhabit rich country, the glens and dingles far from the tossing sea—strip to sow, and strip to plough and strip to reap, if you wish to get in all Demeter's fruits in due season, and that each kind may grow in its season. Else afterwards, you may chance to be in want, and go begging to other men's houses, but without avail; as you have already come to me. But I will give you no more nor give you further measure. Foolish Perses! Work the work which the gods ordained for men, lest in bitter anguish of spirit you with your wife and children seek your livelihood amongst your neighbours, and they do not heed you. Two or three times, may be, you will succeed, but if you trouble them further, it will not avail you, and all your talk will be in vain, and your word-play unprofitable. Nay, I bid you find a way to pay your debts and avoid hunger.

[405] First of all, get a house, and a woman and an ox for the plough—a slave woman and not a wife, to follow the oxen as well—and make everything ready at home, so that you may not have to ask of another, and he refuses you, and so, because you are in lack, the season pass by and your work come to nothing. Do not put your work off till to-morrow and the day after; for a sluggish worker does not fill his barn, nor one who puts off his work: industry makes work go well, but a man who puts off work is always at hand-grips with ruin.

[414] When the piercing power and sultry heat of the sun abate, and almighty Zeus sends the autumn rains [in October], and men's flesh comes to feel far easier—for then the star Sirius passes over the heads of men, who are born to misery, only a little while by day and takes greater share of night—then, when it showers its leaves to the ground and stops sprouting, the wood you cut with your axe is least liable to worm. Then

remember to hew your timber: it is the season for that work. Cut a mortar [for pounding grain] three feet wide and a pestle three cubits long, and an axle of seven feet, for it will do very well so; but if you make it eight feet long, you can cut a beetle [a mallet for breaking clods after ploughing] from it as well. Cut a felloe three spans across for a wagon of ten palms' width. Hew also many bent timbers, and bring home a plough-tree when you have found it, and look out on the mountain or in the field for one of holm-oak; for this is the strongest for oxen to plough with when one of Athena's handmen has fixed in the share-beam and fastened it to the pole with dowels. Get two ploughs ready, work on them at home, one all of a piece, and the other jointed. It is far better to do this, for if you should break one of them, you can put the oxen to the other. Poles of laurel or elm are most free from worms, and a share-beam of oak and a plough-tree of holm-oak. Get two oxen, bulls of nine years; for their strength is unspent and they are in the prime of their age: they are best for work. They will not fight in the furrow and break the plough and then leave the work undone. Let a brisk fellow of forty years follow them, with a loaf of four quarters [a flat bread] and eight slices for his dinner, one who will attend to his work and drive a straight furrow and is past the age for gaping after his fellows, but will keep his mind on his work. No younger man will be better than he at scattering the seed and avoiding double-sowing; for a man less staid gets disturbed, hankering after his fellows.

[448] Mark, when you hear the voice of the crane [middle of November] who cries year by year from the clouds above, for she give the signal for ploughing and shows the season of rainy winter; but she vexes the heart of the man who has no oxen. Then is the time to feed up your horned oxen in the byre; for it is easy to say: 'Give me a yoke of oxen and a wagon,' and it is easy to refuse: 'I have work for my oxen.' The man who is rich in fancy thinks his wagon as good as built already—the fool! He does not know that there are a hundred timbers to a wagon. Take care to lay these up beforehand at home.

[458] So soon as the time for ploughing is proclaimed to men, then make haste, you and your slaves alike, in wet and in dry, to plough in the season for ploughing, and bestir yourself early in the morning so that your fields may be full. Plough in the spring; but fallow broken up in the summer will not belie your hopes. Sow fallow land when the soil is still getting light: fallow land is a defender from harm and a soother of children.

[465] Pray to Zeus of the Earth and to pure Demeter to make Demeter's holy grain sound and heavy, when first you begin ploughing, when you hold in your hand the end of the plough-tail and bring down your stick on the backs of the oxen as they draw on the pole-bar by the yoke-straps. Let a slave follow a little behind with a mattock and make trouble for the birds by hiding the seed; for good management is the best for mortal men as bad management is the worst. In this way your corn-ears will bow to the ground with fullness if the Olympian himself gives a good result at the last, and you will sweep the cobwebs from your bins and you will be glad, I ween, as you take of your garnered substance. And so you will have plenty till you come to grey [early] springtime, and will not look wistfully to others, but another shall be in need of your help.

[479] But if you plough the good ground at the solstice [in December], you will reap sitting, grasping a thin crop in your hand, binding the sheaves awry, dust-covered, not glad at all; so you will bring all home in a basket and not many will admire you. Yet the will of Zeus who holds the aegis is different at different times; and it is hard for mortal men to tell it; for if you should plough late, you may find this remedy—when the cuckoo first calls [in March] in the leaves of the oak and makes men glad all over the boundless earth, if Zeus should send rain on the third day and not cease until it rises neither above an ox's hoof nor falls short of it, then the late-plougher will vie with the early. Keep all this well in mind, and fail not to mark grey spring as it comes and the season of rain.

[493] Pass by the smithy and its crowded lounge in winter time when the cold keeps men from field work—for then an industrious man can greatly prosper his house—lest bitter winter catch you helpless and poor and you chafe a swollen foot with a shrunk hand. The idle man who waits on empty hope, lacking a livelihood, lays to heart mischief-making; it is not an wholesome hope that accompanies a needy man who lolls at ease while he has no sure livelihood.

[502] While it is yet midsummer command your slaves: 'It will not always be summer, build barns.'

[504] Avoid the month Lenaeon [late January, early February], wretched days, all of them fit to skin an ox, and the frosts which are cruel when Boreas blows over the earth. He blows across horse-breeding Thrace upon the wide sea and stirs it up, while earth and the forest howl. On many a high-leafed oak and thick pine he falls and brings them to the

bounteous earth in mountain glens: then all the immense wood roars and the beasts shudder and put their tails between their legs, even those whose hide is covered with fur; for with his bitter blast he blows even through them although they are shaggy-breasted. He goes even through an ox's hide; it does not stop him. Also he blows through the goat's fine hair. But through the fleeces of sheep, because their wool is abundant, the keen wind Boreas pierces not at all; but it makes the old man curved as a wheel. And it does not blow through the tender maiden who stays indoors with her dear mother, unlearned as yet in the works of golden Aphrodite, and who washes her soft body and anoints herself with oil and lies down in an inner room within the house, on a winter's day when the Boneless One [octopus or cuttle] gnaws his foot in his fireless house and wretched home; for the sun shows him no pastures to make for, but goes to and fro over the land and city of dusky men [the southern Aethiopians], and shines more sluggishly upon the whole race of the Hellenes. Then the horned and unhorned denizens of the wood, with teeth chattering pitifully, flee through the copses and glades, and all, as they seek shelter, have this one care, to gain thick coverts or some hollow rock. Then, like the Three-legged One [old man with walking-stick] whose back is broken and whose head looks down upon the ground, like him, I say, they wander to escape the white snow.

[536] Then put on, as I bid you, a soft coat and a tunic to the feet to shield your body—and you should weave thick woof on thin warp. In this clothe yourself so that your hair may keep still and not bristle and stand upon end all over your body. Lace on your feet close-fitting boots of the hide of a slaughtered ox, thickly lined with felt inside. And when the season of frost comes on, stitch together skins of firstling kids with ox-sinew, to put over your back and to keep off the rain. On your head above wear a shaped cap of felt to keep your ears from getting wet, for the dawn is chill when Boreas has once made his onslaught, and at dawn a fruitful mist is spread over the earth from starry heaven upon the fields of blessed men: it is drawn from the ever flowing rivers and is raised high above the earth by windstorm, and sometimes it turns to rain towards evening, and sometimes to wind when Thracian Boreas huddles the thick clouds. Finish your work and return home ahead of him, and do not let the dark cloud from heaven wrap round you and make your body clammy and soak your clothes. Avoid it; for this is the hardest month, wintry, hard for sheep and hard for men. In this season let your oxen have half their usual food, but let your man have more; for the helpful nights are long. Observe all this until the year is ended and you have nights and days

of equal length, and Earth, the mother of all, bears again her various fruit.

[564] When Zeus has finished sixty wintry days after the solstice, then the star Arcturus [late February, early March] leaves the holy stream of Ocean and first rises brilliant at dusk. After him the shrilly wailing daughter of Pandion, the swallow, appears to men when spring is just beginning. Before she comes, prune the vines, for it is best so.

[571] But when the House-carrier [the snail, in early May] climbs up the plants from the earth to escape the Pleiades, then it is no longer the season for digging vineyards, but to whet your sickles and rouse up your slaves. Avoid shady seats and sleeping until dawn in the harvest season, when the sun scorches the body. Then be busy, and bring home your fruits, getting up early to make your livelihood sure. For dawn takes away a third part of your work, dawn advances a man on his journey and advances him in his work—dawn which appears and sets many men on their road, and puts yokes on many oxen.

[582] But when the artichoke flowers [in June], and the chirping grass-hopper sits in a tree and pours down his shrill song continually from under his wings in the season of wearisome heat, then goats are plumpest and wine sweetest; women are most wanton, but men are fee-blest, because Sirius parches head and knees and the skin is dry through heat. But at that time let me have a shady rock and wine of Biblis, a clot of curds and milk of drained goats with the flesh of an heifer fed in the woods, that has never calved, and of firstling kids; then also let me drink bright wine, sitting in the shade, when my heart is satisfied with food, and so, turning my head to face the fresh Zephyr, from the everflowing spring which pours down unfouled, thrice pour an offering of water, but make a fourth libation of wine.

[597] Set your slaves to winnow Demeter's holy grain, when strong Orion [in July] first appears, on a smooth threshing-floor in an airy place. Then measure it and store it in jars. And so soon as you have safely stored all your stuff indoors, I bid you put your bondman out of doors and look out for a servant-girl with no children—for a servant with a child to nurse is troublesome. And look after the dog with jagged teeth; do not grudge him his food, or some time the Day-sleeper [a robber] may take your stuff. Bring in fodder and litter so as to have enough for your oxen and mules. After that, let your men rest their poor knees and

unyoke your pair of oxen.

[609] But when Orion and Sirius are come into mid-heaven, and rosy-fingered Dawn sees Arcturus [in September], then cut off all the grape-clusters, Perses, and bring them home. Show them to the sun ten days and ten nights: then cover them over for five, and on the sixth day draw off into vessels the gifts of joyful Dionysus. But when the Pleiades and Hyades and strong Orion begin to set [the end of October], then remember to plough in season: and so the completed year [constellation cycle] will fitly pass beneath the earth.

[618] But if desire for uncomfortable sea-faring seize you; when the Pleiades plunge into the misty sea [end October, beginning November] to escape Orion's rude strength, then truly gales of all kinds rage. Then keep ships no longer on the sparkling sea, but bethink you to till the land as I bid you. Haul up your ship upon the land and pack it closely with stones all round to keep off the power of the winds which blow damply, and draw out the bilge-plug so that the rain of heaven may not rot it. Put away all the tackle and fittings in your house, and stow the wings of the sea-going ship neatly, and hang up the well-shaped rudder over the smoke. You yourself wait until the season for sailing is come, and then haul your swift ship down to the sea and stow a convenient cargo in it, so that you may bring home profit, even as your father and mine, foolish Perses, used to sail on shipboard because he lacked sufficient livelihood. And one day he came to this very place crossing over a great stretch of sea; he left Aeolian Cyme and fled, not from riches and substance, but from wretched poverty which Zeus lays upon men, and he settled near Helicon in a miserable hamlet, Ascra, which is bad in winter, sultry in summer, and good at no time.

[641] But you, Perses, remember all works in their season but sailing especially. Admire a small ship, but put your freight in a large one; for the greater the lading, the greater will be your piled gain, if only the winds will keep back their harmful gales.

[646] If ever you turn your misguided heart to trading and wish to escape from debt and joyless hunger, I will show you the measures of the loud-roaring sea, though I have no skill in sea-faring nor in ships; for never yet have I sailed by ship over the wide sea, but only to Euboea from Aulis where the Achaeans once stayed through much storm when they had gathered a great host from divine Hellas for Troy, the land

of fair women. Then I crossed over to Chalcis, to the games of wise Amphidamas where the sons of the great-hearted hero proclaimed and appointed prizes. And there I boast that I gained the victory with a song and carried off an handled tripod which I dedicated to the Muses of Helicon, in the place where they first set me in the way of clear song. Such is all my experience of many-pegged ships; nevertheless I will tell you the will of Zeus who holds the aegis; for the Muses have taught me to sing in marvellous song.

[663] Fifty days after the solstice [in July-August], when the season of wearisome heat is come to an end, is the right time for me to go sailing. Then you will not wreck your ship, nor will the sea destroy the sailors, unless Poseidon the Earth-Shaker be set upon it, or Zeus, the king of the deathless gods, wish to slay them; for the issues of good and evil alike are with them. At that time the winds are steady, and the sea is harmless. Then trust in the winds without care, and haul your swift ship down to the sea and put all the freight on board; but make all haste you can to return home again and do not wait till the time of the new wine and autumn rain and oncoming storms with the fierce gales of Notus who accompanies the heavy autumn rain of Zeus and stirs up the sea and makes the deep dangerous.

[678] Another time for men to go sailing is in spring when a man first sees leaves on the topmost shoot of a fig-tree as large as the foot-print that a cow makes; then the sea is passable, and this is the spring sailing time. For my part I do not praise it, for my heart does not like it. Such a sailing is snatched, and you will hardly avoid mischief. Yet in their ignorance men do even this, for wealth means life to poor mortals; but it is fearful to die among the waves. But I bid you consider all these things in your heart as I say. Do not put all your goods in hallow ships; leave the greater part behind, and put the lesser part on board; for it is a bad business to meet with disaster among the waves of the sea, as it is bad if you put too great a load on your wagon and break the axle, and your goods are spoiled. Observe due measure: and proportion is best in all things.

- Proverbs and Customs -

[695] Bring home a wife to your house when you are of the right age, while you are not far short of thirty years nor much above; this is the right age for marriage. Let your wife have been grown up four years, and marry her in the fifth. Marry a maiden, so that you can teach her careful

ways, and especially marry one who lives near you, but look well about you and see that your marriage will not be a joke to your neighbours. For a man wins nothing better than a good wife, and, again, nothing worse than a bad one, a greedy soul who roasts her man without fire, strong though he may be, and brings him to a raw old age.

[706] Be careful to avoid the anger of the deathless gods. Do not make a friend equal to a brother; but if you do, do not wrong him first, and do not lie to please the tongue. But if he wrongs you first, offending either in word or in deed, remember to repay him double; but if he ask you to be his friend again and be ready to give you satisfaction, welcome him. He is a worthless man who makes now one and now another his friend; but as for you, do not let your face put your heart to shame.

[715] Do not get a name either as lavish or as churlish; as a friend of rogues or as a slanderer of good men.

[717] Never dare to taunt a man with deadly poverty which eats out the heart; it is sent by the deathless gods. The best treasure a man can have is a sparing tongue, and the greatest pleasure, one that moves orderly; for if you speak evil, you yourself will soon be worse spoken of.

[722] Do not be boorish at a common [public] feast where there are many guests; the pleasure is greatest and the expense is least.

[724] Never pour a libation of sparkling wine to Zeus after dawn with unwashen hands, nor to others of the deathless gods; else they do not hear your prayers but spit them back.

[727] Do not stand upright facing the sun when you make water, but remember to do this when he has set towards his rising. And do not make water as you go, whether on the road or off the road, and do not uncover yourself: the nights belong to the blessed gods. A scrupulous man who has a wise heart sits down or goes to the wall of an enclosed court.

[733] Do not expose yourself befouled by the fireside in your house, but avoid this. Do not beget children when you are come back from ill-omened burial, but after a festival of the gods.

[737] Never cross the sweet-flowing water of ever-rolling rivers afoot

until you have prayed, gazing into the soft flood, and washed your hands in the clear, lovely water. Whoever crosses a river with hands unwashed of wickedness, the gods are angry with him and bring trouble upon him afterwards.

[742] At a cheerful festival of the gods do not cut the withered from the quick upon that which has five branches with bright steel [i.e. do not cut your fingernails].

[744] Never put the ladle upon the mixing-bowl at a wine party, for malignant ill-luck is attached to that.

[746] When you are building a house, do not leave it rough-hewn, or a cawing crow may settle on it and croak.

[748] Take nothing to eat or to wash with from uncharmed pots, for in them there is mischief.

[750] Do not let a boy of twelve years sit on things which may not be moved [i.e. things which are sacriligeous to disturb, such as tombs], for that is bad, and makes a man unmanly; nor yet a child of twelve months, for that has the same effect. A man should not clean his body with water in which a woman has washed, for there is bitter mischief in that also for a time. When you come upon a burning sacrifice, do not make a mock of mysteries, for Heaven is angry at this also. Never make water in the mouths of rivers which flow to the sea, nor yet in springs; but be careful to avoid this. And do not ease yourself in them: it is not well to do this.

[760] So do: and avoid the talk of men. For Talk is mischievous, light, and easily raised, but hard to bear and difficult to be rid of. Talk never wholly dies away when many people voice her: even Talk is in some ways divine.

- Division of the Month -

[The month is divided into three periods, the waxing, the mid-month, and the waning, which answer to the phases of the moon. Greek months consisted of thirty days and began with a new moon.]

[765] Mark the days which come from Zeus, duly telling your slaves of

them, and that the thirtieth day of the month is best for one to look over the work and to deal out supplies. For these are days which come from Zeus the all-wise, when men discern aright.

[770] To begin with, the first, the fourth, and the seventh—on which Leto bare Apollo with the blade of gold—each is a holy day. The eighth and the ninth, two days at least of the waxing month, are specially good for the works of man. Also the eleventh and twelfth are both excellent, alike for shearing sheep and for reaping the kindly fruits; but the twelfth is much better than the eleventh, for on it the airy-swinging spider spins its web in full day, and then the Wise One [the ant], gathers her pile. On that day woman should set up her loom and get forward with her work.

[780] Avoid the thirteenth of the waxing month for beginning to sow: yet it is the best day for setting plants.

[782] The sixth of the mid-month is very unfavourable for plants, but is good for the birth of males, though unfavourable for a girl either to be born at all or to be married. Nor is the first sixth a fit day for a girl to be born, but a kindly for gelding kids and sheep and for fencing in a sheep-cote. It is favourable for the birth of a boy, but such will be fond of sharp speech, lies, and cunning words, and stealthy converse.

[790] On the eighth of the month geld the boar and loud-bellowing bull, but hard-working mules on the twelfth.

[792] On the great twentieth, in full day, a wise man should be born. Such an one is very sound-witted. The tenth is favourable for a male to be born; but, for a girl, the fourth day of the mid-month. On that day tame sheep and shambling, horned oxen, and the sharp-fanged dog and hardy mules to the touch of the hand. But take care to avoid troubles which eat out the heart on the fourth of the beginning and ending of the month; it is a day very fraught with fate.

[800] On the fourth of the month bring home your bride, but choose the omens which are best for this business.

[802] Avoid fifth days: they are unkindly and terrible. On a fifth day, they say, the Erinyes assisted at the birth of Horcus (Oath) whom Eris (Strife) bare to trouble the forsworn.

[805] Look about you very carefully and throw out Demeter's holy grain upon the well-rolled threshing floor on the seventh of the mid-month. Let the woodman cut beams for house building and plenty of ships' timbers, such as are suitable for ships. On the fourth day begin to build narrow ships.

[810] The ninth of the mid-month improves towards evening; but the first ninth of all is quite harmless for men. It is a good day on which to beget or to be born both for a male and a female: it is never an wholly evil day.

[814] Again, few know that the twenty-seventh of the month is best for opening a wine-jar, and putting yokes on the necks of oxen and mules and swift-footed horses, and for hauling a swift ship of many thwarts down to the sparkling sea; few call it by its right name.

[819] On the fourth day open a jar. The fourth of the mid-month is a day holy above all. And again, few men know that the fourth day after the twentieth is best while it is morning: towards evening it is less good.

[822] These days are a great blessing to men on earth; but the rest are changeable, luckless, and bring nothing. Everyone praises a different day but few know their nature. Sometimes a day is a stepmother, sometimes a mother. That man is happy and lucky in them who knows all these things and does his work without offending the deathless gods, who discerns the omens of birds and avoids transgressions.

THE END

QUINTUS of SMYRNA

Quintus Smyrnaeus
The Fall of Troy
(Selections)

Translated by A.S.Way

Book I

[1] When godlike Hector by Peleides slain passed, and the pyre had ravined up his flesh, and earth had veiled his bones, the Trojans then tarried in Priam's city, sore afraid before the might of stout-heart Aeacus' son: as kine they were, that midst the copses shrink from faring forth to meet a lion grim, but in dense thickets terror-huddled cower; so in their fortress shivered these to see that mighty man. Of those already dead they thought of all whose lives he reft away as by Scamander's outfall on he rushed, and all that in mid-flight to that high wall he slew, how he quelled Hector, how he haled his corpse round Troy—yea, and of all beside laid low by him since that first day whereon o'er restless seas he brought the Trojans doom. Ay, all these they remembered, while they stayed thus in their town, and o'er them anguished grief hovered dark-winged, as though that very day all Troy with shrieks were crumbling down in fire.

[22] Then from Thermodon, from broad-sweeping streams, came, clothed upon with beauty of Goddesses, Penthesileia—came athirst indeed for groan-resounding battle, but yet more fleeing abhorred reproach and evil fame, lest they of her own folk should rail on her because of her own sister's death, for whom ever her sorrows waxed, Hippolyte, whom she had struck dead with her mighty spear, not of her will—'twas at a stag she hurled. So came she to the far-famed land of Troy. Yea, and her warrior spirit pricked her on, of murder's dread pollution thus to cleanse her soul, and with such sacrifice to appease the Awful Ones, the Erinnyes, who in wrath for her slain sister straightway haunted her unseen: for ever round the sinner's steps they hover; none may 'scape those Goddesses.

635

[40] And with her followed twelve beside, each one a princess, hot for war and battle grim, far-famous each, yet handmaids unto her: Penthesileia far outshone them all. As when in the broad sky amidst the stars the moon rides over all pre-eminent, when through the thunder-clouds the cleaving heavens open, when sleep the fury-breathing winds, so peerless was she mid that charging host. Clonie was there, Polemusa Derinoe, Evandre, and Antandre, and Bremusa, Hippothoe, dark-eyed Harmothoe, Alcibie, Derimacheia, Antibrote, and Thermodosa glorying with the spear. All these to battle fared with warrior-souled Penthesileia: even as when descends Dawn from Olympus' crest of adamant, Dawn, heart-exultant in her radiant steeds amidst the bright-haired Hours; and o'er them all, how flawless-fair soever these may be, her splendour of beauty glows pre-eminent; so peerless amid all the Amazons unto Troy-town Penthesileia came. To right, to left, from all sides hurrying thronged the Trojans, greatly marvelling, when they saw the tireless War-god's child, the mailed maid, like to the Blessed Gods; for in her face glowed beauty glorious and terrible. Her smile was ravishing: beneath her brows, her love-enkindling eyes shone like to stars, and with the crimson rose of shamefastness bright were her cheeks, and mantled over them unearthly grace with battle-prowess clad.

[73] Then joyed Troy's folk, despite past agonies, as when, far-gazing from a height, the hinds behold a rainbow spanning the wide sea, when they be yearning for the heaven-sent shower, when the parched fields be craving for the rain; then the great sky at last is overgloomed, and men see that fair sign of coming wind and imminent rain, and seeing, they are glad, who for their corn-fields' plight sore sighed before; even so the sons of Troy when they beheld there in their land Penthesileia dread afire for battle, were exceeding glad; for when the heart is thrilled with hope of good, all smart of evils past is wiped away. So, after all his sighing and his pain, gladdened a little while was Priam's soul. As when a man who hath suffered many a pang from blinded eyes, sore longing to behold the light, and, if he may not, fain would die, then at the last, by a cunning leech's skill, or by a God's grace, sees the dawn-rose flush, sees the mist rolled back from before his eyes—yea, though clear vision come not as of old, yet, after all his anguish, joys to have some small relief, albeit the stings of pain prick sharply yet beneath his eyelids; so joyed the old king to see that terrible queen—the shadowy joy of one in anguish whelmed for slain sons. Into his halls he led the Maid, and with glad welcome honoured her, as one who greets a daughter to her home returned from a far country in the twentieth year; and set a feast before her, sumptuous

as battle-glorious kings, who have brought low nations of foes, array in splendour of pomp, with hearts in pride of victory triumphing. And gifts he gave her costly and fair to see, and pledged him to give many more, so she would save the Trojans from the imminent doom. And she such deeds she promised as no man had hoped for, even to lay Achilles low, to smite the wide host of the Argive men, and cast the brands red-flaming on the ships. Ah fool! but little knew she him, the lord of ashen spears, how far Achilles' might in warrior-wasting strife o'erpassed her own!

[119] But when Andromache, the stately child of king Eetion, heard the wild queen's vaunt, low to her own soul bitterly murmured she: "Ah hapless! why with arrogant heart dost thou speak such great swelling words? No strength is thine to grapple in fight with Peleus' aweless son. Nay, doom and swift death shall he deal to thee. Alas for thee! What madness thrills thy soul? Fate and the end of death stand hard by thee! Hector was mightier far to wield the spear than thou, yet was for all his prowess slain, slain for the bitter grief of Troy, whose folk the city through looked on him as a God. My glory and his noble parents' glory was he while yet he lived—O that the earth over my dead face had been mounded high, or ever through his throat the breath of life followed the cleaving spear! But now have I looked—woe is me!—on grief unutterable, when round the city those fleet-footed steeds haled him, steeds of Achilles, who had made me widowed of mine hero-husband, made my portion bitterness through all my days." So spake Eetion's lovely-ankled child low to her own soul, thinking on her lord. So evermore the faithful-hearted wife nurseth for her lost love undying grief.

[146] Then in swift revolution sweeping round into the Ocean's deep stream sank the sun, and daylight died. So when the banqueters ceased from the wine-cup and the goodly feast, then did the handmaids spread in Priam's halls for Penthesileia dauntless-souled the couch heart-cheering, and she laid her down to rest; and slumber mist-like overveiled her eyes depths like sweet dew dropping round. From heavens' blue slid down the might of a deceitful dream at Pallas' hest, that so the warrior-maid might see it, and become a curse to Troy and to herself, when strained her soul to meet the whirlwind of the battle. In this wise the Trito-born, the subtle-souled, contrived: Stood o'er the maiden's head that baleful dream in likeness of her father, kindling her fearlessly front to front to meet in fight fleetfoot Achilles. And she heard the voice, and all her heart exulted, for she weened that she should on that dawning day achieve a mighty deed in battle's deadly toil. Ah, fool, who trusted for

her sorrow a dream out of the sunless land, such as beguiles full oft the travail-burdened tribes of men, whispering mocking lies in sleeping ears, and to the battle's travail lured her then!

[173] But when the Dawn, the rosy-ankled, leapt up from her bed, then, clad in mighty strength of spirit, suddenly from her couch uprose Penthesileia. Then did she array her shoulders in those wondrous-fashioned arms given her of the War-god. First she laid beneath her silver-gleaming knees the greaves fashioned of gold, close-clipping the strong limbs. Her rainbow-radiant corslet clasped she then about her, and around her shoulders slung, with glory in her heart, the massy brand whose shining length was in a scabbard sheathed of ivory and silver. Next, her shield unearthly splendid, caught she up, whose rim swelled like the young moon's arching chariot-rail when high o'er Ocean's fathomless-flowing stream she rises, with the space half filled with light betwixt her bowing horns. So did it shine unutterably fair. Then on her head she settled the bright helmet overstreamed with a wild mane of golden-glistering hairs. So stood she, lapped about with flaming mail, in semblance like the lightning, which the might, the never-wearied might of Zeus, to earth hurleth, what time he showeth forth to men fury of thunderous-roaring rain, or swoop resistless of his shouting host of winds. Then in hot haste forth of her bower to pass caught she two javelins in the hand that grasped her shield-band; but her strong right hand laid hold on a huge halberd, sharp of either blade, which terrible Eris gave to Ares' child to be her Titan weapon in the strife that raveneth souls of men. Laughing for glee thereover, swiftly flashed she forth the ring of towers. Her coming kindled all the sons of Troy to rush into the battle forth which crowneth men with glory. Swiftly all hearkened her gathering-cry, and thronging came, champions, yea, even such as theretofore shrank back from standing in the ranks of war against Achilles the all-ravager. But she in pride of triumph on she rode throned on a goodly steed and fleet, the gift of Oreithyia, the wild North-wind's bride, given to her guest the warrior-maid, what time she came to Thrace, a steed whose flying feet could match the Harpies' wings. Riding thereon Penthesileia in her goodlihead left the tall palaces of Troy behind. And ever were the ghastly-visaged Fates thrusting her on into the battle, doomed to be her first against the Greeks—and last! To right, to left, with unreturning feet the Trojan thousands followed to the fray, the pitiless fray, that death-doomed warrior-maid, followed in throngs, as follow sheep the ram that by the shepherd's art strides before all. So followed they, with battle-fury filled, strong Trojans and wild-hearted Amazons. And like Tritonis

seemed she, as she went to meet the Giants, or as flasheth far through war-hosts Eris, waker of onset-shouts. So mighty in the Trojans' midst she seemed, Penthesileia of the flying feet.

[238] Then unto Cronos' Son Laomedon's child upraised his hands, his sorrow-burdened hands, turning him toward the sky-encountering temple of Zeus of Ida, who with sleepless eyes looks ever down on Ilium; and he prayed: "Father, give ear! Vouchsafe that on this day Achaea's host may fall before the hands of this our warrior-queen, the War-god's child; and do thou bring her back unscathed again unto mine halls: we pray thee by the love thou bear'st to Ares of the fiery heart thy son, yea, to her also! is she not most wondrous like the heavenly Goddesses? And is she not the child of thine own seed? Pity my stricken heart withal! Thou know'st all agonies I have suffered in the deaths of dear sons whom the Fates have torn from me by Argive hands in the devouring fight. Compassionate us, while a remnant yet remains of noble Dardanus' blood, while yet this city stands unwasted! Let us know from ghastly slaughter and strife one breathing-space!"

[260] In passionate prayer he spake: lo, with shrill scream swiftly to left an eagle darted by and in his talons bare a gasping dove. Then round the heart of Priam all the blood was chilled with fear. Low to his soul he said: "Ne'er shall I see return alive from war Penthesileia!" On that selfsame day the Fates prepared his boding to fulfil; and his heart brake with anguish of despair.

[269] Marvelled the Argives, far across the plain seeing the hosts of Troy charge down on them, and midst them Penthesileia, Ares' child. These seemed like ravening beasts that mid the hills bring grimly slaughter to the fleecy flocks; and she, as a rushing blast of flame she seemed that maddeneth through the copses summer-scorched, when the wind drives it on; and in this wise spake one to other in their mustering host: "Who shall this be who thus can rouse to war the Trojans, now that Hector hath been slain—these who, we said, would never more find heart to stand against us? Lo now, suddenly forth are they rushing, madly afire for fight! Sure, in their midst some great one kindleth them to battle's toil! Thou verily wouldst say this were a God, of such great deeds he dreams! Go to, with aweless courage let us arm our own breasts: let us summon up our might in battle-fury. We shall lack not help of Gods this day to close in fight with Troy."

[290] So cried they; and their flashing battle-gear cast they about them
forth the ships they poured clad in the rage of fight as with a cloak. The
front to front their battles closed, like beasts of ravin, locked in tangl
of gory strife. Clanged their bright mail together, clashed the spear
the corslets, and the stubborn-welded shields and adamant helms. Eac
stabbed at other's flesh with the fierce brass: was neither ruth nor res
and all the Trojan soil was crimson-red.

[300] Then first Penthesileia smote and slew Molion; now Persinou
falls, and now Eilissus; reeled Antitheus 'neath her spear the pride o
Lernus quelled she: down she bore Hippalmus 'neath her horse-hoofs
Haemon's son died; withered stalwart Elasippus' strength. And Derino
laid low Laogonus, and Clonie Menippus, him who sailed long sinc
from Phylace, led by his lord Protesilaus to the war with Troy. The
was Podarces, son of Iphiclus, heart-wrung with ruth and wrath to se
him lie dead, of all battle-comrades best-beloved. Swiftly at Clonie h
hurled, the maid fair as a Goddess: plunged the unswerving lance 'twix
hip and hip, and rushed the dark blood forth after the spear, and all he
bowels gushed out. Then wroth was Penthesileia; through the brawn o
his right arm she drave the long spear's point, she shore atwain the grea
blood-brimming veins, and through the wide gash of the wound th
gore spirted, a crimson fountain. With a groan backward he sprang, hi
courage wholly quelled by bitter pain; and sorrow and dismay thrilled, a
he fled, his men of Phylace. A short way from the fight he reeled aside
and in his friends' arms died in little space. Then with his lance Idome
neus thrust out, and by the right breast stabbed Bremusa. Stilled for eve
was the beating of her heart. She fell, as falls a graceful-shafted pin
hewn mid the hills by woodmen: heavily, sighing through all its boughs
it crashes down. So with a wailing shriek she fell, and death unstrung he
every limb: her breathing soul mingled with multitudinous-sighing winds
Then, as Evandre through the murderous fray with Thermodosa rushed
stood Meriones, a lion in the path, and slew: his spear right to the hear
of one he drave, and one stabbed with a lightning sword-thrust 'twixt the
hips: leapt through the wounds the life, and fled away. Oileus' fiery son
smote Derinoe 'twixt throat and shoulder with his ruthless spear; and on
Alcibie Tydeus' terrible son swooped, and on Derimacheia: head with
neck clean from the shoulders of these twain he shore with ruin-wreak-
ing brand. Together down fell they, as young calves by the massy axe of
brawny flesher felled, that, shearing through the sinews of the neck, lops
life away. So, by the hands of Tydeus' son laid low upon the Trojan plain,
far, far away from their own highland-home, they fell. Nor these alone

died; for the might of Sthenelus down on them hurled Cabeirus' corpse, who came from Sestos, keen to fight the Argive foe, but never saw his fatherland again. Then was the heart of Paris filled with wrath for a friend slain. Full upon Sthenelus aimed he a shaft death-winged, yet touched him not, despite his thirst for vengeance: otherwhere the arrow glanced aside, and carried death whither the stern Fates guided its fierce wing, and slew Evenor brazen-tasleted, who from Dulichium came to war with Troy. For his death fury-kindled was the son of haughty Phyleus: as a lion leaps upon the flock, so swiftly rushed he: all shrank huddling back before that terrible man. Itymoneus he slew, and Hippasus' son Agelaus: from Miletus brought they war against the Danaan men by Nastes led, the god-like, and Amphimachus mighty-souled. On Mycale they dwelt; beside their home rose Latmus' snowy crests, stretched the long glens of Branchus, and Panormus' water-meads. Maeander's flood deep-rolling swept thereby, which from the Phrygian uplands, pastured o'er by myriad flocks, around a thousand forelands curls, swirls, and drives his hurrying ripples on down to the vine-clad land of Carian men these mid the storm of battle Meges slew, nor these alone, but whomsoe'er his lance black-shafted touched, were dead men; for his breast the glorious Trito-born with courage thrilled to bring to all his foes the day of doom. And Polypoetes, dear to Ares, slew Dresaeus, whom the Nymph Neaera bare to passing-wise Theiodamas for these spread was the bed of love beside the foot of Sipylus the Mountain, where the Gods made Niobe a stony rock, wherefrom tears ever stream: high up, the rugged crag bows as one weeping, weeping, waterfalls cry from far-echoing Hermus, wailing moan of sympathy: the sky-encountering crests of Sipylus, where alway floats a mist hated of shepherds, echo back the cry. Weird marvel seems that Rock of Niobe to men that pass with feet fear-goaded: there they see the likeness of a woman bowed, in depths of anguish sobbing, and her tears drop, as she mourns grief-stricken, endlessly. Yea, thou wouldst say that verily so it was, viewing it from afar; but when hard by thou standest, all the illusion vanishes; and lo, a steep-browed rock, a fragment rent from Sipylus—yet Niobe is there, dreeing her weird, the debt of wrath divine, a broken heart in guise of shattered stone.

[411] All through the tangle of that desperate fray stalked slaughter and doom. The incarnate Onset-shout raved through the rolling battle; at her side paced Death the ruthless, and the fearful Fates, beside them strode, and in red hands bare murder and the groans of dying men. That day the beating of full many a heart, Trojan and Argive, was for ever stilled, while roared the battle round them, while the fury of Penthe-

sileia fainted not nor failed; but as amid long ridges of lone hills a lioness, stealing down a deep ravine, springs on the kine with lightning leap, athirst for blood wherein her fierce heart revelleth; so on the Danaans leapt that warrior-maid. And they, their souls were cowed: backward they shrank, and fast she followed, as a towering surge chases across the thunder-booming sea a flying bark, whose white sails strain beneath the wind's wild buffering, and all the air maddens with roaring, as the rollers crash on a black foreland looming on the lee where long reefs fringe the surf-tormented shores. So chased she, and so dashed the ranks asunder triumphant-souled, and hurled fierce threats before: "Ye dogs, this day for evil outrage done to Priam shall ye pay! No man of you shall from mine hands deliver his own life, and win back home, to gladden parents' eyes, or comfort wife or children. Ye shall lie dead, ravined on by vultures and by wolves, and none shall heap the earth-mound o'er your clay. Where skulketh now the strength of Tydeus' son, and where the might of Aeacus' scion? Where is Aias' bulk? Ye vaunt them mightiest men of all your rabble. Ha! they will not dare with me to close in battle, lest I drag forth from their fainting frames their craven souls!"

[449] Then heart-uplifted leapt she on the foe, resistless as a tigress, crashing through ranks upon ranks of Argives, smiting now with that huge halberd massy-headed, now hurling the keen dart, while her battle-horse flashed through the fight, and on his shoulder bare quiver and bow death-speeding, close to her hand, if mid that revel of blood she willed to speed the bitter-biting shaft. Behind her swept the charging lines of men fleet-footed, friends and brethren of the man who never flinched from close death-grapple, Hector, panting all the hot breath of the War-god from their breasts, all slaying Danaans with the ashen spear, who fell as frost-touched leaves in autumn fall one after other, or as drops of rain. And aye went up a moaning from earth's breast all blood-bedrenched, and heaped with corpse on corpse. Horses pierced through with arrows, or impaled on spears, were snorting forth their last of strength with screaming neighings. Men, with gnashing teeth biting the dust, lay gasping, while the steeds of Trojan charioteers stormed in pursuit, trampling the dying mingled with the dead as oxen trample corn in threshing-floors.

[474] Then one exulting boasted mid the host of Troy, beholding Penthesileia rush on through the foes' array, like the black storm that maddens o'er the sea, what time the sun allies his might with winter's Goat-horned Star; and thus, puffed up with vain hope, shouted he: "O

friends, in manifest presence down from heaven one of the deathless Gods this day hath come to fight the Argives, all of love for us, yea, and with sanction of almighty Zeus, he whose compassion now remembereth haply strong-hearted Priam, who may boast for his a lineage of immortal blood. For this, I trow, no mortal woman seems, who is so aweless-daring, who is clad in splendour-flashing arms: nay, surely she shall be Athene, or the mighty-souled Enyo—haply Eris, or the Child of Leto world-renowned. O yea, I look to see her hurl amid yon Argive men mad-shrieking slaughter, see her set aflame yon ships wherein they came long years agone bringing us many sorrows, yea, they came bringing us woes of war intolerable. Ha! to the home-land Hellas ne'er shall these with joy return, since Gods on our side fight."

[500] In overweening exultation so vaunted a Trojan. Fool! he had no vision of ruin onward rushing upon himself and Troy, and Penthesileia's self withal. For not as yet had any tidings come of that wild fray to Aias stormy-souled, nor to Achilles, waster of tower and town. But on the grave-mound of Menoetius' son they twain were lying, with sad memories of a dear comrade crushed, and echoing each one the other's groaning. One it was of the Blest Gods who still was holding back these from the battle-tumult far away, till many Greeks should fill the measure up of woeful havoc, slain by Trojan foes and glorious Penthesileia, who pursued with murderous intent their rifled ranks, while ever waxed her valour more and more, and waxed her might within her: never in vain she aimed the unswerving spear-thrust: aye she pierced the backs of them that fled, the breasts of such as charged to meet her. All the long shaft dripped with steaming blood. Swift were her feet as wind as down she swooped. Her aweless spirit failed not for weariness nor fainted, but her might was adamantine. The impending Doom, which roused unto the terrible strife not yet Achilles, clothed her still with glory; still aloof the dread Power stood, and still would shed splendour of triumph o'er the death-ordained but for a little space, ere it should quell that Maiden 'neath the hands of Aeaeus' son. In darkness ambushed, with invisible hand ever it thrust her on, and drew her feet destruction-ward, and lit her path to death with glory, while she slew foe after foe. As when within a dewy garden-close, longing for its green springtide freshness, leaps a heifer, and there rangeth to and fro, when none is by to stay her, treading down all its green herbs, and all its wealth of bloom, devouring greedily this, and marring that with trampling feet; so ranged she, Ares' child, through reeling squadrons of Achaea's sons, slew these, and hunted those in panic rout.

[545] From Troy afar the women marvelling gazed at the Maid's battle-prowess. Suddenly a fiery passion for the fray hath seized Antimachus' daughter, Meneptolemus' wife, Tisiphone. Her heart waxed strong, and filled with lust of fight she cried to her fellows all, with desperate-daring words, to spur them on to woeful war, by recklessness made strong. "Friends, let a heart of valour in our breasts awake! Let us be like our lords, who fight with foes for fatherland, for babes, for us, and never pause for breath in that stern strife! Let us too throne war's spirit in our hearts! Let us too face the fight which favoureth none! For we, we women, be not creatures cast in diverse mould from men: to us is given such energy of life as stirs in them. Eyes have we like to theirs, and limbs: throughout fashioned we are alike: one common light we look on, and one common air we breathe: with like food are we nourished—nay, wherein have we been dowered of God more niggardly than men? Then let us shrink not from the fray; see ye not yonder a woman far excelling men in the grapple of fight? Yet is her blood nowise akin to ours, nor fighteth she for her own city. For an alien king she warreth of her own heart's prompting, fears the face of no man; for her soul is thrilled with valour and with spirit invincible. But we—to right, to left, lie woes on woes about our feet: this mourns beloved sons, and that a husband who for hearth and home hath died; some wail for fathers now no more; some grieve for brethren and for kinsmen lost. Not one but hath some share in sorrow's cup. Behind all this a fearful shadow looms, the day of bondage! Therefore flinch not ye from war, O sorrow-laden! Better far to die in battle now, than afterwards hence to be haled into captivity to alien folk, we and our little ones, in the stern grip of fate leaving behind a burning city, and our husbands' graves."

[589] So cried she, and with passion for stern war thrilled all those women; and with eager speed they hasted to go forth without the wall mail-clad, afire to battle for their town and people: all their spirit was aflame. As when within a hive, when winter-tide is over and gone, loud hum the swarming bees what time they make them ready forth to fare to bright flower-pastures, and no more endure to linger there within, but each to other crieth the challenge-cry to sally forth; even so bestirred themselves the women of Troy, and kindled each her sister to the fray. The weaving-wool, the distaff far they flung, and to grim weapons stretched their eager hands.

[604] And now without the city these had died in that wild battle, as their husbands died and the strong Amazons died, had not one voice of

wisdom cried to stay their maddened feet, when with dissuading words Theano spake: "Wherefore, ah wherefore for the toil and strain of battle's fearful tumult do ye yearn, infatuate ones? Never your limbs have toiled in conflict yet. In utter ignorance panting for labour unendurable, ye rush on all-unthinking; for your strength can never be as that of Danaan men, men trained in daily battle. Amazons have joyed in ruthless fight, in charging steeds, from the beginning: all the toil of men do they endure; and therefore evermore the spirit of the War-god thrills them through. They fall not short of men in anything: their labour-hardened frames make great their hearts for all achievement: never faint their knees nor tremble. Rumour speaks their queen to be a daughter of the mighty Lord of War. Therefore no woman may compare with her in prowess—if she be a woman, not a God come down in answer to our prayers. Yea, of one blood be all the race of men, yet unto diverse labours still they turn; and that for each is evermore the best whereto he bringeth skill of use and wont. Therefore do ye from tumult of the fray hold you aloof, and in your women's bowers before the loom still pace ye to and fro; and war shall be the business of our lords. Lo, of fair issue is there hope: we see the Achaeans falling fast: we see the might of our men waxing ever: fear is none of evil issue now: the pitiless foe beleaguer not the town: no desperate need there is that women should go forth to war."

[643] So cried she, and they hearkened to the words of her who had garnered wisdom from the years; so from afar they watched the fight. But still Penthesileia brake the ranks, and still before her quailed the Achaeans: still they found nor screen nor hiding-place from imminent death. As bleating goats are by the blood-stained jaws of a grim panther torn, so slain were they. In each man's heart all lust of battle died, and fear alone lived. This way, that way fled the panic-stricken: some to earth had flung the armour from their shoulders; some in dust grovelled in terror 'neath their shields: the steeds fled through the rout unreined of charioteers. In rapture of triumph charged the Amazons, with groan and scream of agony died the Greeks. Withered their manhood was in that sore strait; brief was the span of all whom that fierce maid mid the grim jaws of battle overtook. As when with mighty roaring bursteth down a storm upon the forest-trees, and some uprendeth by the roots, and on the earth dashes them down, the tall stems blossom-crowned, and snappeth some athwart the trunk, and high whirls them through air, till all confused they lie a ruin of splintered stems and shattered sprays; so the great Danaan host lay, dashed to dust by doom of Fate, by Penthesileia's spear.

[671] But when the very ships were now at point to be by hands of Trojans set aflame, then battle-bider Aias heard afar the panic-cries, and spake to Aeacus' son: "Achilles, all the air about mine ears is full of multitudinous cries, is full of thunder of battle rolling nearer aye. Let us go forth then, ere the Trojans win unto the ships, and make great slaughter there of Argive men, and set the ships aflame. Foulest reproach such thing on thee and me should bring; for it beseems not that the seed of mighty Zeus should shame the sacred blood of hero-fathers, who themselves of old with Hercules the battle-eager sailed to Troy, and smote her even at her height of glory, when Laomedon was king. Ay, and I ween that our hands even now shall do the like: we too are mighty men."

[690] He spake: the aweless strength of Aeacus' son hearkened thereto, for also to his ears the roar of bitter battle came. Then hasted both, and donned their warrior-gear all splendour-gleaming: now, in these arrayed facing that stormy-tossing rout they stand. Loud clashed their glorious armour: in their souls a battle-fury like the War-god's wrath maddened; such might was breathed into these twain by Atrytone, Shaker of the Shield, as on they pressed. With joy the Argives saw the coming of that mighty twain: they seemed in semblance like Aloeus' giant sons who in the old time made that haughty vaunt of piling on Olympus' brow the height of Ossa steeply-towering, and the crest of sky-encountering Pelion, so to rear a mountain-stair for their rebellious rage to scale the highest heaven. Huge as these the sons of Aeacus seemed, as forth they strode to stem the tide of war. A gladsome sight to friends who have fainted for their coming, now onward they press to crush triumphant foes. Many they slew with their resistless spears; as when two herd-destroying lions come on sheep amid the copses feeding, far from help of shepherds, and in heaps on heaps slay them, till they have drunken to the full of blood, and filled their maws insatiate with flesh, so those destroyers twain slew on, spreading wide havoc through the hosts of Troy.

[721] There Deiochus and gallant Hyllus fell by Aias slain, and fell Eurynomus lover of war, and goodly Enyeus died. But Peleus' son burst on the Amazons smiting Antandre, Polemusa then, Antibrote, fierce-souled Hippothoe, hurling Harmothoe down on sisters slain. Then hard on all their reeling ranks he pressed with Telamon's mighty-hearted son; and now before their hands battalions dense and strong crumbled as weakly and as suddenly as when in mountain-folds the forest-brakes shrivel before a tempest-driven fire.

[734] When battle-eager Penthesileia saw these twain, as through the scourging storm of war like ravening beasts they rushed, to meet them there she sped, as when a leopard grim, whose mood is deadly, leaps from forest-coverts forth, lashing her tail, on hunters closing round, while these, in armour clad, and putting trust in their long spears, await her lightning leap; so did those warriors twain with spears upswung await Penthesileia. Clanged the brazen plates about their shoulders as they moved. And first leapt the long-shafted lance sped from the hand of goodly Penthesileia. Straight it flew to the shield of Aeacus' son, but glancing thence this way and that the shivered fragments sprang as from a rock-face: of such temper were the cunning-hearted Fire-god's gifts divine. Then in her hand the warrior-maid swung up a second javelin fury-winged, against Aias, and with fierce words defied the twain: "Ha, from mine hand in vain one lance hath leapt! But with this second look I suddenly to quell the strength and courage of two foes—ay, though ye vaunt you mighty men of war amid your Danaans! Die ye shall, and so lighter shall be the load of war's affliction that lies upon the Trojan chariot-lords. Draw nigh, come through the press to grips with me, so shall ye learn what might wells up in breasts of Amazons. With my blood is mingled war! No mortal man begat me, but the Lord of War, insatiate of the battle-cry. Therefore my might is more than any man's."

[767] With scornful laughter spake she: then she hurled her second lance; but they in utter scorn laughed now, as swiftly flew the shaft, and smote the silver greave of Aias, and was foiled thereby, and all its fury could not scar the flesh within; for fate had ordered not that any blade of foes should taste the blood of Aias in the bitter war. But he recked of the Amazon naught, but turned him thence to rush upon the Trojan host, and left Penthesileia unto Peleus' son alone, for well he knew his heart within that she, for all her prowess, none the less would cost Achilles battle-toil as light, as effortless, as doth the dove the hawk.

[782] Then groaned she an angry groan that she had sped her shafts in vain; and now with scoffing speech to her in turn the son of Peleus spake: "Woman, with what vain vauntings triumphing hast thou come forth against us, all athirst to battle with us, who be mightier far than earthborn heroes? We from Cronos' Son, the Thunder-roller, boast our high descent. Ay, even Hector quailed, the battle-swift, before us, e'en though far away he saw our onrush to grim battle. Yea, my spear slew him, for all his might. But thou—thine heart is utterly mad, that thou hast greatly dared to threaten us with death this day! On thee thy latest hour

shall swiftly come—is come! Thee not thy sire the War-god now shall pluck out of mine hand, but thou the debt shalt pay of a dark doom, as when mid mountain-folds a pricket meets a lion, waster of herds. What, woman, hast thou heard not of the heaps of slain, that into Xanthus' rushing stream were thrust by these mine hands? or hast thou heard in vain, because the Blessed Ones have stol'n wit and discretion from thee, to the end that Doom's relentless gulf might gape for thee?"

[807] He spake; he swung up in his mighty hand and sped the long spear warrior-slaying, wrought by Chiron, and above the right breast pierced the battle-eager maid. The red blood leapt forth, as a fountain wells, and all at once fainted the strength of Penthesileia's limbs; dropped the great battle-axe from her nerveless hand; a mist of darkness overveiled her eyes, and anguish thrilled her soul. Yet even so still drew she difficult breath, still dimly saw the hero, even now in act to drag her from the swift steed's back. Confusedly she thought: "Or shall I draw my mighty sword, and bide Achilles' fiery onrush, or hastily cast me from my fleet horse down to earth, and kneel unto this godlike man, and with wild breath promise for ransoming great heaps of brass and gold, which pacify the hearts of victors never so athirst for blood, if haply so the murderous might of Aeacus' son may hearken and may spare, or peradventure may compassionate my youth, and so vouchsafe me to behold mine home again? for O, I long to live!"

[831] So surged the wild thoughts in her; but the Gods ordained it otherwise. Even now rushed on in terrible anger Peleus' son: he thrust with sudden spear, and on its shaft impaled the body of her tempest-footed steed, even as a man in haste to sup might pierce flesh with the spit, above the glowing hearth to roast it, or as in a mountain-glade a hunter sends the shaft of death clear through the body of a stag with such winged speed that the fierce dart leaps forth beyond, to plunge into the tall stem of an oak or pine. So that death-ravening spear of Peleus' son clear through the goodly steed rushed on, and pierced Penthesileia. Straightway fell she down into the dust of earth, the arms of death, in grace and comeliness fell, for naught of shame dishonoured her fair form. Face down she lay on the long spear outgasping her last breath, stretched upon that fleet horse as on a couch; like some tall pine snapped by the icy mace of Boreas, earth's forest-fosterling reared by a spring to stately height, amidst long mountain-glens, a glory of mother earth; so from the once fleet steed low fallen lay Penthesileia, all her shattered strength brought down to this, and all her loveliness.

[858] Now when the Trojans saw the Warrior-queen struck down in battle, ran through all their lines a shiver of panic. Straightway to their walls turned they in flight, heart-agonized with grief. As when on the wide sea, 'neath buffetings of storm-blasts, castaways whose ship is wrecked escape, a remnant of a crew, forspent with desperate conflict with the cruel sea: late and at last appears the land hard by, appears a city: faint and weary-limbed with that grim struggle, through the surf they strain to land, sore grieving for the good ship lost, and shipmates whom the terrible surge dragged down to nether gloom; so, Troyward as they fled from battle, all those Trojans wept for her, the Child of the resistless War-god, wept for friends who died in groan-resounding fight.

[874] Then over her with scornful laugh the son of Peleus vaunted: "In the dust lie there a prey to teeth of dogs, to ravens' beaks, thou wretched thing! Who cozened thee to come forth against me? And thoughtest thou to fare home from the war alive, to bear with thee right royal gifts from Priam the old king, thy guerdon for slain Argives? Ha, 'twas not the Immortals who inspired thee with this thought, who know that I of heroes mightiest am, the Danaans' light of safety, but a woe to Trojans and to thee, O evil-starred! Nay, but it was the darkness-shrouded Fates and thine own folly of soul that pricked thee on to leave the works of women, and to fare to war, from which strong men shrink shuddering back."

[891] So spake he, and his ashen spear the son of Peleus drew from that swift horse, and from Penthesileia in death's agony. Then steed and rider gasped their lives away slain by one spear. Now from her head he plucked the helmet splendour-flashing like the beams of the great sun, or Zeus' own glory-light. Then, there as fallen in dust and blood she lay, rose, like the breaking of the dawn, to view 'neath dainty-pencilled brows a lovely face, lovely in death. The Argives thronged around, and all they saw and marvelled, for she seemed like an Immortal. In her armour there upon the earth she lay, and seemed the Child of Zeus, the tireless Huntress Artemis sleeping, what time her feet forwearied are with following lions with her flying shafts over the hills far-stretching. She was made a wonder of beauty even in her death by Aphrodite glorious-crowned, the Bride of the strong War-god, to the end that he, the son of noble Peleus, might be pierced with the sharp arrow of repentant love. The warriors gazed, and in their hearts they prayed that fair and sweet like her their wives might seem, laid on the bed of love, when home they won. Yea, and Achilles' very heart was wrung with love's remorse to have slain a thing so sweet, who might have borne her home, his queenly bride,

to chariot-glorious Phthia; for she was flawless, a very daughter of the Gods, divinely tall, and most divinely fair.

[923] Then Ares' heart was thrilled with grief and rage for his child slain. Straight from Olympus down he darted, swift and bright as thunderbolt terribly flashing from the mighty hand of Zeus, far leaping o'er the trackless sea, or flaming o'er the land, while shuddereth all wide Olympus as it passeth by. So through the quivering air with heart aflame swooped Ares armour-clad, soon as he heard the dread doom of his daughter. For the Gales, the North-wind's fleet-winged daughters, bare to him, as through the wide halls of the sky he strode, the tidings of the maiden's woeful end. Soon as he heard it, like a tempest-blast down to the ridges of Ida leapt he: quaked under his feet the long glens and ravines deep-scored, all Ida's torrent-beds, and all far-stretching foot-hills. Now had Ares brought a day of mourning on the Myrmidons, but Zeus himself from far Olympus sent mid shattering thunders terror of levin-bolts which thick and fast leapt through the welkin down before his feet, blazing with fearful flames. And Ares saw, and knew the stormy threat of the mighty-thundering Father, and he stayed his eager feet, now on the very brink of battle's turmoil. As when some huge crag thrust from a beetling cliff-brow by the winds and torrent rains, or lightning-lance of Zeus, leaps like a wild beast, and the mountain-glens fling back their crashing echoes as it rolls in mad speed on, as with resistless swoop of bound on bound it rushes down, until it cometh to the levels of the plain, and there perforce its stormy flight is stayed; so Ares, battle-eager Son of Zeus, was stayed, how loth soe'er; for all the Gods to the Ruler of the Blessed needs must yield, seeing he sits high-throned above them all, clothed in his might unspeakable. Yet still many a wild thought surged through Ares' soul, urging him now to dread the terrible threat of Cronos' wrathful Son, and to return heavenward, and now to reck not of his Sire, but with Achilles' blood to stain those hands, the battle-tireless. At the last his heart remembered how that many and many a son of Zeus himself in many a war had died, nor in their fall had Zeus availed them aught. Therefore he turned him from the Argives—else, down smitten by the blasting thunderbolt, with Titans in the nether gloom he had lain, who dared defy the eternal will of Zeus.

[975] Then did the warrior sons of Argos strip with eager haste from corpses strewn all round the blood-stained spoils. But ever Peleus' son gazed, wild with all regret, still gazed on her, the strong, the beautiful, laid in the dust; and all his heart was wrung, was broken down with

sorrowing love, deep, strong as he had known when that beloved friend
Patroclus died.

[984] Loud jeered Thersites, mocking to his face: "Thou sorry-souled
Achilles! art not shamed to let some evil Power beguile thine heart to
pity of a pitiful Amazon whose furious spirit purposed naught but ill to
us and ours? Ha, woman-mad art thou, and thy soul lusts for this thing,
as she were some lady wise in household ways, with gifts and pure intent
for honoured wedlock wooed! Good had it been had her spear reached
thine heart, the heart that sighs for woman-creatures still! Thou carest
not, unmanly-souled, not thou, for valour's glorious path, when once
thine eye lights on a woman! Sorry wretch, where now is all thy goodly
prowess? where thy wit? And where the might that should beseem a king
all-stainless? Dost not know what misery this self-same woman-madness
wrought for Troy? Nothing there is to men more ruinous than lust for
woman's beauty; it maketh fools of wise men. But the toil of war attains
renown. To him that is a hero indeed glory of victory and the War-god's
works are sweet. 'Tis but the battle-blencher craves the beauty and the
bed of such as she!"

[1009] So railed he long and loud: the mighty heart of Peleus' son leapt
into flame of wrath. A sudden buffet of his resistless hand smote 'neath
the railer's ear, and all his teeth were dashed to the earth: he fell upon his
face: forth of his lips the blood in torrent gushed: swift from his body
fled the dastard soul of that vile niddering. Achaea's sons rejoiced there-
at, for aye he wont to rail on each and all with venomous gibes, himself
a scandal and the shame of all the host. Then mid the warrior Argives
cried a voice: "Not good it is for baser men to rail on kings, or secretly
or openly; for wrathful retribution swiftly comes. The Lady of Justice
sits on high; and she who heapeth woe on woe on humankind, even Ate,
punisheth the shameless tongue."

[1027] So mid the Danaans cried a voice: nor yet within the mighty
soul of Peleus' son lulled was the storm of wrath, but fiercely he spake:
"Lie there in dust, thy follies all forgot! 'Tis not for knaves to beard their
betters: once thou didst provoke Odysseus' steadfast soul, babbling with
venomous tongue a thousand gibes, and didst escape with life; but thou
hast found the son of Peleus not so patient-souled, who with one only
buffet from his hand unkennels thy dog's soul! A bitter doom hath swal-
lowed thee: by thine own rascalry thy life is sped. Hence from Achaean
men, and mouth out thy revilings midst the dead!"

[1041] So spake the valiant-hearted aweless son of Aeacus. But Tydeus' son alone of all the Argives was with anger stirred against Achilles for Thersites slain, seeing these twain were of the self-same blood, the one, proud Tydeus' battle-eager son, the other, seed of godlike Agrius: brother of noble Oeneus Agrius was; and Oeneus in the Danaan land begat Tydeus the battle-eager, son to whom was stalwart Diomedes. Therefore wroth was he for slain Thersites, yea, had raised against the son of Peleus vengeful hands, except the noblest of Achaea's sons had thronged around him, and besought him sore, and held him back therefrom. With Peleus' son also they pleaded; else those mighty twain, the mightiest of all Argives, were at point to close with clash of swords, so stung were they with bitter wrath; yet hearkened they at last to prayers of comrades, and were reconciled.

[1062] Then of their pity did the Atreid kings—for these too at the imperial loveliness of Penthesileia marvelled—render up her body to the men of Troy, to bear unto the burg of Ilus far-renowned with all her armour. For a herald came asking this boon for Priam; for the king longed with deep yearning of the heart to lay that battle-eager maiden, with her arms, and with her war-horse, in the great earth-mound of old Laomedon. And so he heaped a high broad pyre without the city wall: upon the height thereof that warrior-queen they laid, and costly treasures did they heap around her, all that well beseems to burn around a mighty queen in battle slain. And so the Fire-god's swift-upleaping might, the ravening flame, consumed her. All around the people stood on every hand, and quenched the pyre with odorous wine. Then gathered they the bones, and poured sweet ointment over them, and laid them in a casket: over all shed they the rich fat of a heifer, chief among the herds that grazed on Ida's slope. And, as for a beloved daughter, rang all round the Trojan men's heart-stricken wail, as by the stately wall they buried her on an outstanding tower, beside the bones of old Laomedon, a queen beside a king. This honour for the War-god's sake they rendered, and for Penthesileia's own. And in the plain beside her buried they the Amazons, even all that followed her to battle, and by Argive spears were slain. For Atreus' sons begrudged not these the boon of tear-besprinkled graves, but let their friends, the warrior Trojans, draw their corpses forth, yea, and their own slain also, from amidst the swath of darts o'er that grim harvest-field. Wrath strikes not at the dead: pitied are foes when life has fled, and left them foes no more.

[1103] Far off across the plain the while uprose smoke from the pyres

whereon the Argives laid the many heroes overthrown and slain by Tro-
jan hands what time the sword devoured; and multitudinous lamentation
wailed over the perished. But above the rest mourned they o'er brave
Podarces, who in fight was no less mighty than his hero-brother Protesil-
aus, he who long ago fell, slain of Hector: so Podarces now, struck down
by Penthesileia's spear, hath cast over all Argive hearts the pall of grief.
Wherefore apart from him they laid in clay the common throng of slain;
but over him toiling they heaped an earth-mound far-descried in mem-
ory of a warrior aweless-souled. And in a several pit withal they thrust
the niddering Thersites' wretched corpse. Then to the ships, acclaiming
Aeacus' son, returned they all. But when the radiant day had plunged
beneath the Ocean-stream, and night, the holy, overspread the face of
earth, then in the rich king Agamemnon's tent feasted the might of Pele-
us' son, and there sat at the feast those other mighty ones all through the
dark, till rose the dawn divine.

Book III

[1] When shone the light of Dawn the splendour-throned, then to
the ships the Pylian spearmen bore Antilochus' corpse, sore sighing for
their prince, and by the Hellespont they buried him with aching hearts.
Around him groaning stood the battle-eager sons of Argives, all, of love
for Nestor, shrouded o'er with grief. But that grey hero's heart was no-
wise crushed by sorrow; for the wise man's soul endures bravely, and
cowers not under affliction's stroke. But Peleus' son, wroth for Antilo-
chus his dear friend, armed for vengeance terrible upon the Trojans. Yea,
and these withal, despite their dread of mighty Achilles' spear, poured
battle-eager forth their gates, for now the Fates with courage filled their
breasts, of whom many were doomed to Hades to descend, whence
there is no return, thrust down by hands of Aeacus' son, who also was
foredoomed to perish that same day by Priam's wall. Swift met the fronts
of conflict: all the tribes of Troy's host, and the battle-biding Greeks,
afire with that new-kindled fury of war.

[24] Then through the foe the son of Peleus made wide havoc: all
around the earth was drenched with gore, and choked with corpses were
the streams of Simois and Xanthus. Still he chased, still slaughtered, even
to the city's walls; for panic fell on all the host. And now all had he
slain, had dashed the gates to earth, rending them from their hinges,
or the bolts, hurling himself against them, had he snapped, and for the
Danaans into Priam's burg had made a way, had utterly destroyed that

goodly town—but now was Phoebus wroth against him with grim fury
when he saw those countless troops of heroes slain of him. Down from
Olympus with a lion-leap he came: his quiver on his shoulders lay, and
shafts that deal the wounds incurable. Facing Achilles stood he; round
him clashed quiver and arrows; blazed with quenchless flame his eyes
and shook the earth beneath his feet. Then with a terrible shout the great
God cried, so to turn back from war Achilles awed by the voice divine
and save from death the Trojans: "Back from the Trojans, Peleus' son!
Beseems not that longer thou deal death unto thy foes, lest an Olympian
God abase thy pride."

[50] But nothing quailed the hero at the voice immortal, for that round
him even now hovered the unrelenting Fates. He recked naught of the
God, and shouted his defiance: "Phoebus, why dost thou in mine own
despite stir me to fight with Gods, and wouldst protect the arrogant
Trojans? Heretofore hast thou by thy beguiling turned me from the fray,
when from destruction thou at the first didst save Hector, whereat the
Trojans all through Troy exulted. Nay, thou get thee back: return unto
the mansion of the Blessed, lest I smite thee—ay, immortal though thou
be!"

[63] Then on the God he turned his back, and sped after the Trojans
fleeing cityward, and harried still their flight; but wroth at heart thus
Phoebus spake to his indignant soul: "Out on this man! he is sense-be-
reft! But now not Zeus himself nor any other Power shall save this mad-
man who defies the Gods!"

[70] From mortal sight he vanished into cloud, and cloaked with mist
a baleful shaft he shot which leapt to Achilles' ankle: sudden pangs with
mortal sickness made his whole heart faint. He reeled, and like a tower
he fell, that falls smit by a whirlwind when an earthquake cleaves a chasm
for rushing blasts from underground; so fell the goodly form of Aeacus'
son. He glared, a murderous glance, to right, to left, [upon the Trojans,
and a terrible threat] shouted, a threat that could not be fulfilled: "Who
shot at me a stealthy-smiting shaft? Let him but dare to meet me face to
face! So shall his blood and all his bowels gush out about my spear, and
he be hellward sped! I know that none can meet me man to man and
quell in fight—of earth-born heroes none, though such an one should
bear within his breast a heart unquailing, and have thews of brass. But
dastards still in stealthy ambush lurk for lives of heroes. Let him face me
then! ay! though he be a God whose anger burns against the Danaans!

Yea, mine heart forebodes that this my smiter was Apollo, cloaked in deadly darkness. So in days gone by my mother told me how that by his shafts I was to die before the Scaean Gates a piteous death. Her words were not vain words."

[98] Then with unflinching hands from out the wound incurable he drew the deadly shaft in agonized pain. Forth gushed the blood; his heart waxed faint beneath the shadow of coming doom. Then in indignant wrath he hurled from him the arrow: a sudden gust of wind swept by, and caught it up, and, even as he trod Zeus' threshold, to Apollo gave it back; for it beseemed not that a shaft divine, sped forth by an Immortal, should be lost. He unto high Olympus swiftly came, to the great gathering of immortal Gods, where all assembled watched the war of men, these longing for the Trojans' triumph, those for Danaan victory; so with diverse wills watched they the strife, the slayers and the slain.

[114] Him did the Bride of Zeus behold, and straight upbraided with exceeding bitter words: "What deed of outrage, Phoebus, hast thou done this day, forgetful of that day whereon to godlike Peleus' spousals gathered all the Immortals? Yea, amidst the feasters thou sangest how Thetis silver-footed left the sea's abysses to be Peleus' bride; and as thou harpedst all earth's children came to hearken, beasts and birds, high craggy hills, rivers, and all deep-shadowed forests came. All this hast thou forgotten, and hast wrought a ruthless deed, hast slain a godlike man, albeit thou with other Gods didst pour the nectar, praying that he might be the son by Thetis given to Peleus. But that prayer hast thou forgotten, favouring the folk of tyrannous Laomedon, whose kine thou keptest. He, a mortal, did despite to thee, the deathless! O, thou art wit-bereft! Thou favourest Troy, thy sufferings all forgot. Thou wretch, and doth thy false heart know not this, what man is an offence, and meriteth suffering, and who is honoured of the Gods? Ever Achilles showed us reverence—yea, was of our race. Ha, but the punishment of Troy, I ween, shall not be lighter, though Aeacus' son have fallen; for his son right soon shall come from Scyros to the war to help the Argive men, no less in might than was his sire, a bane to many a foe. But thou—thou for the Trojans dost not care, but for his valour enviedst Peleus' son, seeing he was the mightest of all men. Thou fool! how wilt thou meet the Nereid's eyes, when she shall stand in Zeus' hall midst the Gods, who praised thee once, and loved as her own son?"

[151] So Hera spake, in bitterness of soul upbraiding, but he answered

her not a word, of reverence for his mighty Father's bride; nor could he
lift his eyes to meet her eyes, but sat abashed, aloof from all the Gods
eternal, while in unforgiving wrath scowled on him all the Immortals
who maintained the Danaans' cause; but such as fain would bring tri-
umph to Troy, these with exultant hearts extolled him, hiding it from
Hera's eyes, before whose wrath all Heaven-abiders shrank.

[162] But Peleus' son the while forgat not yet war's fury: still in his in-
vincible limbs the hot blood throbbed, and still he longed for fight. Was
none of all the Trojans dared draw nigh the stricken hero, but at distance
stood, as round a wounded lion hunters stand mid forest-brakes afraid,
and, though the shaft stands in his heart, yet faileth not in him his royal
courage, but with terrible glare roll his fierce eyes, and roar his grimly
jaws; so wrath and anguish of his deadly hurt to fury stung Peleides' soul;
but aye his strength ebbed through the god-envenomed wound. Yet leapt
he up, and rushed upon the foe, and flashed the lightning of his lance; it
slew the goodly Orythaon, comrade stout of Hector, through his tem-
ples crashing clear: his helm stayed not the long lance fury-sped which
leapt therethrough, and won within the bones the heart of the brain, and
spilt his lusty life. Then stabbed he 'neath the brow Hipponous even to
the eye-roots, that the eyeball fell to earth: his soul to Hades flitted forth.
Then through the jaw he pierced Alcathous, and shore away his tongue:
in dust he fell gasping his life out, and the spear-head shot out through
his ear. These, as they rushed on him, that hero slew; but many a fleer's
life he spilt, for in his heart still leapt the blood.

[191] But when his limbs grew chill, and ebbed away his spirit, leaning
on his spear he stood, while still the Trojans fled in huddled rout of pan-
ic, and he shouted unto them: "Trojan and Dardan cravens, ye shall not
even in my death, escape my merciless spear, but unto mine Avenging
Spirits ye shall pay—ay, one and all -- destruction's debt!"

[199] He spake; they heard and quailed: as mid the hills fawns trem-
ble at a lion's deep-mouthed roar, and terror-stricken flee the monster,
so the ranks of Trojan chariot-lords, the lines of battle-helpers drawn
from alien lands, quailed at the last shout of Achilles, deemed that he
was woundless yet. But 'neath the weight of doom his aweless heart, his
mighty limbs, at last were overborne. Down midst the dead he fell, as
fails a beetling mountain-cliff. Earth rang beneath him: clanged with a
thundercrash his arms, as Peleus' son the princely fell. And still his foes
with most exceeding dread stared at him, even as, when some murderous

656

beast lies slain by shepherds, tremble still the sheep eyeing him, as beside the fold he lies, and shrinking, as they pass him, far aloof and, even as he were living, fear him dead; so feared they him, Achilles now no more.

[218] Yet Paris strove to kindle those faint hearts; for his own heart exulted, and he hoped, now Peleus' son, the Danaans' strength, had fallen, wholly to quench the Argive battle-fire: "Friends, if ye help me truly and loyally, let us this day die, slain by Argive men, or live, and hale to Troy with Hector's steeds in triumph Peleus' son thus fallen dead, the steeds that, grieving, yearning for their lord to fight have borne me since my brother died. Might we with these but hale Achilles slain, glory were this for Hector's horses, yea, for Hector—if in Hades men have sense of righteous retribution. This man aye devised but mischief for the sons of Troy; and now Troy's daughters with exultant hearts from all the city streets shall gather round, as pantheresses wroth for stolen cubs, or lionesses, might stand around a man whose craft in hunting vexed them while he lived. So round Achilles—a dead corpse at last!—in hurrying throngs Troy's daughters then shall come in unforgiving, unforgetting hate, for parents wroth, for husbands slain, for sons, for noble kinsmen. Most of all shall joy my father, and the ancient men, whose feet unwillingly are chained within the walls by eld, if we shall hale him through our gates, and give our foe to fowls of the air for meat."

[247] Then they, which feared him theretofore, in haste closed round the corpse of strong-heart Aeacus' son, Glaucus, Aeneas, battle-fain Agenor, and other cunning men in deadly fight, eager to hale him thence to Ilium the god-built burg. But Aias failed him not. Swiftly that godlike man bestrode the dead: back from the corpse his long lance thrust them all. Yet ceased they not from onslaught; thronging round, still with swift rushes fought they for the prize, one following other, like to long-lipped bees which hover round their hive in swarms on swarms to drive a man thence; but he, recking naught of all their fury, carveth out the combs of nectarous honey: harassed sore are they by smoke-reek and the robber; spite of all ever they dart against him; naught cares he; so naught of all their onsets Aias recked; but first he stabbed Agelaus in the breast, and slew that son of Maion: Thestor next: Ocythous he smote, Agestratus, Aganippus, Zorus, Nessus, Erymas the war-renowned, who came from Lycia-land with mighty-hearted Glaucus, from his home in Melanippion on the mountain-ridge, Athena's fane, which Massikyton fronts anigh Chelidonia's headland, dreaded sore of scared seafarers, when its lowering crags must needs be doubled. For his death the blood of famed Hip-

polochus' son was horror-chilled; for this was his dear friend. With on
swift thrust he pierced the sevenfold hides of Aias' shield, yet touche
his flesh not; stayed the spear-head was by those thick hides and by th
corset-plate which lapped his battle-tireless limbs. But still from that ster
conflict Glaucus drew not back, burning to vanquish Aias, Aeacus' son
and in his folly vaunting threatened him: "Aias, men name thee mightie
man of all the Argives, hold thee in passing-high esteem even as Achille
therefore thou, I wot, by that dead warrior dead this day shalt lie!"

[289] So hurled he forth a vain word, knowing not how far in migh
above him was the man whom his spear threatened. Battle-bider Aia
darkly and scornfully glaring on him, said "Thou craven wretch, an
knowest thou not this, how much was Hector mightier than thou in war
craft? yet before my might, my spear, he shrank. Ay, with his valour wa
there blent discretion. Thou thy thoughts are deathward set, who dar's
defy me to the battle, me, a mightier far than thou! Thou canst not say
that friendship of our fathers thee shall screen; nor me thy gifts shall wil
to let thee pass scatheless from war, as once did Tydeus' son. Though
thou didst 'scape his fury, will not I suffer thee to return alive from war
Ha, in thy many helpers dost thou trust who with thee, like so man
worthless flies, flit round the noble Achilles' corpse? To these death an
black doom shall my swift onset deal."

[309] Then on the Trojans this way and that he turned, as mid long
forest-glens a lion turns on hounds, and Trojans many and Lycians slew
that came for honour hungry, till he stood mid a wide ring of flinchers
like a shoal of darting fish when sails into their midst dolphin or shark, a
huge sea-fosterling; so shrank they from the might of Telamon's son, as
aye he charged amidst the rout. But still swarmed fighters up, till round
Achilles' corse to right, to left, lay in the dust the slain countless, as boars
around a lion at bay; and evermore the strife waxed deadlier. Then too
Hippolochus' war-wise son was slain by Aias of the heart of fire. He
fell backward upon Achilles, even as falls a sapling on a sturdy moun-
tain-oak; so quelled by the spear on Peleus' son he fell. But for his rescue
Anchises' stalwart son strove hard, with all his comrades battle-fain, and
haled the corpse forth, and to sorrowing friends gave it, to bear to Ili-
um's hallowed burg. Himself to spoil Achilles still fought on, till warrior
Aias pierced him with the spear through the right forearm. Swiftly leapt
he back from murderous war, and hasted thence to Troy. There for his
healing cunning leeches wrought, who stanched the blood-rush, and laid
on the gash balms, such as salve war-stricken warriors' pangs.

[338] But Aias still fought on: here, there he slew with thrusts like lightning-flashes. His great heart ached sorely for his mighty cousin slain. And now the warrior-king Laertes' son fought at his side: before him blenched the foe, as he smote down Peisander's fleetfoot son, the warrior Maenalus, who left his home in far-renowned Abydos: down on him he hurled Atymnius, the goodly son whom Pegasis the bright-haired Nymph had borne to strong Emathion by Granicus' stream. Dead by his side he laid Orestius' son, Proteus, who dwelt 'neath lofty Ida's folds. Ah, never did his mother welcome home that son from war, Panaceia beauty-famed! He fell by Odysseus' hands, who spilt the lives of many more whom his death-hungering spear reached in that fight around the mighty dead. Yet Alcon, son of Megacles battle-swift, hard by Odysseus' right knee drave the spear home, and about the glittering greave the blood dark-crimsom welled. He recked not of the wound, but was unto his smiter sudden death; for clear through his shield he stabbed him with his spear amidst his battle-fury: to the earth backward he dashed him by his giant might and strength of hand: clashed round him in the dust his armour, and his corslet was distained with crimson life-blood. Forth from flesh and shield the hero plucked the spear of death: the soul followed the lance-head from the body forth, and life forsook its mortal mansion. Then rushed on his comrades, in his wound's despite, Odysseus, nor from that stern battle-toil refrained him. And by this a mingled host of Danaans eager-hearted fought around the mighty dead, and many and many a foe slew they with those smooth-shafted ashen spears. Even as the winds strew down upon the ground the flying leaves, when through the forest-glades sweep the wild gusts, as waneth autumn-tide, and the old year is dying; so the spears of dauntless Danaans strewed the earth with slain, for loyal to dead Achilles were they all, and loyal to hero Aias to the death. For like black Doom he blasted the ranks of Troy. Then against Aias Paris strained his bow; but he was ware thereof, and sped a stone swift to the archer's head: that bolt of death crashed through his crested helm, and darkness closed round him. In dust down fell he: naught availed his shafts their eager lord, this way and that scattered in dust: empty his quiver lay, flew from his hand the bow. In haste his friends upcaught him from the earth, and Hector's steeds hurried him thence to Troy, scarce drawing breath, and moaning in his pain. Nor left his men the weapons of their lord, but gathered up all from the plain, and bare them to the prince; while Aias after him sent a wrathful shout: "Dog, thou hast 'scaped the heavy hand of death today! But swiftly thy last hour shall come by some strong Argive's hands, or by mine own, but now have I a nobler task in hand, from murder's grip to rescue Achilles' corpse."

[402] Then turned he on the foe, hurling swift doom on such as fought around Peleides yet. These saw how many yielded up the ghost 'neath his strong hands, and, with hearts failing them for fear, against him could they stand no more. As rascal vultures were they, which the swoop of an eagle, king of birds, scares far away from carcasses of sheep that wolves have torn; so this way, that way scattered they before the hurtling stones, the sword, the might of Aias. In utter panic from the war they fled, in huddled rout, like starlings from the swoop of a death-dealing hawk, when, fleeing bane, one drives against another, as they dart all terror-huddled in tumultuous flight. So from the war to Priam's burg they fled wretchedly clad with terror as a cloak, quailing from mighty Aias' battle-shout, as with hands dripping blood-gouts he pursued. Yea, all, one after other, had he slain, had they not streamed through city-gates flung wide hard-panting, pierced to the very heart with fear. Pent there within he left them, as a shepherd leaves folded sheep, and strode back o'er the plain; yet never touched he with his feet the ground, but aye he trod on dead men, arms, and blood; for countless corpses lay o'er that wide stretch even from broad-wayed Troy to Hellespont, bodies of strong men slain, the spoil of Doom. As when the dense stalks of sun-ripened corn fall 'neath the reapers' hands, and the long swaths, heavy with full ears, overspread the field, and joys the heart of him who oversees the toil, lord of the harvest; even so, by baleful havoc overmastered, lay all round face-downward men remembering not the death-denouncing war-shout.

[440] But the sons of fair Achaea left their slaughtered foes in dust and blood unstripped of arms awhile till they should lay upon the pyre the son of Peleus, who in battle-shock had been their banner of victory, charging in his might. So the kings drew him from that stricken field straining beneath the weight of giant limbs, and with all loving care they bore him on, and laid him in his tent before the ships. And round him gathered that great host, and wailed heart-anguished him who had been the Achaeans' strength, and now, forgotten all the splendour of spears, lay mid the tents by moaning Hellespont, in stature more than human, even as lay Tityos, who sought to force Queen Leto, when she fared to Pytho: swiftly in his wrath Apollo shot, and laid him low, who seemed invincible: in a foul lake of gore there lay he, covering many a rood of ground, on the broad earth, his mother; and she moaned over her son, of blessed Gods abhorred; but Lady Leto laughed. So grand of mould there in the foemen's land lay Aeacus' son, for joy to Trojans, but for endless grief to Achaean men lamenting. Moaned the air with sighing

from the abysses of the sea; and passing heavy grew the hearts of all, thinking: "Now shall we perish by the hands of Trojans!" Then by those dark ships they thought of white-haired fathers left in halls afar, of wives new-wedded, who by couches cold mourned, waiting, waiting, with their tender babes for husbands unreturning; and they groaned in bitterness of soul. A passion of grief came o'er their hearts; they fell upon their faces on the deep sand flung down, and wept as men all comfortless round Peleus' mighty son, and clutched and plucked out by the roots their hair, and cast upon their heads defiling sand. Their cry was like the cry that goeth up from folk that after battle by their walls are slaughtered, when their maddened foes set fire to a great city, and slay in heaps on heaps her people, and make spoil of all her wealth; so wild and high they wailed beside the sea, because the Danaans' champion, Aeacus' son, lay, grand in death, by a God's arrow slain, as Ares lay, when She of the Mighty Father with that huge stone down dashed him on Troy's plain.

[489] Ceaselessly wailed the Myrmidons Achilles, a ring of mourners round the kingly dead, that kind heart, friend alike to each and all, to no man arrogant nor hard of mood, but ever tempering strength with courtesy.

[494] Then Aias first, deep-groaning, uttered forth his yearning o'er his father's brother's son god-stricken—ay, no man had smitten him of all upon the wide-wayed earth that dwell! Him glorious Aias heavy-hearted mourned, now wandering to the tent of Peleus' son, now cast down all his length, a giant form, on the sea-sands; and thus lamented he: "Achilles, shield and sword of Argive men, thou hast died in Troy, from Phthia's plains afar, smitten unwares by that accursed shaft, such thing as weakling dastards aim in fight! For none who trusts in wielding the great shield, none who for war can skill to set the helm upon his brows, and sway the spear in grip, and cleave the brass about the breasts of foes, warreth with arrows, shrinking from the fray. Not man to man he met thee, whoso smote; else woundless never had he 'scaped thy lance! But haply Zeus purposed to ruin all, and maketh all our toil and travail vain— ay, now will grant the Trojans victory who from Achaea now hath reft her shield! Ah me! how shall old Peleus in his halls take up the burden of a mighty grief now in his joyless age! His heart shall break at the mere rumour of it. Better so, thus in a moment to forget all pain. But if these evil tidings slay him not, ah, laden with sore sorrow eld shall come upon him, eating out his heart with grief by a lone hearth Peleus so passing dear once to the Blessed! But the Gods vouchsafe no perfect happiness to hapless men."

[528] So he in grief lamented Peleus' son. Then ancient Phoenix made heart-stricken moan, clasping the noble form of Aeacus' seed, and in wild anguish wailed the wise of heart: "Thou art reft from me, dear child, and cureless pain hast left to me! Oh that upon my face the veiling earth had fallen, ere I saw thy bitter doom! No pang more terrible hath ever stabbed mine heart no, not that hour of exile, when I fled from fatherland and noble parents, fleeing Hellas through, till Peleus welcomed me with gifts, and lord of his Dolopians made me. In his arms thee through his halls one day he bare, and set upon my knees, and bade me foster thee, his babe, with all love, as mine own dear child: I hearkened to him: blithely didst thou cling about mine heart, and, babbling wordless speech, didst call me 'father' oft, and didst bedew my breast and tunic with thy baby lips. Ofttimes with soul that laughed for glee I held thee in mine arms; for mine heart whispered me 'This fosterling through life shall care for thee, staff of thine age shall be.' And that mine hope was for a little while fulfilled; but now thou hast vanished into darkness, and to me is left long heart-ache wild with all regret. Ah, might my sorrow slay me, ere the tale to noble Peleus come! When on his ears falleth the heavy tidings, he shall weep and wail without cease. Most piteous grief we twain for thy sake shall inherit aye, thy sire and I, who, ere our day of doom, mourning shall go down to the grave for thee—ay, better this than life unholpen of thee!"

[563] So moaned his ever-swelling tide of grief. And Atreus' son beside him mourned and wept with heart on fire with inwardly smouldering pain: "Thou hast perished, chiefest of the Danaan men, hast perished, and hast left the Achaean host fenceless! Now thou art fallen, are they left an easier prey to foes. Thou hast given joy to Trojans by thy fall, who dreaded thee as sheep a lion. These with eager hearts even to the ships will bring the battle now. Zeus, Father, thou too with deceitful words beguilest mortals! Thou didst promise me that Priam's burg should be destroyed; but now that promise given dost thou not fulfil, but thou didst cheat mine heart: I shall not win the war's goal, now Achilles is no more."

[579] So did he cry heart-anguished. Mourned all round wails multitudinous for Peleus' son: the dark ships echoed back the voice of grief, and sighed and sobbed the immeasurable air. And as when long sea-rollers, onward driven by a great wind, heave up far out at sea, and strandward sweep with terrible rush, and aye headland and beach with shattered spray are scourged, and roar unceasing; so a dread sound rose of moaning of the Danaans round the corpse, ceaselessly wailing Peleus' aweless son.

[590] And on their mourning soon black night had come, but spake unto Atreides Neleus' son, Nestor, whose own heart bare its load of grief remembering his own son Antilochus: "O mighty Agamemnon, sceptre-lord of Argives, from wide-shrilling lamentation refrain we for this day. None shall withhold hereafter these from all their heart's desire of weeping and lamenting many days. But now go to, from aweless Aeacus' son wash we the foul blood-gouts, and lay we him upon a couch: unseemly it is to shame the dead by leaving them untended long."

[603] So counselled Neleus' son, the passing-wise. Then hasted he his men, and bade them set cauldrons of cold spring-water o'er the flames, and wash the corpse, and clothe in vesture fair, sea-purple, which his mother gave her son at his first sailing against Troy. With speed they did their lord's command: with loving care, all service meetly rendered, on a couch laid they the mighty fallen, Peleus' son.

[612] The Trito-born, the passing-wise, beheld and pitied him, and showered upon his head ambrosia, which hath virtue aye to keep taintless, men say, the flesh of warriors slain. Like softly-breathing sleeper dewy-fresh she made him: over that dead face she drew a stern frown, even as when he lay, with wrath darkening his grim face, clasping his slain friend Patroclus; and she made his frame to be more massive, like a war-god to behold. And wonder seized the Argives, as they thronged and saw the image of a living man, where all the stately length of Peleus' son lay on the couch, and seemed as though he slept.

[626] Around him all the woeful captive-maids, whom he had taken for a prey, what time he had ravaged hallowed Lemnos, and had scaled the towered crags of Thebes, Eetion's town, wailed, as they stood and rent their fair young flesh, and smote their breasts, and from their hearts bemoaned that lord of gentleness and courtesy, who honoured even the daughters of his foes. And stricken most of all with heart-sick pain Briseis, hero Achilles' couchmate, bowed over the dead, and tore her fair young flesh with ruthless fingers, shrieking: her soft breast was ridged with gory weals, so cruelly she smote it thou hadst said that crimson blood had dripped on milk. Yet, in her griefs despite, her winsome loveliness shone out, and grace hung like a veil about her, as she wailed: "Woe for this grief passing all griefs beside! Never on me came anguish like to this not when my brethren died, my fatherland was wasted—like this anguish for thy death! Thou wast my day, my sunlight, my sweet life, mine hope of good, my strong defense from harm, dearer than all my

beauty—yea, more dear than my lost parents! Thou wast all in all to me, thou only, captive though I be. Thou tookest from me every bondmaid's task and like a wife didst hold me. Ah, but now me shall some new Achaean master bear to fertile Sparta, or to thirsty Argos. The bitter cup of thraldom shall I drain, severed, ah me, from thee! Oh that the earth had veiled my dead face ere I saw thy doom!"

[659] So for slain Peleus' son did she lament with woeful handmaids and heart-anguished Greeks, mourning a king, a husband. Never dried her tears were: ever to the earth they streamed like sunless water trickling from a rock while rime and snow yet mantle o'er the earth above it; yet the frost melts down before the east-wind and the flame-shafts of the sun.

[667] Now came the sound of that upringing wail to Nereus' Daughters, dwellers in the depths unfathomed. With sore anguish all their hearts were smitten: piteously they moaned: their cry shivered along the waves of Hellespont. Then with dark mantles overpalled they sped swiftly to where the Argive men were thronged. As rushed their troop up silver paths of sea, the flood disported round them as they came. With one wild cry they floated up; it rang, a sound as when fleet-flying cranes forebode a great storm. Moaned the monsters of the deep plaintively round that train of mourners. Fast on sped they to their goal, with awesome cry wailing the while their sister's mighty son. Swiftly from Helicon the Muses came heart-burdened with undying grief, for love and honour to the Nereid starry-eyed.

[685] Then Zeus with courage filled the Argive men, that eyes of flesh might undismayed behold that glorious gathering of Goddesses. Then those Divine Ones round Achilles' corpse pealed forth with one voice from immortal lips a lamentation. Rang again the shores of Hellespont. As rain upon the earth their tears fell round the dead man, Aeacus' son; for out of depths of sorrow rose their moan. And all the armour, yea, the tents, the ships of that great sorrowing multitude were wet with tears from ever-welling springs of grief. His mother cast her on him, clasping him, and kissed her son's lips, crying through her tears: "Now let the rosy-vestured Dawn in heaven exult! Now let broad-flowing Axius exult, and for Asteropaeus dead put by his wrath! Let Priam's seed be glad but I unto Olympus will ascend, and at the feet of everlasting Zeus will cast me, bitterly planning that he gave me, an unwilling bride, unto a man—a man whom joyless eld soon overtook, to whom the Fates are near, with

death for gift. Yet not so much for his lot do I grieve as for Achilles; for Zeus promised me to make him glorious in the Aeacid halls, in recompense for the bridal I so loathed that into wild wind now I changed me, now to water, now in fashion as a bird I was, now as the blast of flame; nor might a mortal win me for his bride, who seemed all shapes in turn that earth and heaven contain, until the Olympian pledged him to bestow a godlike son on me, a lord of war. Yea, in a manner this did he fulfill faithfully; for my son was mightiest of men. But Zeus made brief his span of life unto my sorrow. Therefore up to heaven will I: to Zeus's mansion will I go and wail my son, and will put Zeus in mind of all my travail for him and his sons in their sore stress, and sting his soul with shame."

[728] So in her wild lament the Sea-queen cried. But now to Thetis spake Calliope, she in whose heart was steadfast wisdom throned: "From lamentation, Thetis, now forbear, and do not, in the frenzy of thy grief for thy lost son, provoke to wrath the Lord of Gods and men. Lo, even sons of Zeus, the Thunder-king, have perished, overborne by evil fate. Immortal though I be, mine own son Orpheus died, whose magic song drew all the forest-trees to follow him, and every craggy rock and river-stream, and blasts of winds shrill-piping stormy-breathed, and birds that dart through air on rushing wings. Yet I endured mine heavy sorrow: Gods ought not with anguished grief to vex their souls. Therefore make end of sorrow-stricken wail for thy brave child; for to the sons of earth minstrels shall chant his glory and his might, by mine and by my sisters' inspiration, unto the end of time. Let not thy soul be crushed by dark grief, nor do thou lament like those frail mortal women. Know'st thou not that round all men which dwell upon the earth hovereth irresistible deadly Fate, who recks not even of the Gods? Such power she only hath for heritage. Yea, she soon shall destroy gold-wealthy Priam's town, and Trojans many and Argives doom to death, whomso she will. No God can stay her hand."

[758] So in her wisdom spake Calliope. Then plunged the sun down into Ocean's stream, and sable-vestured Night came floating up o'er the wide firmament, and brought her boon of sleep to sorrowing mortals. On the sands there slept they, all the Achaean host, with heads bowed 'neath the burden of calamity. But upon Thetis sleep laid not his hand: still with the deathless Nereids by the sea she sate; on either side the Muses spake one after other comfortable words to make that sorrowing heart forget its pain.

[770] But when with a triumphant laugh the Dawn soared up the sky, and her most radiant light shed over all the Trojans and their king, then, sorrowing sorely for Achilles still, the Danaans woke to weep. Day after day, for many days they wept. Around them moaned far-stretching beaches of the sea, and mourned great Nereus for his daughter Thetis' sake; and mourned with him the other Sea-gods all for dead Achilles. Then the Argives gave the corpse of great Peleides to the flame. A pyre of countless tree-trunks built they up which, all with one mind toiling, from the heights of Ida they brought down; for Atreus' sons sped on the work, and charged them to bring thence wood without measure, that consumed with speed might be Achilles' body. All around piled they about the pyre much battle-gear of strong men slain; and slew and cast thereon full many goodly sons of Trojan men, and snorting steeds, and mighty bulls withal, and sheep and fatling swine thereon they cast. And wailing captive maids from coffers brought mantles untold; all cast they on the pyre: gold heaped they there and amber. All their hair the Myrmidons shore, and shrouded with the same the body of their king. Briseis laid her own shorn tresses on the corpse, her gift, her last, unto her lord. Great jars of oil full many poured they out thereon, with jars of honey and of wine, rich blood of the grape that breathed an odour as of nectar, yea, cast incense-breathing perfumes manifold marvellous sweet, the precious things put forth by earth, and treasures of the sea divine.

[805] Then, when all things were set in readiness about the pyre, all, footmen, charioteers, compassed that woeful bale, clashing their arms, while, from the viewless heights Olympian, Zeus rained down ambrosia on dead Aeacus' son. For honour to the Goddess, Nereus' child, he sent to Aeolus Hermes, bidding him summon the sacred might of his swift winds, for that the corpse of Aeacus' son must now be burned. With speed he went, and Aeolus refused not: the tempestuous North in haste he summoned, and the wild blast of the West; and to Troy sped they on their whirlwind wings. Fast in mad onrush, fast across the deep they darted; roared beneath them as they flew the sea, the land; above crashed thunder-voiced clouds headlong hurtling through the firmament. Then by decree of Zeus down on the pyre of slain Achilles, like a charging host swooped they; upleapt the Fire-god's madding breath: uprose a long wail from the Myrmidons. Then, though with whirlwind rushes toiled the winds, all day, all night, they needs must fan the flames ere that death-pyre burned out. Up to the heavens vast-volumed rolled the smoke. The huge tree-trunks groaned, writhing, bursting, in the heat, and dropped the dark-grey ash all round. So when the winds had tirelessly fulfilled

their mighty task, back to their cave they rode cloud-charioted.

[834] Then, when the fire had last of all consumed that hero-king, when all the steeds, the men slain round the pyre had first been ravined up, with all the costly offerings laid around the mighty dead by Achaia's weeping sons, the glowing embers did the Myrmidons quench with wine. Then clear to be discerned were seen his bones; for nowise like the rest were they, but like an ancient Giant's; none beside with these were blent; for bulls and steeds, and sons of Troy, with all that mingled hecatomb, lay in a wide ring round his corpse, and he amidst them, flame-devoured, lay there alone. So his companions groaning gathered up his bones, and in a silver casket laid massy and deep, and banded and bestarred with flashing gold; and Nereus' daughters shed ambrosia over them, and precious nards for honour to Achilles: fat of kine and amber honey poured they over all. A golden vase his mother gave, the gift in old time of the Wine-god, glorious work of the craft-master Fire-god, in the which they laid the casket that enclosed the bones of mighty-souled Achilles. All around the Argives heaped a barrow, a giant sign, upon a foreland's uttermost end, beside the Hellespont's deep waters, wailing loud farewells unto the Myrmidons' hero-king.

[863] Nor stayed the immortal steeds of Aeacus' son tearless beside the ships; they also mourned their slain king: sorely loth were they to abide longer mid mortal men or Argive steeds bearing a burden of consuming grief; but fain were they to soar through air, afar from wretched men, over the Ocean's streams, over the Sea-queen's caverns, unto where divine Podarge bare that storm-foot twain begotten of the West-wind clarion-voiced. Yea, and they had accomplished their desire, but the Gods' purpose held them back, until from Scyros' isle Achilles' fleetfoot son should come. Him waited they to welcome, when he came unto the war-host; for the Fates, daughters of holy Chaos, at their birth had spun the life-threads of those deathless foals, even to serve Poseidon first, and next Peleus the dauntless king, Achilles then the invincible, and, after these, the fourth, the mighty-hearted Neoptolemus, whom after death to the Elysian Plain they were to bear, unto the Blessed Land, by Zeus' decree. For which cause, though their hearts were pierced with bitter anguish, they abode still by the ships, with spirits sorrowing for their old lord, and yearning for the new.

[890] Then from the surge of heavy-plunging seas rose the Earth-shaker. No man saw his feet pace up the strand, but suddenly he stood beside

the Nereid Goddesses, and spake to Thetis, yet for Achilles bowed with grief: "Refrain from endless mourning for thy son. Not with the dead shall he abide, but dwell with Gods, as doth the might of Herakles, and Dionysus ever fair. Not him dread doom shall prison in darkness evermore, nor Hades keep him. To the light of Zeus soon shall he rise; and I will give to him a holy island for my gift: it lies within the Euxine Sea: there evermore a God thy son shall be. The tribes that dwell around shall as mine own self honour him with incense and with steam of sacrifice. Hush thy laments, vex not thine heart with grief."

[908] Then like a wind-breath had he passed away over the sea, when that consoling word was spoken; and a little in her breast revived the spirit of Thetis: and the God brought this to pass thereafter. All the host moved moaning thence, and came unto the ships that brought them o'er from Hellas. Then returned to Helicon the Muses: 'neath the sea, wailing the dear dead, Nereus' Daughters sank.

Book V

[1] So when all other contests had an end, Thetis the Goddess laid down in the midst great-souled Achilles' arms divinely wrought; and all around flashed out the cunning work wherewith the Fire-god overchased the shield fashioned for Aeacus' son, the dauntless-souled.

[7] Inwrought upon that labour of a God were first high heaven and cloudland, and beneath lay earth and sea: the winds, the clouds were there, the moon and sun, each in its several place; there too were all the stars that, fixed in heaven, are borne in its eternal circlings round. Above and through all was the infinite air where to and fro flit birds of slender beak: thou hadst said they lived, and floated on the breeze. Here Tethys' all-embracing arms were wrought, and Ocean's fathomless flow. The outrushing flood of rivers crying to the echoing hills all round, to right, to left, rolled o'er the land.

[20] Round it rose league-long mountain-ridges, haunts of terrible lions and foul jackals: there fierce bears and panthers prowled; with these were seen wild boars that whetted deadly-clashing tusks in grimly-frothing jaws. There hunters sped after the hounds: beaters with stone and

dart, to the life portrayed, toiled in the woodland sport.

[27] And there were man-devouring wars, and all horrors of fight: slain men were falling down mid horse-hoofs; and the likeness of a plain blood-drenched was on that shield invincible. Panic was there, and Dread, and ghastly Enyo with limbs all gore-bespattered hideously, and deadly Strife, and the Avenging Spirits fierce-hearted—she, still goading warriors on to the onset they, outbreathing breath of fire. Around them hovered the relentless Fates; beside them Battle incarnate onward pressed welling, and from their limbs streamed blood and sweat. There were the ruthless Gorgons: through their hair horribly serpents coiled with flickering tongues. A measureless marvel was that cunning work of things that made men shudder to behold seeming as though they verily lived and moved.

[44] And while here all war's marvels were portrayed, yonder were all the works of lovely peace. The myriad tribes of much-enduring men dwelt in fair cities. Justice watched o'er all. To diverse toils they set their hands; the fields were harvest-laden; earth her increase bore.

[50] Most steeply rose on that god-laboured work the rugged flanks of holy Honour's mount, and there upon a palm-tree throned she sat exalted, and her hands reached up to heaven. All round her, paths broken by many rocks thwarted the climbers' feet; by those steep tracks daunted ye saw returning many folk: few won by sweat of toil the sacred height.

[58] And there were reapers moving down long swaths swinging the whetted sickles: 'neath their hands the hot work sped to its close. Hard after these many sheaf-binders followed, and the work grew passing great. With yoke-bands on their necks oxen were there, whereof some drew the wains heaped high with full-eared sheaves, and further on were others ploughing, and the glebe showed black behind them. Youths with ever-busy goads followed: a world of toil was there portrayed.

[68] And there a banquet was, with pipe and harp, dances of maids, and flashing feet of boys, all in swift movement, like to living souls.

[72] Hard by the dance and its sweet winsomeness out of the sea was rising lovely-crowned Cypris, foam-blossoms still upon her hair; and round her hovered smiling witchingly Desire, and danced the Graces lovely-tressed.

[76] And there were lordly Nereus' Daughters shown leading their sister up from the wide sea to her espousals with the warrior-king. And round her all the Immortals banqueted on Pelion's ridge far-stretching. All about lush dewy watermeads there were, bestarred with flowers innumerable, grassy groves, and springs with clear transparent water bright.

[84] There ships with sighing sheets swept o'er the sea, some beating up to windward, some that sped before a following wind, and round them heaved the melancholy surge. Seared shipmen rushed this way and that, adread for tempest-gusts, hauling the white sails in, to 'scape the death—it all seemed real—some tugging at the oars, while the dark sea on either side the ship grew hoary 'neath the swiftly-plashing blades.

[93] And there triumphant the Earth-shaker rode amid sea-monsters' stormy-footed steeds drew him, and seemed alive, as o'er the deep they raced, oft smitten by the golden whip. Around their path of flight the waves fell smooth, and all before them was unrippled calm. Dolphins on either hand about their king swarmed, in wild rapture of homage bowing backs, and seemed like live things o'er the hazy sea swimming, albeit all of silver wrought.

[103] Marvels of untold craft were imaged there by cunning-souled Hephaestus' deathless hands upon the shield. And Ocean's fathomless flood clasped like a garland all the outer rim, and compassed all the strong shield's curious work.

[108] And therebeside the massy helmet lay. Zeus in his wrath was set upon the crest throned on heaven's dome; the Immortals all around fierce-battling with the Titans fought for Zeus. Already were their foes enwrapped with flame, for thick and fast as snowflakes poured from heaven the thunderbolts: the might of Zeus was roused, and burning giants seemed to breathe out flames.

[116] And therebeside the fair strong corslet lay, unpierceable, which clasped Peleides once: there were the greaves close-lapping, light alone to Achilles; massy of mould and huge they were.

[120] And hard by flashed the sword whose edge and point no mail could turn, with golden belt, and sheath of silver, and with haft of ivory: brightest amid those wondrous arms it shone. Stretched on the earth thereby was that dread spear, long as the tall-tressed pines of Pelion, still

670

breathing out the reek of Hector's blood.

[127] Then mid the Argives Thetis sable-stoled in her deep sorrow for Achilles spake: "Now all the athlete-prizes have been won which I set forth in sorrow for my child. Now let that mightiest of the Argives come who rescued from the foe my dead: to him these glorious and immortal arms I give which even the blessed Deathless joyed to see."

[135] Then rose in rivalry, each claiming them, Laertes' seed and god-like Telamon's son, Aias, the mightiest far of Danaan men: he seemed the star that in the glittering sky outshines the host of heaven, Hesperus, so splendid by Peleides' arms he stood; "And let these judge," he cried, "Idomeneus, Nestor, and kingly-counselled Agamemnon," for these, he weened, would sureliest know the truth of deeds wrought in that glorious battle-toil. "To these I also trust most utterly," Odysseus said, "for prudent of their wit be these, and princeliest of all Danaan men."

[148] But to Idomeneus and Atreus' son spake Nestor apart, and willingly they heard: "Friends, a great woe and unendurable this day the careless Gods have laid on us, in that into this lamentable strife Aias the mighty hath been thrust by them against Odysseus passing-wise. For he, to whichsoe'er God gives the victor's glory—O yea, he shall rejoice! But he that loseth—all for the grief in all the Danaans' hearts for him! And ours shall be the deepest grief of all; for that man will not in the war stand by us as of old. A sorrowful day it shall be for us, whichsoe'er of these shall break into fierce anger, seeing they are of our heroes chiefest, this in war, and that in counsel. Hearken then to me, seeing that I am older far than ye, not by a few years only: with mine age is prudence joined, for I have suffered and wrought much; and in counsel ever the old man, who knoweth much, excelleth younger men. Therefore let us ordain to judge this cause 'twixt godlike Aias and war-fain Odysseus, our Trojan captives. They shall say whom most our foes dread, and who saved Peleides' corpse from that most deadly fight. Lo, in our midst be many spear-won Trojans, thralls of Fate; and these will pass true judgment on these twain, to neither showing favour, since they hate alike all authors of their misery."

[179] He spake: replied Agamemnon lord of spears: "Ancient, there is none other in our midst wiser than thou, of Danaans young or old, in that thou say'st that unforgiving wrath will burn in him to whom the Gods herein deny the victory; for these which strive are both our chiefest.

Therefore mine heart too is set on this, that to the thralls of war thi
judgment we commit: the loser then shall against Troy devise his deadly
work of vengeance, and shall not be wroth with us."

[190] He spake, and these three, being of one mind, in hearing o
all men refused to judge judgment so thankless: they would none of it
Therefore they set the high-born sons of Troy there in the midst, spear
thralls although they were, to give just judgment in the warriors' strife
Then in hot anger Aias rose, and spake: "Odysseus, frantic soul, why
hath a God deluded thee, to make thee hold thyself my peer in might in
vincible? Dar'st thou say that thou, when slain Achilles lay in dust, wher
round him swarmed the Trojans, didst bear back that furious throng
when I amidst them hurled death, and thou coweredst away? Thy dam
bare thee a craven and a weakling wretch frail in comparison of me, as
is a cur beside a lion thunder-voiced! No battle-biding heart is in thy
breast, but wiles and treachery be all thy care. Hast thou forgotten how
thou didst shrink back from faring with Achaea's gathered host to Ilium's
holy burg, till Atreus' sons forced thee, the cowering craven, how loth
soe'er, to follow them—would God thou hadst never come! For by thy
counsel left we in Lemnos' isle groaning in agony Poeas' son renowned.
And not for him alone was ruin devised of thee; for godlike Palamedes
too didst thou contrive destruction—ha, he was alike in battle and council
better than thou! And now thou dar'st to rise up against me, neither re-
membering my kindness, nor having respect unto the mightier man who
rescued thee erewhile, when thou didst quaff in fight before the onset of
thy foes, when thou, forsaken of all Greeks beside, midst tumult of the
fray, wast fleeing too! Oh that in that great fight Zeus' self had stayed
my dauntless might with thunder from his heaven! Then with their two-
edged swords the Trojan men had hewn thee limb from limb, and to
their dogs had cast thy carrion! Then thou hadst not presumed to meet
me, trusting in thy trickeries! Wretch, wherefore, if thou vauntest thee
in might beyond all others, hast thou set thy ships in the line's centre,
screened from foes, nor dared as I, on the far wing to draw them up? Be-
cause thou wast afraid! Not thou it was who savedst from devouring fire
the ships; but I with heart unquailing there stood fast facing the fire and
Hector ay, even he gave back before me everywhere in fight. Thou—thou
didst fear him aye with deadly fear! Oh, had this our contention been but
set amidst that very battle, when the roar of conflict rose around Achil-
les slain! Then had thine own eyes seen me bearing forth out from the
battle's heart and fury of foes that goodly armour and its hero lord unto
the tents. But here thou canst but trust in cunning speech, and covetest a

place amongst the mighty! Thou—thou hast not strength to wear Achilles' arms invincible, nor sway his massy spear in thy weak hands! But I they are verily moulded to my frame: yea, seemly it is I wear those glorious arms, who shall not shame a God's gifts passing fair. But wherefore for Achilles' glorious arms with words discourteous wrangling stand we here? Come, let us try in strife with brazen spears who of us twain is best in murderous right! For silver-footed Thetis set in the midst this prize for prowess, not for pestilent words. In folkmote may men have some use for words: in pride of prowess I know me above thee far, and great Achilles' lineage is mine own."

[276] He spake: with scornful glance and bitter speech Odysseus the resourceful chode with him: "Aias, unbridled tongue, why these vain words to me? Thou hast called me pestilent, niddering, and weakling: yet I boast me better far than thou in wit and speech, which things increase the strength of men. Lo, how the craggy rock, adamantine though it seem, the hewers of stone amid the hills by wisdom undermine full lightly, and by wisdom shipmen cross the thunderous-plunging sea, when mountain-high it surgeth, and by craft do hunters quell strong lions, panthers, boars, yea, all the brood of wild things. Furious-hearted bulls are tamed to bear the yoke-bands by device of men. Yea, all things are by wit accomplished. Still it is the man who knoweth that excels the witless man alike in toils and counsels. For my keen wit did Oeneus' valiant son choose me of all men with him to draw nigh to Hector's watchmen: yea, and mighty deeds we twain accomplished. I it was who brought to Atreus' sons Peleides far-renowned, their battle-helper. Whensoe'er the host needeth some other champion, not for the sake of thine hands will he come, nor by the rede of other Argives: of Achaeans I alone will draw him with soft suasive words to where strong men are warring. Mighty power the tongue hath over men, when courtesy inspires it. Valour is a deedless thing; and bulk and big assemblage of a man cometh to naught, by wisdom unattended. But unto me the Immortals gave both strength and wisdom, and unto the Argive host made me a blessing. Nor, as thou hast said, hast thou in time past saved me when in flight from foes. I never fled, but steadfastly withstood the charge of all the Trojan host. Furious the enemy came on like a flood but I by might of hands cut short the thread of many lives. Herein thou sayest not true; me in the fray thou didst not shield nor save, but for thine own life roughtest, lest a spear should pierce thy back if thou shouldst turn to flee from war. My ships? I drew them up mid-line, not dreading the battle-fury of any foe, but to bring healing unto Atreus' sons of war's calamities: and thou didst

set far from their help thy ships. Nay more, I seamed with cruel stripes my body, and entered so the Trojans' burg, that I might learn of them all their devisings for this troublous war. Nor ever I dreaded Hector's spear; myself rose mid the foremost, eager for the fight, when, prowess-confident, he defied us all. Yea, in the fight around Achilles, I slew foes far more than thou; 'twas I who saved the dead king with this armour. Not a whit I dread thy spear now, but my grievous hurt with pain still vexeth me, the wound I gat in fighting for these arms and their slain lord. In me as in Achilles is Zeus' blood."

[339] He spake; strong Aias answered him again: "Most cunning and most pestilent of men, nor I, nor any other Argive, saw thee toiling in that fray, when Trojans strove fiercely to hale away Achilles slain. My might it was that with the spear unstrung the knees of some in fight, and others thrilled with panic as they pressed on ceaselessly. Then fled they in dire straits, as geese or cranes flee from an eagle swooping as they feed along a grassy meadow; so, in dread the Trojans shrinking backward from my spear and lightening sword, fled into Ilium to 'scape destruction. If thy might came there ever at all, not anywhere nigh me with foes thou foughtest: somewhere afar mid other ranks thou toiledst, nowhere nigh Achilles, where the one great battle raged."

[357] He spake; replied Odysseus the shrewd heart: "Aias, I hold myself no worse than thou in wit or might, how goodly in outward show thou be soever. Nay, I am keener far of wit than thou in all the Argives' eyes. In battle-prowess do I equal thee haply surpass; and this the Trojans know, who tremble when they see me from afar. Aye, thou too know'st, and others know my strength by that hard struggle in the wrestling-match, when Peleus' son set glorious prizes forth beside the barrow of Patroclus slain."

[369] So spake Laertes' son the world-renowned. Then on that strife disastrous of the strong the sons of Troy gave judgment. Victory and those immortal arms awarded they with one consent to Odysseus mighty in war. Greatly his soul rejoiced; but one deep groan brake from the Greeks. Then Aias' noble might stood frozen stiff; and suddenly fell on him dark wilderment; all blood within his frame boiled, and his gall swelled, bursting forth in flood. Against his liver heaved his bowels; his heart with anguished pangs was thrilled; fierce stabbing throes shot through the filmy veil 'twixt bone and brain; and darkness and confusion wrapped his mind. With fixed eyes staring on the ground he stood still

as a statue. Then his sorrowing friends closed round him, led him to the shapely ships, aye murmuring consolations. But his feet trod for the last time, with reluctant steps, that path; and hard behind him followed Doom.

[389] When to the ships beside the boundless sea the Argives, faint for supper and for sleep, had passed, into the great deep Thetis plunged, and all the Nereids with her. Round them swam sea-monsters many, children of the brine.

[394] Against the wise Prometheus bitter-wroth the Sea-maids were, remembering how that Zeus, moved by his prophecies, unto Peleus gave Thetis to wife, a most unwilling bride. Then cried in wrath to these Cymothoe: "O that the pestilent prophet had endured all pangs he merited, when, deep-burrowing, the eagle tare his liver aye renewed!"

[402] So to the dark-haired Sea-maids cried the Nymph. Then sank the sun: the onrush of the night shadowed the fields, the heavens were star-bestrewn; and by the long-prowed ships the Argives slept by ambrosial sleep o'ermastered, and by wine the which from proud Idomeneus' realm of Crete the shipmen bare o'er foaming leagues of sea.

[409] But Aias, wroth against the Argive men, would none of meat or drink, nor clasped him round the arms of sleep. In fury he donned his mail, he clutched his sword, thinking unspeakable thoughts; for now he thought to set the ships aflame, and slaughter all the Argives, now, to hew with sudden onslaught of his terrible sword guileful Odysseus limb from limb. Such things he purposed—nay, had soon accomplished all, had Pallas not with madness smitten him; for over Odysseus, strong to endure, her heart yearned, as she called to mind the sacrifices offered to her of him continually. Therefore she turned aside from Argive men the might of Aias. As a terrible storm, whose wings are laden with dread hurricane-blasts, cometh with portents of heart-numbing fear to shipmen, when the Pleiads, fleeing adread from glorious Orion, plunge beneath the stream of tireless Ocean, when the air is turmoil, and the sea is mad with storm; so rushed he, whithersoe'er his feet might bear. This way and that he ran, like some fierce beast which darteth down a rock-walled glen's ravines with foaming jaws, and murderous intent against the hounds and huntsmen, who have torn out of the cave her cubs, and slain: she runs this way and that, and roars, if mid the brakes haply she yet may see the dear ones lost; whom if a man meet in that

maddened mood, straightway his darkest of all days hath dawned; so
ruthless-raving rushed he; blackly boiled his heart, as cauldron on the
Fire-god's hearth maddens with ceaseless hissing o'er the flames from
blazing billets coiling round its sides, at bidding of the toiler eager-souled
to singe the bristles of a huge-fed boar; so was his great heart boiling in
his breast. Like a wild sea he raved, like tempest-blast, like the wingèd
might of tireless flame amidst the mountains maddened by a mighty
wind, when the wide-blazing forest crumbles down in fervent heat. So
Aias, his fierce heart with agony stabbed, in maddened misery raved.
Foam frothed about his lips; a beast-like roar howled from his throat.
About his shoulders clashed his armour. They which saw him trembled,
all cowed by the fearful shout of that one man.

[457] From Ocean then uprose Dawn golden-reined: like a soft wind
upfloated Sleep to heaven, and there met Hera, even then returned to
Olympus back from Tethys, unto whom but yester-morn she went. She
clasped him round, and kissed him, who had been her marriage-kin since
at her prayer on Ida's crest he had lulled to sleep Cronion, when his anger
burned against the Argives. Straightway Hera passed to Zeus's mansion,
and Sleep swiftly flew to Pasithea's couch. From slumber woke all na-
tions of the earth. But Aias, like Orion the invincible, prowled on, still
bearing murderous madness in his heart. He rushed upon the sheep, like
lion fierce whose savage heart is stung with hunger-pangs. Here, there, he
smote them, laid them dead in dust thick as the leaves which the strong
North-wind's might strews, when the waning year to winter turns; so on
the sheep in fury Aias fell, deeming he dealt to Danaans evil doom.

[478] Then to his brother Menelaus came, and spake, but not in hear-
ing of the rest: "This day shall surely be a ruinous day for all, since Aias
thus is sense-distraught. It may be he will set the ships aflame, and slay us
all amidst our tents, in wrath for those lost arms. Would God that Thetis
ne'er had set them for the prize of rivalry! Would God Laertes' son had
not presumed in folly of soul to strive with a better man! Fools were we
all; and some malignant God beguiled us; for the one great war-defense
left us, since Aeacus' son in battle fell, was Aias' mighty strength. And
now the Gods will to our loss destroy him, bringing bane on thee and
me, that all we may fill up the cup of doom, and pass to nothingness."

[495] He spake; replied Agamemnon, lord of spears: "Now nay, Mene-
laus, though thine heart he wrung, be thou not wroth with the resourceful

king of Cephallenian folk, but with the Gods who plot our ruin. Blame not him, who oft hath been our blessing and our enemies' curse."

[501] So heavy-hearted spake the Danaan kings. But by the streams of Xanthus far away 'neath tamarisks shepherds cowered to hide from death, as when from a swift eagle cower hares 'neath tangled copses, when with sharp fierce scream this way and that with wings wide-shadowing he wheeleth very nigh; so they here, there, quailed from the presence of that furious man. At last above a slaughtered ram he stood, and with a deadly laugh he cried to it: "Lie there in dust; be meat for dogs and kites! Achilles' glorious arms have saved not thee, for which thy folly strove with a better man! Lie there, thou cur! No wife shall fall on thee, and clasp, and wail thee and her fatherless childs, nor shalt thou greet thy parents' longing eyes, the staff of their old age! Far from thy land thy carrion dogs and vultures shall devour!"

[519] So cried he, thinking that amidst the slain Odysseus lay blood-boltered at his feet. But in that moment from his mind and eyes Athena tore away the nightmare-fiend of Madness havoc-breathing, and it passed thence swiftly to the rock-walled river Styx where dwell the winged Erinnyes, they which still visit with torments overweening men.

[527] Then Aias saw those sheep upon the earth gasping in death; and sore amazed he stood, for he divined that by the Blessed Ones his senses had been cheated. All his limbs failed under him; his soul was anguished-thrilled: he could not in his horror take one step forward nor backward. Like some towering rock fast-rooted mid the mountains, there he stood. But when the wild rout of his thoughts had rallied, he groaned in misery, and in anguish wailed: "Ah me! why do the Gods abhor me so? They have wrecked my mind, have with fell madness filled, making me slaughter all these innocent sheep! Would God that on Odysseus' pestilent heart mine hands had so avenged me! Miscreant, he brought on me a fell curse! O may his soul suffer all torments that the Avenging Fiends devise for villains! On all other Greeks may they bring murderous battle, woeful griefs, and chiefly on Agamemnon, Atreus' son! Not scatheless to the home may he return so long desired! But why should I consort, I, a brave man, with the abominable? Perish the Argive host, perish my life, now unendurable! The brave no more hath his due guerdon, but the baser sort are honoured most and loved, as this Odysseus hath worship mid the Greeks: but utterly have they forgotten me and all my deeds, all

that I wrought and suffered in their cause."

[557] So spake the brave son of strong Telamon, then thrust the sword of Hector through his throat. Forth rushed the blood in torrent: in the dust outstretched he lay, like Typhon, when the bolts of Zeus had blasted him. Around him groaned the dark earth as he fell upon her breast.

[562] Then thronging came the Danaans, when they saw low laid in dust the hero; but ere then none dared draw nigh him, but in deadly fear they watched him from afar. Now hasted they and flung themselves upon the dead, outstretched upon their faces: on their heads they cast dust, and their wailing went up to the sky. As when men drive away the tender lambs out of the fleecy flock, to feast thereon, and round the desolate pens the mothers leap ceaselessly bleating, so o'er Aias rang that day a very great and bitter cry. Wild echoes pealed from Ida forest-palled, and from the plain, the ships, the boundless sea.

[577] Then Teucer clasping him was minded too to rush on bitter doom: howbeit the rest held from the sword his hand. Anguished he fell upon the dead, outpouring many a tear more comfortlessly than the orphan babe that wails beside the hearth, with ashes strewn on head and shoulders, wails bereavement's day that brings death to the mother who hath nursed the fatherless child; so wailed he, ever wailed his great death-stricken brother, creeping slow around the corpse, and uttering his lament: "O Aias, mighty-souled, why was thine heart distraught, that thou shouldst deal unto thyself murder and bale? All, was it that the sons of Troy might win a breathing-space from woes, might come and slay the Greeks, now thou art not? From these shall all the olden courage fail when fast they fall in fight. Their shield from harm is broken now! For me, I have no will to see mine home again, now thou art dead. Nay, but I long here also now to die, that so the earth may shroud me—me and thee not for my parents so much do I care, if haply yet they live, if haply yet spared from the grave, in Salamis they dwell, as for thee, O my glory and my crown!"

[603] So cried he groaning sore; with answering moan queenly Tecmessa wailed, the princess-bride of noble Aias, captive of his spear, yet ta'en by him to wife, and household-queen o'er all his substance, even all that wives won with a bride-price rule for wedded lords. Clasped in his mighty arms, she bare to him a son Eurysaces, in all things like unto his father, far as babe might be yet cradled in his tent. With bitter moan

fell she on that dear corpse, all her fair form close-shrouded in her veil, and dust-defiled, and from her anguished heart cried piteously: "Alas for me, for me now thou art dead, not by the hands of foes in fight struck down, but by thine own! On me is come a grief ever-abiding! Never had I looked to see thy woeful death-day here by Troy. Ah, visions shattered by rude hands of Fate! Oh that the earth had yawned wide for my grave ere I beheld thy bitter doom! On me no sharper, more heart-piercing pang hath come—no, not when first from fatherland afar and parents thou didst bear me, wailing sore mid other captives, when the day of bondage had come on me, a princess theretofore. Not for that dear lost home so much I grieve, nor for my parents dead, as now for thee: for all thine heart was kindness unto me the hapless, and thou madest me thy wife, one soul with thee; yea, and thou promisedst to throne me queen of fair-towered Salamis, when home we won from Troy. The Gods denied accomplishment thereof. And thou hast passed unto the Unseen Land: thou hast forgot me and thy child, who never shall make glad his father's heart, shall never mount thy throne. But him shall strangers make a wretched thrall: for when the father is no more, the babe is ward of meaner men. A weary life the orphan knows, and suffering cometh in from every side upon him like a flood. To me too thraldom's day shall doubtless come, now thou hast died, who wast my god on earth."

[647] Then in all kindness Agamemnon spake: "Princess, no man on earth shall make thee thrall, while Teucer liveth yet, while yet I live. Thou shalt have worship of us evermore and honour as a Goddess, with thy son, as though yet living were that godlike man, Aias, who was the Achaeans' chiefest strength. Ah that he had not laid this load of grief on all, in dying by his own right hand! For all the countless armies of his foes never availed to slay him in fair fight."

[658] So spake he, grieved to the inmost heart. The folk woefully wafted all round. O'er Hellespont echoes of mourning rolled: the sighing air darkened around, a wide-spread sorrow-pall. Yea, grief laid hold on wise Odysseus' self for the great dead, and with remorseful soul to anguish-stricken Argives thus he spake: "O friends, there is no greater curse to men than wrath, which groweth till its bitter fruit is strife. Now wrath hath goaded Aias on to this dire issue of the rage that filled his soul against me. Would to God that ne'er yon Trojans in the strife for Achilles' arms had crowned me with that victory, for which strong Telamon's brave son, in agony of soul, thus perished by his own right hand! Yet blame not me, I pray you, for his wrath: blame the dark dolorous Fate

that struck him down. For, had mine heart foreboded aught of this, this desperation of a soul distraught, never for victory had I striven with him, nor had I suffered any Danaan else, though ne'er so eager, to contend with him. Nay, I had taken up those arms divine with mine own hands, and gladly given them to him, ay, though himself desired it not. But for such mighty grief and wrath in him I had not looked, since not for a woman's sake nor for a city, nor possessions wide, I then contended, but for Honour's meed, which alway is for all right-hearted men the happy goal of all their rivalry. But that great-hearted man was led astray by Fate, the hateful fiend; for surely it is unworthy a man to be made passion's fool. The wise man's part is, steadfast-souled to endure all ills, and not to rage against his lot."

[695] So spake Laertes' son, the far-renowned. But when they all were weary of grief and groan, then to those sorrowing ones spake Neleus' son: "O friends, the pitiless-hearted Fates have laid stroke after stroke of sorrow upon us, sorrow for Aias dead, for mighty Achilles, for many an Argive, and for mine own son Antilochus. Yet all unmeet it is day after day with passion of grief to wail men slain in battle: nay, we must forget laments, and turn us to the better task of rendering dues beseeming to the dead, the dues of pyre, of tomb, of bones inurned. No lamentations will awake the dead; no note thereof he taketh, when the Fates, the ruthless ones, have swallowed him in night."

[711] So spake he words of cheer: the godlike kings gathered with heavy hearts around the dead, and many hands upheaved the giant corpse, and swiftly bare him to the ships, and there washed they away the blood that clotted lay dust-flecked on mighty limbs and armour: then in linen swathed him round. From Ida's heights wood without measure did the young men bring, and piled it round the corpse. Billets and logs yet more in a wide circle heaped they round; and sheep they laid thereon, fair-woven vests, and goodly kine, and speed-triumphant steeds, and gleaming gold, and armour without stint, from slain foes by that glorious hero stripped. And lucent amber-drops they laid thereon, tears, say they, which the Daughters of the Sun, the Lord of Omens, shed for Phaethon slain, when by Eridanus' flood they mourned for him. These, for undying honour to his son, the God made amber, precious in men's eyes. Even this the Argives on that broad-based pyre cast freely, honouring the mighty dead. And round him, groaning heavily, they laid silver most fair and precious ivory, and jars of oil, and whatsoe'er beside they have who heap up goodly and glorious wealth. Then thrust they in the

strength of ravening flame, and from the sea there breathed a wind, sent forth by Thetis, to consume the giant frame of Aias. All the night and all the morn burned 'neath the urgent stress of that great wind beside the ships that giant form, as when Enceladus by Zeus' levin was consumed beneath Thrinacia, when from all the isle smoke of his burning rose—or like as when Hercules, trapped by Nessus' deadly guile, gave to devouring fire his living limbs, what time he dared that awful deed, when groaned all Oeta as he burned alive, and passed his soul into the air, leaving the man far-famous, to be numbered with the Gods, when earth closed o'er his toil-tried mortal part. So huge amid the flames, all-armour clad, lay Aias, all the joy of fight forgot, while a great multitude watching thronged the sands. Glad were the Trojans, but the Achaeans grieved.

[657] But when that goodly frame by ravening fire was all consumed, they quenched the pyre with wine; they gathered up the bones, and reverently laid in a golden casket. Hard beside Rhoeteium's headland heaped they up a mound measureless-high. Then scattered they amidst the long ships, heavy-hearted for the man whom they had honoured even as Achilles. Then black night, bearing unto all men sleep, upfloated: so they brake bread, and lay down waiting the Child of the Mist. Short was sleep, broken by fitful staring through the dark, haunted by dread lest in the night the foe should fall on them, now Telamon's son was dead.

Book XII

When round the walls of Troy the Danaan host had borne much travail, and yet the end was not, by Calchas then assembled were the chiefs; for his heart was instructed by the hests of Phoebus, by the flights of birds, the stars, and all the signs that speak to men the will of Heaven; so he to that assembly cried: "No longer toil in siege of yon walls; some other counsel let your hearts devise, some stratagem to help the host and us. For here but yesterday I saw a sign: a falcon chased a dove, and she, hard pressed, entered a cleft of the rock; and chafing he tarried long time hard by that rift, but she abode in covert. Nursing still his wrath, he hid him in a bush. Forth darted she, in folly deeming him afar: he swooped, and to the hapless dove dealt wretched death. Therefore by force essay we not to smite Troy, but let cunning stratagem avail."

[21] He spake; but no man's wit might find a way to escape their griev-

ous travail, as they sought to find a remedy, till Laertes' son discerned i
of his wisdom, and he spake: "Friend, in high honour held of the Heav-
enly Ones, if doomed it be indeed that Priam's burg by guile must fal
before the war-worn Greeks, a great Horse let us fashion, in the which
our mightiest shall take ambush. Let the host burn all their tents, and sai
from hence away to Tenedos; so the Trojans, from their towers gazing,
shall stream forth fearless to the plain. Let some brave man, unknown
of any in Troy, with a stout heart abide without the Horse, crouching
beneath its shadow, who shall say: "Achaea's lords of might, exceeding
fain safe to win home, made this their offering for safe return, an image
to appease the wrath of Pallas for her image stolen from Troy.' And to
this story shall he stand, how long soe'er they question him, until, though
never so relentless, they believe, and drag it, their own doom, within the
town. Then shall war's signal unto us be given—to them at sea, by sudden
flash of torch, to the ambush, by the cry, 'Come forth the Horse!' when
unsuspecting sleep the sons of Troy."

[48] He spake, and all men praised him: most of all extolled him Cal-
chas, that such marvellous guile he put into the Achaeans' hearts, to be
for them assurance of triumph, but for Troy ruin; and to those bat-
tle-lords he cried: "Let your hearts seek none other stratagem, friends; to
war-strong Odysseus' rede give ear. His wise thought shall not miss ac-
complishment. Yea, our desire even now the Gods fulfil. Hark! for new
tokens come from the Unseen! Lo, there on high crash through the fir-
mament Zeus' thunder and lightning! See, where birds to right dart past,
and scream with long-resounding cry! Go to, no more in endless leaguer
of Troy linger we. Hard necessity fills the foe with desperate courage that
makes cowards brave; for then are men most dangerous, when they stake
their lives in utter recklessness of death, as battle now the aweless sons
of Troy all round their burg, mad with the lust of fight."

[68] But cried Achilles' battle-eager son: "Calchas, brave men meet face
to face their foes! Who skulk behind their walls, and fight from towers,
are nidderings, hearts palsied with base fear. Hence with all thought of
wile and stratagem! The great war-travail of the spear beseems true he-
roes. Best in battle are the brave."

[75] But answer made to him Laertes' seed: "Bold-hearted child of
aweless Aeacus' son, this as beseems a hero princely and brave, daunt-
lessly trusting in thy strength, thou say'st. Yet thine invincible sire's un-
quailing might availed not to smite Priam's wealthy burg, nor we, for all

our travail. Nay, with speed, as counselleth Calchas, go we to the ships, and fashion we the Horse by Epeius' hands, who in the woodwright's craft is chiefest far of Argives, for Athena taught his lore."

[86] Then all their mightiest men gave ear to him save twain, fierce-hearted Neoptolemus and Philoctetes mighty-souled; for these still were insatiate for the bitter fray, still longed for turmoil of the fight. They bade their own folk bear against that giant wall what things soe'er for war's assaults avail, in hope to lay that stately fortress low, seeing Heaven's decrees had brought them both to war. Yea, they had haply accomplished all their will, but from the sky Zeus showed his wrath; he shook the earth beneath their feet, and all the air shuddered, as down before those heroes twain he hurled his thunderbolt: wide echoes crashed through all Dardania. Unto fear straightway turned were their bold hearts: they forgat their might, and Calchas' counsels grudgingly obeyed. So with the Argives came they to the ships in reverence for the seer who spake from Zeus or Phoebus, and they obeyed him utterly.

[106] What time round splendour-kindled heavens the stars from east to west far-flashing wheel, and when man doth forget his toil, in that still hour Athena left the high mansions of the Blest, clothed her in shape of a maiden tender-fleshed, and came to ships and host. Over the head of brave Epeius stood she in his dream, and bade him build a Horse of tree: herself would labour in his labour, and herself stand by his side, to the work enkindling him. Hearing the Goddess' word, with a glad laugh leapt he from careless sleep: right well he knew the Immortal One celestial. Now his heart could hold no thought beside; his mind was fixed upon the wondrous work, and through his soul marched marshalled each device of craftsmanship.

[122] When rose the dawn, and thrust back kindly night to Erebus, and through the firmament streamed glad glory, then Epeius told his dream to eager Argives—all he saw and heard; and hearkening joyed they with exceeding joy. Straightway to tall-tressed Ida's leafy glades the sons of Atreus sent swift messengers. These laid the axe unto the forest-pines, and hewed the great trees: to their smiting rang the echoing glens. On those far-stretching hills all bare of undergrowth the high peaks rose: open their glades were, not, as in time past, haunted of beasts: there dry the tree-trunks rose wooing the winds. Even these the Achaeans hewed with axes, and in haste they bare them down from those shagged mountain heights to Hellespont's shores. Strained with a strenuous spirit at

the work young men and mules; and all the people toiled each at his task obeying Epeius's hest. For with the keen steel some were hewing beams, some measuring planks, and some with axes lopped branches away from trunks as yet unsawn: each wrought his several work. Epeius first fashioned the feet of that great Horse of Wood: the belly next he shaped, and over this moulded the back and the great loins behind, the throat in front, and ridged the towering neck with waving mane: the crested head he wrought, the streaming tail, the ears, the lucent eyes—all that of lifelike horses have. So grew like a live thing that more than human work, for a God gave to a man that wondrous craft. And in three days, by Pallas's decree, finished was all. Rejoiced thereat the host of Argos, marvelling how the wood expressed mettle, and speed of foot—yea, seemed to neigh. Godlike Epeius then uplifted hands to Pallas, and for that huge Horse he prayed: "Hear, great-souled Goddess: bless thine Horse and me!" He spake: Athena rich in counsel heard, and made his work a marvel to all men which saw, or heard its fame in days to be.

[164] But while the Danaans o'er Epeius' work joyed, and their routed foes within the walls tarried, and shrank from death and pitiless doom, then, when imperious Zeus far from the Gods had gone to Ocean's streams and Tethys' caves, strife rose between the Immortals: heart with heart was set at variance. Riding on the blasts of winds, from heaven to earth they swooped: the air crashed round them. Lighting down by Xanthus' stream arrayed they stood against each other, these for the Achaeans, for the Trojans those; and all their souls were thrilled with lust of war: there gathered too the Lords of the wide Sea. These in their wrath were eager to destroy the Horse of Guile and all the ships, and those fair Ilium. But all-contriving Fate held them therefrom, and turned their hearts to strife against each other. Ares to the fray rose first, and on Athena rushed. Thereat fell each on other: clashed around their limbs the golden arms celestial as they charged. Round them the wide sea thundered, the dark earth quaked 'neath immortal feet. Rang from them all far-pealing battle-shouts; that awful cry rolled up to the broad-arching heaven, and down even to Hades' fathomless abyss: trembled the Titans there in depths of gloom. Ida's long ridges sighed, sobbed clamorous streams of ever-flowing rivers, groaned ravines far-furrowed, Argive ships, and Priam's towers. Yet men feared not, for naught they knew of all that strife, by Heaven's decree. Then her high peaks the Gods' hands wrenched from Ida's crest, and hurled against each other: but like crumbling sands shivered they fell round those invincible limbs, shattered to small dust. But the mind of Zeus, at the utmost verge of earth, was ware

of all: straight left he Ocean's stream, and to wide heaven ascended, char-
ioted upon the winds, the East, the North, the West-wind, and the South:
for Iris rainbow-plumed led 'neath the yoke of his eternal ear that stormy
team, the ear which Time the immortal framed for him of adamant with
never-wearying hands. So came he to Olympus' giant ridge. His wrath
shook all the firmament, as crashed from east to west his thunders; light-
nings gleamed, as thick and fast his thunderbolts poured to earth, and
flamed the limitless heaven. Terror fell upon the hearts of those Im-
mortals: quaked the limbs of all—ay, deathless though they were! Then
Themis, trembling for them, swift as thought leapt down through clouds,
and came with speed to them—for in the strife she only had no part and
stood between the fighters, and she cried: "Forbear the conflict! O, when
Zeus is wroth, it ill beseems that everlasting Gods should fight for men's
sake, creatures of a day: Else shall ye be all suddenly destroyed; for Zeus
will tear up all the hills, and hurl upon you: sons nor daughters will he
spare, but bury 'neath one ruin of shattered earth all. No escape shall ye
find thence to light, in horror of darkness prisoned evermore."

[228] Dreading Zeus' menace gave they heed to her, from strife re-
frained, and cast away their wrath, and were made one in peace and ami-
ty. Some heavenward soared, some plunged into the sea, on earth stayed
some. Amid the Achaean host spake in his subtlety Laertes' son: "O
valorous-hearted lords of the Argive host, now prove in time of need
what men ye be, how passing-strong, how flawless-brave! The hour is
this for desperate emprise: now, with hearts heroic, enter ye yon carven
horse, so to attain the goal of this stern war. For better it is by stratagem
and craft now to destroy this city, for whose sake hither we came, and still
are suffering many afflictions far from our own land. Come then, and let
your hearts be stout and strong for he who in stress of fight hath turned
to bay and snatched a desperate courage from despair, oft, though the
weaker, slays a mightier foe. For courage, which is all men's glory, makes
the heart great. Come then, set the ambush, ye which be our mightiest,
and the rest shall go to Tenedos' hallowed burg, and there abide until our
foes have haled within their walls us with the Horse, as deeming that they
bring a gift unto Tritonis. Some brave man, one whom the Trojans know
not, yet we lack, to harden his heart as steel, and to abide near by the
Horse. Let that man bear in mind heedfully whatsoe'er I said erewhile.
And let none other thought be in his heart, lest to the foe our counsel
be revealed."

[261] Then, when all others feared, a man far-famed made answer,

Sinon, marked of destiny to bring the great work to accomplishment. Therefore with worship all men looked on him, the loyal of heart, as in the midst he spake: "Odysseus, and all ye Achaean chiefs, this work for which ye crave will I perform—yea, though they torture me, though into fire living they thrust me; for mine heart is fixed not to escape, but die by hands of foes, except I crown with glory your desire."

[272] Stoutly he spake: right glad the Argives were; and one said: "How the Gods have given to-day high courage to this man! He hath not been heretofore valiant. Heaven is kindling him to be the Trojans' ruin, but to us salvation. Now full soon, I trow, we reach the goal of grievous war, so long unseen."

[279] So a voice murmured mid the Achaean host. Then, to stir up the heroes, Nestor cried: "Now is the time, dear sons, for courage and strength: now do the Gods bring nigh the end of toil: now give they victory to our longing hands. Come, bravely enter ye this cavernous Horse. For high renown attendeth courage high. Oh that my limbs were mighty as of old, when Aeson's son for heroes called, to man swift Argo, when of the heroes foremost I would gladly have entered her, but Pelias the king withheld me in my own despite. Ah me, but now the burden of years—O nay, as I were young, into the Horse will I fearlessly! Glory and strength shall courage give."

[294] Answered him golden-haired Achilles' son: "Nestor, in wisdom art thou chief of men; but cruel age hath caught thee in his grip: no more thy strength may match thy gallant will; therefore thou needs must unto Tenedos' strand. We will take ambush, we the youths, of strife insatiate still, as thou, old sire, dost bid."

[301] Then strode the son of Neleus to his side, and kissed his hands, and kissed the head of him who offered thus himself the first of all to enter that huge horse, being peril-fain, and bade the elder of days abide without. Then to the battle-eager spake the old: "Thy father's son art thou! Achilles' might and chivalrous speech be here! O, sure am I that by thine hands the Argives shall destroy the stately city of Priam. At the last, after long travail, glory shall be ours, ours, after toil and tribulation of war; the Gods have laid tribulation at men's feet but happiness far off, and toil between: therefore for men full easy is the path to ruin, and the path to fame is hard, where feet must press right on through painful toil."

[318] He spake: replied Achilles' glorious son: "Old sire, as thine heart trusteth, be it vouchsafed in answer to our prayers; for best were this: but if the Gods will otherwise, be it so. Ay, gladlier would I fall with glory in fight than flee from Troy, bowed 'neath a load of shame."

[324] Then in his sire's celestial arms he arrayed his shoulders; and with speed in harness sheathed stood the most mighty heroes, in whose healers was dauntless spirit. Tell, ye Queens of Song, now man by man the names of all that passed into the cavernous Horse; for ye inspired my soul with all my song, long ere my cheek grew dark with manhood's beard, what time I fed my goodly sheep on Smyrna's pasture-lea, from Hermus thrice so far as one may hear a man's shout, by the fane of Artemis, in the Deliverer's Grove, upon a hill neither exceeding low nor passing high.

[337] Into that cavernous Horse Achilles' son first entered, strong Menelaus followed then, Odysseus, Sthenelus, godlike Diomede, Philoctetes and Menestheus, Anticlus, Thoas and Polypoetes golden-haired, Aias, Eurypylus, godlike Thrasymede, Idomeneus, Meriones, far-famous twain, Podaleirius of spears, Eurymachus, Teucer the godlike, fierce Ialmenus, Thalpius, Antimachus, Leonteus staunch, Eumelus, and Euryalus fair as a God, Amphimachus, Demophoon, Agapenor, Akamas, Meges stalwart Phyleus' son—yea, more, even all their chiefest, entered in, so many as that carven Horse could hold. Godlike Epeius last of all passed in, the fashioner of the Horse; in his breast lay the secret of the opening of its doors and of their closing: therefore last of all he entered, and he drew the ladders up whereby they clomb: then made he all secure, and set himself beside the bolt. So all in silence sat 'twixt victory and death.

[360] But the rest fired the tents, wherein erewhile they slept, and sailed the wide sea in their ships. Two mighty-hearted captains ordered these, Nestor and Agamemnon lord of spears. Fain had they also entered that great Horse, but all the host withheld them, bidding stay with them a-shipboard, ordering their array: for men far better work the works of war when their kings oversee them; therefore these abode without, albeit mighty men. So came they swiftly unto Tenedos' shore, and dropped the anchor-stones, then leapt in haste forth of the ships, and silent waited there keen-watching till the signal-torch should flash.

[375] But nigh the foe were they in the Horse, and now looked they for death, and now to smite the town; and on their hopes and fears uprose the dawn.

[378] Then marked the Trojans upon Hellespont's strand the smoke upleaping yet through air: no more saw they the ships which brought to them from Greece destruction dire. With joy to the shore they ran, but armed them first, for fear still haunted them then marked they that fair-carven Horse, and stood marvelling round, for a mighty work was there. A hapless-seeming man thereby they spied, Sinon; and this one, that one questioned him touching the Danaans, as in a great ring they compassed him, and with unangry words first questioned, then with terrible threatenings. Then tortured they that man of guileful soul long time unceasing. Firm as a rock abode the unquivering limbs, the unconquerable will. His ears, his nose, at last they shore away in every wise tormenting him, until he should declare the truth, whither were gone the Danaans in their ships, what thing the Horse concealed within it. He had armed his mind with resolution, and of outrage foul recked not; his soul endured their cruel stripes, yea, and the bitter torment of the fire; for strong endurance into him Hera breathed; and still he told them the same guileful tale: "The Argives in their ships flee oversea weary of tribulation of endless war. This horse by Calchas' counsel fashioned they for wise Athena, to propitiate her stern wrath for that guardian image stol'n from Troy. And by Odysseus' prompting I was marked for slaughter, to be sacrificed to the sea-powers, beside the moaning waves, to win them safe return. But their intent I marked; and ere they spilt the drops of wine, and sprinkled hallowed meal upon mine head, swiftly I fled, and, by the help of Heaven, I flung me down, clasping the Horse's feet; and they, sore loth, perforce must leave me there dreading great Zeus's daughter mighty-souled."

[418] In subtlety so he spake, his soul untamed by pain; for a brave man's part is to endure to the uttermost. And of the Trojans some believed him, others for a wily knave held him, of whose mind was Laocoon. Wisely he spake: "A deadly fraud is this," he said, "devised by the Achaean chiefs!" And cried to all straightway to burn the Horse, and know if aught within its timbers lurked.

[427] Yea, and they had obeyed him, and had 'scaped destruction; but Athena, fiercely wroth with him, the Trojans, and their city, shook earth's deep foundations 'neath Laocoon's feet. Straight terror fell on him, and trembling bowed the knees of the presumptuous: round his head horror of darkness poured; a sharp pang thrilled his eyelids; swam his eyes beneath his brows; his eyeballs, stabbed with bitter anguish, throbbed even from the roots, and rolled in frenzy of pain. Clear through his brain the

bitter torment pierced even to the filmy inner veil thereof; now blood-shot were his eyes, now ghastly green; anon with rheum they ran, as pours a stream down from a rugged crag, with thawing snow made turbid. As a man distraught he seemed: all things he saw showed double, and he groaned fearfully; yet he ceased not to exhort the men of Troy, and recked not of his pain. Then did the Goddess strike him utterly blind. Stared his fixed eyeballs white from pits of blood; and all folk groaned for pity of their friend, and dread of the Prey-giver, lest he had sinned in folly against her, and his mind was thus warped to destruction yea, lest on themselves like judgment should be visited, to avenge the outrage done to hapless Sinon's flesh, whereby they hoped to wring the truth from him. So led they him in friendly wise to Troy, pitying him at the last. Then gathered all, and o'er that huge Horse hastily cast a rope, and made it fast above; for under its feet smooth wooden rollers had Epeius laid, that, dragged by Trojan hands, it might glide on into their fortress. One and all they haled with multitudinous tug and strain, as when down to the sea young men sore-labouring drag a ship; hard-crushed the stubborn rollers groan, as, sliding with weird shrieks, the keel descends into the sea-surge; so that host with toil dragged up unto their city their own doom, Epeius' work. With great festoons of flowers they hung it, and their own heads did they wreathe, while answering each other pealed the flutes. Grimly Enyo laughed, seeing the end of that dire war; Hera rejoiced on high; glad was Athena. When the Trojans came unto their city, brake they down the walls, their city's coronal, that the Horse of Death might be led in. Troy's daughters greeted it with shouts of salutation; marvelling all gazed at the mighty work where lurked their doom.

[479] But still Laocoon ceased not to exhort his countrymen to burn the Horse with fire: they would not hear, for dread of the Gods' wrath. But then a yet more hideous punishment Athena visited on his hapless sons. A cave there was, beneath a rugged cliff exceeding high, unscalable, wherein dwelt fearful monsters of the deadly brood of Typhon, in the rock-clefts of the isle Calydna that looks Troyward from the sea. Thence stirred she up the strength of serpents twain, and summoned them to Troy. By her uproused they shook the island as with earthquake: roared the sea; the waves disparted as they came. Onward they swept with fearful-flickering tongues: shuddered the very monsters of the deep: Xanthus' and Simois' daughters moaned aloud, the River-nymphs: the Cyprian Queen looked down in anguish from Olympus. Swiftly they came whither the Goddess sped them: with grim jaws whetting their deadly fangs, on his hapless sons sprang they. All Trojans panic-stricken fled,

seeing those fearsome dragons in their town. No man, though ne'er so
dauntless theretofore, dared tarry; ghastly dread laid hold on all shrink
ing in horror from the monsters. Screamed the women; yea, the mother
forgat her child, fear-frenzied as she fled: all Troy became one shriek of
fleers, one huddle of jostling limbs: the streets were choked with cower
ing fugitives. Alone was left Laocoon with his sons, for death's doom and
the Goddess chained their feet. Then, even as from destruction shrank
the lads, those deadly fangs had seized and ravined up the twain, out
stretching to their sightless sire agonized hands: no power to help had
he. Trojans far off looked on from every side weeping, all dazed. And
having now fulfilled upon the Trojans Pallas' awful hest, those monsters
vanished 'neath the earth; and still stands their memorial, where into the
fane they entered of Apollo in Pergamus the hallowed. Therebefore the
sons of Troy gathered, and reared a monument for those who miserably
had perished. Over it their father from his blind eyes rained the tears
over the empty tomb their mother shrieked, boding the while yet worse
things, wailing o'er the ruin wrought by folly of her lord, dreading the
anger of the Blessed Ones. As when around her void nest in a brake in
sorest anguish moans the nightingale whose fledglings, ere they learned
her plaintive song, a hideous serpent's fangs have done to death, and left
the mother anguish, endless woe, and bootless crying round her desolate
home; so groaned she for her children's wretched death, so moaned she
o'er the void tomb; and her pangs were sharpened by her lord's plight
stricken blind.

[538] While she for children and for husband moaned—these slain, he
of the sun's light portionless—the Trojans to the Immortals sacrificed
pouring the wine. Their hearts beat high with hope to escape the weary
stress of woeful war. Howbeit the victims burned not, and the flames
died out, as though 'neath heavy-hissing rain; and writhed the smoke-
wreaths blood-red, and the thighs quivering from crumbling altars fell
to earth. Drink-offerings turned to blood, Gods' statues wept, and tem-
ple-walls dripped gore: along them rolled echoes of groaning out of
depths unseen; and all the long walls shuddered: from the towers came
quick sharp sounds like cries of men in pain; and, weirdly shrieking, of
themselves slid back the gate-bolts. Screaming "Desolation!" wailed the
birds of night. Above that God-built burg a mist palled every star; and
yet no cloud was in the flashing heavens. By Phoebus' fane withered the
bays that erst were lush and green. Wolves and foul-feeding jackals came
and howled within the gates. Ay, other signs untold appeared, portending
woe to Dardanus' sons and Troy: yet no fear touched the Trojans' hearts

who saw all through the town those portents dire: Fate crazed them all, that midst their revelling slain by their foes they might fill up their doom.

[565] One heart was steadfast, and one soul clear-eyed, Cassandra. Never her words were unfulfilled; yet was their utter truth, by Fate's decree, ever as idle wind in the hearers' ears, that no bar to Troy's ruin might be set. She saw those evil portents all through Troy conspiring to one end; loud rang her cry, as roars a lioness that mid the brakes a hunter has stabbed or shot, whereat her heart maddens, and down the long hills rolls her roar, and her might waxes tenfold; so with heart aflame with prophecy came she forth her bower. Over her snowy shoulders tossed her hair streaming far down, and wildly blazed her eyes. Her neck writhed, like a sapling in the wind shaken, as moaned and shrieked that noble maid: "O wretches! into the Land of Darkness now we are passing; for all round us full of fire and blood and dismal moan the city is. Everywhere portents of calamity Gods show: destruction yawns before your feet. Fools! ye know not your doom: still ye rejoice with one consent in madness, who to Troy have brought the Argive Horse where ruin lurks! Oh, ye believe not me, though ne'er so loud I cry! The Erinyes and the ruthless Fates, for Helen's spousals madly wroth, through Troy dart on wild wings. And ye, ye are banqueting there in your last feast, on meats befouled with gore, when now your feet are on the Path of Ghosts!"

[595] Then cried a scoffing voice an ominous word: "Why doth a raving tongue of evil speech, daughter of Priam, make thy lips to cry words empty as wind? No maiden modesty with purity veils thee: thou art compassed round with ruinous madness; therefore all men scorn thee, babbler! Hence, thine evil bodings speak to the Argives and thyself! For thee doth wait anguish and shame yet bitterer than befell presumptuous Laocoon. Shame it were in folly to destroy the Immortals' gift."

[606] So scoffed a Trojan: others in like sort cried shame on her, and said she spake but lies, saying that ruin and Fate's heavy stroke were hard at hand. They knew not their own doom, and mocked, and thrust her back from that huge Horse for fain she was to smite its beams apart, or burn with ravening fire. She snatched a brand of blazing pine-wood from the hearth and ran in fury: in the other hand she bare a two-edged halberd: on that Horse of Doom she rushed, to cause the Trojans to behold with their own eyes the ambush hidden there. But straightway from her hands they plucked and flung afar the fire and steel, and careless turned to the feast; for darkened o'er them their last night. Within the

horse the Argives joyed to hear the uproar of Troy's feasters setting at naught Cassandra, but they marvelled that she knew so well the Achaeans' purpose and device.

[625] As mid the hills a furious pantheress, which from the steading hounds and shepherd-folk drive with fierce rush, with savage heart turns back even in departing, galled albeit by darts: so from the great Horse fled she, anguish-racked for Troy, for all the ruin she foreknew.

THE END.